NEW EDITION

SAS
SURVIVAL
HANDBOOK

By the same author

THE SAS URBAN SURVIVAL HANDBOOK

NEW EDITION

SAS SURVIVAL HANDBOOK

JOHN 'LOFTY' WISEMAN

How to survive in the wild, in any
climate, on land or at sea

HarperCollinsPublishers
77-85 Fulham Palace Road
Hammersmith, London W6 8JB
www.fireandwater.com

First published by Harvill 1986
This paperback edition published by HarperCollins*Publishers* 2003

2 4 6 8 10 9 7 5 3 1

John Wiseman asserts the moral right to
be identified as the author of this work

ISBN 0 00 715899-8

Printed and bound in Great Britain by
Scotprint

Distributed in the USA by Lewis International Inc.,
2201 NW 102 Place #1, Miami, Florida 33172, USA
Tel: 800 259 5962/305 436 7984
Fax: 800 664 5095/305 436 7985
www.Lewisinternational.com

A catalogue record for this book is available from the British Library

CREDITS/ACKNOWLEDGEMENTS

The colour illustrations were painted by Norman Arlott. Other illustrations were drawn by Steve Cross, Chris Lyon, Andrew Mawson and Tony Spalding. New design on the 2003 edition by Paul Collins.

The editors would also like to thank Howard Loxton and Christopher McLehose.

For my father

T. C. H. WISEMAN

who showed me the value of life
and whose dedication to helping
others I try to follow

CONTENTS

INTRODUCTION

For 26 years, as a professional soldier, I had the privilege to serve with the Special Air Service (SAS). This elite unit of the British Army is trained to carry out arduous operations in all parts of the world, often isolated and far from conventional forces. Working in small groups, often in enemy territory, they have to become their own doctor, dentist, navigator and cook. Frequently, the operational situation makes resupply impossible and they have to live off the land. They have to handle every kind of situation and problem, whether man-made or act of nature, and get back to safety, and must develop skills which enable them to survive anywhere.

After serving throughout the world, I became the survival instructor to the SAS and it became my job to ensure that each and every member of the Regiment could apply these skills. Tested in training and operations, they form the basis of this book.

The need for survival training has never been greater. Not only are we indulging in more exotic holidays, challenging expeditions, and foreign business ventures, but the last twelve years have been particularly unstable. The Berlin wall came down in 1999, followed by the Gulf War, Bosnia, Kosovo, Sierra Leone and Afghanistan. These were all overshadowed by the events of 11th September 2001. This event affected everyone, and our lives will never be the same again.

It's crucial that we are prepared for any eventuality and survival training is the best insurance policy you can take out. Just by following the basic techniques, and knowing what to do in an emergency will make the world a safer place.

You could be isolated anywhere in the world — from the arctic ice to a desert, from tropical rainforest to the open ocean, and the problems of survival are the same for both soldier and civilian. The difference lies in that soldiers may need to hide their presence, whereas civilians will want to attract attention to effect their rescue. Each environment calls for special survival techniques. Mountains, jungles, open plains and swamps can seem hazardous to the survivor, but each offers some form of support and can be exploited for food, fuel, water and shelter — if you know how. The effect of climate is very important. You must know how to cope with intense cold and how to survive in searing heat — they challenge the survivor in different ways. *Survival depends upon applying basic principles and adapting them to the circumstances.*

These basic principles form an essential pyramid of learning for the survivor.

Although initially it may take great physical effort to escape from a dangerous situation, survival is a mental exercise. After the excitement of the incident and the rush of adrenalin has settled it takes great mental resolve to carry on. What keeps us going is the basic instinct, which is best referred to as 'the will to live'. This is the firm foundation that we build all of our training on and try to nourish and increase. It's easy to see how physically fit we are but very difficult to know how mentally fit we are.

This basic instinct is getting weaker as we get more civilized so it's important to practise our skills, and be prepared for any eventuality.

The will to live

The will to live (WTL) means never giving in, regardless of the situation. It's very reassuring to know that there is nothing on this earth that we cannot deal with, and there is no place on earth where we cannot survive. As long as we follow the basic principles, prepare ourselves, and apply this WTL, we will come through. Some people have a stronger will than others, but we can all improve.

Some people turn to religion in times of stress, others think of loved ones. Fear of failure or letting down comrades, all help to strengthen our WTL. Reading of past exploits of survival will also help.

You can have all the knowledge and kit in the world but without the will to live you can still perish.

Knowledge

On top of our foundation we have knowledge. The more we have the easier it is to survive. Knowledge dispels fear, and hopefully this book will supply what we need to know, but we must take this further. Practise these skills till you master them. Look at the locals and see how they survive. Talk to people who have endured and learn from their experiences.

Kit

The tip of our pyramid of learning is Kit. We keep this to a minimum and have a thorough knowledge of its uses and capabilities. There are essential items that you should never leave home without, like Survival tin, knife, compass and radio/phone.

The reader must use his or her own judgement in the application of the methods described in this book. The tests for plant foods, for instance, are the only sure way of being certain whether a particular fruit or leaf is safe or poisonous. The average person is unlikely to come to any harm if they follow the method carefully, but there is risk involved. Individual responses to poisons vary — even small quantities of toxic substances can be very dangerous to some people. Some of the traps described are also very dangerous. They should never be left unsupervised where other people may come to harm and they could inflict self-injury if handled carelessly.

In learning the skills described here, readers must be restrained by the need to conserve our environment and to avoid cruelty to animals, and by laws which it is possible that some of these techniques may contravene. Remember, this is a handbook for the survival situation when self-preservation is paramount and risks may be involved which would be foolish even to consider taking in normal life. Weighing those risks against each other is all part of surviving strategy. The final choice must be yours and no one else can be blamed if you make the wrong one.

Although this is not an official publication, by sharing the survival knowledge that I and my colleagues have gained through experience, I aim to help you to make those decisions correctly. These methods and skills have helped save our lives — they will help you to be a survivor, too.

Finally, I would like to thank the SAS Regiment for providing me with the experience on which this book is based and to thank Howard Loxton and Tony Spalding who helped to bring it to publication. Without their hard work and dedication this book would not have been possible.

J.W.
The Survival School, Hereford

-1-
ESSENTIALS

Begin by preparing yourself to be a survivor. That means preparation in every sense. This section is concerned with making sure that you have the right equipment for any expedition you undertake. It introduces the idea of carrying a pocket-sized kit of carefully selected key survival aids — which should go with you everywhere.

A knife is your most important survival tool. It must be chosen and used carefully and it must be kept in perfect condition.

Equally important is a personal preparedness, so that you are both physically and psychologically equipped to deal with the stresses and hazards of survival conditions. You must have a clear understanding of survival needs, especially of the need for — and ways of obtaining — water and salt.

ESSENTIALS FOR SURVIVAL

The human species has established itself in almost every corner of the Earth. Even in territories too inhospitable to provide a regular home mankind has found a way to exploit their resources, whether by hunting or by taking wealth from the ground, and has often pitted its skills against nature simply for the satisfaction of doing so.

Almost everywhere nature provides the necessities for survival. In some places the provision is abundant, in others very meagre and it takes common sense, knowledge and ingenuity to take advantage of the resources available. Even more important is the will to survive. Men and women have shown that they can survive in the most adverse situations, but they have done so because of their determination to do so — without that, the skills and knowledge in this book will be of little use if you find yourself really up against it.

Survival is the art of staying alive. Any equipment you have must be considered a bonus. You must know how to take everything possible from nature and use it to the full, how to attract attention to yourself so that rescuers may find you, how to make your way across unknown territory back to civilization, if hope of rescue is not on the cards, navigating without map or compass. You must know how to maintain a healthy physical condition, or if sick or wounded heal yourself and others. You must be able to maintain your morale and that of others who share your situation.

Lack of equipment should not mean that you are unequipped, for you will carry skills and experience with you, but those skills and experience must not be allowed to get rusty and you must extend your knowledge all the time.

We are all used to surviving on our home ground — though we may not think of our lives in that way — but the true survivor must learn how to survive when taken from familiar surroundings or when those surroundings are drastically changed by man or nature. Anyone, young or old, from whatever walk of life, can find him- or herself in a survival situation. As more and more people fly the globe, sail small boats or cross the sea in large ones, walk the hills and climb mountains and take their holidays in ever more exotic places, the situations to which they could become exposed are increasingly diversified.

But survival skills are not only concerned with the extremes of the air crash on a mountain peak, a shipwreck in the tropics or a vehicle breakdown in the middle of a desert. Every time you fasten a seat belt in a car you are giving yourself a greater chance of survival. Checking each way before crossing a road or ensuring that an open fire is safe before you go to bed are survival techniques that you carry out instinctively. It is these habits of mind that you must develop as much as acquiring skills.

The main elements of survival are Food, Fire, Shelter, Water, Navigation and Medicine. To put these in order of priority we use the acronym **PLAN**. No matter where you are in the world this will never change be it the arctic, desert, jungle, sea or seashore.

P – for Protection

You must ensure that you are protected from further danger, ie impending avalanche, forest fire or exploding fuel. Always stay on the scene of the incident as long as it is safe to do so and then make sure you are protected from the elements. This means making a shelter and often lighting a fire. There are several reasons why you should always stay at the scene:

1 You can utilize the wreckage for shelter, signaling etc.
2 It's a bigger signature on the ground, making it easier to find.
3 There are probably injured people that cannot be moved.
4 By staying where you are you conserve energy.
5 Because you have booked in and out and have stayed on the route, rescue time will be minimal.

L – for Location

The next step after building a shelter is to put out emergency signals. You must draw attention to your position. Do this as soon as possible to help the rescuers.

A – for Acquisition

While waiting to be rescued, look for water and food to help supplement your emergency supplies.

N – for Navigation

Good navigation will keep you on route and will often avert a survival situation. But if you find yourself stranded, always stay where you are.

Medical

You must become your own doctor and carefully monitor yourself at all times. Treat blisters as they occur, don't let them become sceptic. Keep an eye on your companions and deal with any unusual problems as they arise. If they are limping, falling behind, or behaving strangely, stop and treat immediately.

BE PREPARED

The Boy Scouts' motto is the right one. Anyone setting out on a journey or planning an expedition should follow it by discovering as much as possible about the situations likely to be faced and the skills and equipment called for. It is the most basic common sense to prepare yourself, to take appropriate gear and to plan as carefully as possible.

Your kit could make the difference between failure and success, but, especially when back-packing, many people initially take too much and have to learn from bitter experience what they really need and what they could have done without. There is no fun in struggling with a huge pack full of superfluous items while wishing that you had a torch or can opener with you. Getting the right balance is not easy.

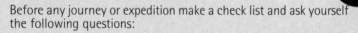

EQUIPMENT CHECK LIST

Before any journey or expedition make a check list and ask yourself the following questions:

– How long will I be away? How much food do I need for this period and do I need to carry water?

– Have I the right clothing for the climate and enough of it? Is one pair of boots enough or, because of the surface conditions and the amount of walking, should I take a standby pair?

– What special equipment do I need for the terrain?

– What medical kit is appropriate?

Make sure that you are fit enough for what you plan to do. The fitter you are, the easier and more enjoyable it will be. If you are going hill-walking, for instance, take regular exercise beforehand and wear in your hiking boots. Walk to and from work with a bag weighted with sand and get your muscles in condition! Mental fitness is another factor. Are you sure that you are up to the task, have prepared enough and have the equipment to accomplish it? Eliminate any nagging doubts before you set out.

Always prepare contingency plans in case anything goes wrong. Things rarely go quite according to plan. What will you do if you are prevented from achieving your objective? What will you do if a vehicle breaks down, or if weather or ground conditions prove more severe than anticipated? If in a party, how will you regroup if separated? What happens if someone becomes ill?

Health checks

Have a thorough medical check and ensure that you have all the necessary injections for the territories through which you intend to travel. There are vaccinations against yellow fever, cholera, typhoid, hepatitis, smallpox, polio, diptheria and tuberculosis, and an anti-tetanus injection is a must. Allow plenty of time for jabs — the full anti-typhoid protection requires three injections over the course of six months. If travelling through a malarial region take an adequate supply of anti-malaria tablets. You must start taking these two weeks before your journey, so that resistance is in the system before you arrive in the risk area, and should keep taking them for a month after your return.

Go to the dentist and get your teeth inspected. Teeth that normally do not hurt can cause considerable pain in cold climates. At least start out in sound condition.

Make up a medical kit that will cover all your likely needs and, if travelling with a group, ensure that any particular individual medical needs are covered. If a potential member of the group is not fit, should they be dropped from the party? A difficult decision among friends, but one that must be made for it is best in the long run. Consider, too, the ability of each member of the group to deal with the challenge of hardship, risk and endurance that you may meet. Stress often brings out the unknown side of a person, and in planning any group expedition some form of selection is needed when choosing your companions.

RESEARCH

You can never have too much information about a place you are going to. Contact people who know it already, read books, study maps — and make sure that you have reliable and up-to-date maps to take with you. Find out about the local people. Are they likely to be friendly and helpful or are they wary of strangers? Are there local customs and taboos?

The more detailed your knowledge of the way people live — particularly in non-westernized societies, where life is linked much more closely to the land — the more survival knowledge you will have if you come to need it. Local methods of shelter building and fire making, wild foods, herbal medicines and water sources will be based on an intimate understanding of the surroundings.

Study your maps carefully, get a feel for the land even before you see it and gain as much knowledge of the terrain as possible: river directions and speed of flow, waterfalls, rapids and difficult currents. How high are hills and mountains, and what are their slopes like — are they snow covered? Which way do the ridges run? What kind of vegetation can you expect, what species of trees and where? What temperatures and how different are day and night? When are first and last light? What is the state of the moon, the time and height of tides, the prevailing wind direction and strength? The weather that can be expected?

PLANNING

For a group expedition get the members together for frequent discussions of what you aim to achieve. Nominate people for particular responsibilities: medic, linguist, cook, special equipment, vehicle maintenance, driver, navigator and so forth. Ensure that everyone is familiar with the equipment and that there are spares where needed — batteries, fuel and bulbs especially.

Divide the project into phases: entry phase, objective and recovery. Clearly state the aim of each phase and work out a time scale. Plan for emergency procedures such as vehicle breakdown, illness and casualty evacuation.

In estimating the rate of progress, especially on foot, allow plenty of time. It is always better to underestimate and be pleasantly surprised by doing better. Pressure to keep up to an over-ambitious schedule not only produces tension and exhaustion but leads to errors of judgement and risk-taking that are frequently the reason for things going wrong. You cannot carry all your water requirement with you but must replenish supplies as you travel. Water sources will be a major factor in planning any route.

When the route is planned and agreed make sure that others know about it so that you can have expectations of rescue if anything goes wrong. If you are hiking in the hills inform the police and local mountain rescue centre. Tell them your proposed plan and give times of departure and expected arrival. If touring by car, log the route with the respective motoring organization. If sailing check with coastguard and port authorities.

Always make sure that someone knows what you are planning to do and when, and keep them informed at prearranged stages so that failure to contact will set alarm bells ringing. Boats and aircraft are strictly controlled in this respect and, if overdue, a search is raised and the route checked out, effecting rescue. Get into the habit of telling people where you are going and what time you expect to return or reach your next destination.

EQUIPMENT

Being prepared for any eventuality is a tall order if you are on foot and have to carry everything you need yourself. Whatever you carry, you must ensure that it is up to the job, versatile and robust. It's a fine balance between what you would like to carry and what you must carry. When preparing for any adventure, you must take into consideration what the dangers are and how you can overcome these. This is what is called contingency planning.

The climate, weather and time of year will all help you to determine what to carry, but you must ensure that everyone with you knows how to use and maintain the specialist kit you decide to take with you. Armed with information from your research you will be able to select your equipment, matching it to objectives and conditions.

Clothing

The correct choice of clothing is so important. If you start out right the chances are that you will succeed. Man is a tropical animal and can only survive as we are born in the tropics. The moment we leave this area we have to provide our bodies with this tropical environment, hence the need for clothes. There is no heat in clothing, it only traps what the body produces.

The wind and rain are the most dangerous elements in a temperate climate and the cold in extreme areas like the polar regions. If the heat that is trapped in the layers of clothing you are wearing, is continuously being replaced by wind and rain, you are in danger of hypothermia. In cold climates layering is the answer so pull on a jersey if it turns cold and waterproofs if it rains. However if you wear an anorak while carrying a heavy pack, there is a danger of wearing through the shoulders and lower lumbar region allowing the ingress of water to soak the body. You need a change of clothing and additional warm garments for when you stop.

In hot climates it is very difficult to get the balance right between comfort and practicality. There has always been a danger of overheating in extreme conditions caused by wearing heavy clothing while carrying out physical activities. When on the move wear the least amount of clothing possible and avoid walking in waterproofs if you are too hot, as the condensation generated will soak the inner layers.

Clothing should give good protection and be well-fitting without being restrictive. They must keep you warm and dry but have plenty of ways to keep the body ventilated so you don't overheat (if it gets colder you can always put on more.)

With all the great breakthroughs in recent years in fabric technology it is worth understanding the pros and cons of the different materials on offer. Gore-tex™ is an excellent material because it is breathable and so keeps you warm and dry while ventilating the body, but it does have limitations. Breathable materials can only work if they are kept clean. Once they get covered in mud and accumulate grime they are less effective. Gore-tex™ is not robust or hard-wearing and must be looked after. The best way to use Gore-tex™ is to walk or climb in windproof garments and when at rest, put on the breathable kit.

Synthetic materials such as fleece are very popular and in certain conditions out perform natural materials like wool, down or cotton. Having a zipped front makes fleeces easy to put on and take off and they are comfortable to walk in. Choose one that is windproof as this is often all that is needed in most conditions. If it gets colder they can be worn under an outer waterproof giving good insulation. There are also garments which act like an animal's skin, using the buffalo system. They have a windproof outer with a man-made fibre pile inside. When wet they perform like a wetsuit. They are good for walking in cold/wet conditions, and are ideal for boating, canoeing and caving.

As for natural fabrics, wool is still an excellent choice for jumpers as it retains its warmth even when wet. The downside is it stretches and becomes heavy, so it's not a good choice for socks. Down is the warmest and lightest of all natural insulating materials but loses all its heat-retaining qualities when wet. Cotton acts as a wick and draws up all the moisture. So it's good to wear in the tropics but not in the cold wet regions.

Footwear is an important consideration and for serious walking give your feet priority. Break in new boots gradually and harden up your skin with surgical spirit, starting two weeks before you set off.

For the enthusiast the major consideration in choosing clothing is cost. Surplus stores are very popular for the younger adventurer who loves to parade in camouflaged clothing. Although ex-military kit is good, and cheap, it is already obsolete. The big drawback of wearing camouflaged or dark clothing is the risk of not being found when lost. The reason soldiers wear it is so they cannot be seen which contradicts what you are trying to do if you get into trouble. Most outdoor clothing is blue or orange, some is reversible, so a contrasting colour will always stand out wherever we find ourselves. Buy the best clothing you can afford, and take advice from a reputable outdoor shop.

Remember: There is no such thing as bad weather, only bad clothing.

Sleeping bags

Two types are generally available. One kind uses hollow fill, man-made fibre, the other (and more expensive) is filled with down. Down is very light and gives much better insulation – provided it stays dry. If it gets wet it loses all its insulating properties and is very difficult to dry out. For conditions that are likely to be wet the man-made fibre will therefore be the better choice. Avoid getting your sleeping bag wet, however, as sleep will seriously be affected.

Excellent bivouac bags made of Gore-tex™ are also available that will keep you dry in place of a tent, but in the long term you cannot beat a tent which can also be used for cooking and communal activities. Keep your sleeping bag inside the bivy bag and stow it inside a compression sack to make it as small as possible. Keep the bag clean and use a kip mat or poncho to lie on.

Packs

You need a strong and comfortable back-pack to carry all your clothing and equipment. Choose the very best you can afford. It should have tough and fully adjustable webbing, well secured to the pack's frame or fabric. Heavy loads can quickly loosen poorly made webbing. It must have a comfortable hip belt. The secret of wearing a pack is to take the weight securely on the hips – the body's strongest pivot – not on the shoulders and back, which quickly strain and tire.

Do you want a pack with an external or an internal frame? Internal frames are lighter and make a pack more easy to stow, but external frames are stronger, ensure a more even distribution of the load and are especially useful for awkward or heavy equipment — including, in an emergency, a sick or injured person. A good external frame should carry the pack high up on your body, putting less strain on hips and shoulders, and it should be designed to allow an airspace between the pack and your back to minimise contact perspiration. A frame adds weight and is more prone to snag on rocky projections or branches, making progress through dense vegetation a little more difficult, but its advantages more than compensate.

Finally, choose a pack made from a tough, waterproof fabric, preferably with a lace-up hood inside the main sack to prevent water leaking in and the contents falling out. Side pockets are always useful, but they must have secure zips rather than straps or drawstrings, which do not hold equipment safely.

Stowing kit

If you expect to get wet, stow everything in polythene bags. Pack so that you know where everything is and so that the first things you need are not buried at the bottom. The sleeping bag is probably the last thing you need so that goes at the bottom. Your tent should be on the top, so should heavy kit such as radios, which are more easily carried there — though try not to make the pack too high, if you have to cope with strong winds, for a very high pack will be more difficult to balance and you will expend a lot of energy just keeping upright.

Pack a stove and brew-kit in a side pocket so that you have easy access when you halt. Make sure that foodstuffs that can easily squash or melt are in suitable containers. In a warm climate you can carry food to eat cold and make plenty of hot drinks. In a cold climate make sure that you have plenty of fats and sugars. The exact rations depend on your taste, but they should be chosen to give a good balance of vitamins, minerals, fats, proteins and carbohydrates. Take into account the extent to which you will be able to live off the land and carry a supply of anything unlikely to be available locally.

G.P.S

A G.P.S (Global Positioning System) is an excellent piece of equipment and has taken a lot of skill away from the navigator. Basically these systems receive radio signals from satellites and can locate your current position, anywhere in the world, and are relatively easy to use. It is also useful to note that they are reported to have 95% accuracy rate. However, in order to work, the satellite transmission must not have any obstructions in its way, such as a tree branch or movement, so to receive a clear signal you need to be standing still and out in the open. It is worth remembering, however, that if we depend solely on technology our basic skills will suffer and we will become unstuck if it becomes unserviceable or is lost. So stick to the basics. Map read and navigate normally and use the G.P.S to confirm your navigation or correct it.

When looking to buy a G.P.S there are several considerations to think about: what you'll be using it for – if walking you will want the unit to be as light as possible and compact; where you'll be using it; and if you need it to be waterproof (this is usually a feature of the heavier models with extra gadgets). Battery life should also be taken into account. Some G.P.S are more complicated than others so choose the model that you're happy with. Most have the facility of being able to put in way points (at sea this means the eastern and northern coordinates and on land these can be campsites, rock formations etc.) and there are many convenient hand held versions and some are even featured on watches.

There is always a danger with any battery-operated equipment that it lets you down when you need it most. Batteries always discharge faster in the cold and with age. Recharging facilities are difficult in the wilderness, and bad connections caused by constant abuse while on the move are a real menace.

Carry the G.P.S around the neck tucked under the jacket. This will minimize the risk of damage and protect it from the weather. Don't place it in your pack or leave it lying around.

When planning your route from the map, choose prominent points that can be used as emergency rendezvous. Have these at regular intervals, preferably every hour of walking. Enter these into the G.P.S and they will keep you on track. Once entered they will offer information as to where you are in relation to these points and tell you what direction to take to reach them.

Radios

For a long expedition in remote territory a radio is a necessity. They tend to be expensive but are well worth the cost; if you cannot afford the radios, you cannot afford the expedition. Choose a model with the least amount of channels available that suit your particular needs. The trouble with multi-channeled sets is that people get confused and tend to use the wrong ones. Have a working channel that everyone uses at established schedules. Have a priority channel that you can switch to in an emergency so no one will break into your transmissions. If working with coastguards/forest rangers etc make sure that your radio is compatible and you know the emergency channel (channel 16); knowing the frequency of the World Service is also useful. Keep your radio in a safe place, ideally on a person and not in a pack.

Prearrange a signals plan with scheduled calls morning and evening, especially when working in a large party. A signals plan entails people manning the radio at base and two-way communication is easily made. Make sure that the chosen frequencies will work in the areas you are going to, and that at least two people in the party are familiar with the working of the radio. Every group on the ground must be in radio contact with base. They should be allocated a call sign and frequency, and a schedule of calls to be made.

Discourage groups talking to each other without going through base. This will cause great confusion if not controlled. Listen out before transmitting otherwise you will interfere with other stations. Everyone has verbal diarrhoea when they talk on the radio so write down what you want to say before making contact and have pencil and paper ready to make notes and take instructions. This will help to keep transmissions to a minimum and preserve the batteries.

REMEMBER: RSVP

Rhythm – don't talk like a darlek

Speed   – talk slowly

Volume – speak softly

Pitch   – pitch voice higher than normal and use the phonetic alphabet when spelling out place names

In the evening give a situation report to base with your location, what you have done and your future intentions. In the morning receive an update on weather conditions, a time check and other information that base can give you. A noon time call can be used to confirm your position.

REMEMBER:

Signals will be weak in a steep gully and valley bottoms and good signals will be received on top of high ground or across water.

If you are tackling a dangerous aspect of the expedition you may want to arrange that base listen out for additional calls so that in an emergency you can call for help and get a response immediately.

REMEMBER:

An emergency plan should always be put into operation when two consecutive calls are missed. Even if all is well, if you have not been able to make contact this will be treated by base as an emergency. You must return to or stay at the last reported location and await contact. If you are really in trouble base will know where you last were and where you planned to go to, and the rescue mission can follow.

Mobiles

The mobile phone is one of the great inventions of the century. In an emergency situation it can be a real life-saver. On expeditions where the radios have failed due to bad weather or the location of the victims, a mobile phone has been used to raise the alarm. A group on Everest got into trouble as they started their descent after summitting. They tried many times to raise base camp but without success. The leader phoned his wife in Hong Kong on a mobile phone and reported their situation. She then alerted Kathmandu, who in turn alerted base camp, Everest and effected a rescue.

Some phones are better than others so it's worth doing some homework; it's also essential to check the network coverage with the service provider before going abroad. Keep one in the car, they are priceless when help is required and a cigar lighter is a convenient charger for the battery, providing you have an adaptor. Charging can be a problem in the wild so use your phone wisely. With radios and phones it takes less power to listen than to transmit, so make your call and listen for a reply. If nothing is heard don't despair. With all electrical kit water/moisture is the enemy. The transmitting side may be working but not the receiving side. Make short calls on the hour. Someone may be picking up your signal so don't give up. Once you receive confirmation that the rescue is under way keep the radiophone on listening watch.

Altimeters

In mountainous areas an altimeter is a good idea. Relating the height recorded can help you determine what contour you are on, and how far it is to the ridge or summit.

You never have enough kit in an emergency. It's nice to have G.P.S, phones etc but you can still manage without as long as you have the ability to improvise and adapt. Learn the basics and use technology for confirmation, rather than depending on them whole heartedly. Communication is of the highest importance and must be given priority. You are safe anywhere as long as you can communicate with the outside world.

Many survival sagas begin because of bad nagivation, with people getting lost. Always plan for the worst eventuality and ask yourself if you are up to it.

REMEMBER:

When things go wrong it's a series of events that compound the situation. The weather deteriorates, the radio is broken, the mobile phone is lost. Two people have multiple injuries and you are out of water. Never given in. Plan for these situations and you will come through.

Vehicles

Motor vehicles need special adjustment and adaptation to deal with high altitudes and extreme conditions, as well as a thorough overhaul to make sure they are in tip-top working order. You will need tanks for extra fuel and water as well as spares and modifications (see *Vehicles* in *Climate and Terrain*).

Boats and planes

Whether travelling privately or on a commercial service you must take note of the emergency procedures. Maritime and aviation authorities rule that passengers must be informed of them and remembering them could save your life.

When you board an aircraft cabin staff point out the emergency exits and advise you on action to take in the event of an emergency. On board ship you will carry out lifeboat drills and be instructed on how to abandon ship if you have to.

The safest place on an aircraft is as far back in the tail as possible. In a crash this frequently breaks off and most survivors are from this portion. If you are a passenger in a light aircraft always ask the pilot about the trip: how long will it take and what sort of ground will you be flying over? Attend to details — they count in an emergency.

THE UNEXPECTED

How can you prepare for what you do not expect? Preparing for expected difficulties and dangers is difficult enough, but what chance have you of equipping yourself for the totally unknown disaster? Yet these are the disasters that immediately spring to people's minds — the shipwreck and the plane crash or forced landing in unfamiliar and difficult terrain.

This is the reason for this book's existence. There are specialized books on mountaineering, sailing or pot-holing, on the desert and the jungle and the polar wastes, and reading them will be part of your preparatory research before taking up these activities or travelling in these areas. Even more important, however, is to know about a whole range of skills which can be applied and adapted to all kinds of situations and to develop a way of thinking that enables you to draw upon them to find the solutions to particular problems. This is the preparation you can make for the unexpected.

But it is not all. You can equip yourself with a few small items which will increase your chances many times over by helping you with some of the basic necessities of survival. This can tip the balance between failure and success. They will fit in a small container slipped into a pocket or bag and can be carried anywhere. They are your survival kit. If there is an emergency you will be glad you always carry it.

More bulky and therefore likely to be left at home, but still compact enough to carry on a belt whenever you are travelling, are a knife and the items which will fit in your survival pouch (see below).

Without the basics, which these two kits provide, you can still improvise but they will give you a head start.

SURVIVAL KIT

A few key items can make all the difference in the fight for survival. Collect the things listed below. They can all be fitted into a small container, such as a 2oz tobacco tin, that will be hardly noticeable when slipped into an anorak pocket. Make a habit of always having it with you. Do not choose something bigger, you may find it inconvenient to carry and leave it out on the one occasion you actually need it. Many people who roll their own cigarettes carry such a tin. But this one is much more useful. It may help to save your life. The smoker is speeding up the end of his.

Experience has proved that each item earns its place, though some are more use in some situations than in others: fish hooks, for instance, may be invaluable in the jungle but useless in a desert.

Polish the inside of the lid to make a mirror-like reflecting surface and seal it, to be waterproof, with a strip of adhesive tape (a) which can be easily removed and replaced. Don't then just forget the tin. Regularly check the contents, changing any which deteriorate, such as matches and medicine tablets. Mark all drug containers with use and dosage and a run-out date when they should be replaced. Pack spare space in the tin with cotton wool, which will keep the contents from rattling and can be used for fire lighting. Fire is vital to survival — four items are for making it.

Matches (1)
Waterproof matches are useful but bulkier than ordinary non-safety, strike-anywhere matches, which can be made 'shower-proof' by dipping the heads in melted candle fat. To save space, snap off half of each matchstick.

It is much easier to use matches than to make fire by other methods but don't waste them, use only when improvised methods fail. Take them from the tin one at a time and replace the lid. Never leave the container open or lying on the ground.

Candle (2)
Invaluable for starting a fire as well as a light source. Shave square for packing. If made of tallow it is also fat to eat in an emergency or to use for frying — but be sure it is tallow; paraffin wax and some other candles are inedible. Tallow does not store well, especially in hot climates.

Flint (3)
Flints will work when wet and they will go on striking long after you

run out of matches. Invest in a processed flint with a saw striker.

Magnifying glass (4)
Can start a fire from direct sunshine and is useful for searching for splinters and stings.

Needles and thread (5)
Several needles, including at least one with a very large eye that can be threaded with sinew and coarse threads. Choose strong thread and wrap it around the needles.

Fish hooks and line (6)
A selection of different hooks in a small tin or packet. Add a few split lead weights. Remember that a small hook will catch both large and small fish but a large hook will only catch big ones. Include as much line as possible, it will also be useful for catching birds.

Compass (7)
A luminous button compass – but make sure you know how to read it, as some small compasses can be confusing. A liquid-filled type is best, but check that it does not leak, has no bubbles in it and is fully serviceable. The pointer is prone to rust. Make sure it is on its pivot and swings freely.

Beta light (8)
A light-emitting crystal, only the size of a small coin but ideal for reading a map at night and a useful fishing lure – expensive but just about everlasting.

Snare wire (9)
Preferably brass wire – 60–90cm (2–3ft) should do. Save for snares, but could solve many survival problems.

Flexible saw (10)
These usually come with large rings at the ends as handles. These take up too much room, so remove them; they can be replaced by wooden toggles when you need to use it. To protect from rust and breakage cover it in a film of grease. Flexible saws can be used to cut even quite large trees.

Medical kit (11)
What you include depends upon your own skill in using it. Pack medicines in airtight containers with cotton wool to prevent

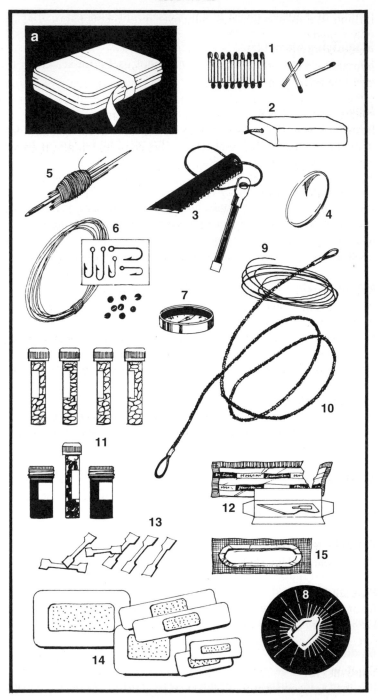

rattling. The following items will cover most ailments but they are only a guide:

Analgesic: A pain reliever for mild and moderate pain. Codeine phosphate is ideal for tooth-, ear- and headaches. DOSE: one tablet every six hours as needed but they can cause constipation as a side-effect so will help in cases of loose bowels. Not to be taken by children, asthmatics or people with liver disorders.

Intestinal sedative: For treating acute and chronic diarrhoea. Immodium is usually favoured. DOSE: two capsules initially, then one each time a loose stool is passed.

Antibiotic: For general infections. Tetracycline can be used even by people hypersensitive to penicillin. DOSE: one 250mg tablet, four times daily, repeated for five to seven days. Carry enough for a full course. If taking them avoid milk, calcium and iron preparations or other drugs containing aluminium hydroxide.

Antihistamine: For allergies, insect bites and stings (may also help in cases of bad reaction to a drug). Piriton is recommended in Britain, Benadryl in the USA. Sleepiness is a side-effect of Piriton, so useful as a mild sleeping pill. Do not exceed recommended dosages or take with alcohol.

Water sterlizing tablets: For use where water is suspect and you cannot boil. Follow manufacturers' instructions.

Anti-malaria tablets: Essential in areas where malaria is present. There are types which require only one tablet taken monthly

Potassium permanganate: Has several uses. Add to water and mix until water becomes bright pink to sterilize it, deeper pink to make an antiseptic and to a full red to treat fungal diseases such as athlete's foot.

Surgical blades (12)
At least two scalpel blades of different sizes. A handle can be made from wood when required.

Butterfly sutures (13)
Use to hold the edges of wounds together.

Plasters (14)
Assorted sizes, preferably waterproof, for minor abrasions and keeping cuts clean. They can be cut and used as butterfly sutures (see *Stitching wounds* in *Health*).

Condom (15)
This makes a good water-bag — holding 1 litre (2pt).

SURVIVAL POUCH

In a car, boat or aircraft don't stow all your kit separately. Pack a survival pouch, too large to carry in your pocket like your survival tin but kept where it can be grabbed quickly in an emergency. If you are on foot keep it outside your back-pack, carried on your belt. It should contain fuel, food, survival bag and signalling kit, all packed into a mess tin which protects the kit and doubles as a cooking utensil. If you fancy a brew or a snack, it is all there for you and in an emergency gives you a first back-up for survival. Anything you use from the pouch on a normal trip must be replenished as soon as possible.

POUCH

The pouch must be made from waterproof material and be large enough to take a mess tin. It must have a positive fastening that will not come undone, and a strong tunnel loop to hold it on your belt. Remember the pouch contains matches, solid fuel and flares — all life savers — but to be treated with care.

Mess tin
This is made from aluminium, which is light and strong. A good cooking utensil, it protects kit packed inside it.

Fuel
Preferably you should have solid fuel tablets in their own stove container (1). Use sparingly when a wood fire is inconvenient. They make excellent fire lighters. The stove simply unfolds to form an adjustable pot stand (2) and holder for burning fuel.

Torch
Pack a small pencil-like torch (3) that takes up little room. Keep batteries inside it, but reverse the last so that, if accidentally switched on, the batteries don't run down. Lithium batteries last a long time.

Flares
Signal flares (4) to attract attention, especially in close country.

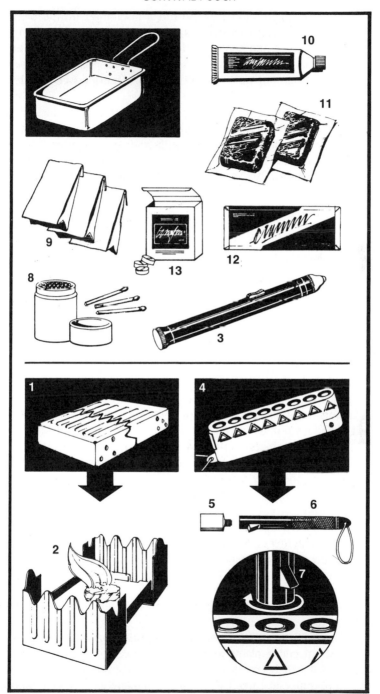

Carry red and green miniflares (5) and a discharger (6) (no bigger than a fountain pen). These are explosive so pack carefully. Simply remove discharger and screw on to flare (7). Withdraw flare and point skywards at arm's length. Pull the trigger to fire. Use with very great care and do not waste. Use to attract attention (see *Rescue*).

Marker panel

A strip or bar of fluorescent material about 0.3 x 2m (1 x 6ft) used to attract attention in an emergency (see *Signalling* in *Rescue*). One bar signals immediate evacuation. Form other signals with panels carried by others in your party. Pack to stop the other items in the pouch rattling.

Matches

Pack as many matches (8) as possible in a waterproof container, you never have enough. Movement against each other can ignite non-safety matches — pack carefully.

Brew kit

There is nothing like a brew-up to restore morale. Pack tea powder and sachets of milk and sugar (9). Tea quenches thirst – coffee aggravates it!

Food

Fat is the hardest food to come by when living off the land. Its extra calories earn it a place in your kit — tubes of butter, lard or ghee (10) are available. Dehydrated meat blocks (11) are nourishing and sustaining, though not very good in flavour. Chocolate (12) is a good food, but does not keep well — check regularly. Salt (13) MUST be included — salt tablets are the compact way to carry it, or, better still, an electrolite powder which contains vitamins, salt and other minerals that the body requires.

Survival bag

A large polythene bag about 200 x 60cm (7 x 2ft) is a lifesaver in the cold. In an emergency get inside to reduce heat loss. Although wet from condensation you will be warm. Even better is a heat-insulated bag of reflective material that keeps you warm and solves the condensation problem.

Survival log

Keep a written log of all events. Do not trust your memory. Record discoveries of edible plants and other resources of what works and what does not. It becomes a valuable reference and making it helps keep up your morale. Later it will be a useful guide for survival training.

KNIVES

A knife is an invaluable asset in a survival situation. The serious adventurer will carry one always. Knives are dangerous, however, and can be used as weapons. They should be surrendered to airline staff when travelling by air as part of standard anti-hijack procedures, and never displayed in tense or awkward circumstances.

Choosing a knife

A multi-bladed folding knife is a useful tool, but, if you carry only one knife, you need something stronger, a general-purpose blade that will do all likely tasks efficiently and comfortably, from cutting trees to skinning animals and preparing vegetables. Some have a compass built into the handle or have the handle hollowed out so that you can carry survival kit inside it. However, these features will be offset by the possibility of a hollow handle breaking and a compass may soon lose its accuracy after the knife has been used on a hardwood tree. If you lose this kind of knife you also lose your survival kit — much better to keep the kit in a separate pouch on your belt or on the sheath.

REMEMBER: YOU ARE ONLY AS SHARP AS YOUR KNIFE. Your knife is such an important piece of survival equipment, that you must keep it sharp to be ready for use. Don't misuse your knife. Never throw it into trees or into the ground. Keep it clean and, if you don't intend to use it for a while, oiled and in its sheath.

When walking through close country, get in the habit of checking your knife. This should become an automatic reflex, especially after negotiating difficult terrain. A check of all pockets and possessions should be second nature.

Folding knives

A folding knife can be valuable, provided it has a good locked position. Always carry one. A blade in a wooden handle is usually more comfortable: it will not slip in a sweaty hand and, if the handle is made from a single piece of wood, is less likely to cause blisters than other types.

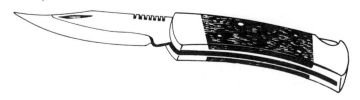

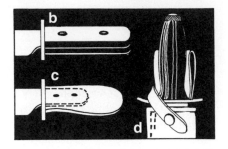

Handle (a) is ideal: a single rounded piece of wood, the knife tang passing through it and fastened at the end. If the handle breaks the tang can be wrapped with cloth or twine. Handle (b) is only riveted to the tang and would cause blisters. Handle (c) could break at the rivets if subjected to heavy work and the short tang would make it difficult to improvise a handle. The sheath (d) should have a positive fastening and a tunnel belt loop.

Parang

This is the Malayan name for a type of knife with a large curved blade like a machete. It is too large to be carried in normal daily life but ideal when going out into the wild.

A parang 30cm (12in) in overall blade length and weighing no more than 750g (1½lb) is best, the blade 5cm (2in) at its widest and end-bolted into a wooden handle. The curved blade enables maximum effort to be applied when cutting timber and the blade arrives before the knuckles, so giving them protection. Even large trees can be cut down with a parang, which is especially useful for building shelters and rafts.

*The parang blade has three different edges: **b** does the heavy work of chopping wood and bone, **a** is finer and used for skinning, **c** is finer still for carving and delicate work. **a** and **c** are easily maintained and **b** is sharp but not so sharp as to chip easily.*

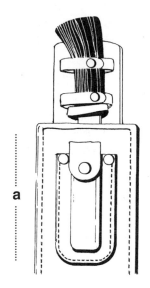

The sheath must have positive fastenings to keep the parang secure, and a loop for fixing to a belt. Some sheaths have a pocket on the front for a sharpening stone.

REMEMBER: *There is a danger that the cutting edge may come through the side. To draw the parang NEVER hold the sheath on the same side as the cutting edge (a). This is dangerous. Get into the habit of gripping the side AWAY FROM THE CUTTING EDGE.*

a

Sharpening a knife

Any sandstone will sharpen tools — a grey, clayey sandstone being best. Quartz, though more rarely found, is good and granite can also be used. Rub two pieces together to make them smooth. A double-faced stone with a rough and a smooth surface is ideal and should be carried in the sheath pocket. Use the rough surface first to remove burrs, then the smooth one to get a fine edge. The object is to get an edge that will last and not chip.

To sharpen the blade, hold the handle in the right hand. Use a clockwise circular motion and apply a steady pressure on the blade with the fingertips of the left hand as you push away. Keep the angle constant. Keep the stone wet. Rock particles on the blade will show the angle you are obtaining. DON'T drag the blade towards you under pressure. This will produce burrs. Reduce the pressure for a finer edge. Work counter clockwise on the other side.

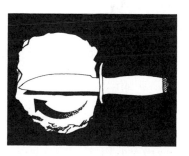

Blade profile: (a) is too steep and will soon wear, (b) is good and (c) is too fine and might chip.

FACING DISASTER

When facing a disaster it is easy to let yourself go, to collapse and be consumed in self-pity. But it is no use giving up or burying your head in the sand and hoping that this is a bad dream that will soon pass. It won't, and with that kind of attitude it will rapidly become much worse. Only positive action can save you.

A healthy, well-nourished person can physically tolerate a great deal, provided that he or she has self-confidence. Even if sick or injured, a determined person can win through and recover from seemingly impossible situations. To do so there are many stresses that must be overcome.

SURVIVAL STRESSES

The survival situation will put you under pressure, both physical and mental. You will have to overcome some or all of the following stresses:

- Fear and anxiety
- Pain, illness and injury
- Cold and/or heat
- Thirst, hunger and fatigue
- Sleep deprivation
- Boredom
- Loneliness and isolation

Can you cope? You have to.

Self-confidence is a product of good training and sound knowledge. These must be acquired before you have to face up to a survival situation. The fact that you are reading this book is an indication that you have the seeds of the determination to equip yourself — and that is the real starting-point. Confidence will enable you to overcome fear, boredom, isolation and loneliness.

Physical fitness plays an important part. The fitter you are the better you will survive. Initially you may have to go without sleep to ensure that you are in a safe location, or make a long march in dangerous conditions. Do not wait until you are forced to go without sleep to see whether you are capable of doing so. Prove it to yourself now by getting into training. Develop the resources to cope with fatigue and loss of sleep.

You will be working hard to procure food and water. They will relieve hunger and thirst. But finding them will tire you and you will need an adequate shelter to enable you to rest and recover from your efforts. Don't overdo it. Rest frequently and assess the situation.

Pain and fever are warning signals that call attention to an injury or physical condition. They are not in themselves dangerous, however distressing and discomforting. Pain can be controlled and overcome. Its biological function is to protect an injured part, to prevent you using it, but this warning may have to be ignored to avoid the risk of further injury or death.

Injured people with multiple fractures, who would certainly have died if they had just lain where they were, hoping for help, have been known to crawl long distances from isolated regions to reach assistance.

Concentration and intense effort can actually stop and reduce feelings of pain for a time, though it is important to treat any injury as soon as possible. Remember that ignoring even a small sore or blister could lead to serious problems later.

BASIC NEEDS

To reiterate, the main elements required for survival are FOOD, FIRE, SHELTER and WATER. Their order of importance will depend upon where you happen to be. In the desert, water will head the list; in polar regions shelter and fire will be the main concerns. Ordering your priorities is one of the first steps to survival.

It takes a healthy person quite a long time to die of starvation, for the body can use up its stored resources, but exposure to wind, rain and cold can be fatal even in temperate climates and death comes in only minutes in the icy waters of the poles. Food is rarely the first priority. Even in those places where it is difficult to find there are usually other problems to face first. Shelter will often be the prime necessity in extremes of climate or temperature — not just in the frozen polar regions or the baking deserts, but for walkers trapped by mist on a hillside. The need for fire is closely linked.

Water is something that most people in the modern world take for granted. They are so used to turning on a tap that until an extreme drought causes water rationing they scarcely think about it. Yet the survivor at sea, or after a flood, though surrounded by water, may be desperate for drinkable water — and there are many places where, unless it rains, no obvious water is available. The other survival necessities are dealt with later in the book, but water is universally important.

WATER

Water is essential to life. All life depends upon it and all living things contain it. The average person can survive for three weeks without food but for only three days without water. It is the number one priority. Don't wait until you have run out of water before you look for it. Conserve what you have and seek a source as soon as possible, preferably fresh running water, though all water can be sterilized by boiling or the use of chemical purifiers.

The human body is 75 per cent water. It is the coolant that keeps the body at an even temperature, it is needed to keep the kidneys functioning to eliminate wastes and it is in some ways the conductor or vehicle for nerve impulses. But the fluids contained in the body are limited. Lost water must be replaced or health and efficiency will suffer.

Water loss

The average person loses 2–3 litres (4–6pt) of water each day – even someone resting in shade loses about 1 litre (2pt). Just breathing loses fluids, and loss through respiration and perspiration increases with work rate and temperature. Vomitting and diarrhoea in illness increase loss further. This must all be replaced to preserve the critical water balance, either by actual water or water contained in food.

HOW TO RETAIN FLUIDS

To keep fluid loss to the minimum, take the following precautions:

- Avoid exertion. Just rest.
- Don't smoke.
- Keep cool. Stay in shade. If there is none erect a cover to provide it.
- Do not lie on hot ground or heated surfaces.
- Don't eat, or eat as little as possible. If there is no water available fluid will be taken from the vital organs to digest food, further increasing dehydration. Fat is hardest to digest and takes a lot of fluid to break it down.
- Never drink alcohol. This also takes fluid from vital organs to break it down.
- Don't talk – and breathe through the nose, not the mouth.

FINDING WATER

The first place to look is in valley bottoms where water naturally drains. If there is no obvious stream or pool, look for patches of green vegetation and try digging there. There may be water just below the surface which will build up in the hole. Even digging in gullies and dry stream beds may reveal a spring beneath the surface, especially in gravelly areas. In mountains look for water trapped in crevices.

On the coast digging above the high water line, especially where there are sanddunes, has a good chance of producing about 5cm (2in) of fresh water that filters down and floats on the heavier salt water. It may be brackish but is still drinkable. Where cliffs fall into the sea look for lush growth of vegetation, even ferns and mosses, in a fault in the rock formation and you may find a soak or spring.

If no freshwater can be found, saltwater can be distilled (see *Solar still* and *Distillation*, this section).

> ## *WARNING*
>
> Be suspicious of any pool with no green vegetation growing around it, or animal bones present. It is likely to be polluted by chemicals in the ground close to the surface. Check edge for minerals which might indicate alkaline conditions. ALWAYS BOIL WATER FROM POOLS. In deserts there are lakes with no outlets; these become salt lakes. Their water MUST be distilled before drinking.

Dew and rain collection

Despite the acid rain produced by industrialized countries, which can cause a build-up of pollution in the soil, rainwater everywhere is drinkable and only needs collecting. Use as big a catchment area as possible, running the water off into containers of every kind. A hole dug in the ground and lined with clay will hold water efficiently, but keep it covered. If you have no impermeable sheeting, metal sheets or bark can be used to catch water in. If you have any doubt about the water you have collected, boil it.

In climates where it is very hot during the day and cold at nights, heavy dew can be expected. When it condenses on metal objects it can be sponged or licked off.

You can use clothing to soak up water and then wring it out. One way is to tie clean cloths around the legs and ankles and walk through wet vegetation. These can be sucked or wrung out.

ANIMALS AS SIGNS OF WATER

Mammals
Most animals require water regularly. Grazing animals are usually never far from water — though some kinds travel thousands of miles to avoid the dry season — as they need to drink at dawn and dusk. Converging game trails often lead to water; follow them downhill. Carnivores (meat eaters) can go for a long period between waterings. They get moisture from the animals on which they prey so are not a positive indication of local water.

Birds
Grain eaters, such as finches and pigeons, are never far from water. They drink at dawn and dusk. When they fly straight and low they are heading for water. When returning from water they are loaded with it and fly from tree to tree, resting frequently. Plot their direction and water can be found.

Water birds can travel long distances without stopping to feed or drink so do not necessarily indicate water nearby. Hawks, eagles and other birds of prey also get liquids from their victims so cannot be taken as a sign of local water.

Reptiles
Not an indicator of water. They collect dew and get moisture from prey, so can go a long time without.

Insects
Good indicators, especially bees: they fly at most 6.5km (4 miles) from their nests or hives, but have no regular watering times. Ants are dependent upon water. A column of ants marching up a tree is going to a small reservoir of trapped water. Such reservoirs are found even in arid areas. Most flies keep within 90m (100yd) of water, especially the European Mason Fly with its iridescent green body.

Human tracks
Will usually lead to a well, bore hole or soak. It may be covered over with scrub or rocks to reduce evaporation. Replace the cover.

REMEMBER: RATION YOUR SWEAT NOT YOUR WATER!
If you have to ration water, take it in sips. After going a long time without water, don't guzzle when you do find it. Take only sips at first. Large gulps will make a dehydrated person vomit, losing even more of the valuable liquid.

CONDENSATION

Tree and plant roots draw moisture from the ground, but a tree may take it from a water table 15m (50ft) or more below, too deep to dig down to reach. Don't try; let the tree pump it up for you by tying a plastic bag around a leafy branch. Evaporation from the leaves will produce condensation in the bag.

Choose healthy vegetation and bushy branches. On trees keep the mouth of the bag at the top with a corner hanging low to collect condensed evaporation.

Placing a polythene tent over any vegetation will collect moisture by evaporation which will condense on the plastic as it cools. Suspend the tent from the apex or support with a padded stick. Avoid foliage touching the sides of the trap or it will divert water droplets which should collect in plastic-lined channels at the bottom.

Even cut vegetation will produce some condensation as it warms up when placed in a large plastic bag. Keep the foliage off the bottom with stones so that water collects below it, and keep the foliage from touching the plastic. Use stones to keep the bag taut. Support the top on a padded stick. Arrange the bag on a slight slope to encourage condensation to run down to the collecting point. When no longer productive carefully replace with fresh foliage.

Solar still

Dig a hole in the ground approximately 90cm (36in) across and 45cm (18in) deep. Place a collecting can in the centre, then cover the hole with a sheet of plastic formed into a cone. The sun's heat raises the temperature of the air and soil below and vapour is produced. As the air becomes saturated, water condenses on the underside of the plastic, running down into the container. This is especially effective in desert regions and elsewhere when it is hot during the day and cold at night. The plastic cools more quickly than the air, causing heavy condensation. This kind of still should collect at least 55cc (1pt) over a 24-hour period.

The still may also double as a trap. Insects and small snakes are attracted by the plastic. They may slide down into the cone or wriggle underneath it and drop into the hole and then cannot climb out.

A solar still can be used to distill pure water from poisonous or contaminated liquids.

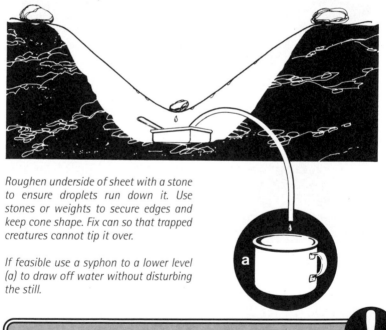

Roughen underside of sheet with a stone to ensure droplets run down it. Use stones or weights to secure edges and keep cone shape. Fix can so that trapped creatures cannot tip it over.

If feasible use a syphon to a lower level (a) to draw off water without disturbing the still.

WARNING

URINE AND SEA WATER

Never drink either — Never! But both can produce drinking water if distilled — and sea water will provide you with a residue of salt.

44

Distillation

Distillation kits are part of the equipment of life-rafts, but they can be improvised. To distill liquid you need to make something to do the job of a laboratory retort. Pass a tube into the top of a water-filled covered container, placed over a fire, and the other end into a sealed collecting tin which, preferably, is set inside another container providing a jacket of cold water to cool the vapour as it passes out of the tube. You can improvise the equipment from any tubing — pack frames, for instance. To avoid wasting water vapour, seal around the joins with mud or wet sand.

An easier method is a variation on the desert still. It takes a little longer for the water to condense but may be easier to set up.

Take a tube from a covered vessel in which polluted/saltwater, or even urine, is to boil. Set the other end under a solar still. A sheet of metal or bark, perhaps weighted down, will cover the vessel. Even a cone of leaf over the water pot will help direct the steam into the tube.

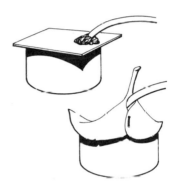

Water from ice and snow

Melt ice rather than snow — it produces a greater volume faster for less heat: twice as much for half the heat. If forced to heat snow, place a little in the pot and melt that first, gradually adding more to it. If you put a lot of snow into the pot, the lower level will melt and then be soaked up into the absorbent snow above it, leaving a hollow beneath which will make the pot burn. Lower layers of snow are more granular than that on the surface and will yield more water.

Water from sea ice

Sea ice is salt — no use for drinking — until it has aged. The more recently frozen, the saltier it will be. New sea ice is rough in contour and milky-white in colour. Old ice is bluish and has rounded edges, caused by weathering.

Good water can be obtained from blue ice — the bluer and smoother the better. But beware of even old ice that has been exposed to salt spray.

45

WATER FROM PLANTS

Water collectors

Cup-shaped plants and cavities between the leaves of bromeliads (many of which are parasitic on the branches of tropical trees) often collect a reservoir of water.

Bamboo often holds water in its hollow joints. Old and yellow stems are more likely to be water bearing. Shake them — if you can hear water slurping around cut a notch at the bottom of each joint and tip the water out.

Pitcher plant is used to describe many kinds of plant which catch and hold water. Strain the liquid to remove insects and debris trapped in the reservoir.

Traveller's Tree Ravenala madagascariensis, one of the banana family, can hold 1–2 litres (2–4pt) of water between the bases of the chevron of leaf stalks.

Vines

Vines with rough bark and shoots about 5cm (2in) thick can be a useful source of water. But you must learn by experience which are the water-bearing vines, because not all have drinkable water and some have a poisonous sap. The poisonous ones yield a sticky, milky sap when cut. You will know not to try that type again — otherwise it is a matter of trial and error and worth trying any species.

Some vines cause a skin irritation on contact if you suck them, so it is better to let the liquid drip into your mouth rather than put your mouth to the stem, and preferable to collect it in a container.

To obtain water from a vine select a particular stem and trace it upwards. Reach as high as possible and cut a deep notch in the stem. Cut off the same stem close to the ground and let the water drip from it into your mouth or into a container. When it ceases to drip cut a section from the bottom and go on repeating this until the vine is drained. Do NOT cut the bottom of the vine first as this will cause the liquid to run up the vine through capillary action.

Roots

In Australia the Water Tree, Desert Oak and Bloodwood have their roots near the surface. Pry these roots out from the ground and cut them up into 30cm (12in) lengths. Remove the bark. Suck out the moisture, or shave to a pulp and squeeze over the mouth.

It is not easy to find some of the most useful desert roots unless you have been shown by someone with experience. Australian Aborigines can identify a tiny twig which grows from a football-like bulbous root, which can be a life-saver — but unless you have been shown how to find them it is not worth expending your energy and resources looking.

Palms

The Buri, Coconut and Nipa palms all contain a sugary fluid which is very drinkable. To start it flowing bend a flowering stalk downwards and cut off its tip. If a thin slice is cut off the stalk every 12 hours the flow will be renewed, making it possible to collect up to a quart each day. Nipa palms shoot from the base so that you can work from ground level, on grown trees of other species you may have to climb up them to reach a flowering stalk.

Coconut milk has considerable water content, but from ripe nuts it is a powerful laxative; drinking too much would make you lose more fluid.

Cacti

Both the fruit and bodies of cacti store water, but not all cacti produce liquid safe to drink — the Saguarro, the giant multi-fingered cactus of Arizona, is very poisonous. Take care to avoid contact with cactus spines, they can be very difficult to remove, especially the very fine hair-like ones, and can cause festering sores if they stay in the skin.

The Barrel cactus *Echinocactus grusoni* (see *Desert plants* in *Food*) can reach a height of 120cm (4ft) and is found in the southern United States through to South America, requires considerable effort to cut through its tough, spine-covered outer skin. The best method is to cut off the top and chop out pieces from the inside to suck, or to smash the pulp within the plant and scoop out the watery sap, which varies from tasteless in some plants to bitter in others. An average-sized, 100cm (3.5ft) Barrel cactus will yield about 1 litre (2pt) of milky juice and this is an exception to the rule to avoid milky-sapped plants.

Saquarro cactus Sereus giganteus of Mexico, Arizona and California, grows to 5m (17ft) high holds large amounts of fluid — but it is poisonous. Collect and place in a solar still to evaporate and recondense during the cold night.

Opuntia cacti — Prickly pears, or Figilinda, have big, ear-like excrescences and produce oval fruits which ripen to red or gold. Their large spines are easier to avoid than those of many cacti. Both fruit and 'ears' are moisture laden.

WATER FROM ANIMALS

Animal eyes contain water which can be extracted by sucking them.

All fish contain a drinkable fluid. Large fish, in particular, having a reservoir of fresh water along the spine. Tap it by gutting the fish and, keeping the fish flat, remove the backbone, being careful not to spill the liquid, and then drink it.

If you need water that badly you should be careful not to suck up the other fish juices in the flesh, for they are rich in protein and will use up water in digestion.

Desert animals can also be a source of moisture. In times of drought in Northwestern Australia, Aborigines dig in dry clay pans for the desert frogs that burrow in the clay to keep cool and survive. They store water in their bodies and it can be squeezed out of them.

SALT

Salt is another essential for human survival. A normal diet includes a daily intake of 10gm (½oz). The trouble starts when you get rid of it faster than you eat it. The body loses salt in sweat and urine, so the warmer the climate the greater the loss. Physical exertion will increase the loss.

INFO.

The first symptoms of salt deficiency are muscle cramps, dizziness, nausea and tiredness. The remedy is to take a pinch of salt in half a litre (a pint) of water. There are salt tablets in your survival kit. Break them up and dissolve an appropriate amount in water. Do not swallow them whole — doing that could cause stomach upsets and harm the kidneys.

What happens if you do not carry salt or your supplies run out? By the coast or at sea there is plenty of saltwater available — a pint of sea water contains about 15gm (¾oz) of salt, but do NOT just drink it as it is. Dilute it with plenty of fresh water. Evaporating sea water will leave you with salt crystals.

Inland salt supplies are more problematic. In farming areas you will find salt licks for cattle — but you will then be close to civilization and not likely to have reached the stage of salt deprivation. However, all animals need salt and observation of them may reveal a natural source. In one part of Africa elephants risk the dangerous depths of a dark cave to lick salt from its sides.

Salt can be obtained from some plants. In North America the best source is the roots of hickory trees, and in south-east Asia those of the Nipa Palm can be used in the same way. Boil the roots until all the water is evaporated and black salt crystals are left.

If no direct salt sources are available to you then you will have to rely on getting it second-hand, through animal blood, which should never be wasted as it is a valuable source of minerals.

-2-
STRATEGY

Whether a small-scale accident or a mammoth disaster – both may bring about a life-or-death situation – the same disciplines and quick thinking are needed.

To show the way in which basic survival strategies are applied to every kind of situation, a series of individual small-scale vehicle incident procedures are outlined.

The same approaches can be seen on a far wider scale in the handling of a major air crash. In these circumstances the survivor is more likely to find himself in unfamiliar territory and involved with a greater number of people for a longer period.

STRATEGY

Good planning and preparation enable the survivor to confront difficulties and dangers that pose a serious threat to survival. They become contingencies for which you are equipped. But you cannot anticipate everything. You must be ready to respond rapidly to the unexpected danger and to deal with potential disaster rationally and realistically. You must overcome the tendency to panic, which such conditions so easily engender and take the action appropriate to the situation.

Sometimes a collision or other accident occurs with no warning of any kind, but in most instances there is a moment of realization that something is going to happen and it is in that moment that instinctive reaction can save lives. In many situations there is a considerable time in which an awareness of potential disaster can develop and that is when the panic reaction is probably most dangerous.

As mist closes in on a hillside, reducing visibility to almost nothing and making it easy to lose any sense of direction, most people would begin to panic at the thought that they are going to be trapped. They begin to do foolish things and increase their danger whereas they should already be assessing the possibilities and looking for some suitable shelter in which to wait until conditions become safe to continue. Keeping calm, in the knowledge that you have the ability to handle the situation, will not only enable you to see it through but also to see other solutions that may present themselves.

Some situations are predictable and knowledge of the techniques for handling them will minimize the risks. Learn them, they may save your life. They may take considerable nerve – like waiting for the right moment to escape from a car that is sinking under water – but they are based on experience and sound principles. The answer to more general survival problems, however, will often lie in inspired improvisation drawing on those skills appropriate to the situation.

Disaster may involve you in a contained situation which you must handle alone – or you may find yourself one of hundreds of people in a large-scale disaster over which there can be no control at all.

There is an enormous difference between coping with motoring accidents and dealing with an air disaster. As these extremes will show, whatever the scale the same resourcefulness and ability to call on a variety of knowledge and skills will apply. BOTH are matters of life and death, however many people they involve.

CAR ACCIDENT SURVIVAL

BRAKE FAILURE

If brakes fail while driving, change gear and apply the handbrake. You must do several things at once: take your foot off the accelerator, flick the switch of your warning lights, pump the footbrake rapidly (it may still connect), change down through the gears and apply handbrake pressure. Don't slam the brake on, begin with gentle bursts, gradually braking harder until you stop.

If there is no time for all this, take your foot off the accelerator and change down through the gears – and grab the handbrake – but DON'T apply maximum pressure until you are sure that you won't skid.

Look out for escape lanes and places where you can leave the road, preferably a soft bank or a turning that has an uphill slope.

If speed remains unchecked, on a steep hill for example, brush the car along a hedge or wall to reduce speed. Take advantage of a vehicle in front and use it to stop you – run into it as gently as the situation allows. Use warning lights, blow your horn and flash your headlights to give the driver in front as much warning as possible that you are on a collision course.

Collision

If collision seems inevitable, stay with it and steer the car to do as little damage to others and yourself as possible. Try to avoid a sudden stop by driving into something which will give. A fence is better than a wall, a clump of small saplings better than a tree – they will eventually stop you but a tree or wall will bring you to a dead stop – and probably very dead.

Seat belts (compulsory in many countries) will help stop you plunging forwards through the windscreen, but unbelted it is better NOT to try to brace yourself against collision. In the rare exception bracing may work, but generally it means only that when the car stops you continue travelling, doing even more damage than if you had gone with the collision, because your deceleration on impact is more sudden. Throw your arms around your head to protect it and twist sideways, away from the steering wheel,while flinging yourself TOWARDS the point of collision. It sounds difficult but, on collision, that steering wheel is like a ram in front of your ribcage.

Back seat passengers should similarly protect their heads and lie against the back of the front seats.

Jumping out

Do NOT try to jump out of a runaway car unless you know it to be headed for a cliff or other substantial drop and will not survive the impact. Then open the door, undo safety belt, begin to roll yourself into a ball – tuck the head tightly into the chest, bring feet and knees together, tightly tuck elbows into the sides, hands up by the ears, then bend at the waist. Drop from the car in a rolling movement. Do not resist the ground but keep balled up and continue the roll.

CAR UNDER WATER

If possible abandon the car before it sinks, for it will not sink immediately and will take time to fill. Water pressure on the outside makes it very difficult to open the door so roll down the window if you can and wriggle out of it. It takes great presence of mind to manage that when subject to the shock and surprise of the 'splash down', but if there are small children in the car it may be possible to push one through. Do not try to save possessions.

If you have not been fast enough CLOSE the window firmly, get children to stand and lift babies near to the roof. Release seat belts and tell everyone by a door to be ready with a hand on the handle. Release at once any automatic door locks or master locks. Water could prevent them from working. Do not attempt to open doors at this stage.

As water fills the interior, air will be trapped near the roof. The water pressure inside the car will nearly equalize the pressure with that of the water outside the car. As the car comes to rest and is nearly full of water tell everyone to take a deep breath, open the doors and swim to the surface, breathing out as they do so. Everyone leaving through the same door should link arms. If you have to wait for someone to get out before you, hold your breath for that moment.

PRECAUTION: Always park alongside water, not running towards it. If you have to park a car facing water then leave it in reverse gear and with the handbrake on (if facing away from water, in first gear with the handbrake on).

CAR ON RAILWAY TRACKS

If a car breaks down on an unmanned level crossing, put it into gear and use the starter motor to jerk it clear. This will work with a manual gear change but not with an automatic. If a train is approaching abandon the car, carry children or infirm persons to safety and keep away – about 45m (50yds) should be far enough – for if a train is travelling at high speed it could fling car wreckage quite a distance.

If there is no train visible, or you can see one several miles in the distance, you must try to avert the collision. If the car can be moved by pushing, push it clear of all tracks – you cannot be sure which one the train will be on. If there is an emergency telephone warn signalmen further down the track of the situation. If not, walk up the track towards the train. Stand well to one side (high speed trains have quite a slipstream) and wave a car blanket or bright coloured garment to warn the driver. If he is doing his job properly he will know that he is approaching a crossing and should look ahead to see that all is clear.

DISASTER IN THE AIR

A plane crash or forced landing in difficult terrain is one of the most dramatic of disaster scenarios. Since it could happen anywhere the individual cannot prepare for any specific situation.

Airline cabin staff are trained for such emergencies and you should follow their instructions. Aircrew will be trying to land the plane as safely as possible; there is nothing you can do except to keep calm and support the crew in calming the other passengers.

To prepare for a crash landing, tighten the seat belt, link arms with people on either side, hold your chin firmly down on your chest, lean forwards over a cushion, folded blanket or coat, interlink legs with your neighbours if seating permits it and brace yourself for impact.

When the aircraft finally stops moving – and not before – evacuate the aircraft as instructed in the pre-flight brief. If a ground landing, then quickly get away from the immediate area of the plane, as there is danger of fire or explosion. Even if there is no fire, keep away until the engines have cooled and any spilled fuel evaporated.

If ditching into water, dinghies will be automatically inflated and anchored on the wings. Do not inflate your own lifejacket while you are in the aircraft. To do so would restrict your exit. Wait until you are in the water and then pull the toggle to inflate it and get into a dinghy.

If the plane is sinking, release the dinghy from its anchorage as soon as passengers and equipment are stowed. As you leave the plane the more kit you can take with you the better. But do not stop to gather personal belongings and luggage. This is when you will be very glad you have a survival kit in your pocket.

NOTE:

If bailing out from a plane by parachute in wild country make your way to the wreck if you can – the wreckage will be much more noticeable to rescuers than a single person or a parachute.

After the crash

However self-disciplined you are, the entry into this kind of survival situation will be dramatic, abrupt and confusing. You will be in a state of shock and may be on the verge of panic. If there is fire or the risk of fire or explosion, keep at a distance until that danger seems to have passed, but no further away than seems necessary for safety. Do not allow anyone to smoke if fuel has been spilled. You must not blunder off into unknown terrain, especially at night, and need to maintain contact with other survivors.

Move injured persons to a safe distance with you and try to account for all the people involved. The immediate treatment of the injured is a priority. Treat cases in order of severity of their injuries and with each individual deal first with breathing difficulties, then in sequence, with major bleeding, wounds, fractures and shock.

Separate the dead from the living if possible – the deaths are part of the frightening strangeness of the event and the survivors will be easier to calm down.

Even with a fire, all may not have been destroyed. Investigate the wreckage and salvage whatever you can of equipment, food, clothing and water. Take NO risks if there is still a chance that fuel tanks could ignite and beware of any noxious fumes from wreckage which has been smouldering.

If you have to wait for fire to burn out, take stock of the location in which you find yourself – which should in any case be the next step in your strategy. Is it practical and safe to remain where you are? If your anticipated route is known – and with a flight it will be

– some kind of search and rescue operation can be expected and there are considerable advantages in staying where you are. Searchers will already have some idea of your location, and even if you have been forced off route they will have a record of your last reported position. The wreckage or grounded plane will be more noticeable from the air, especially in heavily wooded country where even a large group of people will be hidden by the trees.

If you find that you are in a very exposed or dangerous location then a move to a more protected position is necessary. However, do not move at night unless the threat to life outweighs the risks of trying to negotiate unknown terrain in the dark.

NOTE:

Leave an indication on the crash site of the direction in which you have moved off, so that it is possible for rescuers to know that there are survivors and to know in which direction to go on looking.

The usual reason for making an immediate move will be because you are in an exposed position on a mountain or hillside offering no protection from the elements, or at risk from rock falls or other dangers there. Move down, not up the slope, as conditions are likely to be less exposed on lower ground.

Do not all go off looking for a safer location. Send out scouts to investigate the surrounding terrain carefully. They must keep together, working in pairs, and not go off on individual explorations. They can maintain contact vocally and should mark their routes as they proceed so that they can easily retrace their steps.

PROTECTION

The first requirement will probably be some immediate shelter from the elements, especially for any injured. A more extended reconnaissance can follow to choose a proper campsite. Make the most of any natural shelter and augment it by using whatever materials are at hand.

If injuries are too severe for a person to be moved, some kind of shelter must be provided for them on the spot.

On bare ground, if there is no equipment or wreckage which can be utilized, then the only thing to do is dig down.

If possible, find a natural hollow and burrow deeper, using the excavated earth to build up the sides. This will at least get a casualty out of the wind. Get a fire going to provide warmth (it will also help raise morale) and use reflectors to maximize the heating effect, enabling you to conserve fuel.

If the circumstances make movement away unnecessary or impossible, follow similar procedures. Build up rocks, wreckage or equipment to form a wind break if no natural shelter is available. If in a group huddle together, it will reduce the loss of body heat. Survival time for badly injured persons in these circumstances is limited and you must hope for an early rescue. Fit people must go off in search of water, fuel, shelter materials and food – but always in at least pairs. Lay out as many signals as possible to attract attention.

Remember that shelter may be as necessary from sun as it is from wind and cold. Exposure is not only a matter of hypothermia.

LOCATION

If you have a radio or mobile phone you can signal for help – but do not go back on board a damaged and potentially explosive aircraft to do so. Wait until you are sure it is quite safe. The rescue party will want to know your location. Those who were travelling overland should have a good idea of their position – even if temporarily lost – and with a map should be able to give a more accurate fix. If you are the victim of disaster at sea or in the air, however, it will help considerably if you know your planned course and have some idea of your position when disaster struck, as well as of wind or current directions.

As often as not you must light fires – three fires are an internationally recognized distress signal. Make them as large as possible. Lay ground signals to attract attention, use pyrotechnics when you know help is within range and even make a noise when help is very near. This is when you are glad that the responsible authorities were told of your intentions and that you kept precisely to your route. It is only a matter of time before rescue comes. Meanwhile make yourself as comfortable as possible.

However, even the most careful plans may go astray. Navigational instruments could fail, storms, high winds or fog could all throw you off course and there you are, safe in your shelter but with no one knowing where. You could have a longer wait than you anticipate and you need to provide for it.

You also need to assess where you are on a more local scale, to study the terrain for anything it can tell you, not only to pin-point your position – if that is possible – but to see if there are safer and more comfortable locations to pitch camp, sources for fuel, food and water. In the long term you will also be assessing the possibility of making your own way across the land.

At sea you will be looking out for any indications that, rather than staying put, there is land close enough for your survival chances to be greater if you try to reach it rather than holding your present position. But you are at the mercy of wind and current, though you can delay your drift with a sea anchor.

NOTE:

On land, it is seldom most sensible to set out immediately to walk to safety, rather than wait for rescue. However, if you know that no one will be aware that you are missing, if the terrain is so barren that it provides no food, water or shelter, or if you feel convinced that your reserves of energy and rations are sufficient to see you back to civilization, or to a location where you are sure you will be able to live off the land, you may decide to set off as soon as the light is good enough or conditions are otherwise right.

ACQUIRING FOOD AND WATER

On an isolated cliff ledge, cut off by the tide or forced by storm or mist to wait until you can move on, there may be little opportunity to exploit natural resources. Do not tuck into your emergency rations immediately. You may be there for some time and, hungry though you may be, you should ration them out, allowing for a much longer wait than even a pessimistic assessment suggests. Even in such a situation there may be water and food within reach.

Elsewhere save your emergency rations for when there is nothing else and tap nature's resources first. Do not just find one source of food. Seek out a variety of plants for leaves, fruit, nuts, roots and other edible parts. Look for signs of animals which can be trapped or hunted.

When it is your very survival that is at stake there is no place for squeamishness about what you will or will not eat or about how you acquire your food, but that does not mean that you should totally abandon concern for wild life and the environment. When there is an abundance of other choices there is no reason to take already endangered species for your food – animal or vegetable – nor to set traps (which cannot discriminate in what they catch and maim) that will produce more meat than you can eat fresh or preserve. Making the most of nature's resources does not mean plundering them. Over-exploitation will be to your own disadvantage if you have to stay in the area for a long time.

Remember, too, that the most easily obtained nutritious food may be quite different from what you usually eat. If you have already learned to eat an unusual diet as part of your training you will find it much easier to feed yourself and will be able to encourage others to eat the same things.

Fuel for a fire will be needed for boiling water even if the temperature does not demand a fire for warmth – but do not be deluded into thinking that a warm day is going to be followed by a warm night. There can be dramatic temperature changes from day to night in some parts of the world.

NOTE:

In the short-term water is much more vital than food for your survival. If fresh running water is not available there are many other sources you can tap, but sterilize or boil to ensure that it is pure. Make finding water sources a priority.

NAVIGATION

Although in many circumstances it will be best to stay near to the scene of a crash, because there is material and equipment from a plane or vehicle, or its wreckage, which can be used and because your location is more likely to be known to rescuers, if you have made the decision to move you will need skills in direction-finding and in navigating your way through the terrain to safety.

YOU MUST PLAN

Remember this, it may save your life one day:

P Protection
L Location
A Acquisition
N Navigation

PEOPLE

For an expedition, the planning will include a careful selection of compatible personalities, selected for their fitness, both physically and in experience and training, for the particular project. In a disaster situation anyone may react unexpectedly under stress. With a mishap affecting members of the general public there may be a very varied group of people thrown together. Men, women and children, elderly people and babies. There may be pregnant women and people with medical problems or physical disabilities that require particular attention. The accident situations which involve such a varied group are also likely to involve a higher risk of injuries than among a hand-picked group of the trained and fit.

Babies may look very fragile – but they are very tough. However, they must be kept warm. Children will need reassuring and comforting, especially if they have lost the people with them or they are themselves in pain. Often the adventure of the situation will help to keep them from becoming too worried and it will help to keep them occupied, but they should not be allowed to wander, to play with fire or otherwise expose themselves to further danger. Old people are usually mentally tough and can give reassurance to the younger, but they must be kept warm and fed regularly. It often seems true that women handle emergencies much better than men and are able to accept responsibility for others more easily.

With a ship or commercial airline the ship's officers or flight crew can be expected to take charge of the situation, if they are among survivors, but there will not be the military chain of command or the acceptance of leadership and responsibility which can be expected in a compact organized group. Some democratic procedure to make decisions, plan action and maintain morale must be attempted. The trauma of the experience may leave some people eager to follow any leadership which gives them hope, but it will also throw into relief antagonisms and prejudices which must be overcome.

In an air or sea disaster people of different cultures and backgrounds may be thrown together and forced into situations which their own social taboos would not permit. Considerable tact may be necessary to overcome these problems. SURVIVAL, however, must take precedence.

The wider your medical knowledge the better, but giving people the will to survive is important and much of this can be achieved by a good 'bedside manner' – if you can give the impression that you know what you are doing you are half-way there.

Calmness and confidence in yourself will inspire the confidence and cooperation of others. The more knowledge you have the better you will be able to cope.

-3-
CLIMATE & TERRAIN

Although basic survival strategy and techniques are applicable anywhere, conditions vary widely around the world. It is essential to know as much as possible about conditions in any regions in which you expect to travel. A general knowledge of what you may expect in different climates will greatly increase your ability to handle the survival situation, if accident throws you into totally unfamiliar territory.

A few pages in this book cannot provide a world geography. They can only set the scene for the major types of climate and environment and suggest some of the principle ways of overcoming the problems they present.

Advice on specific topics, such as food and shelter, applicable to particular conditions will be found throughout the other sections of the book, supplementing the information given here.

CLIMATE ZONES

People often view an alien environment as an enemy and feel they must fight it. This is not the way to survive — fight it and you will lose! There are dangers against which precautions must be taken, but nature is neutral. Learn to live with each climate and to use what it offers. Climate is not conditioned only by latitude; location within a continent and altitude are equally important.

Polar climates

Polar regions are regarded as those at latitudes higher than 60°33′ north and south, but cold weather skills may be needed at very high altitudes everywhere. Near the Equator, in the Andes for example, the snow line is not reached until an altitude of about 5000m (16,500ft), but the nearer the poles the lower the snow line will be — at the southern tip of South America there is permanent snow at only a few hundred metres (a thousand feet). Arctic conditions penetrate deep into the northern territories of Alaska, Canada, Greenland, Iceland, Scandinavia and the USSR.

Tundra

South of the polar cap, the ground remains permanently frozen and vegetation is stunted. Snow melts in summer, but roots cannot penetrate the hard earth. High altitudes produce similar conditions.

Northen coniferous forest

Between the arctic tundra and the main temperate lands is a forest zone, up to 1300km (800 miles) deep. In Russia, where it is known as the Taiga, the forests penetrate up to 1650km (400 miles) north of the Arctic Circle along some Siberian rivers, but in the Hudson Bay area of Canada the tree line moves an equal distance south of the Circle.

Winters are long and severe, the ground frozen for much of the time, summers short. For only 3–5 months of the year is the ground thawed sufficiently for water to reach the roots of the trees and plants, which especially flourish along the great rivers that flow to the Arctic Ocean. There is a wealth of game: elk, bear, otter, lynx, sable and squirrel, as well as smaller creatures, and many birds.

In summer, where the snow melt cannot drain, it creates swamps. Fallen trees and dense growths of sphagnum moss make the going difficult. Mosquitoes can be a nuisance (but they do not carry malaria).

Movement is easier in winter, if you have warm clothing. Travel along the rivers, where fishing is good, making a raft from the abundant deadfalls.

Temperate climates

The temperate zone of the northern hemisphere, and the similar climates of the southern hemisphere, probably offer the most equitable circumstances for survival without special skills or knowledge. They will be the areas best known to many readers of this book. These territories are also those most heavily urbanized and where the survival ordeal is not likely to be very extended. A fit and healthy person, equipped with basic skills, would not be so cut off that they could not reach help within a few day's trek. Heavy winter conditions may call for polar skills.

Deciduous forest

As the climate gets warmer and winters less severe, deciduous forest replaces the conifers. Oak, beech, maple and hickory are the main species in America; oak, beech, chestnut and lime, in Eurasia. Soil rich in humus supports many plants and fungi. Survival is not difficult, except at very high altitudes where tundra, or snowfield conditions appear. Many of these areas have been cleared by man.

Temperate grassland

Mainly central continental areas with hot summers, cold winters and moderate rainfall, these have become the world's great food producing areas — grain is grown and cattle reared. Water can be a problem in summer and shelter in winter.

Mediterranean regions

The lands bordering on the Mediterranean are semi-arid areas, with long hot summers and short dry winters. There is sunshine most of the year, and drying winds. At one time this region was forested with oaks. When these were cut down the soil eroded, much of the area became covered with evergreen shrub. The Chapparal of California is very similar. Trees are few and water is a problem. At high altitudes, other conditions prevail.

Tropical forests

The land between the tropics includes areas of cultivation and extremes of swamp and desert, but one-third is undeveloped forest: equatorial rain forest, sub-tropical rain forest

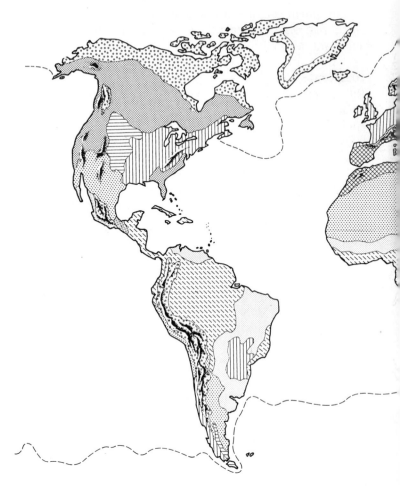

and montane forest. All feature high rainfall and rugged mountains, which drain into large, swift-flowing rivers, with coastal and other low-lying regions often as swampland.

Savannah

This is tropical grassland, lying usually between the desert and the tropical forest. Near the forests the grass is tall, up to 3m (10ft) high, and trees more frequent. Temperatures are high the whole year round. More than one-third of Africa is savannah and large areas of Australia, which are dotted with eucalyptus trees. Similar areas are the llanos of Venezuela and Colombia and the campos in Brazil. Often, water is not easily available but, where it is found, there will be lusher vegetation and plenty of wildlife. In Africa large herds of animals can be found.

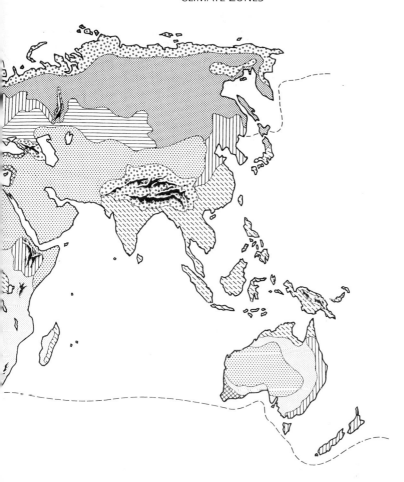

Deserts

One-fifth of the earth's land surface is desert — dry barren land where survival is very difficult. Deserts occur where air currents, which rose at the Equator and have already shed their moisture, descend and are rewarmed as they near the earth, taking what little local moisture is present. There are rarely any clouds to give protection from the sun or to retain heat at night so that great extremes of temperature occur from the highest shade temperatures (58°C/136°F in the Sahara) to below freezing point at night. Only small parts of the world's deserts are sand (about one-tenth of the Sahara), the greater part is flat gravel cut by dried up water courses (wadis). The wind has blown the sand away, piling it up in low-lying areas. Elsewhere there may be wind-carved mountains, dried mudflats and larva flows.

POLAR REGIONS

Antarctica is covered with a sheet of ice. In the Arctic the Pole is capped by deep ice floating on the sea and all the land north of the timber line is frozen. There are only two seasons – a long winter and a short summer – the day varying from complete darkness in midwinter to 24 hours daylight at midsummer.

Arctic summer temperatures can rise to 18°C (65°F), except on glaciers and frozen seas, but fall in winter to as low as –56°C (–81°F) and are never above freezing point. In the northern forests summer temperatures can reach 37°C (100°F), but altitude pushes winter temperatures even lower than in the Arctic. In Eastern Siberia –69°C (–94°F) has been recorded at Verkhotansk! Temperatures in the Antarctic are even lower than in the Arctic.

Antarctic winds of 177kmph (110mph) have been recorded and, in the Arctic autumn, winter winds reach hurricane force and can whip snow 30m (100ft) into the air, giving the impression of a blizzard – even when it is not snowing. Accompanied by low temperatures, winds have a marked chilling effect – much greater than the thermometer indicates. For instance, a 32kmph (20mph) wind will bring a temperature of –14°C (5°F) down to –34°C (–30°F) and one at 64kmph (40mph) would make it –42°C (–34°F) with even greater drops at lower temperatures. Speeds over 64kmph (40mph) do not appear to make a greater difference.

TRAVEL

Experience shows the best policy is to stay near an aircraft or disabled vehicle. If the spot is hazardous establish a safe shelter as close by as possible. A decision to walk-out will be based on nearness to civilisation and probability of rescue.

Decide early what to do – while you can still think clearly. Cold dulls the mind.

Movement in a blizzard is out of the question and, at all times, navigation is difficult on featureless ice and tundra. Ice movement pushes up ridges which make the going treacherous. Summer melt water makes the tundra boggy and even sea ice slushy underfoot.

Mosquito, black-fly, deerfly and midges can all be a nuisance in the arctic summer. Their larvae live in water – avoid making shelter nearby. Keep sleeves down, collar up, wear a net over the head and burn green wood and leaves on the fire – smoke keeps them at bay. When it turns colder, these nuisances are less active and they disappear at night.

In Alaska, northwestern and northeastern Canada, Greenland, Iceland, Scandinavia, Novaya Zemlya, Spitzbergen and on other islands there are mountains where ice cliffs, glaciers, crevasses and avalanches are hazards. Near the Arctic coastline frequent fog from May to August, sometimes carried far inland, increases navigation problems.

Navigation

Compasses are unreliable near the Poles, the constellations are better direction-finders and nights light enough to travel by. By day use the shadow tip method (see *Reading the signs*).

Travelling on sea ice do NOT use icebergs or distant landmarks to fix direction. Floes are constantly moving — relative positions may change. Watch for ice breaking up and, if forced to cross from floe to floe, leap from and to a spot at least 60cm (2ft) from the edge. Survivors have been rescued from floes drifting south but sooner or later ice floating into the warmer oceans will melt — though that chance may be worth taking.

AVOID icebergs, they have most of their mass below the water. As this melts, they can turn over without warning, particularly with your added weight.

AVOID sailing close to ice-cliffs. Glaciers may 'calve' huge masses of ice, often thousands of tons, which break off into the sea without warning.

Bird observations can aid navigation. Migrating wildfowl fly to land in the thaw. Most seabirds fly out to sea during the day and return at night.

Sky reflections help to determine distant terrain. Clouds over open water, timber or snow-free ground appear black below; over sea ice and snowfields, white. New ice produces greyish reflections, mottled ones indicate pack ice or drifted snow.

Snow shoes

All polar travel is strenuous and should only be attempted by a fit person. On snow with a hard crust skis are the best means of travel, though difficult to improvise. Skiing in deep loose snow takes great effort and, in soft snow, snow shoes are better. To walk in snow shoes lift each foot without angling it, unlike a normal stride, keeping the shoe as flat to the ground as possible.

Bend a long green sapling back on itself to form a loop and secure ends firmly. Add crosspieces and twine — the more the better — but do not make the shoes too heavy. You will not be able to walk far without getting very tired. Allow a firmer central section to attach to your foot.

Follow rivers

Travel downstream — by raft in summer, on the ice in winter — except in northern Siberia where rivers flow north.

On frozen rivers keep to smoother ice at the edges and to outer curve on the bends. Where two rivers join follow the outside edge or take to the outer bank. If the river has many bends, leave the ice and travel by higher ridges.

WARNING

ICE COLD WATER IS A KILLER
Falling into icy water knocks the breath out of you. The body curls up with loss of muscular control and violent shivering. Exposed parts freeze in about 4 minutes, consciousness clouds in 7, death follows in 15-20.

RESIST! Take violent action on hitting the water. Move fast for land. Then roll in snow to absorb water. Get to shelter and into dry kit immediately.

CLOTHING

Severe cold and harsh winds can freeze unprotected flesh in minutes. Protect the whole body, hands and feet. Wear a hood — it should have a drawstring so that it can partly cover the face. Fur trimming will prevent moisture in the breath freezing on the face and injuring the skin.

Outer garments should be windproof, with a close enough weave to prevent snow compacting, but porous enough to allow water vapour to escape — NOT waterproof, which could create condensation inside. Under layers should trap air to provide heat insulation. Skins make ideal outer clothing.

Openings allow heat to escape, movement can drive air out through them. If clothing has no draw strings, tie something around sleeves above cuffs, tuck trousers into socks or boots.

If you begin to sweat loosen some closures (collar, cuffs). If still too warm remove a layer. Do so when doing jobs like chopping wood or shelter building.

Only a plane crash or forced landing is likely to leave someone in polar regions unequipped. Try to improvise suitable clothing before leaving the plane.

Wear wool — it does not absorb water and is warm even when damp.

Spaces between the knit trap body heat. It is best for inner garments.

Cotton acts like a wick, absorbing moisture. When wet, it can lose heat 240 times faster than when dry.

Feet

Mukluks, boots of waterproof canvas with a rubber sole which comes up to the caulk and with a drawstring to adjust fitting, are ideal. Ideally they should have an insulated liner.

Insulate feet with three pairs of socks, graded in size to fit over each other and not wrinkle. If necessary, improvise foot coverings with several layers of fabric. Canvas seat covers can make improvised boots.

Trenchfoot can develop when the feet are immersed in water for long periods, as in the boggy tundra during the summer months (see *Cold climate hazards* in *Health*).

Snow glare

Protect the eyes with goggles or a strip of cloth or bark with narrow slits cut for eyes. The intensity of the sun's rays, reflected by snow, can cause snow blindness. Blacken beneath the eyes with charcoal to reduce glare further.

C.O.L.D.

The key to keeping WARM

Keep it – **C**LEAN – Dirt and grease block air spaces!
Avoid – **O**VERHEATING – Ventilate!
Wear it – **L**OOSE – Allow air to circulate!
Keep it – **D**RY – Outside and inside!

SHELTER

You cannot stay in the open to rest. GET OUT OF THE WIND! Look for natural shelter you can improve on, but AVOID the lee side of cliffs where snow could drift and bury your shelter, or sites where rock fall or avalanche is likely. Avoid snowladen trees — the weight could bring down frozen branches — unless the lower boughs are supported on the snow. There may be a space beneath the branch which will provide a ready-made shelter (see *Shelter* in *Camp Craft*).

REMEMBER: Don't block EVERY hole to keep out draughts. You MUST have ventilation, especially if burning a fire inside your shelter. Otherwise you may asphyxiate.

FIRE

Essential for polar survival. Fuel oil from wreckage can provide heat. Drain oil from sump and reservoir on to the ground as soon as possible — as it cools it will congeal and become impossible to drain. High octane fuel does not freeze so quickly — leave it in the tanks.

In the Antarctic and on the Arctic ice, seal and bird fat are the only other fuel sources. On coasts driftwood can sometimes be collected — Greenlanders used to build homes from timber which drifted across the Arctic from Siberian rivers. In the tundra low, spreading, willow can be found. Birch scrub and juniper also grow beyond the forests. Birch bark makes excellent kindling — the wood is oily. Feather a branch and it will burn even when wet.

Casiope is another low, spreading heather-like plant that Eskimos use for fuel. Evergreen, with tiny leaves and white bell-shaped flowers, and only 10-30cm (4-12in) high. It contains so much resin that it, too, burns when wet.

Casiope

WATER

Even in the cold you need over a litre (2pt) daily to replace losses. In summer water is plentiful in tundra lakes and streams. Pond water may look brown and taste brackish but vegetation growing in it keeps it fresh. If in doubt BOIL.

In winter melt ice and snow. Do NOT eat crushed ice, it can injure your mouth and lips and also cause further dehydration. Thaw snow sufficiently to mould into a ball before attempting to suck it.

REMEMBER: if already cold and tired eating snow will further chill your body.

FOOD

Antarctic: Lichens and mosses, growing on dark, heat-absorbing rocks on some northern coasts, are the only plants. Seas are rich in plankton and krill which support fishes, whales, seals and many seabirds. Most birds migrate in autumn, but flightless penguins stay. They make good eating. Most of the year they take to the water at the first sign of danger but, when incubating eggs, sit tight on their burrows or scrapes.

Arctic: Ice provides no habitat for plants or ground animals, even polar bear are likely only where they can find prey — and they are difficult and dangerous to hunt. Seabirds, fish and seals, where there is water, are the potential foods. Foxes — the Arctic fox turns white in winter — sometimes follow polar bears on to sea ice to scavenge their kills. Northern wildlife is migratory and availability depends on season.

Tundra and forest: Plants and animals can be found in winter and summer and the northern forests offer even more wildlife. Tundra plant species are the same in Russia as in Alaska. All are small compared to warmer climate plants: ground spreading willow, birch and berry plants with high vitamin content. Lichens and mosses, found widely, form a valuable food source — especially reindeer moss.

Poisonous plants

The majority of Arctic plants are edible, but AVOID Water Hemlock — the most poisonous. AVOID the fruit of the Baneberry. AVOID small Arctic buttercups. Other temperate poisonous species found far north include Lupin, Monkshood, Larkspur, Vetch (Locoweed), False hellebore and Death camas. Best avoid fungi too — make sure you can distinguish lichens from them! There are no Arctic plants which are known to produce contact poisoning.

Animals for food

Bark and greenery stripped from trees is evidence of feeding animals. Caribou (reindeer) are common from Alaska to west Greenland and found across northern Scandinavia and Siberia. Shaggy musk-ox roam in northern Greenland and, in the islands of the Canadian archipelago, Elk (Moose) are found — where there is a mixture of forest and open ground.

Wolves are common in northern Canada, Alaska and Siberia (but rare and protected in most European countries). Foxes, living in the tundra in summer and open woodland in winter, are an indication of other, smaller prey — mountain hares, squirrels and other small rodents which burrow beneath the snow to find seeds. Lemmings make runways beneath the snow. Beaver, mink, wolverines and weasels can all be found in the Arctic.

Bears roam the barren lands of the north as well as the forests. They can be dangerous. Give them a wide berth.

The best chances for survival are along coasts where the sea provides a dependable source of food. Seals are found on coasts, pack ice and in the open water.

Walruses may look cumbersome but are also very dangerous. LEAVE THEM ALONE UNLESS YOU ARE ARMED.

Hunting and Trapping

Tracks are clear in snow and easy to follow — but leave a trail of fluttering flags of bright material from wreckage to find your way back to your shelter. Make them high enough not to be covered by a fresh snowfall.

Caribou can be very curious and may sometimes be lured by waving a cloth and moving on all fours. Imitating a four-legged animal may also bring wolves closer, thinking you might be prey. Ground squirrels and marmots may run into you if you are between them and their holes. Some prey animals can be attracted by the sound made by kissing the back of your hand. It is like the noise made by a wounded mouse or bird. Make it from a concealed position and downwind. Be patient. Keep on trying.

Stalking animals is difficult in the exposed Arctic. If you have a projectile weapon — gun, bow, catapult — which can be fired from ground level, lie in ambush behind a screen of snow. To be more mobile make a screen of cloth which can stand in front of you, and slowly be moved forward.

In winter, owls, ravens and ptarmigans — the birds available in the north — are usually 'tame' and can be approached slowly, without sudden movements. Many polar birds have a 2–3 week summer moult, which makes them flightless — they can be run down. Eggs are among the safest foods and are edible at any stage of embryo development.

Seals

A main source of food on polar ice, some seals remain there right through the winter. The antarctic Weddel seal, most southerly of mammals, can dive for 15 minutes before coming up to breathe from pockets of air beneath the ice, or at small holes which it keeps open by nibbling around the edges. Most seals must breathe more frequently. Few are as formidable as the Elephant seal, which can rear up to twice a man's height in attack or defence.

Seals are most vulnerable on the ice floes with their young pups (produced between March and June in the Arctic according to species). Newborn seals cannot swim and are easy to catch — thousands are massacred by hunters and in culls each year by simply walking among them on the ice and clubbing them.

Out of the breeding season, breathing holes in the ice are the best place to catch seals; recognize them by their cone shape (narrower on the upper surface). In thicker ice they will be surrounded by flipper and toothmarks where the seal has been keeping the hole open. You have to be patient, yet ever ready, for the visits to the hole are brief. Club the animal then enlarge the hole to recover the carcass.

Seals provide food, clothing, moccasins and blubber for fires. Adult males have a strong odour early in the year, but it does not affect their meat.

Eat all except the liver, which at some times of the year has DANGEROUS concentrations of vitamin A. Cook seal meat to avoid Trichinosis.

POLAR BEARS

Confined to the high Arctic — in Europe only resident on Spitzbergen — they have a keen sense of smell and are tireless hunters on sea ice and in the sea. Feeding mainly on seals, with some fish, they swim well and can stay submerged for two minutes. Rarely found on land — though in summer they may feed on berries and lemmings. Like many cold-climate animals they are larger than their warmer-climate relatives. Most are curious and will come to you — but treat these powerful animals with respect and caution.

Always cook meat: muscles always carry Trichinosis worm. NEVER eat polar bear liver which can have lethal concentrations of vitamin A.

Preparing meat

Bleed, gut and skin while the carcass is still warm. Roll hides before they freeze. Cut meat into usable portions and allow to freeze. Do not keep reheating. Once cooked, eat leftovers cold (that's why you cut it up). Leave fat on all animals except seals. Fat is essential in cold areas but, if you eat a lot, make sure you take plenty of fluids. Except in extreme cold (when it will freeze) remove seal fat and render it down before it turns rancid. It can also be useful fire fuel.

When food is scarce animals will steal it — so cache it carefully. If there are signs of would-be thieves look out for them — they could be your next meal.

Rodents, especially squirrels, and rabbits and hares, can carry Tularemia, which can be caught from ticks or handling infected animals. Wear gloves when skinning. Boiled flesh is safe.

ARCTIC HEALTH

Frostbite, hypothermia and snow blindness are the main hazards, while efforts to keep warm and exclude draughts can lead to lack of oxygen and carbon monoxide poisoning.

It is easy to withdraw from reality, layered in clothing and with the head wrapped in a hood. Thinking can become sluggish and obvious things overlooked. Keep 'switched on'. Keep active — but avoid fatigue and conserve energy for useful tasks. Sleep as much as possible — the cold will wake you before you freeze unless you are completely exhausted and cannot regenerate the heat you lose to the air.

AVOIDING FROSTBITE

- Wrinkle face to stop stiff patches forming, pulling muscles in every direction. Exercise hands.

- Watch yourself and others for patches of waxy, reddening or blackened skin, especially on faces, ears, hands.

- AVOID tight clothing which will reduce circulation.

- Dress inside warmth of sleeping bag (if you have one).

- Never go out without adequate clothing — however briefly. Avoid getting clothing wet, through sweat or water. Dry it as soon as possible if this happens.

- Knock snow off before entering shelter, or leave outer clothing at entrance. Snow will melt in warmth giving you more clothing to dry.

- Wear gloves and keep them dry. NEVER touch metal with bare hands.

- AVOID spilling petrol on bare flesh. In sub-zero temperatures it will freeze almost at once and does even more damage than water because of its lower melting point.

- Be especially careful if you have been working hard and are fatigued. If you are sick — REST.

Don't let the cold demoralize you. Think up ways to improve the shelter, how to make a better pair of gloves, for instance. Exercise fingers and toes to improve circulation.

Don't put off defecation — constipation is often brought on that way. Do try to time it conveniently before leaving your shelter, so that you can take waste out with you.

MOUNTAINS

Mountain peaks are exposed to high winds and often covered in snow. They provide neither food nor shelter. Climbing rock and negotiating ice and snowfields calls for special skills, which are best learned firsthand in mountaineering schools and practised under supervision. No inexperienced person should think of trying to tackle real mountaineering territory, except as a learner with a properly organized party. But disaster may leave you on a mountainside or force you to cross a mountain range to get to safety.

If no rescue is likely, the first aim in daylight should be to get down into the valleys where food and shelter are available. At night and in bad visibility this is too dangerous. Some kind of shelter must be found until visibility improves.

Dig into the snow if there is no shelter among rocks and no wreckage to provide cover. If below the snow line you must cover yourself to prevent exposure. A plastic bag will make an improvised sleeping bag, if you have no survival kit. Salvage blankets or covering from a crashed plane or use any clothing to cover yourself as much as possible, but do not pull clothes too tightly round you; air within the clothes will provide insulation.

On a slope, sleep with your head uphill; on rough and stony ground sleep on your stomach for greater comfort.

Judging terrain

As you descend a mountainside it will often be difficult to see what is below you. Can you move around a valley or along a spur to look back at what was below? The opposite side of a valley will give you some idea of what is on your side too.

Be cautious if you find you are looking at a distant slope beyond a foreground bluff, the ground is likely to fall steeply between. Scree slopes can be particularly deceptive and appear continuous until you are very close to a cliff.

Descent

Negotiating cliffs without a rope is extremely dangerous. On the steepest cliffs it is necessary to come down facing the cliff and very difficult to see footholds below. If there is an adjoining slope, a colleague can observe and give directions. Once down, you can then point out holds to others from below. A high cliff should never be attempted. In the case of a plane crash there is probably more risk in climbing than waiting for rescue.

To climb down rock faces which are less steep and with deeper ledges, adopt a sideways position using the inside hand for support. For easier crags, descend facing outwards with the body bent and where possible carry weight on the palms of the hands.

Ascent

Climbing upwards, holds are easier to see, but it is always safer to go round than over obstacles if you are travelling without knowing the route. You could get stuck with an impossible descent.

Always work out your route from the bottom and in climbing keep the body away from the rock and look up. Move only one hand or one foot at a time — always keep three points of contact. Keep your weight evenly balanced on the feet rather than hang from the hands. Do not overstretch.

With the feet firmly planted on the rock and one hand grasping a good hold, reach with the other for a hold just above the head. Test it and then look for another hold for the other hand or the feet. Use small intermediate holds, avoid becoming spread-eagled and let the legs do most of the work. Always place the feet as flat as possible to make maximum contact with the rock.

To climb vertically up fissures, use the chimney technique. Place your back against one surface and wedge your legs across the gap to the other. Slowly move up. If a chimney opens out you may have great difficulty in transferring to one face and have to descend again.

Descending by rope

With a rope firmly anchored at the upper level, it is possible to descend the sheerest cliff. The technique, known as abseiling or rappelling, can involve a special sit sling and a karabiner for the rope to pass through, but the basic method uses just a doubled rope. The rope does not move — you move down it. It is not comfortable, even with the body correctly angled, but it is the safest way to negotiate steep or very slippery slopes. Friction can damage clothing and skin, so if you can, pad out your shoulders and groin, and wear gloves.

The length of the rope controls the amount of descent and there must be a firm anchor point, a rock, or tree which can carry the weight and not

INFO.

Make sure that you are in a firm position before hauling the rope down — its sudden weight could affect your balance — and be sure that you have planned your next move. Once the rope is down you may have no way of retracing your steps.

cut the rope. If a series of platforms with firm anchors can be found, a slope can be negotiated in stages — but if several people are involved there must be room for all of them to wait at each stage.

After an abseil the rope can be pulled down after you. If someone is left above to untie the rope, or you are prepared to leave it behind, an undoubled rope can be used — making twice the descent possible with the same rope. Getting over the edge is often the most difficult part. You may have to climb down a few steps to gain a good position and sufficient confidence.

ABSEILING

Loop rope around firm anchor (test it with full body weight). Avoid sharp edges that could cut rope. Pass both ends of rope between legs from front, bring around to left of body and across chest, over right shoulder and down across back. Hold rope in front with left hand and at back with right. Plant feet about 45cm (18in) apart, firmly against slope and lean back. Let rope around body carry your weight. Do not try to support yourself with your upper hand. Step slowly downwards. The lower hand controls rate of descent. Pay the rope out one hand at a time.
CAUTION: *Abseiling can be dangerous. If not trained in the technique, NEVER attempt it, unless accompanied by an expert or in a survival situation.*

Using a cradle

On an unobstructed vertical descent, a cradle made from a bowline-on-the-bight (see *Knots* in *Camp Craft*) can be used to lower people down, or haul them up. Use this technique to rescue anyone who has fallen down a crevasse.

Ascending with ropes

Belaying is a method of helping others to climb up. First, one person must make the ascent with a rope (this could be a light line to haul up the actual rope afterwards) attached around the waist with a bowline. At each stage of the ascent there must be a platform or ledge to accommodate all the party and a secure anchor for the rope. If there are a number of lengths of rope a series of stages could be operated at the same time to handle a larger party.

Test that the anchor is firm — a tree, spike of rock or thread (a hole through rock, or a stone or small boulder firmly wedged in a crevice). Anchor the rope with a loop tied in a figure-of-eight or an overhand knot.

Belayer ties on with a bight or two bights to steady himself, and passes climbing rope over head and down to hips, making a twist around the arm closest to the anchor and takes up any slack. Climber ties on with a bowline around waist and begins to mount. Belayer takes in rope to keep it taught.

TAKING UP ROPE
Pull with both hands so that rope passes behind back (pull in with right hand, push away with left). Slide right hand out for more rope. Bring hands together and hold both parts of rope in right hand, while the left slides in towards body to take up slack. Begin again, pulling in with right hand, pulling rope around body with left. Be ready to arrest rope, in case climber falls. Bring rope tight around body by bringing hands together.

Anchor, belayer and climber should be in a straight line. If a spike is used it should be higher than the belayer's head. If this is not possible standing, the belayer should work from a secure sitting position.

Older people and children should be roped around the chest. Small children are best carried papoose-style on another climber's back.

Note: Belaying without an anchor is risky and requires more strength. The rope should then only pass through the belayer's fingers, NOT around the back, lest the belayer be pulled down by the climber.

> ## WARNING
> **FALLING ROCK CAN KILL!**
> On loose rock always test holds gently and never pull outwards on a loose hold.
> Be careful that your rope does not dislodge rocks. Even small falling rocks can inflict serious injury. If you knock a piece down, shout a warning to those below.

SNOW AND ICEFIELDS

Sophisticated equipment is available for climbing in snow and ice, but on snow some of the mountaineer's ice-axe techniques can be improvised with a stout stick — a handled walking stick may give more grip than a simple shaft. If not equipped with proper ice axe and crampons and skilled in their use, try to keep clear of mountain ice.

An ice axe or stick, driven into the snow when climbing, gives stability. On steep slopes climb in zig-zags, kicking steps and digging stick in sideways. Dig in heels and use stick on slighter slopes. On gentle slopes use heels and stick as a walking stick. On steep slopes descend backwards driving stick into snow for support and as a brake if you slip. Sliding down a snow slope is exhilarating, but dangerous.

Digging in the heels will help control speed and a stick driven into the snow is an additional brake — but there is always a risk that you have not seen a precipice ahead! Never use this method where there is any risk of avalanche.

Security ropes on ice

Any party moving across a glacier should be tied together, at not less than 9m (30ft) intervals. The leader should probe the snow with a stick, for any slight depression could indicate a crevasse.

Ropes fixed to a firm anchor at both ends can steady movement across ice patches which have to be traversed. Use as a hand hold, or tie a short rope in a bowline around the waist and secure to the rope with a prusik knot. This will slide along the rope to allow descent but if you slip will arrest your fall. This is a technique also useful on scree and loose descents for children and the less able.

Ice and snow bollards

If no firm rock is available for belaying, an upper anchor can be cut from the ice. Cut in a mushroom shape where natural ice formation makes it easiest. Make diameter at least 40cm (18in) and depth at least 15cm (6in). Discard and start again at the slightest sign of a crack in the ice.

A snow bollard must be much bigger: at least 30cm (1ft) deep and from 1m (40ft) wide in hard snow to 3m (10ft) in soft. Pack equipment and baggage around it to prevent rope cutting through.

Crevasses

Crevasses are found where a glacier starts at a valley wall, changes direction or spreads out in a widening valley. Travel slowly, probing the ground. If one of the group falls through the snow he is belayed by a rope and can be hauled out.

Pressure of rope on chest can cause asphyxiation. Pass a rope down with a loop to put a foot in to take the weight. If faller is unconscious it will take three people to heave him out. Manharness hitches will enable them to pull together. Temperature in a crevasse is very low and the victim will rapidly weaken. Speed is important.

AVALANCHES

Avalanches are a serious hazard in all high mountain regions. They most frequently occur on slopes of between 20° and 60°, and especially between 30° and 45°, usually within 24 hours of a snow fall.

Several things trigger avalanches, like temperature, ground conditions and noise. If you find yourself in avalanche prone areas be aware of these causes. Avoid if possible areas where fresh snow has just fallen on steep ground. After a major fall, waiting 24 hours for it to settle will help. The majority of victims of avalanches start them off themselves.

Rain, or a rise in temperature, after a snow fall greatly increases the risk. The melting process helps to lubricate the slide. Heavy snow falling during low temperature can also avalanche because it does not have enough time to stabilize.

Slopes with irregular surfaces are safest and timbered slopes are also stable. Steep rocks at the top of a slope make it more prone to slipping, because falling snow, rocks or icicles can set it in motion. On a convex slope the gravitational movement downward compacts the snow at the bottom and creates tension at the top making it more likely to slip. Where snow is building up on the lee side of a ridge or the head of steep gullies, it's under tension and the slightest disturbance can cause it to slide. Slopes with rocky outcrops and trees are safer to cross than bare ones. Carefully choose the best place to cross and before committing yourself test the snow. Dig in your stick/ice axe and see if it's compacted or in layers. Throw rocks and make noise to try to encourage a slide, making sure you are well protected. On all dangerous ground it is best to rope together and use belays. Keep at least 50 feet apart to help spread the load. If possible, let one person go across the more dangerous areas alone paying out the rope as he goes. When he is across he belays himself before the next person crosses.

MAIN AREAS OF DANGER

- Snow-covered convex slopes. Here the snow is under tension.

- Lee slopes where snow has accumulated. They are unstable.

- Deep snow-filled gullies.

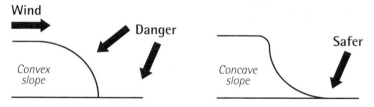

Never make camp on the lee side of a convex slope, a concave slope is safer.

As a precaution always carry a location beacon that omits a signal that rescuers can use to find you. Also carry an avalanche tape that can be streamed out in an emergency. It is made of bright nylon tape and makes detection easier if buried.

PRECAUTIONS

- The heat of the sun on the snow can cause avalanches so before noon travel in shaded areas — keep off those exposed to the sun.

- After noon, keep to slopes that have been exposed, avoiding those that are now in sun for the first time.

- Avoid small gullies and valleys with steep side walls.

- Stick to ridges and high ground above avalanche paths — you are more likely to trigger a slide but, if you do, have a better chance of being on top of the debris or not being carried down at all.

- Always look out for avalanche activity, even if you do not see it happening. Assess where avalanches started, their direction, how long ago they took place. They will be a guide to where other avalanches are likely.

A mud slide is very similar to an avalanche, but instead of tons of snow, masses of mud sliding on water bury all in it's path. Avoid low-lying areas and water courses. Stay on the spurs and ridges. If caught up in a slide, use swimming actions to stay on top and go feet first.

SEASHORES

Most seashores offer abundant sources of food and excellent prospects for survival. Even where they appear bleak and barren, there is food to be had. Coastal waters are the home of many life forms — seaweeds, fish, seals, birds, molluscs and the plankton that supports the marine animals. Inland lakes and waterways of all kinds will also teem with life, with the exception of the Dead Sea and other areas of extreme salination, and those heavily polluted by man.

Coasts can range from sheer cliffs to long and gently sloping beaches. From the sea a towering cliff offers no opportunity to escape the water. Even a stretch of beach at its foot is likely to be cut off by high tide in tidal waters, though it could offer a few hours of respite before swimming off to find another landing place. All kinds of shore, however, offer resources to exploit and there are few better places to be stranded.

Sandy beaches

Sandy shores tend to be gentle and sloping. The tide goes out a long way, revealing large areas which are the habitat of burrowing species, left below the exposed sand. They include many worms and molluscs and they also attract feeding birds. Look for signs of buried molluscs. It is usually easier to spot the marks left by the syphons of buried bivalves under the shallow water at the sea's edge.

Where the sand is not inundated by the tide and is blown into dunes, it may be possible to find fresh water and it is here that plants will grow.

Sand is easily blown by the wind and gets into everything. Dunes also tend to be full of aggravating insects — so do not choose them for making camp or building shelter, if you can move beyond.

Muddy shores and estuaries

Where a slow-moving river joins the sea it deposits sediment, rich in nutrients, forming large mud flats. These can support many species of worms and molluscs and provide a rich feeding ground for birds and animals.

Rocky shores

Rocky shores, if their cliffs are not too sheer, trap pools of water when the tide recedes. These pools may teem with life. Rocks form a strata to which the many univalve shells can cling, an anchor for weed and sea urchins and crevices where octopus and other cephalopods can live.

Soft rocks, such as chalk, marl and limestone, erode quickly and their surfaces are smooth, but hard rocks fracture in chunks and provide good nesting sites for birds.

Pebble beaches

Stretches of pebble beach, often found between sandy and rocky sections of the shore, sustain least life. The continual movement of pebbles makes a difficult habitat for most plants and animals.

Tides

Tides vary considerably according to both location and time of year for they are caused by the counter-gravities of the sun and moon. In enclosed seas, such as the Mediterranean, they range over only a few metres. The Bay of Fundy, between Nova Scotia and New Brunswick, has a difference of 16m (53·5ft) between low tide and high tide.

A line of debris along the beach; a change in appearance and texture from the long dry sand to that which is daily inundated; weed, shells and colour changes on vertical rock faces, all these will help to indicate the level to which the water is likely to rise.

Always check access to and from a beach or rocky shore — keep an eye on the rising water level so that you do not run the risk of being cut off.

Tides not only scour the beach but throw up valuable flotsam and jetsam, often providing fuel for fires, and may leave large fish stranded in rock pools along with their usual inhabitants.

SHORE SAFETY

- Never underestimate the power and danger of the sea. Time the tides and become familiar with their pattern, then you will be less likely to be cut off by an incoming tide or swept out by the ebb. It is easy to be caught, when some way offshore.

- Cliffs offer problems of access. If there is only one way down make sure you can get back to it.

- Look out for strong currents, especially off headlands. Sand banks and submerged rocks are also dangerous. Where a beach falls steeply into deep water there will be a strong undertow. If you are forced to enter the water to rescue someone or retrieve kit, have a safety line around the waist and someone anchoring you on shore — or tie the line to a firm anchor.

Swimming

If caught in the undertow of a large wave, push off the bottom and swim to the surface. Swim to shore in the trough between waves. When the next large wave comes, face it and submerge. Let it pass and swim in the next trough shorewards.

When fishing or swimming stay within your depth, if you are not a strong swimmer. Watch out for large waves which can knock you off your feet and carry you further out. If this happens do not panic. People tend to panic when they do not know how deep water is, but are reassured when they do. It does not really matter for you can drown in 10cm (4in) of water as effectively as in 10m (30ft). If you want to test the depth place your arms above head, point your toes and dive feet first. It may not be as deep as you thought!

If a strong current forces you offshore do NOT fight against it — you will lose. Swim ACROSS it, using side stroke, and make for land further along the coast. Side stroke is not the strongest or fastest stroke — but it is the least tiring.

If in the sea and being swept on to rocks, face shorewards and adopt a sitting position with your feet in front. They will absorb the initial shock and enable you to grab hold and scramble ashore. This is also useful for exploring water that may conceal hidden rocks — keep your shoes on and at least one layer of clothing.

Floating

A relaxed body floats best — so try to stay calm. It is difficult to sink in salt water. The main danger is swallowing salt water and choking on the vomit.

Women are more bouyant than men (they have an extra layer of fat) and float naturally on their backs. Men float naturally face down — but don't forget to lift your head out to breathe!

WATER

Fresh water along the coast is best obtained from small river outlets — large rivers tend to be full of silt and may be polluted by industry or other human activity upriver.

On sandy shores with no freshwater outlets there may be pools among dunes. Digging above the high water mark on any beach, especially if there is vegetation, may bring results. Dig down until you reach moist sand. Let water accumulate. Freshwater floats on top of salt. Scoop the lighter layer off the top.

Rock pools are unlikely to be freshwater. Even above the high water mark, they may be the result of wave splash, but you can sometimes identify fresh water by the growth of green algae which is not grazed by molluscs, as it would be elsewhere on the beach. Saltwater molluscs cannot survive in the reduced salinity.

Look for water trickling through rock faces, especially where there are ferns or mosses growing out of them, it will be drinkable. If stranded on a rocky outcrop off the shore, the only reliable source of water will be the sea itself — but NEVER drink sea water without distilling it. Far from quenching your thirst, it will take valuable body fluids away from the vital organs and eventually cause the kidneys to pack up.

Saltwater can be used for cooking — but do not eat until you have an adequate supply of fresh water. The residue of salt from distilled sea water can be used for preserving meat and fish.

FOOD

Seashore plants will differ according to the climate, but they will be available when weather or tide prevent you gathering food from the sea. In the water, you will find seaweeds of one kind or another where there is rock to give them purchase and water shallow enough to allow the sun to reach them. Seaweeds (more correctly called algae) are very valuable as food. In many parts of the world they form a major part of the diet and many are considered a delicacy from the cuisine of Japan to the laver bread of Wales. Seaweeds can be dried and stored for months.

Seafood

The best hunting for fish and molluscs will be at low tide, when rock pools can be inspected and buried molluscs and other creatures dug from sandy shores.

WARNING

Seaweeds are a valuable contribution to diet — but do NOT eat the blue-green algae sometimes found on freshwater pools. It is very poisonous.

Bivalves, which feed by filtering water through their digestive systems, can build up dangerous concentrations of toxic chemicals in areas polluted by industry or sewage.

In tropical zones, mussels are poisonous during the summer, especially when seas are reddish or highly phosphorescent. In the Arctic, black mussels can be poisonous at any time of year. Learn to recognize the cone shells, which shoot out a poisonous barb, in a few species potent enough to kill you. There are more than 400 types of cone shell, mainly found in the tropical Indo-Pacific with about 12 species off the southeast of USA and in the Caribbean. They are all identified by their shape. Tenebra or Auger and Turrid shells also have poison darts. Their venom is not dangerous to man, but a sting may still be painful.

Only eat molluscs collected live. Bivalves, such as oysters, clams and mussels, should close tightly if tapped gently. Gastropods, such as winkles and whelks, have a 'trap-door' (the operculum) to close the entrance to the shell. It should close tightly if the shell is shaken.

Other gastropods, such as limpets and Abalones, have no operculum but are tightly anchored to the rocks. Use a knife under the edge of the shell to prise them off. If they are hard to dislodge, they are good to eat. If they come off easily, they are probably dead or sick. After high tide any limpet found still fastened is good food – the tide washes away sick or dead specimens.

Cook shell foods by plunging them into boiling water and boiling for at least five minutes.

If you eat shell foods raw you expose yourself to parasites and pollutants which they may carry.

Fishing

Fish and sea snakes require more catching. Some fish are dangerous and all sea snakes are venomous. Distinguish snakes from eels by their scales and their broad flattened tails. They are said not to bite swimmers. Bites usually occur, and then only rarely, when fishermen are removing fish from nets in which the snakes are also caught.

On most coasts the best time to fish from the shore is about two hours after high water. If you fish when the tide is still coming in you are constantly retreating and probably getting wet. Remember that saltwater will rot boots and clothing.

Sea fishing requires a larger hook than freshwater fishing. A wide variety of bait can be used. Limpets, for instance, can often be found clinging to the rocks, or lugworms (*Arenicola*) can be dug up on sandy and muddy beaches. At low tide look for the coiled worm casts that show you where their L-shaped burrows are.

Make use of the tide to help you catch fish by building large arrow-shaped fish traps from stakes or rocks. Point them away from the shore. Fish will be caught when the tide recedes.

Octopus and squid

Octopus can be hunted at night, when they are in search of their own prey. Attract them with a light, then spear them. In daytime empty shells around a hole are an indication that an octopus may live inside. Drop in a baited hook, wait until it is taken and pull sharply up. The best way to kill an octopus is to turn it inside out: place a hand inside the fleshy hood, grab the innards and pull hard. Try it on a small octopus first! It takes practise so until you are proficient stab the octopus between the eyes or bang it against a rock.

All octopuses have a hard, parrot-like beak, and a few can give a poisonous bite. The worst is the Blue-ringed octopus of eastern Australia — its venom can be lethal. AVOID IT!

Octopus flesh is tough but chewy and very nourishing. Pounding it will help make it more tender. Boil the body and roast the smaller tentacles.

In the open sea squid can be huge, but a few small squid may occur inshore. Look for them in rock pools attached to seaweed. Catch them at night with a bright light, by jigging. Cuttlefish do not come close inshore but can be caught at sea in the same way.

Echinoderms

Another useful source of food, the echinoderms include the starfish (not worth bothering with as food), the sea urchins and the sea cucumbers. Sea cucumbers creep about on the seabed or burrow in the sand. They look like warty black cucumbers, up to 20cm (8in) long. There are also spiky white sea gerkins and worm cucumbers (which burrow into sand). Sea cucumbers should be boiled for five minutes before eating.

Sea urchins, or sea eggs as they are sometimes called, are usually prickly balls which cling on to rocks, just below the low water mark but they have burrowing relations, the cake and heart urchins and the sea potato, which can be found beneath the sand. Split open and eat the egg-like 'yolk' inside. You can eat it raw, but it is safer to boil. AVOID any if their spines do not move when touched or if they smell badly when opened.

SEA URCHINS

Handle carefully. Their spines can inflict a painful wound — especially if you tread on them with bare feet! If you get pricked and the spine breaks off don't try to squeeze it out, it may push the spine in deeper. With luck spines will begin to work their way out of the skin after a few days.

Crustaceans

These include the crabs, crayfish, shrimp and prawns, all of which make their homes in rock pools. Lobsters are usually found beyond the tidal zone but sometimes can be found in deep pools or crevices.

Look under stones and seaweeds — though you'll have to be quick to catch them! A net would help. Improvise one from clothing and a piece of wire or a sapling.

Sand crabs are abundant in the tropics. Active at night, they can be chased back to their burrow at the top of the beach and dug out. Some even climb trees and can be knocked down.

Freshwater crabs, crayfish and shrimps are also found in many parts of the world. They are smaller than sand crabs and usually found in shallow water.

All crustaceans spoil quickly and they may contain harmful parasites. They must be eaten as soon as possible — so keep them alive in water until you are ready to cook them. They are cooked alive — either by plunging into boiling water, so that they die almost immediately, or by putting them in cold water and heating it up, which is claimed to lull them to unconsciousness so that they feel no pain. Boil for 20 minutes.

Crabs have poisonous sections which must be removed: Twist off claws and legs, then, with the crab on its back, place your thumbs under the flap at the tail and push upwards. Pull the flap up and away from the body and lift it off. This prevents the stomach contents from touching the flesh. Next press on the mouth with the thumbs, pushing down and outwards. This makes mouth and stomach come away in one piece. The lungs (known as 'Dead men's fingers'), which are harmful to eat, can then be pulled out and discarded.

Lobster is easier to prepare. Cut along the back towards the head and split open. The stomach lies just behind the mouth and is removed with the head and intestinal cord.

Turtles

Turtle meat is highly nutritious, and turtle eggs another good source of food — if you are lucky enough to have turtles come ashore. (See *Reptiles* in *Food*.)

Seabirds

Most ocean coasts are alive with seabirds. Fish for them. Leave baited hooks among offal on flat rocks, even throw baited hooks into the air to be taken on the wind. Try wrapping bait around stones. The sudden change in weight can make birds 'crash'.

Ground nesting birds can provide a rich source of eggs. Look for the ones that are easy to collect before risking raiding nests on cliffs. You can also try to catch the birds themselves at night when roosting — but do NOT risk climbing.

DANGERS

Unless very still, water higher than your thighs will be too murky to see through. You'll risk stepping on something unpleasant and waves could sweep you on to rocks or coral.

Wear shoes when foraging in the water — you need soles if you are improvising foot coverings. Cloth wrapping is NOT enough to protect from spines.

- Jellyfish are often swept inshore after a storm. Some, especially in the tropics, sting severely. The Sea wasps, or Box jellies, of northern Australian beaches, are the most dangerous. The bell-shaped body of the largest reaches only 25cm (10in) but its tentacles can reach 9m (30ft). Almost transparent, and difficult to see, each tentacle is armed with millions of stinging cells. Although their venom is one of the most deadly known and high concentrations cause skin lesions and death, usually only a very high dose is fatal to humans. Some jellyfish are not venomous but beware — size is not an indication of potency! If stung do NOT pull the tentacles off or wipe away the slime with your hand — you will only get stung more. Use seaweed, cloth etc to wipe the sting with sand.

- Portuguese-man-of-war, looks like a jellyfish but is actually a colony of polyps. It, too, can have tentacles 9m (30ft) long but, though its stings may cause irritation for several days, they are rarely fatal. Treat as for jellyfish.

- Weaverfish lie buried in the sand off the shores of Europe, West Africa and the Mediterranean. Their spines are venomous. Apply very hot water to sooth spine wounds.

- Stingrays occur inshore everywhere, but especially in warm waters, and electric rays in warm to temperate zones. Superbly camouflaged, some like rocky and pebbly places, they don't only hide in sand. Play safe — prod the bottom with a stick as you go. Stingray wounds can be soothed with very hot water.

- Moray eels may be found in shallow water. They have a savage bite and guard their holes tenaciously. Keep clear of any you see and do NOT put your hands into crevices!

- Giant clams on tropical reefs can be big enough to trap a limb if they snap shut on it.

- Fish with venomous spines often live in very shallow waters. Most common, and most dangerous, in the tropics, a few occur in temperate waters. Bottom-dwelling kinds are almost impossible to detect and are often superbly camouflaged. Zebra fish are easier to see, but equally dangerous to contact. Use a stick to stir up the sand and rocks in front of you.

- Sea snakes often occur in some numbers close in shore in the tropical Pacific and Indian Oceans. They are inoffensive and bites are rare — but their venom is the most toxic of all snake venom. Keep clear of snakes in the water. Found on shore, pin them with a forked stick — they make a good meal.

- Many corals are sharp and can easily cut you. Some, such as the fire corals, sting on contact. Always approach a reef with caution. Exploit other sites for food first. Both the reef and its inhabitants — which may include cone shells — can present dangers.

- Sharks Although most sharks feed mainly in deep waters, some species frequent shallow waters and swim up rivers and any might come onshore looking for an easy meal. Most shark attacks on humans occur in very shallow water. Be watchful!

- Lagoons Reefs are often formed around tropical islands or out from the shore, making a breakwater which leaves still waters in a lagoon. Fish in the lagoon are often of the poisonous varieties. Barracuda and Red snapper, which are edible in the open sea, should be avoided if caught in lagoons — their eating habits cause them to become toxic. Fish from the reef on the seaward side.

ISLANDS

Islands offer a special challenge to the survivor, especially small islands and those lacking resources. The feeling of loneliness is emphasized on an island and the sense of isolation acute. The problems are mental as well as physical. To help overcome them explore the island thoroughly and establish a daily routine.

Climb to the highest point to make a sketch of the island and get a mental picture of the terrain. Explore every creek, cranny, bay and beach of the coastline. Then take your reconnaissances inland until the island is familiar.

The island may have been inhabited in the past — remains of buildings offer a basis for shelter. Fence posts and wire will be useful to repair your boat or build a raft. Vegetables may still be found growing and rats seem to follow man everywhere — sometimes they are the only permanent wildlife to be found.

Shelter will make life seem better and even a scrape in the ground will give some protection. If you find caves ensure that they are not tidal before you decide to use one. Remember that even caves that seem safe may be flooded or cut off by spring tides, which are higher than normal.

On a barren rocky outcrop shelter may simply mean finding a place out of the wind. Water may depend upon collecting rainfall and distillation. Food will be whatever clings to the rocks, birds and birds' eggs if you are lucky, and what you can haul from the sea.

Resources

On any small island resources will be limited. Take care not to over-exploit any one of them. Water is often a problem – lack of it is the reason many islands are uninhabited. Lush vegetation will draw attention to springs and streams. Digging above the high water mark may produce water. Catch and store rainwater.

To desalinate sea water by distillation you need a lot of fuel, which may be scarce. Driftwood may be available and some seaweeds will burn when dried – but you need wood to get the fire going. Seal blubber also makes good fuel. Have a fire only when you really need one. Search beaches after every tide – not just for wood. Everything has a use to the survivor.

Once familiar with your island, venture out at night – more creatures can be seen and foraging may be more rewarding.

Coconuts

Tropical islands are rarely desert islands – they will usually offer plenty to eat, both ashore and in the water. The coconut palm is found right through the tropics and subtropics and can provide: fronds for shelter, husks for ropes, growing points, which taste like cabbages, the milk and meat, and the shell (which you can also use as cups and containers).

To remove the fibrous husk around the coconut force it over a sharpened stake or split it with a hand axe. Extract the milk by piercing one of the dark 'eyes' of the nut itself before smashing the nut open to get at the meat.

Coconut milk is a safe and refreshing drink – a large nut may hold 1 litre (2pt). Do not drink from very young (green) or old (dark brown) nuts, their liquid will give you diarrhoea. The meat itself is indigestible in large amounts – eat only a little at a time.

Extract coconut oil by exposing chopped white meat to heat – sun or fire – and collecting oil as it runs off, or by boiling and skimming the oil as it rises to the surface. Rub it on to protect from sunburn, and chafing from saltwater, to repel insects, as a salve for sores and blisters or, mixed with wood ash, as a substitute for soap.

Climbing palms: If coconuts don't fall on your head and you can't knock them down, or if you need to reach some high bananas, don't try to climb the tree trunk like a rope. Instead, tie a strong bandage of cloth into a strap and slip it around your ankles. Adjust it to hold your feet close to the trunk and then you can press the soles of your feet inward and grip with them.

ATTRACTING RESCUE

- Lay out signals to attract searchers by arranging rocks, seaweed — anything that contrasts with its surroundings.

- Sand is excellent for polishing metal to make mirrors to signal with.

- If you can see a ship you can try and make contact on a VHF radio.

Moving on

In a group of islands, you may be able to move on to another when the first's resources are exhausted. In warmer climates it may be possible to swim, but build a raft in cold climates. If there is nothing to build a raft from, make some kind of flotation aid — even if it is only an empty box or coconuts.

If there are seals on your island you could use them to make a raft. From autumn through to spring, when the seal stores a lot of fat in its body, a seal carcass will float. If several are lashed together they will support your weight.

Study tides and currents between islands carefully, they can be treacherous. Float something you can observe and note its progress. Time your swim so that the ebb takes you out from your island and the high tide takes you in to the new island.

ARID REGIONS

Most desert lands were once fertile and some of the creatures that lived there then adapted to the new conditions. Like them, the survivor must learn to make the most of any available shade, to create protection from the sun, reduce moisture loss and restrict activity to the ends of the day and the night. Learn from the peoples who live or travel through the deserts.

In some deserts, especially the Sahara, the deserts of the Middle East, of Peru and northern Chile and parts of the Gobi Desert in

Mongolia, there are great temperature differences between night and day. At night condensation of any moisture in the air can make some water available — and in the Namib desert of southern Africa fog coming in from the sea often provides moisture for life. Elsewhere, in such deserts as those of Western Australia, northern Mexico and the Mohave of the southwestern USA, where the temperature changes are comparatively slight, there is very little condensation and consequently both plants and game are very rare. Sometimes, as in the Kalahari, there will be sparse grass and thorny bushes and, even in the most barren conditions, some kind of life seems to survive, though often invisible if you do not know where to look.

Dust and sand storms may occur at certain times of year, reducing visibility to zero and demanding maximum protection to prevent sand entering every orifice. Dust devils — desert whirlwinds like tornadoes — are quite common.

When rain does come — and in some territories years may pass with none at all — it may be in torrential downpours which create flash floods, before being quickly absorbed into the parched ground. This provides for a brief blossoming of vegetation and the emergence of species, such as the Spadefoot Toad of Arizona, for rapid reproduction.

Desert rainfall and temperature

Typical of desert extremes are conditions in the Rub'al Khali, the 'Empty Quarter', of southern Arabia. For most of the year there is only a trace of rain but over 30mm (1¼in) may fall on a single day in the winter. July temperatures may reach over 48°C (120°F), dropping to 15°C (60°F) at night, and December extremes range from 26° to –6.6°C (79-20°F).

WATER

Water needs are paramount. Finding it is VITAL. If you have it, ration it immediately. If you are stranded by mechanical failure during a planned desert crossing, you will have plotted your route with an awareness of oases, wells and waterholes. Wells can be very deep and the water level require a container lowered on a line to reach it. Small water holes in wadi bottoms are often seasonal. They are usually covered with a stone or brushwood.

Away from known waterholes, try digging at the lowest point of the outside bend of a dry stream bed or at the lowest point between dunes. Do NOT dig in the heat of the day, the exertion will use up too much fluid and you may find none to replace it. You must always balance fluid loss against possible gain.

Exploit cactus and roots as water sources and, in deserts where the day/night temperature range is great, exploit this to produce water by condensation. (See *Water* in *Essentials.*)

Life expectancy

Life expectancy depends upon the water available and your ability to protect the body from exposure to the sun to minimize perspiration. Allow a slight negative balance. Drink 1·5 litre for every 2 litre lost (3:4pt) and then drink at the rate the body is sweating. Efficiency is then impaired little and no water is wasted. Less fluid will not result in less sweating. Sweating is a cooling mechanism, not a way of losing moisture. If more fluid is drunk than needed it will be excreted and used to no purpose.

Without water you will last about 2½ days at 48°C (120°F) if you spend the whole time resting in the shade, though you could last as long as 12 days if the temperature stays below 21°C (70°F).

If you are forced to walk to safety the distance you cover will relate directly to water available. With none, a temperature of 48°C (120°F), walking only at night, resting all day, you could cover 40km (25 miles). Attempting to walk by day you would be lucky to complete 8km (5 miles) before collapse. At the same temperature, with about 2 litres (4pt) of water you might cover 56km (35 miles) and last 3 days. Your chances are not appreciably increased until available water reaches about 4.5 litres (8pt) per person, though training and a determination to survive could contradict predictions.

SHELTER AND FIRE

Make a shelter from the sun and rest in its shade. You'll also need protection from winds and low night temperatures. Do NOT stay in a metal vehicle or aeroplane which may rapidly become overheated. Use it to support a shelter or make use of the shadow beneath an aircraft's wing. Make use of rock outcrops and the shadow provided by the sides of a wadi. Use the double layer technique to aid cooling (see *Tropical Regions*).

In a sand desert you may even be able to use wreckage to make a shelter beneath the sand. Many desert creatures spend the day beneath the surface, where the day temperature is much lower and night much warmer than outside. Sand will not permit tunnelling and you have to make a support structure.

Having provided immediate shade, build your shelter in the cool of the evening to conserve energy and fluids. Pile rocks to make a windbreak and make use of wadi walls (except when rain, and consequent flash floods, seem likely).

If using fabrics, leave the bottom edges lifted and loose by day to increase air circulation. Weight them down with rocks at night. Avoid lying directly on hot ground. If you make a raised bed air can circulate beneath you.

You will need fire for warmth at night, and for boiling water. Smoke will also be very noticeable and useful for signalling. Desert scrub is dry and burns easily. If the land is totally barren, vehicle fuel and oil mixed with sand in a container will burn well (and is an easy way to light other fires) or use a string wick. Camel, donkey and other animal droppings burn well.

CLOTHING

Clothing helps reduce fluid loss and gives protection from sunburn — as well as warmth at night and a barrier against insect bites and thorns. In the desert it should be light and loose fitting, with air space between the garments and the body to provide insulation. Copy the flowing, layered garments of the Arab world. Trousers give more protection from insects than shorts (and guard against serious burns on the legs if forced into daytime exposure). Cover the head and feet.

KEEP COVERED

Do not strip off your clothes. Apart from the risk of severe sunburn, an uncovered body will lose sweat through evaporation requiring even more to cool it — but keep the covering as loose as possible so that there is a layer of insulating air. Sweating will then cool you more efficiently.

Headgear

Any hat with a piece of cloth attached to the back will give some protection to the head and back of the neck but it is better to copy the headgear of desert peoples. You need a piece of material about 120cm (4ft) square, a smaller piece, such as a handkerchief, and a piece of cord or cloth (a tie is ideal) to keep them in position.

Make the handkerchief into a wad on top of the head. Fold the large cloth diagonally, place it over the handkerchief, the long edge forward. Tie cord or cloth around the head to secure them.

Allowed to fall freely this will protect from the sun, trap pockets of air, take advantage of breezes and protect from sandstorms. At night wrap it around the face for warmth.

Eye protection

Sunglasses or goggles will help — though many made for use in temperate climes may offer insufficient protection. Soot from the fire smeared below the eyes will reduce glare reflected from the skin. Shield the eyes from glare and windborne sand with a strip of material. Cut narrow slits to see through.

Footwear

Do not walk barefoot on hot sand until your feet have become hardened. It will burn and cause blisters. Do not wear sandals which leave the top of the foot exposed. Improvise coverings if you have none. Putees will help keep sand out of boots or could be extended to wrap round the foot over open sandals.

FOOD

Heat usually produces a loss of appetite — so do not force yourself to eat. Protein foods increase metabolic heat and increase water loss and liquids are needed for digestion. If water is scarce, keep eating to a minimum and then try to eat only moisture-containing foods, such as fruit and vegetables.

Food spoils very quickly in the desert and any stores, once opened, should be eaten straight away or kept covered and shaded. Flies appear from nowhere and settle upon uncovered food.

Plants

Vegetation, away from oases and waterholes, is likely to be little more than scrub and grasses — even in the semi-desert — but grasses are edible and sometimes plentiful. The Acacia tree in the scrub provides edible beans. Beware of the Acacia's thorns but try all its soft parts: flowers, fruit, seeds, bark and young shoots.

The grasses of the Sahara and Gobi are neither nutritious nor palatable, but in the Sahara and the Asian deserts you may find the Desert Gourd, a member of the Squash family. Its vine can run over the ground for 4·5m (15ft). Chew its water-filled shoots and eat its flowers and orange-sized fruits, the seeds of which are edible roasted or boiled.

The Mescal plant (an Agave from which tequila is made) of the Mexican desert, grows with a rosette of thick, tough, sharp-tipped leaves. Its central stalk, which rises like a candle to a flowering head, can be eaten. Cut the ends of the leaves to suck out water.

Animals

Deserts often support a variety of animal life which burrows into the sand or hides in any available shade during the day. Insects, reptiles, small rodents and specially adapted mammals such as the Fennec Fox of North Africa, the Australian Bandicoot, a hedgehog in the Gobi and the Jack Rabbit of North America — all of which have big ears to act as cooling aids.

There are geckoes, lizards and snakes. Tortoises and amphibians survive from when these were once well-watered lands. The Sahara has gerbils and gerboas; the Middle East, caracals and hyenas; the New World, kangaroo rats and coyotes. In the Kalahari there is a squirrel that uses its tail for shade. There are even Gazelles that manage to get all the moisture they need from the sap of leaves, though most large mammals are an indication that there is a water supply within daily reach of their grazing areas.

Birds' feathers give them good insulation against heat and many live and breed long distances from their water supplies.

HEALTH

Most desert illnesses are caused by excessive exposure to sun and heat. They can be avoided by keeping head and body covered and remaining in shade until sundown.

- Constipation and pain in passing urine are common and salt-deficiency can lead to cramps.

- Continued heavy sweating on the body, coupled with rubbing by clothing can produce blockages in the sweat glands and an uncomfortable skin irritation known as prickly heat.

- Heat cramps, leading to heat exhaustion, heat stroke and serious sunburn are all dangers. A gradual increase in activity and daily exposure to the sun will build up a defence — provided that plenty of drinking water is available.

- Various micro-organisms attack the moist areas of the body — the crevices of the armpits, groin and between the toes. Prevention and treatment are to keep these areas clean and dry.

WARNING – DESERT SORES

In the desert even the most trivial wound is likely to become infected if not dealt with straight away. Thorns are easily picked up and should be pulled out as soon as possible. Where the skin is broken a large and painful sore may develop which could prevent walking. Bandage all cuts with clean dressings and use what medical aids are available.

TROPICAL REGIONS

Everything in the jungle thrives, including disease — germs breed at an alarming rate — and parasites. Nature provides water, food and plenty of materials for making shelters. Indigenous peoples have lived for millennia from hunting and gathering, but for the outsider it can take a long time to get used to the conditions and the non-stop activity.

Native peoples wear little, except as ornament, but the newcomer, uninured to insects and leeches and unaccustomed to moving through dense jungle growth, needs to keep as covered as possible. Clothing may become saturated by perspiration but it is better than being stung, scratched and bitten all over. Do not remove wet clothing until you halt and then, with humidity at 80-90 per cent, there is no point hanging it up to dry except in the sun or by a fire. Clothes saturated regularly by perspiration will rot.

Except at high altitudes, both equatorial and subtropical regions are characterized by high temperatures, heavy rainfall and oppressive humidity. At low altitudes, temperature variation is seldom more than 10°C (50°F), and is often 37°C (98°F). At altitudes over 1500m (5000ft) ice often forms at night. The rain has a slightly cooling effect but, when it stops, the temperature soars.

Rainfall is heavy, often with thunder and lightning. Sudden rain beats on the tree canopy, turning trickles into raging torrents and rivers rise at an alarming rate, but — just as suddenly — it is gone. Violent storms may occur, usually towards the end of the 'summer' months. Hurricanes, cyclones and typhoons develop over the sea and rush inland causing tidal waves and devastation. In choosing camp sites, make sure you are above any potential flooding. Prevailing winds create variation between winter and summer with the dry season (rain once a day) and the monsoon (continuous rain). In southeast Asia, winds from the Indian Ocean bring monsoon, but it is dry when the wind blows from the landmass of China.

Tropical day and night are of equal length, darkness falls quickly and daybreak is equally sudden.

Equatorial rain forests

The climate varies little in these forests, spread across the equator in the Amazon and Congo basins, parts of Indonesia and several Pacific islands. Rain of 1·5-3·5m (60-149in) is distributed evenly throughout the year. Temperatures range from 30°C (86°F) to 20°C (68°F) at night.

Where untouched by man, jungle trees rise from buttress roots to 60m (200ft), bursting into a mushroom of leaves. Below them, smaller trees produce a canopy so thick that little light reaches the jungle floor. Seedlings struggle beneath them to reach light and masses of vines and lianas twine up to the sun. Ferns, mosses and herbaceous plants push through a thick carpet of leaves and a great variety of fungi grow on leaves and fallen trunks.

It is fairly cool in this PRIMARY JUNGLE, with little undergrowth to hamper movement, but visibility is limited to about 50m (170ft). It is easy to lose a sense of direction and also difficult to spot anyone from the air.

Smoke is diffused by the tree canopy and may not be seen, especially if there is mist about as well. Set signals in a clearing, more often found near river bends, or − better − out on rafts on the river itself.

RESCUE SIGNALS

Smoke is diffused by the tree canopy and may not be seen, especially if there is mist about as well. Set signals in a clearing, more often found near river bends, or − better − out on rafts on the river itself.

Secondary jungle

Growth is prolific where sunlight does penetrate to the jungle floor − mainly along river banks, on jungle fringes and where primary jungle has been cleared by man for slash and burn farming. When abandoned, this is reclaimed by a tangled mass of vegetation − look out for cultivated food plants which may survive among the others.

Grasses, ferns, shrubs and vines of secondary jungle reach heights of 2–3m (7–10ft) in a single year. Moving is slow, often hacking a way with a machete or parang − hot work, with visibility only a few metres (see *On the Move*). Jungle vegetation seems to be covered with thorns and spikes and bamboo thickets can be impenetrable barriers.

Sometimes, as in Belize in Central America, the jungle trees are low. Light does reach the fertile ground, producing abundant undergrowth even in primary jungle.

Sub-tropical rain forests

Found within 10° of the Equator, in Central and South America, Madagascar, western India, Burma, Vietnam, southeast Asia and the Phillipines, these forests have a season of reduced rainfall even drought, with the rain coming in cycles − monsoons. With more marked seasons there are more deciduous trees so that more light reaches the forest floor and undergrowth is dense.

Montane forests

When altitudes reach about 1000m (3000ft) in the tropics, and the areas bordering them, tropical forest begins to give way to montane forest. It becomes true montane at about 1240m (4900ft), as in the Monts Gotel in Cameroon, the Amhara Plateau of Ethiopia or the Ruwenzori Range of central Africa. The Ruwenzori — the 'Mountains of the Moon' — are typical: sharply contoured slopes making a crater-like landscape covered in moss between ice-capped peaks.

Plant growth is sparse, trees stunted and distorted, their branches low and difficult to walk beneath. Nights are cold, day temperatures high with lots of mist and long periods of cloud cover. Survival is difficult in this terrain. Leave it and make your way down the mountainside to the tropical rain forest.

Saltwater swamps

Where coastal areas are subject to tidal flooding, mangrove trees thrive. They can reach heights of 12m (40ft) and their tangled roots are an obstacle both above and below the waterline. Visibility is poor and passage difficult — it may take 12 hours to cover 900m (1000ft). Sometimes channels are wide enough to raft, but generally progress is on foot.

There are mangrove swamps in West Africa, Madagascar, Malaysia and the Pacific Islands, Central and South America and at the mouth of the Ganges. The swamps at the mouths of the Orinoco, Amazon and rivers of Guyana consist of stinking mud and trees which offer little shade. Tides can rise as much as 12m (40ft).

Everything in mangrove swamps seems hostile, from water leeches and insects, to cayman and crocodiles. Avoid them if you can. If forced there by mishap look for a way out. Where there are river channels intersecting the swamp you may be able to make a raft.

You won't starve among the mangroves. There is plenty of fish and vegetation. At low water crabs, molluscs, catfish and mudfish can be found. Arboreal and aquatic animals include water opposum, otter, tapir, armadillo and, on firmer ground, peccaries.

Inland of the mangroves, nipa palm swamp is common — all the palm's growing points are edible.

If forced to stay in a swamp, determine the high-tide level, by the line of salt and debris on the trees, and fit up a raised bed above it. Cover yourself for protection against ants and mosquitoes.

In any swamp a fire will have to be built on a platform. Use standing deadwood for fuel. Decay is rapid in a swamp. Choose wood that is not far decayed.

Freshwater swamps

Found in low-lying inland areas, their mass of thorny undergrowth, reeds, grasses and occasional short palms makes going difficult and reduces visibility to only a few metres — but wildlife abounds and survival is easy. A freshwater swamp is not such a bad place once you get used to it. It will often be dotted with islands and you are not chest-deep in the water ALL the time. There are often navigable channels and raw materials available from which to build a raft.

SHELTER

There are ample materials for building shelter in most tropical regions (see *Shelter* in *Camp Craft*). Where temperatures are very high and shelters directly exposed to the sun, make roofs in two layers with an airspace in between to aid cooling. Much of the heat will dissipate on striking the upper layer, and with the air passing between this lowers the temperature of the layer beneath. The distance between should be 20–30cm (8–12in). Double layers of even permeable cloth will help keep out rain if well angled (see *Camp Craft*).

FIRE

Everything is likely to be damp. Take standing dead wood and shave off the outside. Use that to start your fire. Dry bamboo makes excellent tinder (store some), so does a termite's nest.

FOOD

A large variety of fruits, roots and leaves are available. Banana, papaya, mango and figs are easily recognized. (Papaya is one of the few plants with white sap that is edible.) The large, thorny fruit of the Durian, of southeast Asia, smells disgusting, but is good to eat.

Palms provide an edible growing point and manioc produces massive tubers – though they must be cooked before eating. Taro, wild potato and some kinds of yam must also be prepared to remove poisons before they are eaten. You may find the wealth of tropical foods hard to identify, if you're not sure use the tests described in *Food*, before you risk eating them.

Animal foods
Deer, pigs, monkeys and a wide range of animals can be hunted and trapped according to location (see *Traps and trapping* in *Food*) .

In primary jungle, birds spend most of their time in the tree canopy among the fruit and berries. Place traps in clearings and lure birds with fruit. Some, such as the Asian Hornbill, also feed on lizards and snakes. Near rivers, traps can be baited with fish or offal for Fish Eagles and similar species which patrol rivers for prey.

Parrots and their relatives abound in the tropics — their mad screeching makes their presence known from early morning. They are cunning — get them used to taking bait before setting the trap.

Snakes are easier to catch — go for the non-poisonous constrictors — and very tasty. Catch them using a forked stick (see *Hunting* in *Food*).

Food from rivers

Rivers support all kinds of life: fish, plants, animals and insects. If you have no fishing tackle small pools can be dammed and then emptied with a bailer — fish and turtles in surprising numbers can be found in the mud. Try constructing traps or crushing certain roots and vines to stupefy the fish (see *Fishing* in *Food*).

Fish are easily digested and have good protein content. Many jungle people depend on them for nourishment, but in the tropics they spoil quickly. Clean thoroughly, discard entrails and eat as soon as possible, do not preserve them by smoking or drying. Fish from slow moving water are more likely to be infested with parasites. If suspect, boil for 20 minutes. In areas where locals use the water as their sanitation system, fish may carry tapeworms and other human parasites and the water itself could be infected with amoebas which cause dysentery. Always boil water.

Rivers can bring dangers too. Piranha may be found in the Amazon, Orinoco and Paraguay river systems of South America. A similar fish is found in Burma. Electric eels are slow-moving and not aggressive, but they can grow very large and discharge 500 volts or more. Stingrays also occur in some tropical South American and West African rivers. Look out for crocodiles or alligators and water snakes and take care in handling catfish, which have sharp dorsal fins and spines on their gill covers, the Electric catfish can also deliver a powerful shock.

DANGERS

Cover your feet

Good footwear and protection for the legs is essential — they are most exposed to leeches, chigoe, and centipedes. Wrap bark or cloth around the legs and tie it to make puttees.

Insect attack!

Slashing your way through jungle you may disturb bee, wasp or hornet nests. They may attack, especially hornets, whose stings can be especially painful. Anywhere left bare, including your face, is vulnerable to attack. Run! Goggles would help protect the eyes.

Perspiration is a problem, insects desperate for salt will fly to the wettest parts of your body. However, they also sting. Protect armpits and groin.

Beware invaders

Keep clothing and footwear off the ground, then scorpions, snakes and other nasties are less likely to invade them. Always shake out clothing and check boots before putting them on and be wary when putting hands in pockets. On waking, take care. Centipedes tend to curl for warmth in some of the more private body regions.

Beware caterpillars too!

If mosquitoes and leeches sucking your blood, painful bites from centipedes and the risk or scorpion and snake bites are not enough (see *Bites* in *First Aid*) look out for hairy caterpillars. Be careful to brush them off in the direction they are travelling or small irritant hairs may stay in your skin and cause an itchy rash, which may fester in the heat.

Mosquito protection

Wear a net over your head, or tie a tee-shirt or singlet over it, especially at dawn and dusk. Better, take a strip of cloth long enough to tie around your head and about 45cm (18in) deep and cut it to make a fringe of vertical strips hanging from a band that will hang around your face and over your neck and impregnant your clothes and bags etc with repellent.

At night keep covered, including your hands. Use bamboo or a sapling to support a little tent of clothing plus large leaves, rigged over your upper half. Oil, fat or even mud spread on hands and face may help to repel mosquitoes. In camp a smoky fire will help keep insects at bay. If you are bitten make sure you don't scratch as this may let infection in.

Leeches

Leeches lie on the ground or on vegetation, especially in damp places, waiting to attach themselves to an animal (or person) to take a meal of blood. Their bite is not painful but they secrete a natural anti-coagulant that makes it messy. Left alone, they drop off when they have had their fill — but if you are covered in them you must do something! Do NOT pull them off. There is a risk the head will come off leaving the jaws in the bite, which could turn septic. Remove with a dab of salt, alcohol, an ember or a flame.

Beware the candiru!

This minute Amazonian catfish, about 2·5cm (1in) long, very slender and almost transparent, sucks blood from the gills of other fish. It is reported to be able to swim up the urethra of a person urinating in the water — where it gets stuck by its dorsal spine. The chance of this happening is remote but the consequences could be dire! Cover your genitals and don't urinate in the water.

VEHICLES

For desert travel, fit long-range fuel tanks and make provision for storing drinking water. Carry further supplies of both in jerry cans. A jack is no use in soft sand and an air bag should be carried which is inflated by the exhaust. Extra filters will be needed in the fuel line and air intake. Sand tyres must be fitted and sand channels carried to get you moving again when bogged down in loose sand.

For high altitudes the carburettor needs adjustment. In scrub country, thorn gaiters will reduce puncture risks. Antifreeze and suitable wheels and chains are needed for snow and ice. The engine will need special tuning to match climatic conditions and its own spares. A spare wheel and a good tool kit are obvious requirements.

HOT CLIMATES
Even when you have had modifications made to prepare your vehicle for hot climate conditions you may still find that you have problems.

In crossing some deserts the considerable temperature change from day to night can put a strain on any metal and increase the risk of leaks.

WARNING: *NEVER leave a sleeping or injured person or any animal in a closed car in a hot climate – or even on a sunny day in temperate regions. Always leave windows open to ensure ventilation (heat exhaustion can be lethal) even if parked in the shade, as the sun will move.*

Overheating: *Stop and allow the engine to cool. If you are driving a particularly tricky stretch and stopping is out of the question, switch on the heater. This will give greater volume to the cooling water and, although the inside of the car will get even hotter, the engine will cool. When convenient stop and open up the bonnet. Do not undo the radiator cap until the temperature drops. Check the radiator and all hoses for leaks. If the radiator is leaking, adding the white of an egg will seal small holes. If there is a large* *hole, squeeze that section of the copper piping flat to seal it off. It will reduce the size of the cooling area but, if you drive very steadily, you will be able to keep going.*

Metal gets hot: *Be careful! All metal parts of a car can become hot enough to cause blisters.*

Care in sandy conditions: *When adding fuel, sand and dust can get into the tank. Rig a filter over or just inside the inlet to the tank.*

COLD CLIMATES
Low temperatures not only make driving conditions difficult. They can make starting and maintenance difficult and hazardous.

Starting: *Always try to park on a gradient so that you can use a bump start to back up the starter. Once you get the engine going keep it running – but check that the handbrake is firmly on and never leave children or animals in an unattended vehicle with the engine running.*

Demisting: *Don't try to drive looking through a small clear patch on a misty screen. Onion or raw potato rubbed on the inside of the screen will stop it misting up.*

Cover the outside of windscreen and windows with newspaper to prevent frost building up on them. If damp, however, paper will stick.

Coddle the engine: Wrapping a blanket around the engine may help to stop it from freezing up – but remember to remove it before you start the engine. Cover lower part of the radiator with cardboard or wood so that it does not freeze as you go along. If very cold, leave covered. Otherwise remove to prevent overheating.

Cover metal: Don't touch ANY metal with bare hands. Your fingers could freeze to it and tear off skin. Where handling metal components with gloves is awkward, wrap fingers with adhesive tape. Treat radiator cap and dip stick in this way to ease your daily checks.

Diesel engines: Diesel contains water and freezes solid at low temperatures. Always cover front of engine, but check for overheating. Always wrap engine at night or when left standing. Some lorry drivers light small fires under frozen tanks. Only you can judge if the risk is worth taking.

CUT OFF IN SNOW

If you are trapped by a blizzard, stay in the car. If you are on a regular traffic route you will probably soon be rescued. Going for help could be too risky.

Run the engine for heat if you have fuel. Cover the engine so that as little heat as possible is lost directly – but make sure that the exhaust is clear. Take no risk of exhaust coming into the car. If you feel drowsy stop the engine and open a window. Do NOT go to sleep with the engine running.

Switch off the heater as soon as you have taken the chill off the interior. Start it again when the temperature drops. If there is no fuel to run the engine wrap up in any spare clothing, rugs etc, and keep moving inside the car.

If you have to leave the car to go a short distance, when you know help is very close for instance, rig up a signpost – a bright scarf or garment on a stick to help you find it again.

When the blizzard stops, and if it is daylight (otherwise wait until morning), it is worth walking out if there is a clear guide to the route (such as telegraph poles).

If miles from anywhere and off normal routes, and if the snow is building up to bury the car, it is worth getting out and building yourself a snow cave – where you may be warmer than in the car and can sit out several days. When the blizzard stops scrape large signs in the snow and use other signals to attract attention.

GENERAL

Clutch slip: Often caused by oil or grease getting on the clutch plates. To degrease these plates use the fire extinguisher. Squirt it through the inspection plate opening.

Fan belts: Improvise one with a pair of tights, a tie or even string.

HT leads: If a high tension lead breaks, you may be able to replace it with a willow twig. Any plant stem with water content can be used to carry current from the coil to the distributor. Spit on the ends and insert into the push-fit contacts. DANGER! When you switch on, there is a current of about 1300 volts. DO NOT TOUCH. Replace twig frequently as it dries out.

Dead battery: You don't need the battery if you can get up enough speed. A tow or a steep slope will do. On a vehicle with four gears, use gear two or three when releasing the clutch to try for ignition.

Half-shaft breakage: Not much you can do on a front or back wheel drive but, if your vehicle is 4-wheel drive, remove the half-shaft. Disconnect the drive and keep motoring on the other axle.

-4-
FOOD

You need to have some understanding of your body's nutritional needs and how you can meet them. In most circumstances plant foods will be the most readily available — but you need to know which plants to avoid. Colour illustrations provide a miniature field guide to some of the most useful plants. From this nucleus you can extend your plant knowledge.

Almost any animal can provide food and you must get used to eating unusual ones, such as worms and insects, which are easily obtained. A wide range of effective snares and traps will catch food, while you gather plants, collect water or carry out other survival tasks.

To hunt you may first have to improvise your own weapons. Learn how to do so and practise using them.

Meat needs preparation to make it convenient to handle and safe to cook. Learn how to preserve it when there is a surplus.

Fish offers another source of food, so simple methods are described which require no prior angling skills.

FOOD AND FOOD VALUES

The body needs food to supply heat and energy and to provide the materials with which it can build new tissues, whether for growth, repair or reproduction. A healthy body can survive for a time on reserves stored in its tissues, but lack of food makes it increasingly difficult to keep warm, to recover after hard work or injury and to fight off disease.

Fortunately human beings are omnivores — we can digest both flesh and plants — and we can eat almost anything from the animal and vegetable kingdoms. With a little care, those things that are poisonous or dangerous are easily avoided. We enjoy food, so a good meal is an excellent morale booster, and when there are not other pressing priorities it is worth taking the trouble to cook food, which will make it more tasty, and to seek out foods with interesting flavours.

Do not rely on the easiest source of food, for a balanced diet is as important to the long-term survivor as having enough to eat in the first place. If you are camped in the middle of a rabbit warren, and dinner almost jumps into the pot, you could die from deficiencies not supplied by rabbit meat. Your diet MUST be made up of a wide range of elements which provide the right proportions of nutrients and sufficient energy to get you through the day. These nutrients must include proteins, carbohydrates, fats, minerals and other trace elements and vitamins.

ENERGY NEEDS

Without making a physical effort of any kind, the average person in a completely restful state requires 70 calories per hour to maintain their basic metabolism — the involuntary functions such as breathing and blood circulation that we do not even have to think about. A calorie is a unit of heat — it is the amount needed to raise the temperature of one litre of water by one degree centigrade — and is the way in which energy is expressed when discussing nutrition.

Calories are not produced equally by all kinds of foods. The energy values of the basic types are:

Carbohydrates	1g (.035oz) produces 4 calories
Fat	1g (.035oz) produces 9 calories
Protein	1g (.035oz) produces 4 calories

The simplest domestic activities — standing up, sitting down, lighting a fire and so forth — that make up an ordinary day demand another 45 calories per hour. That makes a total of about 2040 calories a day without any work or other major activity, which could burn up a further 3,500 calories daily. Since not only physical effort but mental effort and anxiety also use up calories, keep calm and relax and, if food is scarce, DO NOT SQUANDER ENERGY.

Carbohydrates

Carbohydrates form the bulk of the diet and are the main source of energy, not just for physical effort but for fuelling internal functions and the running of the nervous system. Carbohydrates are made up of carbon, hydrogen and oxygen and are synthesized by plants. They are very easily converted into energy by the body and do not require a large water intake. They prevent ketosis — indigestion, vomiting and nausea caused by the excessive breakdown of body fats during starvation — but have two disadvantages: they do not contain vitamin B and they may cause constipation.

There are two types of carbohydrates:

Sugars are found in sugar, syrup, honey, treacle and fruits.
Starches are found in cereals, roots and tubers. Starch granules are insoluble in cold water but heat causes them to rupture — this is why roots and tubers are always cooked.

Fats

Fats contain the same elements as carbohydrates but combined differently. They also are a concentrated source of energy, providing twice as many calories as carbohydrates, stored in the body as a layer of fat under the skin and around the organs. They are insoluble in water and before they can be absorbed by the body require a lengthy digestive process which demands an adequate intake of water. Fats heat and insulate the body, protect organs, lubricate the alimentary tract and build an energy reserve. They are found in animals, fish, eggs, milk, nuts and some vegetables and fungi.

Proteins

Proteins are the basic chemical units of living matter. They are the only food constituent containing nitrogen and therefore essential for the growth and repair of the body, and are made up of complex chemical structures known as amino acids, combined in thousands of different ways.

The main sources of protein are meat, fish, eggs and dairy produce, and plants in the form of nuts, grains and pulses. It is also found in small quantities in some tubers and other vegetables. Fungi can be an important source of protein. Animal protein contains all the amino acids humans need, but individual plant foods do not unless a sufficient range is eaten.

If carbohydrates and fats are missing from the diet, protein is used to generate energy but at the expense of the body's other needs, so that in starvation the body burns up its own tissues.

Minerals

Minerals include some which one requires in quantity, such as calcium, phosphorus, sodium, chlorine, potassium, sulphur and magnesium, and others, including iron, flourine and iodine, which are required in much smaller amounts. Calcium is needed for bones and teeth but has other roles in muscular function and blood clotting. All minerals have vital roles in body functions.

Trace elements

Trace elements include strontium, aluminium, arsenic, gold and other chemicals in tiny amounts. Their exact function is not yet understood.

Vitamins

Vitamins are essential to health and have an important role not only in maintaining the body but in protection from illness. There are about 40 different vitamins, of which about a dozen are essential for humans, found in minute amounts in many kinds of food. Vitamin D can be synthesized in the skin when it is exposed to the sun's rays and vitamin K can be synthesized by bacteria in the gut, but others must be obtained from external sources. Beri-beri, scurvy, rickets and pellagra are all the result of vitamin deficiency. Vitamin A aids vision and prevents eye disease.

FOOD PLANTS

There are few places in the world where you will be far from some kind of vegetation — bush, vine, creeper, flower, grass or lichen — which can be eaten to provide nourishment. In Europe alone there are 10,000 edible wild plants. The only skill required in making use of them is knowing which is which and where to find them. Some, though edible, have very little food value, so learn which yield the most nourishment, especially those which are widespread and available throughout the year — and learn which are poisonous, in order to avoid them.

Plants contain essential vitamins and minerals, and are rich in protein and carbohydrates. Some plants also contain fat and all provide roughage essential to keep the body in good working order.

Do NOT eat large quantities of any one plant at a time and if you are not used to eating a plant start by nibbling a fresh specimen and adding some to stews, and build up your intake gradually. If you give your stomach a chance to get used to a new food it will adjust and not reject it.

Do NOT assume that because birds, mammals or insects have eaten a plant that it is edible by humans. Monkeys are some indication, but no guarantee, that plants are suitable for human consumption.

TESTING NEW PLANTS

Always adopt the following procedure when trying out potential new food plants, only one person testing each plant. NEVER take short cuts — complete the whole test. If in any doubt, do NOT eat the plant. Should stomach trouble occur, relief can be gained by drinking plenty of hot water; do not eat again until the pain goes. If it is severe, induce vomiting by tickling the back of the throat. Charcoal is a useful emetic. Swallowing some will induce vomiting and the charcoal may also absorb the poison. White wood ash mixed to a paste with water will relieve stomach pain.

Inspect
Try to identify. Ensure that a plant is not slimy or worm-eaten. It will be past its best, with little food value other than the grubs or worms upon it. Some plants, when old, change their chemical content and become toxic.

Smell
Crush a small portion. If it smells of bitter almonds or peaches — DISCARD.

Skin Irritation

Rub slightly or squeeze some of the juice onto a tender part of the body (under the arm between armpit and elbow, for instance). If any discomfort, rash or swelling is experienced — DISCARD, reject in future.

Lips, Tongue, Mouth

If there is no irritation to the skin proceed in the following stages, going on to the next only after waiting five seconds to check that there is no unpleasant reaction:

- Place a small portion on the lips
- Place a small portion in the corner of the mouth
- Place a small portion on the tip of the tongue
- Place a small portion under the tongue
- Chew a small portion

In all cases: if any discomfort is felt, such as soreness to throat, irritation or stinging or burning sensations — DISCARD, reject in future.

Swallow

Swallow a small amount and WAIT FIVE HOURS. During this period eat or drink NOTHING else.

Eating

If no reactions such as soreness to the mouth, repeated belching, nausea, sickness, stomach pains, griping pains in the lower abdomen or any other distressing symptoms are experienced, you may consider the plant safe.

GATHERING PLANTS

It is easy to pick plants here and there, but it is better and safer to gather them systematically.

Take a container on foraging trips — an empty bag, a piece of cloth folded into a sack, a birch-bark box or large leaves stitched together. This stops harvest being crushed, which makes it go off quickly.

Leaves and Stems

Young growth, usually paler green, will be tastier and more tender. Older plants are tougher and more bitter. Nip off leaves near the stem. Leaves simply torn off are easily damaged. They may wilt and loose goodness before they reach the pot.

Roots and Tubers

Choose larger plants. Some are very difficult to pull up. To lessen chance of breaking them dig around the plant to loosen, then prise them out with a sharpened stick.

Fruit and Nuts

Choose larger plants. Pick only ripe, fully coloured fruits. Hard, greenish berries are indigestible, even after long cooking. Many fruits, especially in the tropics, have tough, bitter skins. Peel them. Nuts lying at the base of a tree are a sign they are ready. Others can be shaken down if the tree is a small one. You may be able to knock others down by throwing a stick.

Seeds and Grains

PRECAUTION: Some contain deadly poisons. Tasting will not harm you but DO NOT SWALLOW. Carry out the edibility test, reject any seed that is unpalatable, bitter or with a hot, burning taste (unless a positively identified pepper or spice).

Heads of some grain plants may have black spurs in place of normal seeds. These carry ergot poisoning, a fungal disease that turns the grain into enlarged, black, bean-like structures. It is a source of an hallucinogen, and is very poisonous — sometimes fatal.

REJECT THE WHOLE HEAD!

Fungi

Medium-sized are easier to identify and less likely to suffer from insect damage. Pick the whole fungus. If the stem is left on the ground it will be harder to identify the fungi gathered. Keep fungi separate. If a poisonous kind has been picked it will not then contaminate other food.

PLANTS TO AVOID

WARNING

POISON! There are two fairly common poisons in the plant world, but both are easily detectable:

HYDROCYANIC ACID (Prussic acid) has the taste and smell of bitter almonds or peaches. Most notable example is the Cherry Laurel (*Prunus laurocerasus*), with laurel-like leaves, which contains a closely allied poison. Crush the leaves and remember the smell. Discard ALL plants with this smell.

OXALIC ACID, whose salts (oxalates) occur naturally in some plants, for instance Wild Rhubarb (mostly in the leaves) and Wood Sorrel (*Oxalis acetosella*). Recognizable by the sharp, dry, stinging or burning sensation when applied to the skin or tongue. Discard ALL plants which fit this description.

- **AVOID** any plant with a milky sap, unless positively identified as safe (such as dandelion).

- **AVOID** red plants, unless positively identified, especially in the tropics. The red-streaked stalk of Wild Rhubarb is edible but its leaf is poisonous. Hemlock has reddish-purple splotches on its stem.

- **AVOID** fruit which is divided into five segments, unless positively identified as a safe species.

- **AVOID** grasses and other plants with tiny barbs on their stems and leaves. With a magnifying glass you can see them as hooks rather than straight hairs and they will irritate the mouth and digestive tract.

- **AVOID** old or wilted leaves. The leaves of some trees and plants develop deadly hydrocyanic acid when they wilt — including blackberry, raspberry, cherry, peach and plum. All may be safely eaten when young, fresh and dry.

- **AVOID** mature bracken (*Pteridium aguilinium*). It destroys vitamin B in the body, setting up a peculiar blood condition which can cause death. Eat only tightly coiled 'fiddle heads'. All 250 varieties of north temperate ferns are edible when young, although some are too bitter to be palatable and some have irritating hairs which must be removed before eating. Break off the tips as low as they remain tender, close your hand over the stalk and draw the frond through to remove the 'wool'.

IDENTIFYING PLANTS

Only a small selection of the world's many plants can be described and illustrated here and only a specialist botanist could identify more than a handful of plants in far-flung corners of the world. Begin by learning a few plants that can be found in most conditions and at most times of year. Close familiarity with even one or two could make all the difference between survival and starvation. Learn these first and learn them thoroughly.

Temperate zones: dandelions, nettles, docks, plantains

Sub-tropical and tropical zones: palms, wild figs, bamboo

Arid and desert zones: mescal, prickly pears, baobabs, acacias (but not in North or South America)

Polar zones: spruces and willows (north), lichens (north and south). In summer in north as for temperate zones

Coasts: kelps and lavers

IDENTIFICATION AIDS:

- Location: Plants grow only in suitable conditions, if you know what habitats they like, and geographical distribution, you can reduce the possibilities immediately.

- Shape and size: Is plant tall and woody like a tree or shrub? short and soft-stemmed? bushy and branched or only one or a few stems?

- Leaves: Are they large or small? spear-shaped, rounded or strap-like? with toothed, or lobed edges? made up of several leaflets? uniform in colour?

- Flowers: Seasonal, but if present note colour, size, shape, single or clustered, where on plant.

- Fruits and seeds: Are they fleshy, hard and cased like a nut, or small and tough like a seed? Note colour, size, shape, whether singly or in clusters, in pods or capsules.

- Roots: Rarely help identification — unless unusual.

ANIMALS FOR FOOD

All animals can be a source of nourishment. A few, including worms and insects, can be collected with little skill, but most must be trapped or hunted, demanding both knowledge and expertise of animals and of methods.

The more you know of animals the better, but general natural history knowledge must be used to help you find out more by observation in the wild. There is no one way to do things — you must learn by trial and error.

You must study each species' habits, find out where it sleeps, what it eats and where it waters. You must learn how best to make a kill, what traps to set and balance your humanitarian instincts against the expediencies of survival.

The best animals for flavour and amount of meat are mature females. The younger the animal, the more lean the meat. An adult male is at his fattest just before the mating season (which varies according to species and climate). During the mating season the male becomes progressively poorer, the fat is run off and even the normally rich bone marrow suffers. Animals put on fat to see them through the winter and trim down for the summer. The older the animal the more fat it has and the tougher the meat becomes.

FINDING GAME

There are very few places on earth where there are no wild animals, but sometimes the signs of their presence are far from obvious. If you can recognize and read the signs that animals leave, and identify the animal, you will know what methods to adopt in hunting and trapping your prey, what bait to use and what kind of traps to set.

Most mammals are mainly on the move at first and last light. Only the larger and more powerful venture out during the day. Larger herbivores need a whole day of grazing to satisfy their appetites. Some very small ones have to eat so frequently that they are intermittently active all day long — but most smaller mammals, such as rabbits, eat mainly at night and only change their habits when the weather is bad. Animals that feed on other animals hunt at the times that their prey is active. So must you, if you intend to hunt them, but you can find out a great deal without ever seeing a living animal and can set traps to catch them when they are about.

Tracks and signs

Most animals are creatures of habit and use regular routes between their watering spots, feeding places and homes. Look out for the signs of these trails. Tracks will be more obvious on wet ground, snow and damp sand, and other signs are more noticeable in heavy vegetation. The size of the impression left is in proportion to that of the animal. The age of the track can be accurately judged by its sharpness and moisture content. Has water seeped into it or has rain filled it? Has it become smudged? The clearer the track the more likely it is to be recent.

In the early morning tracks can be checked by looking at them from ground level. If dew and spider's webs have been disturbed, the tracks are, at most, a few hours old. Some animals, such as rabbits, never range very far and any tracks are likely to indicate that they are in the area. Some animals make tunnels through dense undergrowth. Their height indicates the size of the animal that made them. The height of broken twigs along a track will also suggest an animal's size. Check to see how fresh they are: Have trampled leaves wilted? Are broken twigs still green and supple? Marks on trees and logs, feeding signs and discarded food are other useful indications. Droppings indicate the type of animal that left them.

Feeding signs

The way in which bark has been stripped from trees, the gnawed shells of nuts, partially eaten fruits, bitten off shoots and the remains of prey animals of carnivores or the destruction of the nests of prey are all indications of species living or hunting in the vicinity.

Discarded fruits or nuts are often found when food is plentiful — an animal finds one piece not to its liking and drops it to try another. They not only reveal an animal's presence but suggest baits for traps.

A skilled eye can often identify the species by the pattern left by tooth or beak marks on a nut, or the way in which a pine cone has been stripped to get at its seeds.

Bark, twigs and buds, especially of young trees and bushes, form an important part of the diet of many animals, including several species of deer and goats, hares, squirrels and numerous other small rodents. In most cases the marks made by the animal's teeth will show clearly in the bark.

Many deer will bite offshoots leaving a torn and frayed edge. (Hares for instance, leave a clean bite.) Bark pulled off in long shreds, completely exposing the wood is another sign of deer, when eating in summer — in winter the bark is attached more firmly and is eaten in patches, so that usually only sections on one side of the trunk are affected and large toothmarks are clearly visible. Deer also scrape their antlers against trees to remove the velvet and as part of marking their territory — leaving frayed bark and wood with long scratches from the antler points.

Sheep and goats also bark trees. Their toothmarks generally run obliquely, those of deer vertically. Low level gnawing will usually be that of rodents — stripped roots are probably the work of vole-like animals. Severed stumps with conical tops that look as though they have been chopped with a small axe are the felling work of beaver.

Squirrels strip bark higher up the tree, pieces often falling to the ground beneath. A scattering of cone pieces on the ground is often a sign of squirrels too. Beneath a tree, nutshells may also indicate a squirrel — perhaps its nest is overhead, but if nuts or cones are also wedged into the trunk that shows the work of nut-eating birds. Near a pile of empty shells you may also find a rodent's burrow.

If sapling growth looks as though it has been trimmed level like a clipped hedge, or the lower branches of trees look neatly trimmed below a certain height, you may guess this to be the work of browsing animals such as deer.

Droppings

Droppings give one of the best indications of an animal's type. Size can be judged from their size and quantity; dryness is an indication of how long since they were passed. Old droppings will be hard and odourless — fresh, wet and still smelling. Flies draw attention to droppings.

Mammals: Many mammal droppings have a strong scent, produced by glands in the anus. This plays an important role in marking territory and giving sexual signs. It can be used to advantage in baiting snares.

Animals that live on vegetation, such as cattle, deer and rabbits, produce roundish and strawy droppings. Meat eaters, such as wild cats and foxes, produce long tapering ones. Some animals, including badgers and bears, have mixed diets. Break open a dropping to see if there are any clues to what the animal has been eating, then bait accordingly.

Birds: Also fall into two groups: flesh eaters and seed/fruit eaters, which can be distinguished by their droppings. Smaller seed-eating birds' droppings are small and mostly liquid, whereas the owls and hawks produce pellets which may contain indigestible parts of the meal taken, be it fish, bird, insect vole or rodent. Loose droppings are an indication that water is probably within a reasonable range, for small birds need to be close to it. Birds of prey, however, do not need to be close to water. Roosts and nesting sites will often be indicated by copious droppings on the boughs or ground beneath. Birds generally feed in older trees where there is some decay and plenty of grubs.

Rootings

Some animals root up the ground in search of insects and tubers. Pigs, especially, turn over large areas of earth. If the earth is still crumbly and fresh an animal is likely to have been active on the spot quite recently. A big muddy wallow is usually a sign of pigs. Small scratches may be where a squirrel has been digging for shoots.

Scent and Smell

Listen to the noises around you, register the smells. They are certain to include indications of the wildlife present, and where one kind of animal exists there will be others — where there are prey species there will be predators. Many people neglect their sense of smell — but you must try to redevelop it. Some animal smells are very strong, particularly those of foxes. Keep your eyes sharp too. In cold climates, for example, the breath of large animals forms a cloud of condensation. This 'smoke' can be seen some way off if you are in a good vantage point.

Burrows and Dens

Many animals make their homes in burrows, usually on high ground away from water. Some, such as rabbits and ground squirrels, take little trouble to conceal them, although one or two exits will be hidden for use in an emergency. Rabbits' emergency holes are easily dug out, or a piece of bramble or barbed wire can be pushed down the hole to hook the rabbit out.

Predatory animals normally hide their holes, which are generally in wooded country. Tracks or droppings nearby may give their location away — and are an indication that a hole is in use (although some animals, such as badgers, use regular toilet sites elsewhere).

MAMMALS

NOTE: Where tracks are shown, no scale has been imposed on them. Most are typical of a whole family of animals, but will vary greatly in size according to species. Track 1 is right front. Track 2 is right hind.

WILDCATS

Range from domestic size to the tiger. Occur on all continents except Australia and Antarctica, but nowhere common. Secretive and generally nocturnal, they avoid man. You will see lions in a wildlife reserve but seldom encounter cats elsewhere. All are potential food — but don't take on the larger ones. Kills of big cats may be scavenged if unattended — but BEWARE — the owner is likely to be nearby. Meat may be stringy, stew thoroughly, but small cat meat tastes like rabbit. Sinews strong, good for bowstrings.

Traps: *Powerful spring snares, platforms or baited-hole-noose. Bait with offal, blood or meat. Cats have very fast reactions and may leap clear of deadfalls.*

Tracks and signs: *Walk on toes, leaving marks of four well-developed pads and a larger pad to rear. Claws (except in Cheetah) retracted when walking. Droppings elongated, tapering, but usually hidden. Urine strong smelling.*

WILD DOGS

Foxes and other wild dogs are found widely, from deserts to the Arctic but, not in New Zealand, Madagascar and some other islands. Wolves are now mostly confined to wilderness North America and north and central Asia.

Superb senses make it pointless to stalk canines at close quarters but their curiosity will tempt them to traps. Moving on all fours may attract them — they may think YOU potential food! Chewy. Remove anal glands. Dog is a delicacy in the Far East.

Traps: *Snare for foxes, try stepped-bait or toggle, bait-release, baited-hole-noose. Minimize human scent in area.*

Tracks and signs: *Walk on toes. Print shows four pads and claw tips — outer pad shorter than inner with large main pad to rear. Elongated, tapering droppings show remains of fur, bones, insects depending on diet. Fox droppings pungent, as is earth (den) — in soft ground earth can be dug out.*

Hyenas: *Scavengers (not true dogs) of Africa east to India. Can be very dangerous. Boil thoroughly, risk of parasites in flesh.*

Civets: *Scavengers of tropical Africa and Asia, trap as dogs and remove anal glands before cooking.*

BEARS

Solitary animals of North America, Eurasia and some northern parts of South America, preferring well-wooded country (except Polar Bear). Strong and fast-running they may scavenge a campsite. Most kinds can climb trees. Bears can kill a man with ease. Give them a WIDE berth. Potential rich food with nutritious fat, if you can trap one, but hunting with improvised weapons is foolhardy. Cook thoroughly to eliminate parasites. Do NOT eat liver of Polar Bear — it contains lethal level of vitamin A.

Traps: Deadfall and spear, but only largest work — bears tear off most snares. Must kill or completely incapacitate — wounded bears very dangerous.

Tracks and signs: Prints may be 30cm (1ft) x 18cm (9in), with five long-clawed toes. Toe pads close together, claw marks distinct. Rear paws taper and could be mistaken for human prints. Bears eat almost anything and grub up ground, rip up stumps and break into insect nests in search of food.

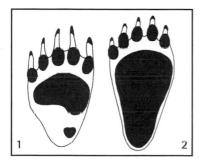

OTTERS

Difficult to see or trap, spending time in water or bolt holes along riverbanks, but curious, so riverside spring snare, baited with fresh fish may tempt them.
Tracks and signs: Five-toed, webbed, almost circular 7·5cm (3in) x 6cm (2⁵/₈in). Fishy-smelling elongated droppings on regular sites, usually stones.

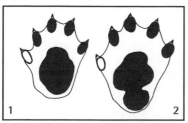

WEASEL GROUP

Weasels, stoats, mink, martens and polecats are secretive — but may be an important food source in the far north. Beware of their sharp teeth.
Traps: Spring snares with bait bars, deadfalls. Bait with offal or birds' eggs.
Tracks: Indistinct except in soft ground. Five well-spaced claws and toes, hair on main pad often smudges. Gait bounding, so fore and rear prints overlap. Weasels are the smallest.

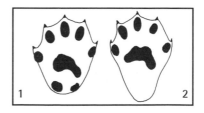

WOLVERINES (Gluttons)

Chunky, badger-shaped animals of the far north, quite capable of pulling down a caribou though mainly carrion eaters. Nowhere common. Don't take one on unless you are armed!
Traps: Strong baited-spring snare or hole-noose — if you can find bait in the tundra.
Tracks: Average 8cm (3¹/₄in) x 7cm (2³/₄in), five toes with powerful claws. Hair on sole may obscure main pad.

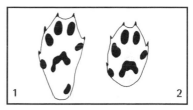

BADGERS

Stocky, nocturnal creatures of habit of North America, Africa and Eurasia east to Indonesia. Hibernate in colder areas. Well-worn runs and toilet sites make good trapping places. Can be fierce, with a disabling bite. Do not get close. Young badger tastes like pork.

Traps: Leg spring snares, baited release and deadfalls, hole noose. Make them tough.

Tracks and signs: Five-toed with prominent claws and large rear pad. Could be confused with small bear. Stride length averages 50cm (20in). Droppings like dog's but in shallow excavated scoop. Uprooted ground and insect nests torn open may indicate badgers.

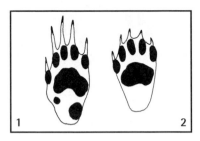

SKUNKS
North and South American, skunks look like small badgers with a hairy tail. When threatened they spray a foul-smelling fluid from glands by the anus. Look for an easier meal.

MONKEYS/APES
Almost entirely confined to tropics, generally living in extended family groups, often in trees. Even small monkeys can inflict a bad bite. Intelligent and difficult to stalk – they set up a howling long before you can get close – but bold and curious, which can be to your advantage. Very edible.

Traps: Perch or baited spring spear trap, spring snare or hole noose. Bait with fruit or anything likely to arouse curiosity.

Signs: Activity will lead you to them – few take trouble to conceal themselves and most are noisy.

SEALS

Track shows belly drag in centre. Arrow indicates direction of travel.

(See *Polar Regions* in *Climate and terrain*.)

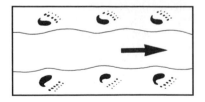

BATS
Found in all except very cold climates. Active at night. Hibernate in temperate areas. Meat-eaters take insects, fish, small animals include a blood-sucking Vampire bat of South America, which can transmit rabies. Keep WELL covered when sleeping rough in bush within its range. Fruit eaters (also known as flying foxes) are larger, some with 1m (40in) wing span, found from tropical Africa east to Australasia. Good eating, especially plump fruit bats. Remove wings and legs, gut and skin like rabbit.

Traps: Net a fruit tree where flying foxes feed. Knock others from roosts when sleeping during day.

Signs: Roosting colonies easy to spot, often in caves, fruit bats also in trees.

CATTLE
Cattle live in herds and need access to water. Bison and other wild cattle are found in wilderness areas of North America, Africa and southern Asia. The few buffalo remaining in Europe and America are protected. Introduced water buffalo are wild in northern Australia. Stray domestic cattle may occur, particularly in Africa.

Big cattle can be dangerous – particularly cunning old solitary bulls.

Traps: Only the most powerful snares, spring traps and deadfalls, except for young animals.

Tracks and signs: Heavy, two distinct

hoofmarks, narrow at top, bulbous at rear. Droppings rather like familiar cowpats — they make excellent fuel.

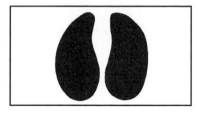

WILD SHEEP/GOATS

Sheep generally live in small flocks on high alpine pastures and steppes in North America, parts of Europe and north Africa (rare) through Arabia to mountains of central Asia. Alert, nimble and liking inaccessible places — making them impossible to approach.

Goats are few in Europe and North Africa, and mainly found in mountains of central Asia. Even more sure-footed than sheep. Good to eat.

Traps: *Snares or spring snares on trails. In rocky areas natural obstructions give good places for deadfalls. But don't expect great success!*

Tracks and signs: *Cloven hooves, two slender pointed marks not joined, tip always splayed in sheep, sometimes in goats. Goats' more rounded at front which is narrower than rear. Illustration below shows, in scale, Domestic sheep (left), Chamois (right). Globular droppings like those of domestic sheep.*

DEER/ANTELOPES

Deer, found in well-wooded country on every continent except Australia, vary from the Moose of the north to tropical forest deer only 45cm (18in) high. Antelopes and gazelles occur in equal variety in Africa east to India with one, the Pronghorn, in North America. Shy, elusive, with superb hearing and smell, they usually live in groups. Most active at dawn and dusk and — except for those in arid areas — never far from water. Excellent meat which smokes well. Hides of deer particularly supple, horns and antlers useful implements.

Regard their horns as WEAPONS. Large animals can be aggressive and can gouge and stab with great power.

Traps: *Snare or deadfall for small types, leg spring snares, spear traps and deadfalls for larger. Bait with offal — curiosity will draw them.*

Tracks and signs: *Cloven hooves form two oblongs. Reindeer noticeably rounded. Illustration below shows, in scale, Roe Deer front and hind track (top) and Reindeer (bottom). Note dew-claw impressions on reindeer track. Walking animals' prints overlap front and rear, running animals' spaced. Droppings oblong to round pellets, usually in clumps. In temperate area, winter droppings lighter and more fibrous. Scrapes on saplings, nibbled and frayed bark.*

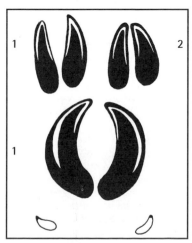

WILD PIGS

Pigs, peccaries and other hogs vary in size. Many are thickly haired, but all have piggy shape, long snout and two large teeth, or tusks, at the side of the mouth. They live in family groups, usually in wooded country – though Warthogs prefer savannah. Difficult to stalk, though not so alert as deer, except when lying up during heat of day when you have more chance. Listen for their snores. Large boars and those guarding young need little provocation to charge and can knock a man down. Tusks inflict severe injury, often dangerously close to the femoral artery on the upper leg. Meat good, with plenty of fat in winter, but must be thoroughly boiled because of parasites.

Traps: *Strong spring snares, deadfalls, pig spear traps on the game trail or hope for a passing group. Pigs eat virtually anything, so bait with whatever is available.*

Tracks and signs: *Cloven hooves leave marks like deer. On soft ground the short side toes distinguish them. Young animals have more pointed hooves. Droppings often rather shapeless, never long, firm or tapering. Ground disturbed by rooting, mudwallows best signs. Warthogs have large, burrow-like sleeping holes.*

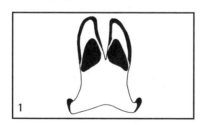

CAMELS

Range wild in deserts of north Africa, east to central Asia, and have been introduced to Australia – but they require a very powerful spear trap or projectile weapon. Camels can spit and could inflict a powerful bite on your hands, face or body.

LLAMAS

Alpacas, Guacanos and Viçunas of the Andes, south to Patagonia, can be trapped like antelopes. Semi-domesticated, Llamas and Alpacas indicate that people are probably not far away.

TAPIRS

Shy animals of the deep forests of tropical America and south-east Asia, they resemble large, hairless pigs with floppy snouts. Snare or trap with spear traps or deadfalls on their trails.

RABBITS/HARES

Widely spread by man and found from well-inside the Arctic Circle to deserts and jungles. In most areas these are the first animals to try to trap – Arctic (snowshoe) hares and Jackrabbits of the far north could save your life. Rabbits are easier to catch, most live in burrows, often in large numbers and using well-worn runs – the places to set snares. Young rabbits will often lie quite still and can be picked up. Hares do not live in burrows and tend not to have regular runs. Myxamatosis has led to many rabbits also living above ground.

Traps: *Simple snares – though a spring snare will take the animal off the ground and reduce the chance of your meal being stolen.*

Tracks and signs: *Hairy soles leave little detail on soft ground but combination of long hind and shorter front feet is distinctive. Hares have five toes on front feet, but inner is short and seldom leaves a mark. Hind foot*

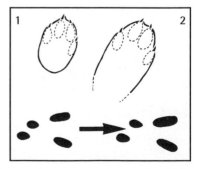

narrower, four toed. Rabbit similar but smaller (4 x 2·5cm (1³/₄ x 1in). Running leaves hind in front of forefeet instead of side by side. Droppings small, hard, round pellets. Bark nibbled at bottom of trees leaving two incisor marks. Rabbits thump a warning sounding like someone hitting a cushion.

DANGER

RABBIT STARVATION!

Rabbits can provide the easiest of meals but their flesh lacks fat and vitamins essential to man. The Hudson Bay Company recorded cases of trappers dying of starvation although eating well on an easily available diet of rabbit.

The body uses its own vitamins and minerals to digest the rabbit and these are then passed out in the faeces. If they are not replaced weakness and other symptoms of vitamin deficiency appear. If more rabbit is eaten, the condition becomes worse. Trappers literally ate themselves to death when eating vegetation would have ensured their survival. This situation often occurs when vegetation has been buried by snow and survivors rely on rabbits for food.

Myxamatosis, a viral disease that causes swelling of the mucous glands, especially on the head, makes rabbits sluggish and often blind. Their appearance is off-putting but the disease does not harm man. Once skinned the only indication of it will be white spots in the liver.

Rabbits and many rodents carry Tularemia (see *Rodents*).

SMALL RODENTS

The largest group of animals and some of the easiest to catch, though most are too small for a snare. Tracks of different kinds are not easy to distinguish. Rats and mice occur almost everywhere. They may be tempted into cage traps or under deadfalls. Rats carry disease. When gutting take care not to rupture the innards and cook thoroughly. Unwelcome, except as food; try to catch them if they invade your camp.

Guinea pigs and cavies: *are widely domesticated in the Andes, where they live. They can be tempted to traps baited with fruit and leafy vegetables and make excellent eating.*

Capybara: *found in tropical lowlands in parts of South America grow to the size of a small sheep and live in family groups. Semi-aquatic, they are easily panicked into traplines or ambushes if their escape route to water is cut off. Meat is lean and tasty.*

Copyu: *similar to capybara and also from South America, is smaller. Occurs ferally in Europe. Tasty.*

PORCUPINES

Various kinds are found in Americas, Africa and tropical Asia. Some climb trees. Ground-living ones are bumbling — easily run down and speared. Quills can inflict injury.

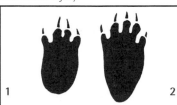

BEAVERS

Chunky, dam-building aquatic animals with scaly, paddle-like tails. Found in North America and northern Eurasia using regular runs along streams, where they can be trapped. Good to eat, especially the tail.

Traps: *Strong net or line of nooses across water run. Spring snares or* deadfalls where they emerge to chew trees.

Tracks and signs: *Five toes with claw marks, often only four show. Rear track webbed, roundish, larger 15 x 10cm (6 x 4in). Look out for dam building and lodges, felled and chewed saplings, bark and shavings near water.*

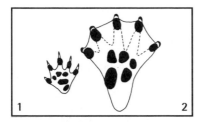

HEDGEHOGS

Shy, mainly nocturnal animals of Eurasia and Africa east to Indonesia they lie in well-concealed nests during the day and hibernate in temperate regions. They move fairly slowly so can be run down. Those that curl up are easiest to catch. Edibility fair, handle carefully usually parasite infested. Skin can be removed with spines intact. Cook thoroughly.

Traps: *Snares are unlikely to grip. Use deadfall — hedgehogs like to snuffle about obstructions.*

Tracks: *Five toes with long claws but usually only four show.*

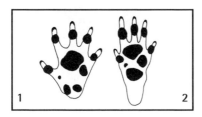

SQUiRRELS

Squirrels and Prairie dogs occur everywhere except Australasia and Poles, hibernating in colder areas. Alert and nimble, most are active by day and night — feeding on nuts, fruits, shoots

etc and some on birds' eggs. Raid their nests in tree hollows for young — beware of their sharp teeth they are savage in defence. Ground-living kinds live in burrows, often in large colonies. Most are excellent eating.

Traps: *Small spring snares attached to bait bars. Use split fruit or a bird's egg to attract. For tree squirrels set 5cm (2in) loop snares along a pole and lean against trunk of squirrels' trees — even when one has been caught they will go on using it as a short cut.*

Tracks and signs: *Four slender toes, with claws on front foot, five on rear. Chewed bark, gnawed nuts, cones beneath tree or an untidy nest of twigs in a fork may indicate squirrels.*

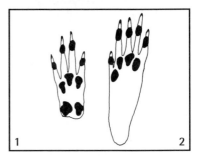

KANGAROOS

With wallabies and other relatives kangaroos are limited to Australia, Tasmania and parts of Papua New Guinea. Large kinds can strike powerfully with hind feet. Some adept tree climbers. Too fast to run down. Most active at night, some shelter in caves etc during day. Plains kangaroos range far from water. Edibility fair, but not easy to catch!

Traps: *Deadfalls, spring snares — though in open country no trail to set them on. Tempt tree kangaroos down with fruit, leaves and roots.*

Tracks and signs: *Only two prints, resembling giant rabbit tracks (front legs not used for support) or locomotion.*

OPOSSUMS

Small nocturnal scavengers of southern US to South America. Similar but unrelated animals in Australasia. Good tree climbers. Possum pie a traditional US dish.

Traps: Bait with juicy fruit, eggs; or anything to hand. They are inquisitive.

WOMBATS

Plump, badger-size animals of Australia. Eucalyptus forest, dry country and Tasmanian forms. Live in burrow. Emerge at night to forage. Trap as badger.

RACCOONS

Cat-sized, with bushy banded tail and black mask, found widely in North America. Prefer woodland near water. Introduced parts of northern Europe. Inquisitive, nocturnal, emerge at night from tree or rock hole to hunt frogs, molluscs, insects; small mammals, berries nuts. Crab-eating Raccoon of tropical America is related.

Traps: Bait a spring snare.

Tracks: Five long toes with clear claw marks; front foot small rounded, rear larger, tapering.

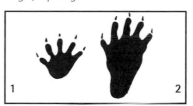

REPTILES

CROCODILES/ALLIGATORS

Members of this group are found in most subtropical and tropical regions. Those under about 1·3m (4ft) are potential food. Larger ones should be avoided – they are virtually armour-plated and some such as the cunning and aggressive estuarine crocodile of Indo-Australasia, can grow to enormous size. In areas where they live ALWAYS assume they are about for they have excellent camouflage and can lie underwater for long periods waiting for an incautious meal to step within range. Their tails can inflict a scything blow, almost as damaging as their teeth. The best meat comes from the tail and is firm and very tasty.

Traps: Set by water for small crocs or catch on line with a stick wedged in the bait to lodge in gullet. Kill with a sharp with a stick wedged in the bait to lodge in gullet. Kill with a sharp blow between the eyes.

LIZARDS

Gila monsters and Beaded lizards are docile but venomous (see Poisonous and dangerous animals in Health), but all lizards can be eaten. Most are timid though some big iguanas and monitors can inflict a bad bite and have powerful claws. Do NOT tangle with the giant Komodo dragon (2m/6ft long), confined to a few Indonesian islands.

Try to catch lizards by the tail, but small lizards move fast. They can sometimes be trapped in a pit, look out for them in a solar still. Set traps for larger ones.

TURTLES/TORTOISES

All these reptiles are good eating. Most spend their lives largely in salt or fresh water, emerging to lay eggs, but a few are terrestrial, the box turtle not even entering the water to mate. Some

129

turtles are encountered far out at sea, a bonus for the sea survivor. Net or drag them from the water. On land use a stick to turn them on their backs — keep out of the way of jaws and flippers. Then it will be defenceless. Kill with a blow to the head. Cut through belly and discard guts, remove head and neck (some have poison sack in neck). Best boiled. Very rich, so eat in small amounts. Blood even richer. Eggs found inside females can be eaten. Tortoises can retract their heads — you will probably have to stab into it. Roast ungutted in embers, when the shell splits they are ready.

Tracks: Females coming ashore to lay eggs leave tractor-like tracks on sand. They will lead to where the eggs are buried, but you may have to go quite deep to find them. Boiled, they will keep for a few days.

AMPHIBIANS

Frogs are all edible, from tiny tree frogs to African giants with legs as big as a chicken's, but some have poisons under the skin so remove skin before cooking. Active at night, their croaking will locate them, always near water. Dazzle with a light — a firebrand will do — and club. In daytime hunt with hook and line and an insect-like lure. The legs of large frogs are a particular delicacy and taste like chicken.

Toads have warty skins and may be found far from water. Bad-tasting, most have highly toxic skin secretions. Do NOT eat.

Salamanders and newts, found in and near water, can be caught like frogs and are just as edible.

SNAKES

Overcome your fear and learn their habits. A snake is a steak! But do NOT try to catch one you know is highly poisonous, if it is too large to tackle safely or you are ill-equipped.

The large constrictors — the pythons of Africa, Asia and Australasia, and the boas, like the anaconda of South America can be very large up to 10m (30ft). They tend to be timid and even the largest would find an adult human too big to swallow. Easy to catch — but do NOT tackle large ones! They are not poisonous but their back-raked teeth can give a very serious bite. If you can prise open the jaws, rather than pulling the snake off, the results will be less severe.

Snakes have excellent camouflage, often only movement gives them away. You may pass many every day without noticing them.

Use a forked stick to pin snake down just behind head. Strike the back of the head with another stick. Tree snakes can be clubbed and then knocked to the ground. Club them again to make sure!

Coiled snakes with head concealed present a problem. Pin one fat coil and watch it unwind before going for the head.

NEVER pick up — or even get close to a snake until you are sure it is dead. A few, including poisonous ones, can feign death convincingly.

BIRDS

All birds are edible, but some taste very much better than others. They occur everywhere — open sea, deserts, high in mountains and in polar regions — but are not always easy to catch.

Game birds make best eating: pheasants, grouse, partridges, quail, ducks, geese, jungle fowl — but they are wary and many are superbly camouflaged. Birds of prey need thorough boiling to tenderize and to destroy parasites. Sea birds can be oily and fishy-tasting.

Traps: Easiest to trap are birds of prey,

such as eagles and hawks; carrion eaters, such as vultures; inquisitive scavengers, such as crows and gulls.

Cage traps, deadfalls and spring snares can be used for birds that take bait, nooses on branches may catch roosting birds. In wooded country site traps in clearings or by river banks. Bait with meat, fruit or berries. Most birds are light — so set delicately.

Use also pole-nooses, lines with baited hooks and gullet jammers.

Small birds are easy to lime and can be attracted by bait, but making a dummy owl can be more effective. Small birds come to mob it — even a crude model works.

Tracks and signs: Except for those with webbed feet, tracks are broadly similar and indicate only the size of the bird, with a few exceptions. However, in desert and on snow, tracks may help to locate birds hiding in close cover. Calls and flights are much more useful. Alarm calls may help locate other animals. Droppings may indicate a night roost.

Autumn moult: Birds go through a complete moult in autumn and are unable to fly, or can manage only short distances. Some, especially ducks, geese and game birds are much easier to catch at this time. If not far out on water, you can run them down.

Bird nesting: Eggs are easily available from ground nesters — and many nest in colonies. Approach carefully — crawling not walking — and you may get within stone-throwing or clubbing distance.

Some, such as gulls, guard nests tenaciously. If you enter a colony be prepared to be attacked.

Burrow nesters: Puffins, petrels and a few other birds nest in burrows, usually in inaccessible places on rocky coasts and small islands. They feed at sea during the day, but can be pulled or dug out of their burrows at night.

Flightless birds: Ostriches (in Africa), Rheas (South America) and Emus and Cassowaries (Australia) are large and flightless but treat them with caution: an ostrich, in particular, can deliver bone-breaking kicks. Fairly rare — but their eggs will feed a large group and make useful containers.

INSECTS

Insects are likely to be the survivor's most reliable source of animal food. Although usually very small they occur almost everywhere and are often so plentiful that enough for a meal can soon be gathered.

Weight for weight they give more food value than vegetables. Rich in fat, protein and carbohydrates they are lifesavers, especially their larvae — those succulent grubs. You'll soon overcome your squeamishness — remember that some people consider them a delicacy. You have certainly eaten them unknowingly in food.

GATHERING

The most useful are termites, ants, beetles, grasshoppers, locusts, crickets, honey bees, caterpillars and various aquatic insects.

Many insects are inactive during the heat of the day, although most will emerge to collect moisture when it rains. Look for them in nooks and crannies of trees and behind their bark, in the tissue and seed pods of plants, in any moist shady spots and on the beds of pools and streams. Ants' and termites' nests are often immediately recognizable mounds.

Look for beetle grubs — usually pale in colour with three short legs, they range from tiny larvae to juicy 'sausages' 15·5cm (7in) and weighing 84g (3oz). You will find them on trees with peeling bark, and in decaying stumps. Some tropical palms and bamboos are infested with them. If you have a knife, cut material away until you find them under the surface.

Collect only living specimens. AVOID any that look sick or dead, have a bad smell or produce skin irritation rash when handled.

Take care when foraging for insects. Their hiding places may also harbour unwelcome creatures such as scorpions and spiders or, in larger crannies, snakes.

WARNING

Do **NOT** gather insects feeding on refuse, carrion or dung — they are likely to carry infection.

REMEMBER: Brightly coloured insects — including their caterpillars — are usually poisonous. Their bright colours are the warning sign.

AVOID: Grubs found on the underside of leaves — they often secrete poisonous fluids. Bad smelling and slimy to touch, they can be used as fish bait.

BEWARE: Large beetles often have powerful jaws, handle them with respect!

PREPARATION

Most insects are edible raw and usually more nutritious that way but they are more palatable cooked. Boiling is safest, it destroys harmful bacteria and parasites, but roasting is easier if proper containers are not to hand. Just place your dinner on hot stones or in the embers of a fire.

Remove legs and wings from larger insects such as locusts, grasshoppers and crickets. Hairs on the legs can irritate or even block the digestive tract. Fine hairs on some caterpillars can cause rashes. If you want to eat a hairy caterpillar squeeze it to extract the innards — don't eat the skin. Take the armour-like casing off beetles.

Smaller insects such as ants and termites can be mashed to a paste and then either cooked or dried to a powder. Use this to thicken other foods or for storage — it will keep for some time. People who cannot abide the idea of insects in their food will find a powder easier to eat, especially in soups or mixed with other food.

TERMITES

Found in the warmer parts of the world, termites are nutritious and tasty. Most eat only vegetation but big ones have sharp jaws and will bite at anything. You can turn this to advantage by inserting a twig into the nests and gently withdrawing it. The termites will bite it and then hang on — but you will not collect very many in this way.

Flying termites, and flying ants, often take wing during thundery weather. At such times quite large quantities can be gathered from leaves and twigs where they settle.

Remove the wings from large termites before eating. They can be boiled, fried or roasted but are more nutritious eaten raw. Their eggs have good food value too.

Gathering: Termites build large mounds, often several feet high and honeycombed with passages and chambers. Although rock hard, pieces can be broken off with a stone or stick and then dunked in water to force the termites out.

A piece of termites' nest put on the coals of a fire will produce fragrant smoke that will keep mosquitoes and similar insects away. It will smoulder all night and help to keep the fire going.

When fishing, suspend a piece of nest above a pool; termites falling from it will be good ground bait.

BEES AND WASPS

All are edible – pupae, larvae and adult – but the honeybee also provides honey. This is the finest of all natural foods, easily digestible and highly nutritious – but NOT easy to collect for bees will guard their nest tenaciously.

During the day worker bees venture far from the nest, but all gather there at night. Then is the time to strike. Make a torch from a bundle of grass and hold it very close to the entrance so that the nest fills with smoke. Then seal the hole. That kills the bees, providing an immediate meal, and making their honey safely available. Remove wings, legs – AND STING – before eating the bees. Boiling or roasting improves the flavour.

Honey can be drained from the combs inside the nest. Even though it may harden, it will keep for years. Honey gives instant energy. Because it is so rapidly assimilated by the body it is an excellent restorative in cases of exhaustion. The comb itself can also be eaten but its wax is also useful for waterproofing clothing, softening pelts and making candles.

In some parts of the world there is a slight risk that honey may contain concentrations of plant poisons. This is likely only in areas where bees are dependent on a single plant source, as with dense stands of rhododendrons in the Himalayas. Smell will be one guide, but if in doubt use the edibility test given for plants.

Wasps are much more dangerous than honeybees, but they and other kinds of social bee, which do not produce honey, can be collected and eaten in the same way together with their larvae. There are also many solitary wasps and bees which do not make communal nests.

Locating: Wasps' nests are usually found suspended from tree branches. Frequently the size and shape of a football, they may also be pear-shaped. The entrance is at the base. Bees' nests are most frequently found in a hollow tree or cave or under an overhanging rock.

HORNETS

Are actually types of social wasp. If you can find their nest without the adults finding you, then you have a ready source of food – both larvae and pupae are highly nutritious. But be warned: hornets guard their nest ferociously. They sting on sight and the pain is extreme. Unless you are desperate – and hornets do occur in areas where other food is scarce – go in search of a safer meal.

There are two main kinds of hornet: those active by day and those active at night. Day hornets can be collected at night, in the same way as honeybees. Night hornets (which you could collect by day) inflict a sting like a white-hot rivet being driven into the body, and usually go for the face. They are best left well alone!

Locating: Hornets make large globular nests, generally in trees.

ANTS

Ants quickly gather round the merest scrap of food, where they can be collected, or you can break into a nest. Take care. Most ants have a stinging bite and some large jungle ants can inflict one that will lay the victim out for 24 hours. Go for the smaller ones.

Some ants, such as the Melanophus species, have a distended abdomen full of nectar. Known as honey- or sugar-pot ants, they make much better eating.

WARNING

Some ants have a bite that feels like a nettle sting. Some fire formic acid. Ants MUST therefore be cooked for at least six minutes to destroy the poison. They are then quite safe to eat.

LOCUSTS/CRICKETS/GRASSHOPPERS

All kinds have plump bodies and well-muscled legs. Some grow to 15cm (6in) long. In some areas they are abundant.

Swat them with a leafy branch or a piece of clothing. Remove the wings, antennae and leg spurs, then eat raw or roasted. Roasting not only kills any parasites they may carry but gives them a delicious taste.

AQUATIC INSECTS

Collect adults and larvae of water beetles, mayflies, stoneflies, caddisflies, damselflies, dragonflies and the rest of the great variety of water insects, only from fresh water. Although small they are found in large numbers.

Place a screen of fine material – a shirt or other piece of cloth – in the water to act as a 'net'. Secure with sticks if necessary. Walk towards it, from upstream in flowing water, stirring up the bottom as you go. The current will carry the insects with it and they will collect in the net. If you do not want to enter the water trawling the surface may produce a harvest.

It is best to boil thoroughly all insects caught in the water, just in case the water is polluted.

SNAILS/WORMS

Snails, slugs, worms and similar creatures should not be ignored. Many cuisines rate snails a delicacy and most people will eat water molluscs such as mussels or oysters without qualms. As for worms – think what they do for birds! Both land and water snails and other shell foods must be fresh. There are a few which can be dangerous to eat. Others which, at no risk to themselves, may have eaten something harmful to humans, require preparation.

SNAILS

Found in fresh water, salt water and from deserts to alpine meadows. There is a giant snail in Africa 20cm (8in) long. They are rich in proteins and minerals. When collecting land snails, avoid any with brightly-coloured shells – they may be POISONOUS. Sea snails, especially in tropical waters, are trickier and should be left alone unless positively identified. The cone shells Toxoglossa, for example, of Pacific and Caribbean coasts, have a venomous sting like a hypodermic needle. Some kinds can kill.

Starve snails for a few days, or feed only on herbs and safe greens so that they can excrete any poisons, and then put them in a saltwater solution to clear out their guts before cooking. Boil for 10 minutes adding herbs for flavour.

Hibernating snails can be eaten provided that the operculum (the seal at the entrance to the shell) has not receded.

SLUGS

Slugs are simply snails without shells. Prepare and cook them in exactly the same way as snails.

WORMS

Contain the highest class of protein with a large proportion of essential amino acids and are easily collected. Starve them for a day before you eat them or squeeze them between the fingers to clear muck out of them. Worms can be sun- or force-dried – one easy method is to leave them to dry on a hot stone – and then ground into a powder to add to other food as required. This will make eating them more 'acceptable' and dried they will also keep for some time.

DANGERS

Carriers of disease

The numerous diseases carried by mosquitoes, ticks and other insects, the unseen dangers of parasites you may pick up from food or water and various waterborne diseases are much more serious dangers than attacks by animals.

DANGEROUS CONFRONTATIONS

Attacks by animals are rare but large animals can be dangerous. Keep out of their way. If you confront one it will be as surprised as you. Self-control will be needed or you may unintentionally provoke the animal to attack.

- If you come face to face with a large animal — FREEZE. Slowly back off and talk in a calm manner. In most cases the animal will back off too. Avoid making sudden movements and remember that animals can smell fear — many a hunter has fouled his breeches and given himself away. Do your best to calm yourself.

- If an animal appears to charge it may be that you are blocking its escape route. Move out of the way.

- If an animal seems determined to give chase (or you haven't got the nerve to freeze or sidestep), zig-zag when you run — animals such as rhinos charge in a straight line and have poor eyesight.

- A skilled nocturnal predator such as a leopard or tiger has excellent vision if you are on the move — though their colour vision is poor and they cannot see stationary objects well. Freeze if you have not already been sighted.

- Shouting and making a commotion may put off a predator.

- Taking to a tree is the final option — but you may be 'treed' for a long time if the animal is persistent. Don't choose a thorn tree if you can help it. In your panic you may get yourself very badly scratched and become trapped on an extremely painful perch.

EDIBLE PLANTS

There are many temperate edible plants in addition to those illustrated in colour, including the wild forms of cultivated plants such as currants and gooseberries. The following are a further selection of the food plants available.

If you are unlucky enough to find none of the plants illustrated or described here use the standard tests for edibility on the plants that are available.

REMEMBER that although one part of a plant can be eaten another may be poisonous. Test leaves, stems, roots and fruits separately.

FRUITS

Currants and Gooseberries *(Ribes)*, *found in woods, scrub and waste places, are medium-sized usually bushy shrubs with toothed leaves resembling those of a maple, small, greenish-white to purple five-petalled flowers and red, purplish black or yellow berries. Ripe currants are edible raw; cook gooseberries.*

Plums *(Prunus) exist in many varieties in scrub and woodland in virtually all temperate areas. Small shrubs or trees, similar to wild cherries, their fruits are larger, downy, blackish-purple, red or yellow; some are too tart to be edible raw.*

ROOTS, LEAVES AND STEMS

Horseradishes *(Armoracia) grow to 50cm (20in) in damp waste places with large, long-stalked, wavy-edged oval leaves and clusters of tiny white flowers. Chop up the hot-tasting root and add to stews; the young leaves are edible raw or boiled.*

Common Evening Primrose *(Oenothera biennis) is a tall plant of drier open areas, leafy, hairy, with spear-shaped, crinkly-margined leaves and sometimes reddish flower-stalks topped with large yellow, four-petalled flowers. The roots are edible boiled, changing the water to ease their pungency. Peel young leaves and treat likewise. The plants overwinter as rosettes.*

Limes or Basswoods *(Tilia) are tall trees, up to 26m (80ft) high, which like damp woods, with large, heart-shaped, toothed leaves and clusters of scented yellow flowers. Young leaves and unopened leaf buds are edible raw; the flowers can be used in tea.*

Hops *(Humulus), climbing plants of woody and scrubby places have long twisting stems, toothed leaves, deeply cut into three lobes, and green, cone-shaped female flowers. Peel, slice and boil the young shoots, brew up the flowers.*

Thistles *(Cirsium) have spiny, often ridged stems, oblong or spear-shaped, prickly, deep-cut leaves and large brush-like heads of purplish flowers. Remove prickles and boil young leaves. Peel tender shoots and eat raw or boiled. Roots of younger, stemless plants can be cooked and the base of each flowerhead contains a nutritious 'nut' which can be eaten raw.*

Saxifrages *(Saxifraga) grow to 90cm (3ft), usually much less, often liking open, rocky country, up into mountains. Most have rounded tapering or long-stalked leaves arcing from the base, often reddish stems and clusters of five-petalled flowers, usually white. Leaves edible raw or cooked.*

Great Burnet *(Sanquisorba officinalis) reaches 60cm (2ft) in damper grassy places, with toothed, spade-shaped leaflets in opposite* pairs and oblong heads of tiny, deep red flowers. Eat the tasty young leaves raw or boiled. Take an infusion for stomach complaints.

Redleg or **Lady's Thumb** (Polygnum persicaria) reaches 60cm (2ft). With reddish mature stems, narrow, spear-shaped, usually dark-spotted leaves and spikes of tiny pink flowers. Often common on waste ground. Young leaves are edible raw or cooked like spinach.

Wild Rhubarb (Rheum palmatum), found in open grassy places and margins from southern Europe east to China, resembles cultivated rhubarb, but its leaves are more ragged and dissected. The large flowerstalks are edible boiled; other parts are harmful. Eat ONLY the stalks.

Bladder Campion (Silene vulgaris), grows to 45cm (18in) in grassy places, is grey-green, with pointed oval, stalkless leaves, clusters of white flowers with a swollen balloon-like base. Boil the young leaves for 10 minutes.

Field Pennycress (Thlaspi arvense) grows to 45cm (18in) in open grassy places, with broad, toothed, spear-shaped leaves clasping the stem, a head of tiny white flowers and distinctive, notched, coin-like seed pods. Leaves are edible raw or boiled.

Clovers (Trifolium) abundant in grassy areas, recognized by their distinctive trefoil leaflets and dense rounded heads of small flowers, ranging from white through greenish-cream to shades of red. Leaves edible raw but better boiled.

Stork's Bill (Erodium cicutarium) reaching 30cm (1ft), in open grassy places, is hairy, often pungent, with fern-like, twice-cut leaves and heads of tiny, five-petalled pinkish to white flowers whose fruits form a long, twisting 'bill'. Eat leaves raw or boiled.

Burdocks (Arctium), medium to large, bushy plants of open waste areas, have floppy oval leaves, often arching stems and many purplish thistle-like flowerheads that develop into clinging burs. Eat leaves and peeled stalks raw or boiled. Boil pitch of peeled root. Change the water to remove bitterness.

Violet (Viola) are small flowers found in many areas, including damp and wooded ones. Veined, crinkly, often heart-shaped leaves rise on long stalks with flowers in shades of blue-violet, yellow or white, made up of five unequal petals. Cook young leaves. Rich in vitamins A and C.

Corn Salad or **Lamb's Lettuce** (Valerianella locusta) grows to 10–20cm (4–8in) in bare rocky and grassy places. Well-branched, with oblong, stalkless leaves and clusters of tiny lilac-bluish flowers; its leaves are edible raw or cooked like spinach. A particularly useful plant to know because it appears from late winter onwards.

Ox-eye daisies (Leucanthemum) often common in open areas, average 90cm (3ft) tall, with narrow dark green, lobed leaves, the lower ones rounded, and large white and yellow daisy-like flowers. Overwinters as a rosette. Eat young leaves (a lighter green) raw.

Cuckoo Flower or **Lady's smock** (Cardamine) pratensis grows on damp ground to 50cm (20in) with many small leaflets in opposite pairs, roundish on the basal ones which form a rosette, and clusters of lilac or white, four-petalled flowers. Young leaves are tasty raw, older ones rather peppery.

Brooklime (Veronica) grows in shallow water and swamps. Its creeping to upright stems carry pairs of thick, oval, toothed leaves, from the stalk bases of which spring 7–25cm (3–10in) spikes of four-petalled blue flowers with two prominent stamens. Eat young shoots before flowering and leaves after. Slightly bitter (especially the European form V. beccabunga) but eat like watercress.

In spring and summer young shoots are tender and easy to pick. Some can be eaten raw, but many are better gently cooked, especially Solomon's seal, Willowherb, Cat's-tail and bracken. Wash them in clean water, rub off any hairs and boil in a little water so that they cook mainly in the steam.

Leaves are very rich in vitamins and minerals. Together with young shoots they are the survivor's easiest source of food. Most will taste better cooked but do not overcook them or you will destroy the vitamins they contain: C, E, K, B and large amounts of A.

1 White Mustard *(Synapsis alba) grows to 60cm (2ft), with a hairy stem, crinkly, deeply lobed leaves and pale yellow flowers; in waste and grassy places in Eurasia. The young, peppery leaves and flowers are edible raw; the whole plant is tasty cooked. Pick young specimens.*

2 Shepherd's Purse *(Capsella bursa-pastoris) may reach to 60cm (2ft), with a rosette of lobed, spear-shaped leaves and a spike of small white flowers; common in waste places. Boil the leaves, which taste like cabbage, and mix with other plants.*

3 Primroses *(Primula) are found in grassy and shady places. Identified by their rosette of crinkly, tapering basal leaves and long-stalked, five-petalled flowers which range from pale to bright yellow and, in some forms, pink. All parts are edible but the young leaves are best part to eat. The primulas include the Cowslip (3a) and the Oxslip (3b).*

4 Dandelions *(Taraxacum) occur in many forms almost everywhere. Look for the large, yellow to orange flowerhead or the rosette of deeply lobed leaves. Eat the young leaves raw; boil the older ones, changing the water to remove their bitter taste. Boil the roots or roast for coffee. Dandelion* *juice is rich in vitamins and minerals.*

5 Chicory *(Cichorium intybus) is common in grassy and waste places. It grows 1·3m (4ft), with thick hairy, deeply basal leaves and leafy spikes of clear blue dandelion-like flowers. Prepare as Dandelion.*

6 Wild Sorrel *(Rumex acetosa) is common in waste and grassy places, reaching 1m (3ft), with long, arrow-shaped leaves and spikes of tiny reddish and green flowers. Gather young plants. Their mineral-rich leaves are edible raw but cooking will reduce the sharp taste.*

7 Buckwheat *(Fagopyrum esculentum) occurs in open grassy places in most temperate parts. Its 60cm (2ft) stems are usually red, with spear-shaped leaves and clusters of small pink or white flowers. Its seeds make good edible grain.*

8 Curled Dock *(Rumex crispus) grows to over 1m (3ft), with long narrow, wavy-margined leaves and whorls of small greenish flowers; in grassy and waste places. Boil the tenderest leaves from young plants, changing the water to remove the bitterness. Rubbing with dock leaves will soothe nettle stings. There are many other Docks temperate and tropical; prepare as here but use sparingly.*

Some plants have edible stems, although many are too woody to eat. If they are soft, peel off the outer, stringy parts, slice and then boil. The inner pith of some stems is nutritious and sweet, elder, for example. In this case the stem must be split open and the pulp extracted.

Stems produce fewer nutrients for the survivor than the roots, shoots and leaves so put them at the bottom of the food choices and exploit their other uses. Fibrous stems, like those of stinging nettles, make good twine.

1 Good King Henry *(Chenopodium bonus-henricus)* is spiky, to 60cm (2ft) tall, with dull green triangular leaves, sometimes reddening, and spikes of tiny greenish flowers; common on waste ground. Leaves and young shoots are edible raw or boiled as spinach; peel the shoots to remove the stringy parts.

2 Fat Hen or Lamb's Quarters *(Chenopodium album)* is spiky, to 1m (3ft) high, with often reddish stems, dull green, mealy, oval to spear-shaped leaves and spikes of tiny greenish flowers; abundant on waste ground. Cook the tasty leaves like spinach.

3 Chickweed *(Stellaria media)* is straggling, to 30cm (1ft) high, with a line of hairs on the main stem, pointed, oval leaves and tiny white, five-petalled flowers, common in waste places. Boil the delicious tender leaves.

4 Watercress *(Roripa nasturtium aquaticunn)* occurs, often abundantly, by running fresh water. It is creeping, semi-aquatic, with shiny leaves in opposite pairs and small, white, four-petalled flowers. Do NOT confuse with Water Hemlock. Leaves and stems are edible raw but boil if the water looks contaminated.

5 Rosebay Willowherb or Fireweed *(Epilobium angustifolium)* is found in open woods, waste and rocky places. It is tall, to over 1·5m (5ft), with spear-shaped leaves in opposite pairs and a spike of brilliant pinkish flowers. Young leaves, flowers and stems are edible raw but better boiled. Mature stems have a sweetish inner pulp.

6 Sweet Cicely *(Myrrhis odorata)* is sweet-smelling, grows to 1·5m (5ft), with slightly hairy and often purplish stems, feathery, fern-like leaves flecked with white and heads of tiny white flowers; in open woods, bare and rocky places in Europe. Do NOT confuse with Hemlock. Roots, stems and leaves taste of aniseed and can be boiled.

7 Dead-nettles *(Lamium) are smaller than Stinging Nettles, with heart-shaped leaves and no stinging hairs, and white (7) or pinkish-purple (7a) flowers. Prepare as Chickweed.*

8 Stinging Nettles *(Urtica) are abundant for most of the year. Look for the toothed, narrow oval leaves covered in stinging hairs and the spikes of green flowers. Pick young growth or young plants 15–20cm (6–8in) high — BOIL for minimum six minutes to destroy the formic acid in the hairs. Leaves can be dried and stored; crushed stems provide fibres for rope.*

9 Plantains *(Plantago) are common in most areas. Ribwort or English Plantain (Plantago lanceolata) has spear-shaped leaves and much shorter flower-spikes than the Greater Plantain; it likes dry ground. Prepare as Greater Plantain.*

10 Buck's-horn Plantain *(Plantago coronopus) is small, star-shaped, with narrow, jagged leaves and shorter flower-spikes; in dry sandy and rocky places, often near the sea. Prepare as Greater Plantain.*

11 Greater or Rat's-tail Plantain *(P. major) has broad, oval leaves and distinctive upright spikes of tiny yellowish-green and brown flowers; in waste and grassy places. Prepare the rather bitter young leaves like spinach; use their expressed juice for wounds, or a decoction of the whole plant for chest complaints.*

FLOWERS

The flowers of some plants are edible. These include limes or basswoods, roses, hops, elder, primrose and camomile. But they are only a seasonal supply and contain few nutrients compared with other parts of the plant. They are best used for teas and in medicinal infusions.

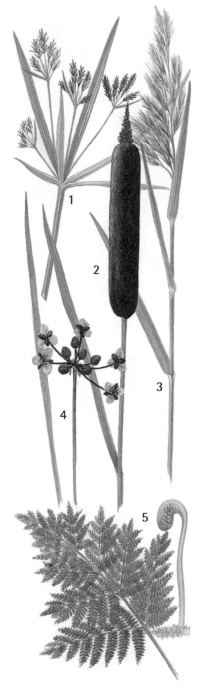

1 Galingale, Nutgrass or Chufa *(Cyperus) grows to 1·5m (5ft), with three-angled stems, long, strap-like leaves and a forking, clustered olive-brown flowerhead turning yellow with fruit; in and by fresh water almost everywhere. Peel and boil its nutty tubers, or dry and grind for flour or a coffee substitute.*

2 Cat's-tail or Reedmace *(Typha) grows to 2–5m (6–15ft), with long, narrow, greyish leaves and a conspicuous, dark brown, sausage-shaped flowerhead; in and by fresh water. The rootstock and stems are edible raw or boiled; cook leaves like spinach and young shoots like asparagus. The pollen can be mixed with water to make a dough and baked or cooked on a griddle or the end of a stick.*

3 Reeds *(Phragmites) grow to 4m (13ft), with greyish-green leaves and spreading, brownish-purple flowerheads on tall canes, in and by fresh water almost everywhere. Cook the edible root, punctured canes exude an edible, sugar-rich gum.*

4 Flowering Rush *(Butomus umbellatus) grows to 1·5m (5ft), with very long, strap-like, three-angled leaves arising from the roots and pink, three-petalled flowers; in and by fresh water in Eurasia. Peel and boil the edible rootstock.*

5 Bracken *(Pteridium aquilinum) is common almost everywhere often in large clumps. Older fronds are harmful; eat ONLY the strong-tasting young shoots, or 'fiddlesticks', drawing off their woolly parts and boiling for half an hour. Eat sparingly. The roots are edible boiled or roasted.*

10 Sweet Flag *(Acorus calamus) grows to 1·3m (4ft), with three-angled stems, wavy-margined, spear-shaped, strap-like leaves and a finger-like flower spike arising from the stem; in and by fresh water. Slice the pungent, aromatic rootstock and boil down to a syrup.*

Many familiar kitchen herbs grow wild. Their smells help to identify them. They can be dried and will keep well — but do not dry them in direct sunlight or they lose their essential oils.

6 Tansy *(Tanacetum vulgare) grows to 90cm (3ft), with toothed dark green, feathery leaflets and a cluster of button-like, bright yellow flowers, in waste and grassy places. Strong-smelling, with a hot, bitter taste. Use sparingly as a potherb, poisonous in quantity, leaves and flowers make a wormifuge tea. Its smell keeps flies away.*

7 Marjoram *(Origanum vulgare) is slightly downy and grows to 60cm (2ft), with small, oval, stalked leaves and clusters of small purplish-pink flowers; in warmer, dry, grassy places in Eurasia, introduced elsewhere. A sweet-tasting herb for stews; use an infusion for coughs and digestive complaints; chewed leaves relieve toothache.*

8 Ramsons *(Allium ursinum) is one of many wild garlics. It has broad, light green leaves like a Lily-of-the-valley and a cluster of white star-like flowers at the top of the stem; in woody places in Eurasia, revealed by its strong garlicky smell. Use any part as a potherb.*

9 Borage *(Borago officinalis) is round-stemmed, hairy, to 30–60cm (1–2ft), with pointed oval leaves, blue star-shaped flowers and a cucumber smell; in waste grassy places in Eurasia. All parts are edible raw or cooked, use an infusion for fevers. The stems produce salt when cooked.*

11 Wild Angelicas *(Angelica) grow to 1·5m (5ft), with hollow stems, sometimes purplish, broad, toothed leaves in opposite pairs and heads of tiny greenish, white or pink flowers; in damp grassy and woody places. The aromatic leaves, stems and roots are edible boiled; use an infusion for colds or externally for stiffness. Do NOT confuse with Water Hemlock.*

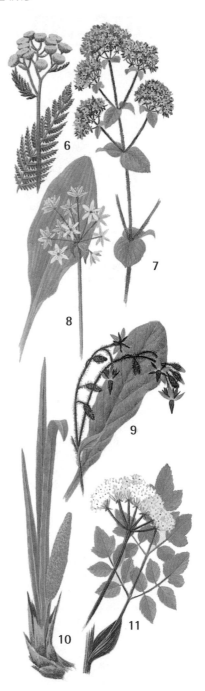

ROOTS AND TUBERS

Roots and tubers are invaluable survival food. They are full of nutrition, particularly starch. All roots should be thoroughly cooked if in any doubt as to their identity.

1 Bistorts or Knotweeds *(Polygonum) average 30–60cm (1–2ft) with narrow, triangular leaves and a slender spike of pink or white flowers; in grassy and woody places, into the far north. Soak roots to remove bitterness, then roast.*

2 Spring Beauties *(Montia) average 15–30cm (6–12in) with a pair of oval, long-stalked leaves halfway up the stem and small white or pink flowers; in disturbed, especially sandy, places. Dig out tubers with a sharp stick, peel and boil. Young leaves are edible and supply vitamins A and C.*

3 Silverweed *(Potentilla anserina) is small, creeping, with silver-white undersides to its segmented leaves and solitary, five-petalled yellow flowers; in damp places. The fleshy roots are edible raw but better cooked. Use an infusion of the leaves externally for haemorrhoids and internally for digestive complaints.*

4 Sweet Vetch or Liquorice Root *(Astralagus glycophyllos) is straggling, to 30–60cm (1–2ft), with small oval leaves in opposite pairs and greenish-cream flowers; in grassy, scrubby and sandy places. The root is edible raw, tasting of carrots when cooked.*

5 Wild Parsnips *(Pastinaca sativa) are hairy, pungent, averaging 1m (3ft), with toothed leaflets and dense heads of tiny yellow flowers; in waste and grassy places. The roots are edible raw or cooked.*

6 Comfrey *(Symphytum officinale) is coarse, hairy, growing to 1m (3ft), with spear-shaped leaves tapering on to the stem and clusters of cream or mauve bell-shaped flowers; in ditches and* damp places. The root is edible raw or cooked. Other parts are medicinal (see Natural Medicine in Health). Do NOT confuse with Foxglove.

7 Salsify or Oyster Plant (*Tragopogon porrifolius*) averages 60–90cm (2–3ft), with long, grass-like leaves running down on to the stem and large, solitary, purple, dandelion-like flowers; in dry waste places. The bulb-like root and young leaves are edible cooked.

8 Woolly Lousewort (*Pedicularis lanata*) is hairy, low-spreading, with rose-pink flowers and a yellow root edible raw or cooked; widespread on the northern American tundra. CAUTION: some other louseworts are poisonous.

Roots are at their starchiest between autumn and spring. In spring some of the starch converts into sugar to sustain new growth. Some edible roots can be several centimetres thick and a metre or more in length. Tubers are swollen, bulb-like roots — a large one may sustain a survivor for a long time. Don't forget edible bulbs, like the onion — but beware, some bulbs, including the Wild Onion-like Death Camas of North America are poisonous.

Many roots are particularly tasty roasted. Parboil them until they are just becoming tender, then roast on hot stones in the embers of a fire. Some, including Galingale and Dandelion (see earlier illustrations), are fine substitutes for coffee when roasted and ground. Others, such as Wild Calla, can be ground and used as flour.

The root of Comfrey is particularly valuable. It is so rich in starch that after boiling it sets as hard as plaster of Paris and makes an ideal splinting agent for broken limbs.

145

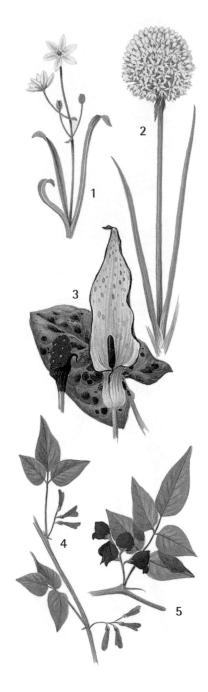

1 Star of Bethlehem or Starflower *(Ornitholgallum umbellatum) averages 10–30cm (4–12in), with grass-like leaves with a white midrib arising from the roots and white, six-petalled flowers, each petal green-striped; in grassy areas. The root is harmful raw and MUST be cooked. Avoid other parts.*

2 Wild Onions *(Allium) occur in most parts, easily detectable by their smell. Long, grass-like leaves arise from the base; a cluster of six-petalled pink, purplish or white flowers tops the stem. The edible bulb may be up to 25cm (10in) underground.*

3 Lords and Ladies or Cuckoopint *(Arum maculatum) grows to 15–40cm (6–16in), with dark green, arrow-shaped, sometimes dark-spotted leaves and a purple finger-like flowering organ enclosed in a pale leaf-like hood from which red berries arise, in shady and woody places in Eurasia. The root is harmful raw and MUST be cooked. Do NOT eat any other part.*

4 Hog-peanut *(Amphicarpa bracteata) occurs in moist places in North America: twining, vine-like, thin-stemmed, with light green oval leaves and lilac to white flowers. Extract each seed from its brown pod (underground) and boil.*

5 Groundnut *(Apios americana) is small, vine-like, with oval, sharp-pointed light green leaflets and maroon to brownish flowers; in moist, usually woody places in North America. Peel the small tubers then roast or boil.*

6 Jerusalem Artichoke *(Helianthus tuberosus) resembles a Sunflower, very tall, hairy, with large, rough, oval leaves and large, disc-like yellow flowers; wild in waste ground in North America, widely introduced elsewhere. The cooked tubers are delicious. Do not peel them or you lose food value.*

AQUATIC AND WATERSIDE ROOTS

7 Wild Calla or Bog Arum *(Calla palustris)* is small, with long-stalked, heart-shaped leaves and a greenish finger-like flowering organ enclosed in a leaf-like hood pale on the inside, from which red berries arise; always by water. The roots are harmful raw and MUST be cooked. AVOID OTHER PARTS.

8 Arrowheads *(Sagittaria)* are aquatic, averaging 30–90cm (1–3ft), with large leaves varying from sharply arrow-shaped to spear-shaped and sometimes strap-like below the water, and flowers with three rounded petals; always by fresh water. Tubers are edible raw but much better cooked.

9 Water Chestnut *(Trapa natans)* is aquatic, with diamond-shaped floating leaves and divided, feathery submerged ones, and small white flowers; widespread in fresh water in Eurasia. The grey, hard 2·5cm (1in), two-horned seeds are edible raw or roasted.

It is best to cook all roots before eating, as some are harmful raw — not just well known ones, like the tropical cassava and taro, but many temperate species. Most roots will need cooking to make them tender enough to eat. Scrub in clean water and boil until soft. Some potato-like roots have their vitamins and minerals near the surface of the skin and so should NOT be peeled. Roots will cook more rapidly if you cube them first. Use a sharpened stick to test them. If it goes in easily they are ready.

FRUIT

From summer on, fruits and nuts are one of the survivor's most important foods. Many will be familiar in their cultivated forms or from the traditional hedgerow harvest. Some are abundant, even on the tundra of the far north.

1 Barberry *(Berberis vulgaris), found in scrub and dry moorland grows to 3m (9ft), with oval leaves, yellow flowers and fierce thorns in groups of three on its stems. Its bright red, very acid berries are rich in vitamin C.*

2 Wild Roses *(Rosa) are found in most temperate areas. They resemble straggly, unshowy garden roses with thorned stems and simple white or pink flowers. Their hips (seedcases) contain more vitamin C than any other fruit. Chew to extract the juices and obtain maximum vitamin content, or crush and boil in water until only a syrup is left.*

3 Brambles (Blackberries) and Wild Raspberries *(Rubus) occur in scrub, woods and on open ground; leaves toothed and flowers white or sometimes pinkish in blackberries. Look for straggly bushes with arching thorny stems and juicy segmented berries, which ripen from green through red to purplish black berries, borne in late summer. Raspberries, less straggly and with fewer prickles, ripen to a rich red earlier in the summer. All are edible raw. Bramble canes can be used to pull rabbits out of sleeper holes.*

4 Dewberries *(Rubus) are like brambles but their berries are smaller and with fewer segments than the blackberry.*

5 Wild Strawberries *(Fragaria) are small, scrambling plants of dry grassy places and woodland whose fruits resemble small cultivated strawberries. You may have to look under the leaves* to find the sweet, delicious fruit. Some kinds occur high in mountains. The fruits are rich in Vitamin C and best eaten fresh.

6 Hawthorns (Crataegus) are spiny shrubs or small trees found in scrub and waste places, with deeply lobed leaves, clusters of white or pink flowers and, in autumn, reddish fruits. Their flesh is creamy and edible raw. Young spring shoots are edible, too.

7 Crab Apples (Malus) are short, rather spiny trees of scrubland and woods, with oval, toothed, often downy leaves, usually reddish-brown twigs and white, pink or red flowers. Fruit, often very bitter, looks like the cultivated apples. It can be sliced and dried for storage. Too many of the yellowish-green (sometimes red), pectin-rich apples will produce diarrhoea and are best cooked with other fruits.

8 Wild Cherries (Prunus) occur in woodland in most areas, growing to 24m (80ft) with small, pale green to reddish leaves, usually shiny reddish-brown bark, and white or pinkish flowers. The fruits are red or black depending on the kind; some kinds taste sour.

9 Blackthorn or Sloe (Prunus spinosa) is a large bush, growing to 4m (13ft) with dark brown twigs, long thorns, oval leaves and white flowers, in woodland and scrub over Eurasia. The small blue-black fruits are very acid and better cooked down to a jelly.

Fruits supply essential food values, particularly vitamins A, B2 and C. They are the staple diet of many animals and birds — so, where you find fruit, you will find animals too.

1 and 2 Bilberries, Cranberries, Cowberries and Huckleberries *(Vaccinium and Gaylussacia) are abundant on northern moors, bogs tundra, and sometimes in woods. Variable in size, but all are woody and shrubby with smallish oval leaves and small globe-shaped flowers varying from white to pink or greenish. The cranberry prefers marshy ground, the closely related, ground-hugging Cowberry (or Mountain Cranberry, 2) grows on moors. The spherical berries may be black (Bilberry, 1), dark blue (Huckleberry), mottled red (Cranberry) or red (Cowberry). They are edible fresh, cooked or dried for storage like raisins. The woody stems make useful fuel.*

3 Chokeberries *(Pyrus) are North American shrubs growing up to 2.4m (8ft) but usually much less, with spear-shaped, finely toothed leaves and five-petalled, pinkish or white flowers; in wet or dry woody areas, or on swampy ground. The red, purplish or black spherical berries, which grow in clusters, are excellent raw, dried or jellied. Do not confuse with the poisonous Buckthorns (Rhamnus).*

4 European Elder *(Sambucus nigra) occurs in scrub and woods, growing to 7m (23ft) with spear-shaped toothed leaves and clusters of tiny whitish flowers. The bunches of small purplish-black berries are best cooked down to a syrup. There are similar edible elders in other parts, but avoid the smaller ones as their red berries may be toxic.*

5 Juniper *(Juniperus communis) occurs in mountainous and northern areas, a woody shrub 5m (15ft) tall or a small prostrate bush with grey-green, needle-like leaves. Avoid young green berries; the ripe blue-black ones are best cooked with other food.*

6 Rowans or Mountain Ashes *(Sorbus) are common in woody and rocky places, growing to 15m (50ft)* with smooth greyish bark, small toothed leaflets, white flowers and clusters of small orange berries. These are edible but sharp-tasting raw and can be cooked down to a jelly.

7 Wild Mulberries (Morus) average 6–20m (18–60ft), with oval leaves, sometimes deeply lobed, flowers on catkins, the red or black fruits look like large blackberries, 5–7cm (2–3in) long. They are edible raw. Found in woody areas in many temperate parts.

8 Wild Grapes (Vitis) are straggly, high-climbing, with large, heart-shaped coarsely toothed leaves, greenish flowers and bunches of amber to purplish grapes. Very widespread in the warmer parts of the world. As well as the fruit, young leaves are excellent boiled.

PRESERVING FRUIT

Fresh fruits soon go off, but they can be kept by making them into jellies. Most kinds contain an ingredient called pectin, which reacts with the acid in the fruit to help it settle into a jelly after boiling.

TO MAKE JELLY

First boil the fruit and then simmer until mushy. Some fruits have less pectin than others. These can be supplemented by adding another fruit rich in pectin, such as Crab Apple. The boiling action kills off any bacteria that would turn the fruit. Allow to cool and keep in a clean, if possible airtight, container.

Some fruits can be dried for storage, although this will take a week to ten days. Lay them in a single layer on a sheet, not in direct sunlight, and protect them from any moisture — both rain and dew.

NUTS

Nuts supply proteins and fat.

1 Pines *(Pinus) are the familiar cone-bearing trees with clusters of slim evergreen needles; in most temperate and northerly areas. Heat mature cones to release the seeds. They are tasty raw but delicious roasted. Roasted nuts can be ground for flour and can be stored. Young catkin-like cones are just about edible boiled. Needles and bark are also edible.*

2 Walnuts *(Juglans) grow to 30m (90ft), with leaves composed of many toothed, narrow leaflets and furrowed bark. The blackish brown nuts are at first enclosed in a thick green husk. In most temperate areas. One tree can yield up to 58kg (140lb) of nuts. Walnuts contain 18% protein, 60% fat and provide 6600 calories per kilo (3000 per pound)!*

3 Butternut *(Juglans cinerea) is another North American relative, smaller, with more greyish bark and oblong, sticky fruit husks.*

4 Pecan *(Carya illinoinensis) reaches 36m (120ft), with dark ridged bark and many small leaflets in opposite pairs, in moist places in North America. The oval, thin-husked nuts are richer in fat than any other vegetable product.*

5 Hazels *(Corylus) are tall shrubs of thickets and waste ground, with toothed, oval to heart-shaped leaves and brownish-yellow catkins. The highly nutritious nuts come in ovoid, leafy, bristly or hairy husks.*

6 Sweet Chestnuts *(Castanea) range from 5–30m (15–90ft), spreading, with large, toothed hairless leaves and bearing catkins, in wooded areas. Nuts, in some forms 2–3 together, are borne in globe-shaped, thick prickly green husks. Smash open husks, peel nuts, boil and mash. Do not confuse with*

Horse Chestnut which has large palmate leaves, like the fingers on a hand, and poisonous nuts.

7 Beeches *(Fagus)* are very tall and spreading, with smooth lightish bark and thick-veined, wavy-margined sharp oval leaves; in broad-leaved woodland. Nuts small, triangular, 2–4 in each hairy husk depending on the species. Protein-rich; edible raw, roasted or crushed for oil.

8 Oaks *(Quercus)* occur in great variety in wooded areas. Many have deeply lobed leaves but all bear unmistakable acorns. Shell them and boil several times, changing the water to ease their bitterness, or steep in cold water for 3–4 days. Alternatively, bury them with ash and charcoal, watering from time to time. Then roast; roasted acorns make good flour or coffee substitute.

9 Pistachios *(Pistacia)* grow wild in warmer parts from the Mediterranean east to Afghanistan; introduced elsewhere. Trees, to 10m (30ft), with many small oval leaflets and clusters of nuts with a green kernel and reddish skin. Eat raw or parch on the embers.

10 Almonds *(Prunus)* grow wild in warm, arid parts of Europe and Asia, widely introduced elsewhere. Resemble large peach trees, with sprays of blossom, small spear-shaped leaves and clusters of nuts in green leathery husks. Avoid bitter ones, which contain prussic acid.

Extract oil from rich nuts such as beech. Crack open, separate meat from shells. Boil gently in water, skimming off the oil as it rises to the surface or allow to cool and separate. Store somewhere cool and dry, preferably in an airtight container. A yield of 270ml (3fl oz) of nutritious oils can come from 450g (1lb) of nuts.

POISONOUS PLANTS

Compared to the many edible ones, there are few poisonous plants in temperate areas. Learn well the ones shown.

CONTACT POISONS
Contact with Poison Sumac, Poison Ivy and Poison Oak produces severe irritation and rashes. Wash effected parts immediately (see Poisons in Health).

1 **Poison Sumac** *(Toxicodendron vernix) reaches 2–6m (6–18ft), hairless, with many oval leaflets in opposite pairs, dark-spotted smooth bark and clusters of white berries; in swamplands in south-eastern North America.*
2 **Poison Oak** *(Toxicodendron quercifolium) resembles Poison Ivy but is smaller, always upright, and with oakleaf-shaped leaflets and white berries, in wooded parts of North America.*
3 **Poison Ivy** *(Toxicodendron radicans) is smaller, 0.6–2.1m (2–7ft), trailing or upright, with three-part very variable leaves, but always with greenish flowers and white berries; in wooded areas of North America.*
4 **Jewelweed** *(Impatiens), often found near Poison Ivy, with pale yellow or orange spotted flowers and seed pods that pop, provides a juice to ease irritation from contact with these and other plants.*

POISONS BY INGESTION
5 **Death Carnas** *(Zigadenus venosus) reaches 30–60cm (1–2ft), with long, strap-like leaves arising from the base and loose clusters of greenish-white, six-part flowers; in North America, in grassy, rocky and lightly wooded places. DEADLY: do not confuse with Wild Onions or Lilies.*
6 **Thorn-apple or Crimson Weed** *(Datura stramonium) averages 90cm*

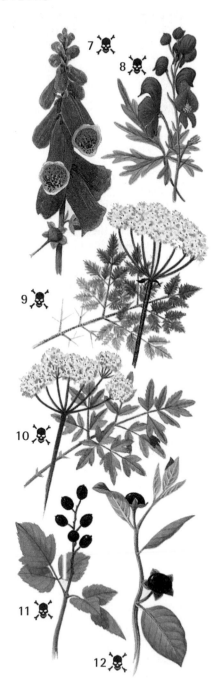

(3ft), with jagged-toothed oval leaves and large solitary trumpet-shaped white flowers and spiny fruits; widespread in most temperate areas and also in the tropics. Sickly smelling. All parts DEADLY poisonous.

7 Foxgloves *(Digitalis) grow to 1.5m (5ft), with a rosette of basal leaves topped by a tall, leafy spike of purple, pink or yellow tube-shaped flowers; widespread in waste and disturbed places. ALL parts are highly toxic, affecting the heart.*

8 Monk's-hood *(Aconitum) reaches 1.5m (5ft), leafy, with palm-shaped, deeply segmented leaves and hairy, hood-like purplish-blue or yellow flowers; in damp woods and shady places. The most common kinds have purplish-blue flowers. VERY poisonous.*

9 Hemlock *(Conium maculatum) may reach 2m (6ft), much branched, with hollow purple-spotted stems, coarsely toothed leaves, lighter below, dense clusters of tiny white flowers and white roots; in grassy waste places. Bad-smelling. Very poisonous.*

10 Water Hemlocks or Cowbanes *(Cicuta) average 0.6-1.3m (2-4ft), branching, with purple-streaked stems, a hollow-chambered rootstock, small 2-3 lobed, toothed leaflets and clusters of tiny white flowers, always found by water. Smells unpleasant. ONE MOUTHFUL CAN KILL.*

11 Baneberries *(Actaea) reach 30-60cm (1-2ft), with leaves made up of several toothed leaflets, small, usually white flowers clustered at the end of a stem, and white or black berries; mostly in woods. ALL parts cause dizziness, Vomiting and severe internal irritation.*

12 Deadly Nightshade *(Atropa bella-donna) may reach 1m (6ft), well branched, with oval leaves, solitary, bell-shaped, purplish or greenish flowers and shiny black berries, in woodland and scrub in Eurasia. ALL parts, especially berries, are VERY poisonous.*

155

Some poisonous plants are easy to mistake for food plants if you are not careful in your identification. Do not take risks.

Hemlock and Water Hemlock are the two most important poisonous plants to learn, found in both Eurasia and the Americas in a wide range of country. Both are umbellifers, of which there are many kinds, and with many tiny flowers in dense clusters, like an umbrella inside-out and difficult to tell apart.

The umbellifers include some edible plants, but NEVER collect any unless certain they are neither of these two, which can be lethal in very small amounts.

Learn to recognize the following common poisonous plants in addition to those illustrated.

Buttercups *(Ranunculus) occur in great variety, from a few centimetres to over a metre tall, in north and south, including far into the Arctic. All have glossy, waxy bright yellow flowers with five or more over-lapping petals. AVOID all, they cause severe inflammation of the intestinal tract.*

Lupins *(Lupinus), 30–90cm (1–3ft) tall, like the garden kind, growing in clearings and grassy places. Often with small leaflets in a palm shape or radiating like the spokes of a wheel, and spikes of 'pea-flowers': blue, violet, occasionally pink white or yellow. Any part can cause fatal inflammation of stomach and intestines.*

Vetches or **Locoweeds** *(Astalagus and Oxytropis), 15–45cm (6–18in) tall, growing in grassland and mountain meadows, usually with many small spear-shaped leaflets in opposite pairs and showy spikes of five-petalled 'pea-flowers': yellowish-white, pink to lavender and purplish. Some are very poisonous. AVOID all.*

False Helleborines *(Veratrum)* *60cm–2.6m (2–8ft), grow in wet, swampy places, some species in grassy ones. Oval ribbed leaves resemble a lily-of-the-valley's, drooping clusters of whitish or greenish-yellow flowers. Can be lethal.*

Henbane *(Hyoscyamus niger) medium to large, growing on bare ground, often near sea (Europe). Sticky hairs, toothed oval leaves (upper ones unstalked), creamy flowers streaked purple. Unpleasant smell. Deadly poisonous.*

POISONOUS BERRIES

Canadian Moonseed *(Menispermum canadense) North American vine-like climber, clusters of soft black berries. Could be mistaken for Wild Grape but lacks tendrils and has only a single crescent-like seed in each berry.*

Nightshades *(Solanum) medium to large, untidy, bushy plants liking scrubby places, leaves usually long-stalked, spear-shaped. Berries ripen from green to black, red, yellow or white. Plants producing similar but edible berries are usually more compact and woody, the berries smaller and more numerous. If in any doubt assume to be poisonous and AVOID.*

Virginia Creeper *(Parthenocissus guinquefolia) vine-like North American climber (introduced to Europe). Long-stalked, palm-shaped leaves, toothed leaflets, tendril and clusters of small blue berries, smaller than wild grapes. No plant with edible blue berries is vine-like and with tendrils.*

Buckthorns *(Rhamnus), shrubs sometimes small trees growing in scrubby and woody places, sometimes damp. Leaves oval, finely toothed; berries black and bitter tasting, clustered along stems. Can be violently purgative.*

There are many field guides available which will help you extend your knowledge of temperate plants, detailing many local forms.

TREES

Trees provide other nourishing foods, as well as fruit and nuts, which can be invaluable to the survivor, particularly in areas where there is little other plant life available.

The following refers to the trees of temperate and northern regions. Tropical trees, such as palms, are included in the section on tropical plants.

Bark

The thin inner bark (cambium) of certain trees is both edible and nutritious, but best in the spring, when sap has started to flow. Choose bark from near the bottom of the tree or from exposed roots. Peel it back with a knife to reveal the inner layer. This is mildly sweet and can be eaten raw — but can be made more digestible by long boiling, which will reduce it to a gelatinous mass. It can then be roasted and ground for use as flour.

Outer bark has too much tannin to be edible, but some kinds have medicinal uses.

Trees with best inner bark

Slippery Elm *(Ulmus rubra), of northern America, grows to a maximum 18m (60ft). Twigs are hairy and rough, oval, toothed leaves are hairy below.*

Basswood *(Tilia americana), a North American lime with large, heart-shaped leaves and dark, grooved bark which becomes smooth grey on upper parts.*

Birches *(Betula), which are often abundant in colder areas. They can be identified by their long delicate twigs and shiny, flaky bark that is often broken up into plates.*

Aspens *(Populus tremula), small to medium trees resembling poplars. They have rounded leaves on very, very long stalks that quiver in the wind.*

Tamarack *(Larix laricina), is found in cold parts of North America. It grows to 24m (80ft) with a pointed shape, bears cones and has needles in tufts along the twigs.*

Poplars *(Populus) have triangular leaves and prominent catkins. They*

occur in many northern areas.

Maples *(Acer) grow widely and are recognized by their distinctive lobed leaves in three parts and by the two-winged fruits.*

Spruces *(Picea) are evergreen trees of cold climates. They are shaped like steeples, bear cones and have stiff, four-sided needles that grow all around the twigs.*

Willows *(Salix) are broad-leaved trees or shrubs with toothed leaves, lighter on the underside, and distinctive yellow or green catkins. There are many kinds, including ground-hugging arctic ones.*

Pines *(Pinus) are widely found evergreen trees bearing cones and clusters of long needles. Their inner bark is rich in vitamin C.*

Hemlocks *(Tsuga) are evergreens, resembling spruces, with sprays of foliage, flat needles and short, oblong cones. They bear no relation to the poisonous plant of the same name.*

NOTE: In addition to the inner bark, the buds and shoots of all these trees can be eaten raw or cooked — EXCEPT for those of Tamarack and Hemlock, which are POISONOUS.

Other uses for inner bark

The inner bark of some trees is very strong but pliable. It is easily torn into strips for lashings. The bark of the mohoe tree, for example, is made into 'grass' skirts by Pacific islanders, having first been steamed in a hangi (see *Fire* in *Camp Craft*).

Birch bark can be removed from the tree in large sheets and forms an ideal material for roofing shelters or for making small containers. The North American Indians clad their canoes with it.

SPRUCE TEA

Steep spruce needles in hot water to make a tea. Collect only fresh, green needles and boil. The liquid produced is rich in vitamin C. The vitamin can be obtained more directly by chewing tender young needles, whose starchy green tips are particularly pleasant in spring. Spruces occur far into the north and are an important source of nourishment when little other plant life is available.

Gums and resins

With some trees, when cut, sap seeping out on to the bark hardens into a lump. If this is soluble in water it is a gum; if not, it is a resin. Both are very nutritious, rich in sugars and a useful survival food. A few have medicinal properties and others are highly inflammable and make excellent material for lighting fires.

Birch and maple syrup

Tap birch or maple in the same way as a rubber tree. Cut a V-shape in the bark to collect the sugary sap that runs out. Below the V make a hole in the trunk to insert a leaf as a drip spout to run the sap into a container.

Collect sap daily and boil it. It will give off lots of steam but thicken down into a syrup. This is instant energy and well worth the effort.

POISONOUS TREES

The following trees contain irritant or poisonous substances. Do NOT eat any part of them, except for the meaty roots of hickory, which are edible.

Yews (*Taxus*) are straggling evergreen trees or shrubs with flaky bark, dark green needles and red berry-like fruits. The fruits are particularly poisonous.

Cedars (*Cedrus*), originally from the Mediterranean and Himalayas, the true cedars are large, spreading, scented evergreens with erect cones.

Horse Chestnuts and Buckeyes (*Aesculus*) are tall with hand-shaped leaves, sticky buds and white, pink or yellow flowers. Do not confuse their poisonous, spiky-cased nuts with those of Sweet Chestnut which has narrow, toothed leaves and much more densely prickled seed cases.

Laburnums (*Laburnum*) are small, broad-leaved trees with three-part leaves and long sprays of yellow flowers.

Black Locust (*Robinia pseudoacacia*) is a North American tree with dark grey bark, oval leaflets in opposite pairs, clusters of white flowers and bean-like seed pods.

California Laurel or Oregon Myrtle (*Umbellularia californica*), is a short-trunked North American evergreen, averaging 16m (50ft) with oval leathery leaves, clusters of yellowish flowers and greenish to purple berries. Foliage is pungently aromatic.

Moosewood or Moosebark (*Acer pensylvanicum*), of north-eastern North America averages 12m (40ft), with light, white-striped bark, oval to spear-shaped leaves, olive to brownish above, broad-petalled, yellow-greenish flowers and winged fruits.

Hickories (*Carya*) have divided, often palm-shaped leaves, catkins and, usually, rounded nuts. The nuts of some kinds are edible, as are the sap and roots, but do not eat unless the species is positively identified.

(See also *contact poison* in *Poisonous Plants* and *Tropical Poisonous Plants*.)

FUNGI

Fungi make good eating, but MUST be positively identified as of an edible kind. There is no room for error. Unlike vegetable plants, on which the 'edibility test' can be used, they must be either identified or left well alone. The deadly kinds do not taste unpleasant and no symptoms may appear until several hours after eating.

Wild fungi are a great delicacy — if you know which ones to pick. Fungi are composed of many thread-like cells which, in the case of ground fungi, form a subterranean web of which only the reproductive part — what we call the fungus — appears above the ground. This edible part appears only at certain times of year.

Most fungi grow directly from the ground — alone, in rings, sometimes in clumps. They consist of a cup- or bowl-shaped cap topping a stem. The underside bears gills of spongy tissue containing spores. The form and colour of this tissue is an important clue to identify. A few fungi, such as truffles, grow completely underground — but they are very hard to find. Others grow on the sides of trees and stumps; some are known — from their shape — as bracket fungi, others grow large and singularly.

Food value

Fungi come between meat and vegetables in the nutritional table. They contain more protein than vegetables and, in some cases, more fat.

The better kinds, Boletus edulis for example, provide a similar amount of calories to the same weight of vegetables. As for minerals: fungi have more phosphorous than carrots, cauliflowers and spinach, but less calcium. Vitamin B complex is present in tiny amounts in most fungi, vitamin C occurs occasionally and D is present in many in appreciable amounts. *Cantharellus cibarius* contains vitamin A.

The great advantage of fungi is their abundance. At the right time of year, usually summer and autumn, you can quickly gather enough for a meal.

Preparing fungi

Reject suspicious, discoloured or maggoty parts, clean, slice and boil. Many bracket fungi are bitter and tough and must be cooked thoroughly. It helps to steep them in cold water first. Tender ground fungi can simply be added to soups and other foods.

Storing fungi

Fungi have high water content and are easily dried. Collect all you can when they are available and add them to your foodstore. Separate caps from stems and place on rocks in the sun, caps gill-side up. With *Boletus* species, first remove the spongy tissue under the cap. When thoroughly dry, store in airtight containers if possible. Eat raw (soak them in water first to let them swell up) or add to soups and stews.

IDENTIFYING AMANITAS

The poisonous Amanitas – and their particularly deadly species the Death Cap and the Destroying Angel – can be mistaken for edible kinds. ALWAYS FOLLOW THESE RULES:

- AVOID any fungi with white gills, a volva (a cup-like appendage at the base of the stem) and stem rings

- AVOID any fungi that are wormy or decomposing

- Unless positively identified – DISCARD

Differences between Amanita and Agaricus fungi:

	AMANITA	AGARICUS
SPORES	White	Purplish-brown
CAP AND STEM	Unchanging	Some kinds stain yellow when bruised
CAP	Slimy with loose patches	Always dry, with only a few small scales
MATURE GILLS	White	Greyish-red, pink or chocolate
GILLS	Partly or wholly veiled	Not veiled
SMELL	Potato or radish	Almonds or marzipan
LOCATION	Never in grassy open areas	

EDIBLE FUNGI

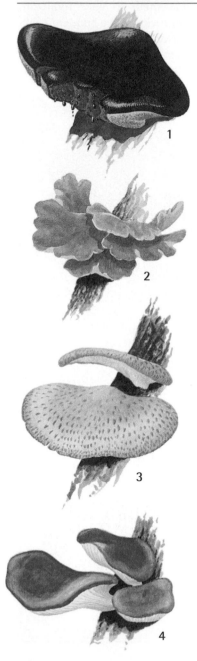

1

2

3

4

There are no reliable rules for identifying fungi, poisonous or edible. Ignore folk tales to the effect that a fungus is not poisonous once peeled, or that toxic kinds change colour when cooked. They do not. Nor does cooking destroy their poisons.

Learn to recognize a small number — those illustrated here — and stick to them. Learn also the Amanita family — they include fungi which can kill you. Then build up your knowledge.

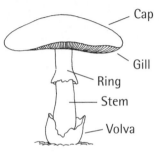

TREE FUNGI
Tree fungi grow off the ground, on the sides of trees and stumps. They are often large and leathery, but are not harmful and are fairly common.

1 Fistulina hepatica *(Beefsteak Fungus) is often found on oaks. It is reddish above, pinkish below and rough-textured, resembling a large tongue; its red flesh exudes a blood-coloured juice. Tough and bitter; young specimens are better. Soak to soften then stew thoroughly. Occurs in autumn.*
2 Polyporus sulphureus *grows to 30–40cm (12–16in) across, a bright orange-yellow fading to yellowish-tan, with spongy, yellowish flesh. On broad-leaved, especially Oak, and evergreen trees from summer on.*
3 Polyporus squamosus *(Dryad's Saddle) grows to 60cm (2ft) across, often*

in clumps, its ochre cap flecked with dark scales to resemble cork and a whitish underside. On broad-leaved trees, especially Elm, Beech and Sycamore, from spring to autumn. Choose young ones and stew them thoroughly.

4 Pleurotus ostreatus *(Oyster Fungus) grows in clumps, with deep blue-grey shell-shaped caps 6–14cm (2¹/₂–5³/₄in) wide, white gills and white rubbery flesh. On broad-leaved trees for most of the year. Tasty; slice and stew. Also dries well.*

5 Armillaria mellea *(Honey or Bootlace Fungus) has tawny-yellowish brown-flecked caps 3–15cm (1¹/₄–6in) across, white gills later speckled with brown, white flesh and bootlace-like 'roots.' On broad-leaved and coniferous trees and stumps from spring to autumn. Slice and stew.*

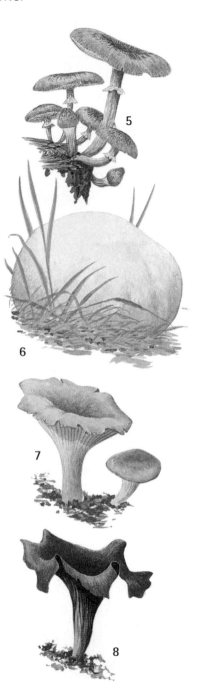

GROUND FUNGI
Ground fungi live in the soil. There are many kinds, some VERY poisonous.

6 Lycoperdon giantea *(Giant Puffball) resembles a football, up to 30cm (1ft) across, smooth, white and leathery, yellowing with age and may weigh up to 9kg (20lb). In woods and grassy places from late summer to autumn. Choose young ones with spongy, pure white flesh. Very tasty; simmer or fry.*

7 Cantharellus cibarius *(Chanterelle) is apricot-scented, egg yellow, funnel-shaped, 3–10cm (1¹/₄–4in) across, with pronounced, forking gills. It grows in groups under trees, especially Beech, from summer on. Very tasty; stew for ten minutes. Do NOT confuse with* Cortinarius speciosissimus.

8 Craterellus cornucopioides *(Horn of Plenty) is horn- or funnel-shaped, with a rough, crinkly, dark brown cap 3–8cm (1¹/₄–3in) across and a smooth, tapering grey stem. In broad-leaved woods, especially Beech, in autumn. Stew well, or dry.*

WARNING
Fungi make excellent eating but should be attempted ONLY if identified with certainty.

Agaricus fungi: AVOID any that stain yellow when cut (see A. xanthoderma below). Some young 'buttons' are hard to tell apart and can be confused with the deadly Amanitas.

1 **Agaricus arvensis** *(Horse Mushroom) resembles A. campestris but with a cap to 15cm (6in). Young ones have light pink gills, later turning pinkish-brown; in same places as A. campestris. Edible raw or cooked.*
2 **Agaricus augustus** *has a scaly, light brownish cap to 20cm (10in) across, young gills pink later turning dark, and a ringed stem; in clusters in woodland clearings in summer and autumn. Tasty; smells of anise.*
3 **Agaricus campestris** *(Field Mushroom) resembles the familiar cultivated kind, with a white cap to 10cm (4in) across, browning slightly in older specimens, and pink gills later turning dark brown; in grassy places in autumn, rarely by trees. Edible raw or cooked.*
4 **Agaricus sylvestris** *(Wood Mushroom) resembles A. arvensis but is found in woodland, often with conifers. Edible raw or cooked.*
5 **Agaricus xanthoderma** *(Yellow Staining Mushroom) resembles other Agaricus species, but shows a yellow stain when bruised and is strongly yellow at the base. It is POISONOUS and smells of carbolic. In both woody and grassy places in summer and autumn. AVOID.*
6 **Lepiota procera** *(Parasol Mushroom) has a brownish cap, later with darker scales, to 30cm (1ft) across, with creamy-white gills and a slender stem with a double*

white ring and brown bands. By broad-leaved woodland and in grassy clearings from summer to autumn. It tastes of almonds or Brazil nuts.

7 Coprinus comatus *(Shaggy Ink Cap) has a cylindrical cap with whitish or pale brownish scales and gills that begin white, turn pinkish and finally dissolve into a black, inky mess. In groups in open grassy areas in summer and autumn. Gather young ones whose gills are still pale. POISONOUS if eaten with alcohol.*

8 Tricholoma nudum *(Wood Blewit or Blue Cap) has a lilac-blue cap, later turning reddish-brown and wavy-edged, to 10cm (4in) across, bluish gills and a stocky, fibrous bluish stem. In rings in mixed woodland from autumn to mid winter. Tasty and sweet-smelling. Produces an allergic reaction in a few people.*

9 Boletus edulis *(Cep) is brownish with a cap to 20cm (8in), a swollen stem and white flesh; in woodland clearings in autumn. All Boletes have a sponge-like layer of pores or tubes instead of gills. Many edible species — they dry well — occur around the world. AVOID any with pink or red spores unless positively identified. Some are poisonous.*

OTHER USES FOR FUNGI

- Many bracket fungi make excellent tinder — once lit they will smoulder for hours.
- Razor-strop fungus is so tough that it can be used to sharpen knives, or chopped up for corks, corn plasters and kindling.
- Giant puffball is styptic — it will staunch and soothe bleeding wounds.
- Tree fungi are rich in tannin and can be used in treating burns.

POISONOUS FUNGI

WARNING
The following are among the worst of the poisonous fungi but there are many others. Do NOT use any fungi you cannot positively identify as a survival food. Some Amanita fungi are among the most deadly of all. They have a cup, or volva, at the base.

1 Amanita virosa *(Destroying Angel)* is *wholly white, with a large volva, a scaly stem and a cap to 12cm (5in) across, in woodland in summer and autumn. Sweet- and sickly-smelling and DEADLY poisonous. Young ones may resemble young Agaricus fungi.*

2 Amanita phalloides *(Death Cap)* *has a greenish-olive cap to 12cm (5in) across, a paler stem, large volva, and white gills and flesh; usually in woodland, especially with Oak or Beech. The MOST DEADLY of all.*

3 Amanita pantherina *(Panther Cap)* *has a brownish, white-flecked cap to 8cm (3in), white gills and 2–3 hoop-looking rings at the base of the stem; in woodland, especially with Beech. Poisonous, often FATAL.*

4 Amanita muscaria *(Fly Agaric) has a distinctive bright red cap, flecked with white, to 22cm (9in) across. Found in autumn, typically in Pine and Birch woods.*

5 Entoloma sinnuatum *(Leaden Entoloma) has a dull greyish-white, deeply convex cap to 15cm (6in) across, yellowish gills turning salmon-pink and firm white flesh smelling of meal, bitter almond and radish; in groups in grassy places and woods, especially with Beech and Oak, in summer and autumn. Poisonous, can be DEADLY. Confusable with an Agaricus, but has no ring on the stem.*

6 Inocybe patouillardii *begins whitish then turns yellowish-brown, with a cap to 7cm (2³/₄in), often split at the margin, and whitish gills turning olive-*

brown; stains red when bruised. In broad-leaved woods, especially Beech, in summer and autumn. Lacks a ring on the stem, but when young confusable with an *Agaricus*. DEADLY poisonous.

7 Paxilus involutus *has a solid yellow-brown cap with a rolled rim, to 12cm (5in) across, yellow-brown gills and a straight, stout stem. Very common in woodland, especially Birch. DEADLY: do NOT confuse with edible yellowish fungi such as the Chanterelle.*

8 Cortinarius speciosissimus *is reddish- to tawny-brown, with a flattish cap 2–8cm (³/₄–3¹/₄in) across, and rusty-brown gills, in coniferous wood in autumn. Not common but very poisonous. Slightly lighter-coloured, C. orelanus, also poisonous in broadleaved woodland. Both have a radish like smell. Do not confuse with the Chanterelle. DEADLY.*

(See also Agaricus xanthoderma, illustrated with edible species)

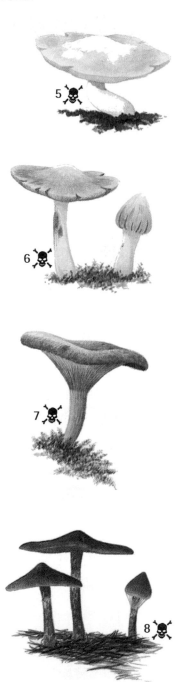

POISON SYMPTOMS
Poisonous fungi produce a variety of symptoms but the following are fairly typical:

Death Cap/Destroying Angel: *Symptoms develop slowly, 8–24 hrs after eating: vomiting, diarrhoea, excessive thirst, sweating and convulsions. Apparent recovery after one day, then a relapse and, in 90% of cases, death from liver failure in 2–10 days. No known antidote.*

Muscarine poisoning: *Caused by several fungi. Effects vary, toxins all attack nervous system.*

Amanita muscaria produces severe gastro-intestinal disturbance, delirium, vivid hallucinations, uncontrollable twitching and convulsions, followed by coma-like sleep. The victim usually recovers. Inocybe patouillardii and its relatives produce vertigo, blindness, sweating, low temperature, very dilated pupils, followed, in the worst cases, by delirium and death.

ARCTIC AND NORTHERN PLANTS

In addition to these hardy arctic plants, many temperate species occur in summer in the far north.

1 Red Spruce *(Picea rubens) reaches 23m (70ft), with dark or yellow-green needles all around its hairy twigs, rough dark bark and pendant cones; in drier areas of North America. Young shoots are edible raw or cooked; infuse the needles for teas and boil the edible inner bark.*

2 Black Spruce *(Picea mariana) is smaller than Red Spruce, with shorter needles; in moist areas of North America. Many similar spruces occur in North America and northern Eurasia. Use all as Red Spruce.*

3 Labrador Tea *(Ledum groenlandicum) is a fragrant evergreen shrub averaging 30–90cm (1–3ft), with narrow leaves with rolled edges, whitish or hairy below, and five-petalled white flowers, in North America. The leaves make a revivifying tea.*

4 Arctic Willows *(Salix) are mat-forming tundra shrubs averaging 30–60cm (1–2ft), with rounded, leaves, shiny above, and yellow catkins. Spring shoots, leaves, inner bark and young peeled roots are all edible. The leaves have 7–10 times more vitamin C than an orange.*

5 Ferns *occur in moist places in summer in far northern woods and by the tundra. Eat ONLY young fiddleheads up to 15cm (6in) long, remove any hairs. Steaming is the best way to cook them.*

6 Cloudberries *(Rubus chamaemorus) seldom reach 30cm (1ft). Bramble-like, with palm-shaped leaves, white flowers and berries at the top of the plant — pink, ripening through orange to amber. The berries are edible raw.*

7 Salmonberry *(Rubus spectabilis) resembles a small Wild Raspberry,* thornless, with three-part leaves, purplish-red flowers and juicy red or yellow berries, edible raw. In North America, now in parts of Europe.

8 Bearberry *(Arctostaphylos uvaursi)* in arctic regions is small, mat-forming, woody, with club-shaped evergreen leathery leaves, pink or white flowers and clusters of red berries, edible cooked.

9 Iceland Moss *(Cetraria islandica)* is a lichen, forming tufted leathery, grey-green or brownish mats up to 10cm (4in) high, composed of many strap-shaped branches. Soak for several hours then boil well.

10 Reindeer Moss *(Cladonia rangiferina)*, lichen growing 5–10cm (2–4in), often in large clumps, with hollow, roundish, greyish stems and branches resembling antlers. Soak for several hours, boil well.

11 Rock Tripes *(Umbillicaria)* are lichens, forming roundish, blister-like greyish or brownish growths attached to rocks by a central stalk; some kinds warty and pebble-like, others smooth. Very nutritious, soak for several hours then boil well.

Lichens are an important survival food, not only in arctic regions — though vital there because they are probably more nutritious than other arctic plants. Explorers have survived on Rock Tripe for long periods. But beware! They can cause painful irritation if eaten raw because they contain a bitter acid. Remove it by soaking them in water overnight and then boiling thoroughly. A further roasting will crispen them up if you prefer a crunchy texture.

If you successfully hunt a caribou eat the fermented lichens in its stomach. They are easily digested and some Eskimos count them a great delicacy.

DESERT PLANTS

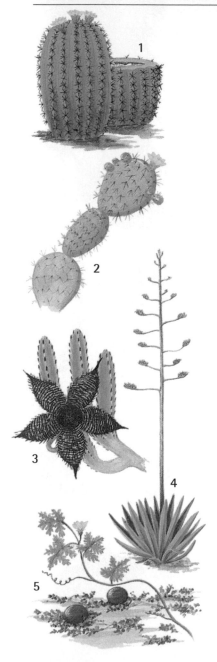

Desert survival depends upon water. Learn the water-bearing trees and cacti before considering food plants. Do not eat if you have no water; digestion will further deplete the body's liquid reserves and accelerate dehydration.

1 Barrel Cacti *(Ferocactus) of south-west North America average 1·2m (4ft), at that size yielding over 1 litre (2 pt) of edible, sometimes bitter, milky sap. This is an exception to the rule to avoid milky sap. Slice off the top and smash the inner pulp, then drink. Only worth doing in an emergency.*

2 Prickly Pears *(Opuntia) have thick, jointed, pad-like leaves, yellow or red flowers and egg-shaped pulpy fruits. Peeled fruits are edible raw; peel and cook tender young pads – cutting away the spines, roast seeds for flour, tap the stems for water. Originally from North America, now in many arid areas. Very prickly, treat with great care. In Africa do NOT confuse with spurges; unlike this plant, they have milky sap.*

3 Carrion Flowers *(Stapelia) are found in some variety in southern and tropical Africa. They are large odd-looking plants with short succulent stems that branch off into leaves like fat spines, with distinctive star-shaped flowers, which may be covered in thick shaggy hairs. Mature flowers give off a powerful stench of rotting meat, an unmistakeable, if not very pleasant clue to identification. Tap the stems for their water.*

4 Mescals *(Agave) have a rosette of thick, leathery, spiky leaves with a sharp tip from which arises a very long, columnar flower stalk. Stalks not yet in flower are edible cooked. In Africa, Asia, southern Europe, Mexico and the southern United States, and parts of the Caribbean. Grows in moist tropical areas as well as desert country.*

5 Wild Gourds *(Cucurbitaceae) occur in the Kalahari and Sahara east to*

India, cultivated elsewhere. The plant is mat-forming, resembling a vine, with orange-sized fruits. Boil the unripe fruit to make it more edible, roast the seeds, cook young leaves. The flower may be eaten raw, and stems and shoots chewed for their water.

6 Date Palms (Phoenix) grow wild, always near water, from India to North Africa; introduced elsewhere. They are tall slender palms crowned with a tuft of leaves up to 4m (16ft) long. The fruits and growing tip of the palm are edible raw young leaves are edible cooked. Sap from the trunk is rich in sugar and can be boiled down.

7 Baobabs (Adansonia) are large trees with huge, swollen, heavily ridged trunks found from Africa to Australia. The trunk of a mature tree can be 9m (30ft) in diameter. Tap the roots for water. The pulpy fruits, 10–20cm (4–8in) long, and seeds are edible raw; boil tender young leaves.

8 Acacias (Acacia) occur abundantly from Africa to northern Australia. There are many different kinds, all thorny, scrubby, medium-sized trees with very small leaflets their flowers usually forming small (1cm/¹/₂in) globular flowerheads, white, pink or yellow, according to species. Their roots may be tapped for water, the seeds roasted and young leaves and shoots boiled.

9 Carob (Ceratonia siliqua) grows in arid land around the Mediterranean and from the Sahara across Arabia to India. It is almost the only tree on Malta. Height can reach 15m (50ft). Shiny, evergreen leaves are paired, two or three to a stem. Small red flowers produce flat leathery seed pods containing a sweet, nutritious pulp, which can be eaten raw, and hard brown seeds which can be ground and cooked as porridge. Also known as St John's or Locust Bread because these pods were thought to have been the 'locusts' on which John the Baptist lived in the wilderness.

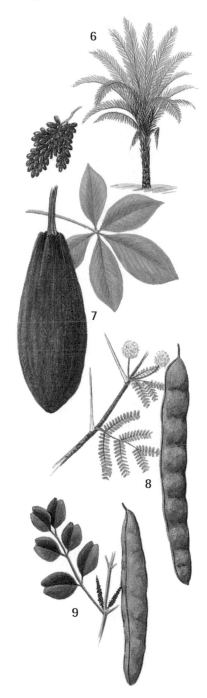

171

TROPICAL PLANTS

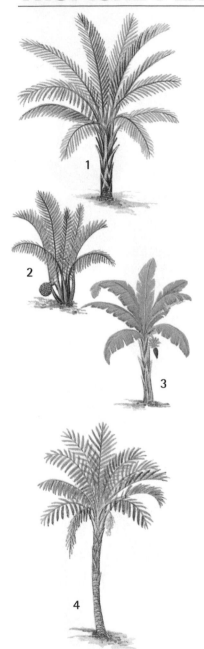

Edible plants abound in tropical areas, but unless you are already familiar with them it is better to begin with to eat palms, bamboos and the commoner fruits.

1 Sago Palms *(Metroxylon) come from the damp lowlands of southeast Asia; introduced elsewhere. Medium, to 10m (30ft), spiny-trunked; leaves long, delicate and arching. The spongy, starchy inner pith of the trunk provides the sago.*

2 The Nipa Palm *(Nifpa fruticans) grows to 6m (20ft), with long, fern-like leaves swelling and clustering at the base to form the 'trunk'; in brackish estuaries in South-east Asia. It yields sugary sap, delicious fruits and an edible 'cabbage' or growing tip.*

3 Bananas or Plantains *(Musa) are spread all over the tropics: 3–10m (9–30ft) tall, with very large, strap-like, usually split light green leaves. Hard plantain fruits are only edible cooked. They have more starch but less sugar than the soft kinds. Eat buds, growing tips, young stems and inner parts of roots as well as fruit.*

4 Sugar Palm *(Arenga pinnata) reaches 12–20m (38–65ft), with a rough scaly trunk topped by fairly erect, Sago-like leaves and yellow, branch-like fruiting parts; wild in Malaysia and Indonesia. To obtain sugar, collect sap and boil down to a thick syrup.*

5 Rattan Palms *(Calamus) are robust climbers, hooking themselves on to trees with a fish-hookshaped appendage on the midrib of the leaves; often common in Old World tropics. The swollen stems, seeds and growing tip are edible; the roots make excellent lashings.*

6 Fish-tail Palms *(Caryota) average 10m (30ft), with a smooth, ringed trunk and long arching leaves of many oval or wedged-shaped leaflets. There* are many similar kinds in the Old World tropics. Use as Sago Palm. Do NOT eat fruit.

7 Coconut Palms *(Cocos nucifera) occur all over the moist tropics, growing to over 30m (90ft), with large clusters of nuts hanging at the base of the leaves. The fibrous 'coconut' is inside a large, smooth husk. The growing tip, milk and flesh of the nut are edible. The rich sap can be boiled down for sugar.*

These are only some of the tropical palms. Others include:

− Piva Palm *(Guiliema utilis) of America, has a slender trunk banded with alternating dark and light spines. Boil or roast the red or yellow fruits.*
− Baccaba and Patawa Palms *(Iessenia and Oemocarpus) of Brazil and the Guianas, have small purplish fruit 2cm (³/₄in) long. Eat both pulp and kernel of seed.*
− Assai Palm *(Euterpe oleraccea) of tropical South America, which likes swampy places, especially along tidal rivers. Edible fruit has soft purple pulp.*

The growing tip, enclosed by a crown of leaves or the sheathing bases of the leaf stems, is edible in most palms − eat any that are not too bitter. Fruit should be AVOIDED if not positively identified, especially in the far east − some contain crystals which cause intense pain.

8 Papaya or Pawpaw *(Carica papaya) is a small tree, 2−6m (6−18ft) tall, with a soft hollow trunk and large, dark green, melon-like fruits that ripen to orange or yellow; in moist conditions in all tropical parts. The fruit is edible raw and settles an upset-stomach; young leaves, flowers and stems are edible boiled. Change the water AT LEAST once. Although it will tenderize tough, stringy meat, do not get the milky sap of unripe fruit in the eyes.*

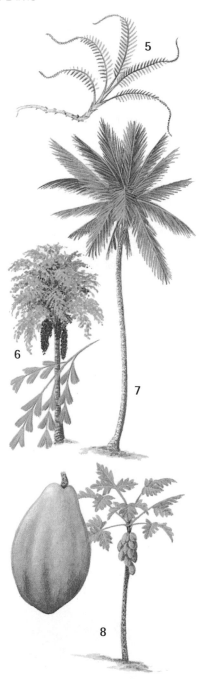

173

1 Horseradish Tree *(Moringa oleifera) grows to 10m (30ft), with small oval leaflets, yellow-white flowers and 25–38cm (10–15in), narrow, three-sided brown seed pods; wild in East Africa and South Asia but now elsewhere. Leaves and young fruits are edible raw or cooked; slice older pods and cook like string beans; use the root for seasoning like true Horseradish. The expressed juice of leaves and roots is good for treating inflammations.*

2 Mango *(Mangifera indica) grows in moist places almost everywhere, a medium to large evergreen tree with clusters of narrow dark green leaves. The oval, 7·5-13cm (3–5in) fruits ripen from green to orange, are edible raw and contain a long flat stone. Mango leaves can cause an allergic reaction in some people.*

3 Sweet Sop *(Annona squamosa) is a 5–6m (15–18ft) tree with oval to spear-shaped leaves and Magnolia-like flowers. The aromatic, pulpy, globe-shaped green-grey fruit is made up of many parts. Originally from the New World tropics but now in most parts; two edible relatives in Central and South America are the Cherimoya (A. cherimola) and Bullock's Heart (A. reticulata).*

4 Sour Sop *(Annona muricata) is similarly widespread, growing to 12m (38ft), with large Avocado-shaped fruits, green, leathery, spiny, weighing up to 2kg (4·4lb). A very refreshing acid taste.*

5 Wild Figs *(Ficus) exist in great variety in tropical and subtropical areas, a few species in deserts. They are straggly trees, with aerial roots and leathery evergreen leaves rounded at the base. The pear-shaped fruits are edible raw and grow direct from the branches. Avoid any that are hard and woody or with irritant hairs.*

6 Breadfruits *(Artocarpus) are trees, growing to 15–20m (48–56ft), with* large, deeply lobed leaves, glossy above, milky sap and very large warty-skinned fruits; now in most tropical parts. The starch-rich fruits are edible raw if the skin is scraped away and the tougher inner bits discarded.

7 Sterculias (Sterculia) are found in Central and South America, and elsewhere in the tropics. Large trees, up to 30m (100ft) high, with buttressed roots and hand-shaped leaves, their fruits consist of pods containing black, peanut-like seeds that can be eaten raw after removing the irritant hairs.

8 Bael Fruit (Aegle marmelos) is a tree of 2·5–4·5m (7–15ft), with dense prickly growth and rounded, yellowish or greyish fruits up to 10cm (4in) across; in parts of the Himalayas, India and Burma. A relative of the citruses, the fruits are edible raw and very rich in vitamin C.

9 Bignays (Antidesma) are evergreen shrubs, 10–13m (30–40ft) tall, with shiny 15cm (6in) leaves, in the forests of South-east Asia. The fleshy, many seeded, currant-like fruits are about 1cm (¹/₂in) across and mature from green to white to red and finally black. Edible raw, but better jellied.

In primary tropical forest most fruits are carried in the canopy, unreachable unless you climb the trees or chop them down, though elsewhere fruit can prove a valuable food. More accessible is the vine-like Rattan, which can be cut and then hauled down to obtain the growing tip. Peel off the outer sheath for about 2m (7ft), cut into lengths and roast in the embers of a fire. The inner heart of some is very tasty, although slightly bitter.

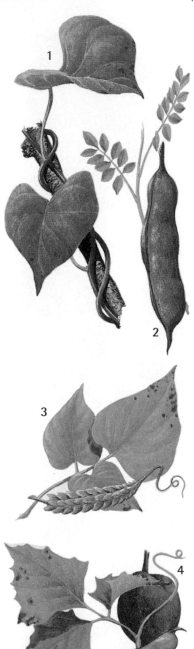

1 Ceylon Spinach *(Basella alba)* is trailing, vine-like, with thick circular to oval or heart-shaped leaves, from greenish to purplish-red, and fleshy purplish flowers; now in most tropical areas. Young leaves and stems are edible cooked and rich in vitamins.

2 Tamarind *(Tamarindus indica)* is a densely branched tree to 25m (80ft), with evergreen leaves formed of many leaflets, pale yellow red-streaked flowers and brown seed pods. The pulp of the pods is edible raw and rich in vitamin C. Seeds and young leaves can be used as a potherb, and the bark peeled and chewed. Now in many areas.

3 Goa Beans *(Psophocarpus)* are climbing plants of the Old World tropics, with spear-shaped leaves, blue flowers and 20cm (8in) long, four-angled, scaly seedpods. Boil young pods lightly, they taste like beans, the young seeds like peas, or roast older seeds. Young leaves, which taste like spinach, are edible raw. Thicker roots, richer in protein than potato or cassava, are edible raw or can be boiled, fried, baked or roasted like potatoes.

4 Yam Beans *(Pachyrrhizus and Sphenostylis)* are climbing plants with irregular, three-part leaves and a knotty turnip-like root, in large patches in most of the tropics. The edible tubers are crisp, sweet, juicy, tasting of nuts. The seeds are harmful raw and must be well boiled.

5 Peanut *(Arachis hypogaea)* is not a true nut and its fruits ripen underground. A small, bushy plant with pairs of bluntly oval leaves, yellow flowers and stalks leading to the wrinkled pods. Very nutritious, the 'nuts' keep well. Now in most tropical and subtropical parts.

6 Cassava or Manioc *(Manihot esculenta)* is a staple throughout the tropics, growing on well-drained ground to 5m (15ft) with jointed stems and long-stalked leaves divided into 5–9 blades. The fat tubers are lethally POISONOUS raw and MUST be cooked. Keeps well, particularly when ground as flour.

7 Ti Plant is a shade-loving shrub, 2–5m (6–15ft), with whorls of shiny, leathery, sometimes reddish leaves and, when ripe, red berries; now widespread in tropical parts particularly Pacific islands. Boil the starch-rich fleshy roots.

8 Taro *(Colocasia)* occurs on wet ground all over the tropics, up to 1·5m (5ft), with large, very long-stalked heart- or arrow-shaped leaves arising from the roots and an orange-yellow flower. The tubers taste like potatoes but are harmful raw and MUST be cooked.

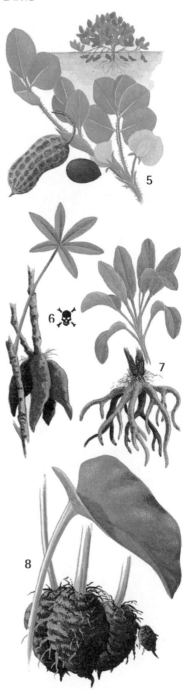

In tropical forests the best places to forage will be along streams and watercourses. Anywhere that the sun can penetrate the jungle floor will produce a mass of vegetation but river banks often offer the clearest area, where plants can thrive.

While climbing spurs take the chance to look out over the jungle canopy below. Good views are obtained where a deadfall has crashed down and cleared an area. Palms and other recognizable food plants can be seen among the canopy. Their position can be noted and they can then be felled when required. A tree will provide a considerable supply of food.

If weak and short of food do NOT expend effort felling a tree. You will use up too much energy and there will be easier food available.

Do not pick more food than you need. Food deteriorates rapidly in tropical conditions. Leave food on the growing plant until you need it and eat if fresh.

1 Water Spinach *(Ipomoea aquatica) is trailing, with light green leaves and white flowers; always by fresh water, usually as a floating plant, mainly in south-east Asia. Older stems are stringy, but young leaves and shoots can be boiled.*

2 Lotus *(Nelumbium nuciferum) is aquatic, with long-stalked, bell-shaped bluish-green leaves standing clear of the water and pink, white or yellow flowers. Young leaves and peeled stems are edible boiled. Boil or roast ripe seeds, first removing the bitter embryo, and the rootstalk. Mainly Asia, and in parts of Africa and North America.*

3 Water Lilies *(Nymphaea) grow in lakes, rivers and streams in tropical Africa, India and America, and also in some temperate areas, with heart-shaped leaves floating on the water. They have large, starch-rich edible tubers, stems which can be cooked, and bitter but nourishing seeds.*

4 Wild Yams *(Dioscorea) occur in great variety in light forest and clearing in both tropical and subtropical parts. Twining, vine-like stems, some kinds bearing edible aerial tubers, lead to one or more large underground tubers. If kept dry, yams store well. Some Wild Yams are poisonous raw: for safety ALWAYS cook — peel tubers, boil and mash.*

5 Wild Rice *(Oryza and in North America Zizania) is a coarse grass growing to 90–120cm (3–4ft), widespread in the tropics and many temperate areas. Thresh and winnow the grains to remove the tough, hairy husks, then boil or roast and pound for storage as flour.*

6 Sugarcanes *(Saccharum) are cultivated all over the tropics and occasionally occur wild. A coarse, tall, aromatic, thick-stemmed grass, the canes can be chewed raw to extract their sweet juice.*

7 Millets *(Panicum, Pennisetum and others)* are tropical cereals, sometimes found wild in drier areas. They are grasses, several feet tall, with sausage-like heads of grain, each one about the size of a mustard seed. Pound to a meal and use in stews or as porridge.

8 Bamboos are giant grasses of most moist areas. The rapidly growing, edible young shoots are at the base of the plant; split the tough outer sheath and cook like asparagus. The seeds of a flowering bamboo are also edible. Bamboos have a great many uses as building materials, for making rafts, even as cooking utensils, as well as their use as food. Take care when collecting: some plants are heavily stressed and may shatter or whiplash.

In addition to the plants illustrated and listed here there are others that you will recognize from their similar cultivated varieties, such as the Avocado (Peresea americana) of tropical South America, where it is a favourite food of many animals — including the jaguar! — the Christophine (Sechium edule), native to Brazil, and the whole family of citrus fruits, with about 60 wild species in Indo-Malaya and China, some growing at quite high altitudes. But BEWARE. Strychnine has fruits that look like oranges but which are DEADLY POISONOUS.

In the tropics you will usually have a choise of plant foods so stick to the ones you can identify and know are safe. If you need to eat unknown plants always apply the edibility test, using very small amounts.

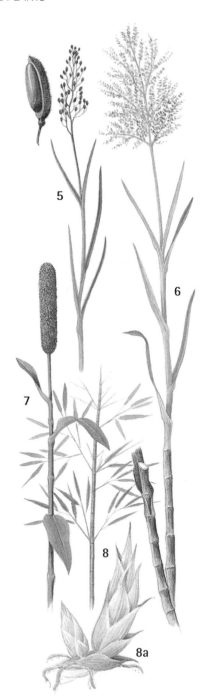

These are some of the many other edible plants which you might find, all are good to eat if prepared as suggested:

PALMS

Palmyra or **Borassus palm** *(Borassus flabellifer)*, growing in drier parts of tropical Africa, southern India and Burma, resembles a Date Palm, with similar fan-like leaves. Sort insides of the three-part nuts are edible, sap makes a pleasant drink and flowering parts can be tapped for their sugary juice.

Saw palmetto *(Serenoa repens)*, common on sandy ground from southern USA into Central America. Average 1–2m (3–7ft) tall, with long, stiff fan-shaped groups of leaves, clusters of white flowers and oblong black fruits. Growing tip (palm heart) edible raw or cooked.

Yuccas *(Yucca)* of many kinds grow on sandy ground, from USA into Central America. Evergreen, woody-stemmed, with stiff sword-like leaves off a stem or in a cluster at the top. Petals of six-petalled white flowers and ripe pulp of oblong gerkin-like fruits are edible raw or cooked.

NUTS

Brazil Nut *(Bertholletia excelsa)* is widespread on dry ground in forests of tropical South America, 30–40m (100–130ft) high, with long, crinkly margined, oval leaves and yellow flowers. Pot-shaped, lidded capsules contain 15–30 edible nuts. In the same area Sapucaya *(*Lecythis urnigera*)* nuts come in similar capsules and are equally tasty.

Cashew Nut *(Anacardium occidentale)*, originally native to north-eastern South America, now grown all over tropics, are shrubs or medium-sized trees with evergreen, broadly oval, leathery, prominently veined leaves in opposite pairs and pinkish-yellow flowers. Eat ONLY nuts, borne on the end of a pear-shaped, reddish, fleshy fruit stalk. Harmful unless peeled and cooked. BEWARE: smoke or steam from cooking can cause blindness.

Indian Almond *(Terminalia catappa)*, found in scrubby, especially coastal, area over almost all the tropics, has very large, leathery, club-shaped leaves. Mature trees spread to 10m (30ft), young ones have distinctive circles of horizontal branches. Hard edible nuts in a fibrous, thick green, fleshy shell, cluster at the branch tips.

Queensland Nut *(Macademia ternifolia)* grows in north-eastern Australia on a tree about 12m (40ft) tall with many narrow, spear-shaped leaves. Round nuts in greenish husks come in clusters.

FRUITS

Guava *(Psidium guajava)* of Central and South America, widely introduced elsewhere, are small gnarled trees, up to 10m (30ft), with peely, light brown bark, oval leaves in pairs (slightly hairy below), white flowers and large crabapple-like light yellow fruits with a whitish to pinkish, creamy, seed-filled pulp. Edible raw or cooked and rich in vitamin C.

Persimmon *(Diospyros)* found in waste places and dry woods of warm temperate east Asia and southern USA, introduced elsewhere, can reach 20m (63ft). Small, sometimes crinkly, spear-shaped leaves make good tea, rich in vitamin C. Round, yellow to reddish or purplish, tomato-like, 5–7·5cm (2–2^{1}/$_{2}$in) fruits are edible raw or cooked.

Rambutan *(Nephelium lappaceum)* grows in forests in parts of south-east Asia reaching 20m (63ft). Bushy, with dark brown bark, many small dark green leaflets, small greenish flowers and clusters of small, soft-spined, hairy-looking fruits ripening to red.

Fleshy white inner pulp — not seed — is edible raw and rich in vitamin C. Pulasan (N. mutabile) is a smaller tree in the same area with equally good blunt-spined fruits with a yellowish pulp.

Durian (Durio zibethinus), 40m (130ft) trees, native to Malaysia and Borneo, widely introduced in south-east Asia, with long, spear-shaped, bronze to olive green leaves and large, spiky-surfaced, distinctive yellow fruits. Cream-coloured pulp (not seeds) is foul smelling but delicious to eat.

Malay Apple or **Pomerac** (Syzygium malaccensis) reaches 15m (50ft), with glossy green, broadly spear-shaped leaves, clusters of bright pink flowers and smallish 5cm (2in) red, apple-like fruits, smelling of roses and edible raw.

Rose apple (S. aqueum) is similar but with yellowish or white pear-shaped fruits tasting of apricots. Both native to rain forest and scrubby places in Malaysia, widely introduced elsewhere.

Carambola (Averrhoa carambola) grows in Indonesian forests. Small, average 8m (24ft) height, with many light green, small, spear-shaped leaves, clusters of small whitish-pink flowers and yellow, ribbed fruits 7·5–12·5cm (3–5in) long, edible raw, though sometimes acid.

Mangosteen (Garcinia mangostana) of south-east Asian forests, reach 12m (40ft), with long, leathery, dark green leaves in pairs large yellow and purple flowers and round, tomato-shaped purplish-brown fruits whose five segments of inner white pulp are edible raw. There are several kinds.

Passion Fruit or **Granadilla** (Passiflora edulis), climbing plant, native to Brazil, introduced elsewhere, with long twining stems, three-lobed leaves, distinctive tendril-like white and purple flowers and egg-shaped purple fruits with a many-seeded, slightly acid pulp. Many kinds of edible passion fruits grow in tropical America.

Jackfruit (Artocarpus heterophyllus) of southern India, now found widely in south-east Asia, is like breadfruit. A tree reaching 25m (80ft), with dark green, leathery, bluntly oval leaves and huge warty fruits up to 32kg (70lb) in weight, edible raw but better cooked; seeds can be roasted.

VEGETABLES

Okras (Abelmoschus) There are many species of this bushy herb. A cluster of up to 40 yellow, five-petalled flowers produce the 'lady's fingers' which are a good food for those with stomach trouble and can be eaten raw. Roast the seeds inside.

Potato (Solanum tuberoisum) grows wild in the Andes, but BEWARE of its tomato-like fruits — which in this case are poisonous. The wild tomato looks so similar that it is safer to avoid it. Always cook potato tubers.

Sweet Potatoes (Ipomoea) are now found in many parts of the world but are especially abundant in the tropics, where they are widely cultivated. They are straggly, creeping, vine-like plants, often with heart-shaped leaves, and sometimes large, spindly tubers. These can be boiled or roasted. They may exude a milky juice, but this is not poisonous.

Beans (Phaseolus) occur widely in huge variety, many as escapees from cultivation. All are twining scrambling plants with 'pea-flowers' in various colours and beans in long pods, like the domestic type. Seeds highly nutritious — boil them.

Snake Gourds (Tricosanthes) of Indo-Malaysia and Australia are straggling, vine-like plants with lobed leaves and very long, thin, snake-like fruits up to 2m (6½ft) long. A common kind has bright red fruits. Slice them, then boil.

POISONOUS TROPICAL PLANTS

The proportion of poisonous plants in the tropics is no greater than in any other part of the world. Watch out for the following — they are either poisonous to eat or irritate on contact.

1 White Mangrove *(Avicennia marina) is slender, growing to 6m (18ft) in mangrove swamps and estuaries from tropical Africa east to Indonesia and Australasia. It has pale bark, many pencil-like roots spear-shaped to oblong leaves, yellow flowers and small round white berries. The sap blisters the skin and will blind if it gets in the eyes.*

2 Nettle Trees *(Laportea), widespread in the tropics, often by water, are smallish, with crinkly, spear-shaped, sharply-toothed leaves and drooping spikes of flowers — like an ordinary nettle. There are many kinds, including temperate ones. The burning sting is like a nettle's, but much worse. The seeds are very poisonous.*

3 Cowhage *(Mucuna pruriens), of scrub and light woodland, is trailing, vine-like, with oval leaflets in groups of three, spikes of hairy dull purplish flowers and brown hairy seedpods. Contact with pods and flowers causes irritation, blindness if in the eyes.*

4 Pangi *(Pangium edule) a tree reaching 20m (60ft) in jungle in south-east Asia, mainly Malaysia, with heart-shaped leaves in spirals, spikes of green flowers and clusters of large brownish pear-shaped fruits. All parts are poisonous, especially the fruits — the seeds contain prussic acid.*

5 Physic Nut *(Jatropha curcas) a shrub or small tree of wooded country throughout the tropics, has large, lobed, ivy-like leaves, small greenish-yellow flowers and yellow apple-sized fruits containing three large seeds. The seeds taste sweet but their oil is* *violently purgative, hence its name, and the remains of the pressed seeds very poisonous. Has equally dangerous relatives.*

6 Strychnine *(Strychnos nuxvomica) a small tree with oval leaves in opposite pairs and white to yellowish-red, orange-like fruits whose seeds, containing strychnine, are DEADLY. S. Nuxvomica is found mainly in India but other strychnine species occur throughout the tropics.*

7 Castor Oil Plant *or* **Castor Bean** *(Ricinus communis), is found throughout the tropics in scrubby and waste places, is shrub-like, its leaves arranged like the fingers of a hand, with spikes of yellow flowers and prickly three-seeded pods. Seeds are violently purgative, sometimes fatally.*

8 Duchesnia *(Duchesnia indica) resembles an ordinary edible strawberry, trailing, with three-part leaves, red strawberry-like fruits and yellow, not white, flowers; on waste ground in the warmer parts of Asia, introduced to North America. The fruits are highly poisonous, sometimes fatal.*

These are only some of the poisonous tropical species. Among others which you should avoid are:

Renghas Trees *(Gluta) of parts of India east to south-east Asia, which have severely irritant sap.*

Beachapple or Manzanillo *(Hippomane mancinella) of the New World tropics, a small tree with smooth pale bark and small apple-like poisonous fruits, which also has irritant sap.*

Sandbox Tree *(Hua crepitans), also of the New World, a large, spiny tree whose sap can irritate or temporarily blind — its segmented fruits, which look rather like miniature pumpkins, are poisonous.*

SEASHORE PLANTS

These plants thrive in salty conditions — but at the right time of year, many other edible plants occur near the coast.

1 Oraches *(Atriplex)* average 90cm *(3ft)*, pale-stalked, with pale green spear-shaped or triangular leaves and spikes of small greenish-white flowers; on salty ground, some kinds well inland. Cook the young leaves.

2 Sea Beet *(Beta vulgaris)* is sprawling, red-tinged, with leathery, long-stalked dark green leaves and clusters of small green flowers; on European coasts. The leaves are edible raw or boiled.

3 Sea Rockets *(Cakile)* average 30cm *(1ft)*, with fleshy, blue-green lobed leaves, lilac or purplish flowers and egg-shaped seedpods. The peppery leaves and young pods can be eaten raw or as a potherb.

4 Glassworts or **Marsh Samphire** *(Salicornia)*, often widespread in saline areas, have plump, greenish-yellow jointed stems up to 30cm (1ft) high. Some grow in great density on mud flats as single shoots 15cm (6in) high. Minute flowers are scarcely visible at the junction of the stems. **Rock Samphire** *(Crithmum maritimum)*, squat and bushy, with umbels of yellow flowers, is no relation but grows on shingle as well as cliffs. Its thick, hairless stems and fleshy, grey-green leaves, cut into narrow leaflets, are both edible. Cook and suck away the fleshy parts.

5 Scurvy-grasses *(Cochlearia)* average 25cm *(10in)*, with dark green, fleshy, heart- or kidney-shaped leaves and small white or pink flowers; often abundant on coasts. Very bitter, best leached in water, but so rich in vitamin C that the survivor should eat it if encountered.

6 Sea Kale *(Crambe maritima)* is cabbage-like, with thick grey-green leaves, four-petalled white flowers and

184

globular seedpods; on European coasts. The very tough leaves are better cooked; the underground stems can be sliced and thoroughly boiled.

7 Sea Holly *(Eryngium maritimum)* is thistle-like, averaging 60cm (2ft), with spiky, white-veined, ice-blue leaves and a blue thistle head; on north European coasts. Dig out the long roots, slice, boil.

8 Oyster Plant *(Mertensia maritima)* is sprawling, mat-forming, blue-green and fleshy, with oval leaves and clusters of pink to blue-purple flowers; on north European coasts. The leaves are edible raw or cooked.

9 Scots Lovage *(Ligusticum scoticum)* is stocky, celery-scented, to 90cm (3ft), often purple-stemmed with bright green leaves and heads of tiny white flowers, on north European coasts. Raw leaves are rich in vitamin C; or add these and chopped stems to other foods. Several similar lovages occur elsewhere.

TROPICAL SHORES

Tropical shore vegetation is likely to consist principally of palm trees, though in the Old World tropics it may be possible to find:

Screw Pines *(Pandanus),* so-called because of their thin, spirally grouped, leaves. They can often be distinguished by the many aerial roots at the base of the trunk. Knobbly, globular, many-segmented fruits are available all year round and in some kinds make good eating.

Wild plums *(Spondias)* may also be found near the coast.

Sour Plum *(Ximenia caffra),* a small usually thorny tree whose plum-like yellow fruits have edible pulp. There are several different kinds throughout the tropics.

Other plants could include **Passionfruit**, often found near the shore in the tropical Americas, and the fleshy stemmed **Seaside Purslanes** *(Sesuvium)* which grows near beaches and salt water, of which the whole plant can be eaten.

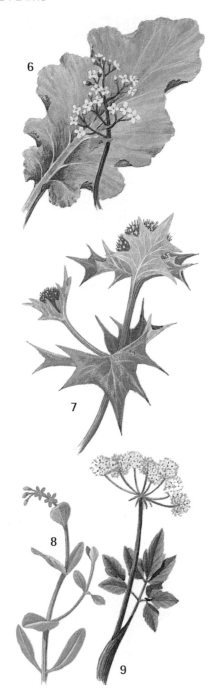

SEAWEEDS AND ALGAE

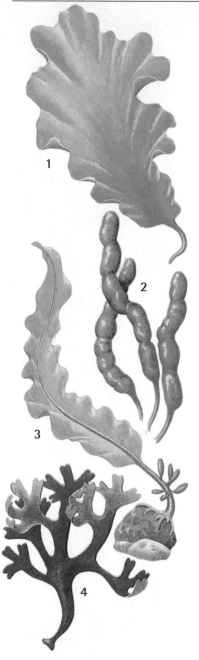

Most varieties of seaweed found in shallow waters, anchored to the bottom or a rock, but there are some that float on the surface in the open oceans. Coastal weeds are usually found stratified with green forms growing in surface waters, red in shallow water and brown a little deeper.

1 Sea Lettuce *(Ulva lactuca) is light green, resembling garden lettuce, and is found on rocks and stones in the Atlantic and Pacific, especially where water runs into the sea. Wash and boil.*
2 Enteromorpha intestinalis *is pale green, with pod-like, unbranched fronds up to 50cm (2ft) long, usually less. Often abundant on rocks in rock pools and also on saltmarshes, in cooler waters around the world. The whole plant is edible, either fresh or dried and pulverized. It is best picked in early spring.*
3 Kelps *(Alaria and Laminaria) have a short cylindrical stem and thin, wavy, olive-green to brown fronds, often very long; on rocky shores of the Atlantic and Pacific. Edible raw but better boiled.*
4 Irish Moss *(Chondrus crispus) consists of forking, lobed purplish to olive-green fronds, often in dense beds on Atlantic shores. Wash and boil. Cooled, the residue will set like gelatine. Fronds may be dried for storage; leave them in the sun until they have bleached white.*
5 Sugarwrack *(Laminaria saccarina) has long, flat, wavy-margined, yellow-brown fronds attached to stones and rocks; common in the Atlantic, and off China and Japan. Young fronds are edible raw, better cooked. Sweet-tasting.*
6 Dulse *(Rhodymenia palmata) has purple-red, short-stemmed, lobed, fan-shaped fronds, and occurs in the Atlantic and Mediterranean. Leathery but sweet; boil it. Dulse can be dried*

and rolled for chewing tobacco.

7 Lavers *(Porphyria) have thin, irregularly shaped, satiny, red, purplish or brown fronds and are found in both the Atlantic and Pacific. Boil until tender, then mash. Use as a relish or combine with grains to make cakes. Very tasty.*

Rich in vitamins and minerals, seaweeds are an ideal survival food. Those shown here are common and safe to eat.

There are no poisonous seaweeds but some contain acids which irritate the digestive tract and some are violent purgatives. If not identified as a known edible species try only small amounts. Even with the more edible varieties eat only a little until you become used to them. Do NOT eat seaweeds if short of water. If possible wash them in freshwater before eating, to remove some of the salt.

Collect growing weed, firm and smooth to the touch, not pieces washed up on the beach. Reject any that smells bad. Some which contain irritating acids can be detected by crushing between the fingers and leaving for five minutes, by which time they give off an unpleasant smell. All seaweeds decay rapidly out of water. Use soon after collection or dry for later use.

FRESHWATER ALGAE
8 Nostoc *(Nostoc) is a freshwater algae of North America and Eurasia, forming green, round, jelly-like, marble-sized globules in pools, from spring on. Dry and use as a thickener. EAT ONLY bright green fresh-looking algae. AVOID ALL BLUE GREEN ALGAE, IT IS POISONOUS. It is found in freshwater, not in the seas and oceans, floating on the surface of stagnant pools. Identify by its blue-green colour and by its gassy smell.*

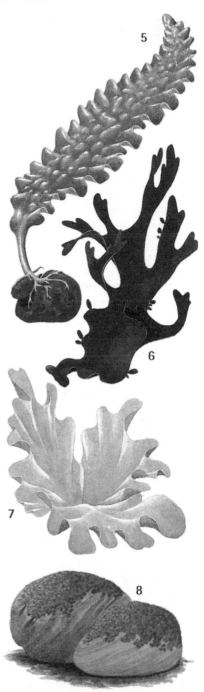

5

6

7

8

TRAPS AND TRAPPING

It is easier to trap most small prey than to hunt them. Even if you spot a small animal it offers very little target and can easily take cover. Trapping requires less skill and leaves you free to spend time foraging for other food. Nevertheless be ready to take advantage of sitting prey if you get the chance.

There are many elaborate traps with complicated mechanisms. They take time to build and demand physical effort. The survivor needs simple traps that are easy to remember and easy to construct. However, because each animal has different habits, a wide variety of types are essential. If one type fails, an alternative can be set — it is a matter of trial and error.

The survivor's own preservation must take precedence over humanitarian principles and unfortunately some of the easiest traps can cause considerable suffering to the animal. A trap which could bring quick death to the species for which it is intended, perhaps by strangulation, may catch another animal by a limb and leave it suffering for hours. Regular checking is essential. Leaving a trap line unchecked will prolong an animal's pain and increase the risk that your catch may be poached by an animal predator or that the prey will have managed painfully to struggle free — animals are known to bite off a limb or inflict other self-mutilation to get away from a trap.

A great deal of error can be eliminated by studying the animals and their habits. Choice of baits and sites is important. If one does not work, try another. BE PATIENT. Give the traps time. Animals will be very suspicious at first but with time will come to accept them — and that is when they will run into them.

Even when on the move, a few simple traps, quickly set up overnight, may be productive, and if you are making a more permanent camp you will be able to set up well-planned lines of traps. The more you set, the more chance you have of success.

Establish as large a trap line as you can manage in your area. Inspect it at first and last light. Collect the game and reset the traps. Repair any traps as necessary and move those that are repeatedly unfruitful. To be effective a trap must be very sensitive, so may be fired accidentally. You will probably have several empty traps for every success, but this does not mean that you are doing things wrong. You must accept a proportion of failures — they are no cause for disappointment. If a trap has not fired, but the bait has gone, it is an indication either that the bait was not sufficiently securely fixed or that the trigger mechanism is too tight. Check both when you reset the trap.

By doing the rounds regularly you effectively patrol an area, noting the many signs of activity or change which help to build up knowledge of your surroundings. At the same time you can forage for plants and other food, or note what is available for later collection.

INFO.

Baiting a trap will attract the game. In a survival situation food may be scarce but, if you know there are animals to trap, a little used as bait may bring large rewards.

Where to trap

Find the game trails or runs, which lead from an animal's home to where it feeds or waters. Look for any natural bottleneck along the route where it will have to pass through a particular position — a deadwood fall or a place where the track goes under an obstruction will be ideal places to set a trap.

Do not place a trap close to an animal's lair. That is where it sits and listens and sniffs the air. If at all suspicious it will either stay put or use a less obvious route. Don't place a trap close to its watering place either. There, too, the animal is on its toes and alert, more likely to notice anything unusual.

If you lay traps down the side of natural pastures the animals will not go near them but use other routes. However, when alarmed they panic and will take the shortest route to cover. That is when the crudest and most obvious of traps will be successful. Rabbits are easily caught by causing them to panic.

Trap construction

The simpler traps and snares are made of string or wire. It will be easier to keep a loop open in the air if you use wire and the wire in your survival tin is ideal. Even the most sophisticated need nothing more than a knife to make them out of available wood. The choice of materials is important. Use strong, springy wood. Do not use dead wood or wood found on the ground. Hazel takes a lot of beating: it is easy to carve and retains its spring and strength.

Types of trap

Trap mechanisms make use of the following principles:

MANGLE   STRANGLE   DANGLE   TANGLE

The deadfall mangles. The snare strangles. Springy saplings can make a trap more efficient and take the game up in the air — it dangles. The higher the sapling the more effectively it lifts the animal. A net tangles. Some traps combine two or more of these principles.

RULES FOR TRAPS

When setting traps, follow these basic rules:

1 Avoid disturbing the environment
Don't tread on the game trail. Do all your preparation off the trail and don't leave any sign that you have been there.

2 Hide scent
When constructing or handling traps don't leave your scent on them. Handle as little as possible and wear gloves if you can. Do not make a trap from pinewood and set it in a wood of hazel. Each tree gives off its own smell — and the animals you are trying to trap have a very high sense of smell, many times sharper than yours. Although they fear fire they are familiar with the smell of smoke and exposing a snare to the smoke from a camp fire will mask any human scent.

3 Camouflage
Hide freshly cut ends of wood with mud. Cover any snare on the ground to blend in as naturally as possible with its surroundings.

4 Make them strong
An ensnared animal is fighting for its life. It exerts a lot of energy in an attempt to escape. Any weakness in the traps will be exposed.

SNARES

Snares are the simplest of traps and should be part of any survival kit. They are made of non-ferrous wire with a running eye at one end through which the other end of the wire passes before being firmly anchored to a stake, rock or tree. A snare is a free-running noose which can catch small game around the throat and larger game around the legs.

A snare can be improvised from string, rope, twine or wire. Consider the kind of animal you are trying to trap when you place the snare. A rabbit, for instance, tends to sit in cover and observe. When satisfied that all is well it hops along. Setting the snare a hand's length from a fall or obstruction on the trail accommodates this hop. If the snare is closer to an obstruction the rabbit may brush it aside.

A wire snare can be supported off the ground on twigs, which can also be used to keep a suspended string noose open.

USING A SIMPLE SNARE

For rabbits and small animals. Use your judgement to scale up these proportions for larger creatures, such as foxes and badgers.

- Make the loop a fist width wide.

- Set it four fingers above the ground, and...

- one hand's width from an obstruction on the trail.

- Check that it is securely anchored, with twigs to support the loop in position if necessary.

Snares under tension

Make a snare more effective by using a sapling under tension to lift the game clear of the ground when it is released. This robs the animal of purchase in its struggle to free itself and also helps to keep it out of reach of predators.

Spring snare

When game is caught the trigger bar disengages and prey is lifted off the ground. Good for animals such as rabbits and foxes, it will trap game coming in both directions and is ideally situated on the game trail by a natural bottleneck caused by a dead fall or a rocky outcrop.

Cut notch in trigger bar (a) to fit notch in upright (b). Drive upright into ground. Attach snare to trigger bar and use cord to sapling to keep tension.

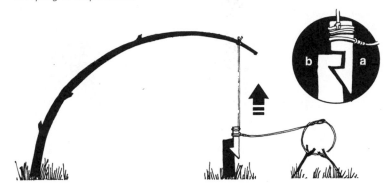

Baited spring snare

Mechanism as for spring snare, but here the quarry is tempted with a tasty morsel. The noose is laid on the ground, the bait strung above. As the game takes the bait the trigger is released.

Suitable for medium-sized animals such as foxes, this trap can be located in an open area as the bait will attract attention. Small clearings in woods are good sites.

The bait support stake should be only lightly driven into the ground as this must fly away with the noose.

Baited spring leg snare

The prongs of a natural fork of wood, or two sticks tied together, are pushed firmly into the ground. The line from a bent sapling is tied to a toggle and to the snare and the toggle then passed under the fork. When the game takes the bait, which is on the end of a separate bar, the bar disengages and the toggle flies up carrying the snare (and hopefully the game). This is a trap for larger game such as deer, bears and large felines. For the herbivorous deer, bait with blood or scent glands, which will arouse its curiosity.

The upper end of the toggle presses against the fork and the lower end is prevented from pulling back through by a bait bar between it and the fork – the pressure of the toggle holding it in position.

Spring tension snare

The upward counter thrust from the keeper stick (a) on which the snare arm (b) rests prevents the switch from pulling it up. When the game becomes ensnared the snare arm is dislodged from the keeper stick and the switch line slips off the other end. Suitable for small animals such as rabbits. Site it on the game trail.

Note how the switch line secures one end of snare arm (b), while the other rests on the keeper stick (a). Keep the switch line near the end of the snare arm (c).

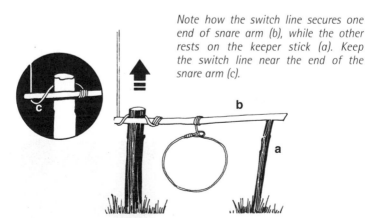

Trapeze spring snare

This snare can be used to cover two game trails in open country. The arm carries two snares and is held in a notch by the tension of the switch line.

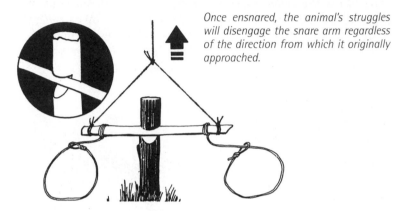

Once ensnared, the animal's struggles will disengage the snare arm regardless of the direction from which it originally approached.

Roller spring snare

A rounded grip holds the snare arm here, the switch line is best pulled back at a slight angle to keep it in place. Suitable for animals such as rabbits and foxes. Although tensed in one direction, the bar will be dislodged by an animal's struggles.

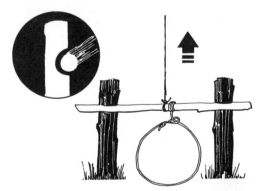

A wide area can be covered by employing several snares on a long horizontal bar. Use where the game trail widens or offers options.

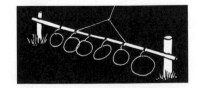

The platform trap

This trap is ideally sited in a small depression on the game trail. Snares are placed on the platforms on either side. When the platform is depressed the trigger bar is released and the game held firmly by the leg. Ideal for larger game — such as deer, bears or large cats. A platform of sticks, stiff bark or other firm materials rests on bottom bar, upper bar fits in notches. A similar mechanism (a) to that of the platform trap, but using a large snare and no platform, is activated by displacement of either toggle or bottom bar to catch small game by the neck.

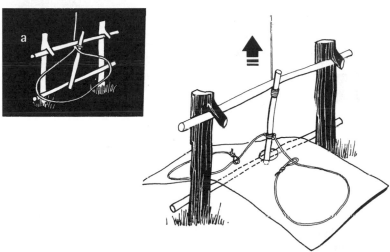

Stepped bait release snare

Two forked sticks hold down a cross-bar which engages with a baited notched upright (attached to a line in tension), which holds it in place and carries the snares. Site this trap in clearings to catch small carnivores and pigs.

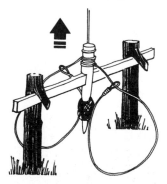

Retaining bar, or at least a section of it, should be squared off to fit a square-cut notch on the bait stick.

Double-ended figure 4 snare

A bait bar is set at right angles across an upright, the faces cut square, and a short trigger lodged between them to maintain their position. The trigger is linked to a springy sapling and the same line carries snares. When the bait bar is dislodged the trigger is released. Four snares will effectively cover both directions on a game trail, or use in clearings to snare small carnivores.

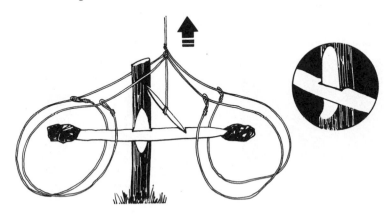

Double spring snare

Two saplings are notched to interlock when bent towards each other over the game trail. A vertical bait bar is lashed near the end of one of them. Two snares can be attached to each sapling, they need to be fairly stiff wire to hold their positions. This is another trap suitable for use in clearings to catch small carnivores. When the bait is taken the game is held in the air between the saplings.

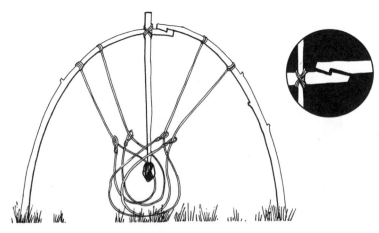

Toggle and bait release snare

A bait bar is wedged between an upright and the lower part of a toggle, the upper part pressing against a retaining bar. The principle is like the platform snare with the bait bar replacing the platform. Movement of the bait bar releases the toggle which flies upward under tension from a sapling above, carrying snare with it.

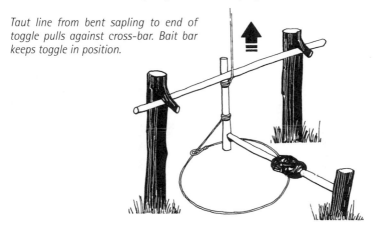

Taut line from bent sapling to end of toggle pulls against cross-bar. Bait bar keeps toggle in position.

DEADFALL TRAPS

These traps all work on the principle that when the bait is taken a weight falls on the prey. All are good for pigs, foxes and badgers. Larger versions can be used for bigger animals such as bears.

WARNING

The large versions of these deadfall traps can be extremely dangerous for humans as well as for the prey for which they are intended. The toggle release and deadfall traps have trip wires and are easily set off accidentally. Even in a survival situation ensure that everyone knows exactly where they are. In survival practise keep people a way from them and never leave such a trap set up at the end of an exercise.

You cannot set a large deadfall trap on your own. Keep the mechanism to the side of the trail, well away from the dropping weight, or setting it will be too risky. Balance is critical — you are unlikely to get it right first time.

Toggle trip-release deadfall trap

This uses the same kind of mechanism as the toggle-release snare — though this time the release bar keeping the toggle in position presses one end of the toggle upwards. A line from the toggle passes over a tree limb to support a bundle of logs or other heavy weight above the trail. From the release bar a trip line (usually a vine) runs above the ground beneath the suspended weight to a firm securing point.

Run the trip line under a forked stick (a) so that it will pull the trigger bar sideways when operated.

Balance log

A forked stick, its ends sharpened to dislodge rapidly and one fork suitably baited, supports one end of a cross-bar, the other end of which rests on a fixed support, held there by the weight of the heavy logs or rock which rest on the bar. When the bait is taken the whole trap collapses.

Angle bait beneath the trap.

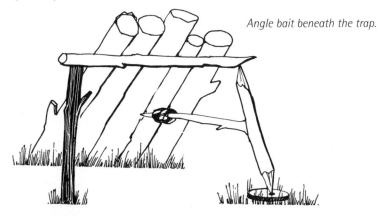

Squared-face release trap

Similar to the balance log trap but using a notched upright as the support, the lower face of the notch squared off. Fit cross-bar against the squared-off lower face of the bar supporting the weight.

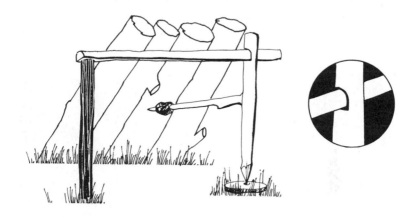

Toggle and bait release deadfall trap

A rock or a group of logs lashed together is supported by a prop which is balanced over a fixed forked stick. The other end of the prop is clear of the ground and held down by a short line attached to a toggle which is wrapped around the upright stick. The toggle is kept in place by a bait stick wedged between it and the dead fall weight. Dislodging the bait stick brings the whole lot down.

The forked stick is driven into the ground first.

199

Deadfall trap

The weight of a log or other weight suspended over the game trail pulls the line carrying it against a retaining bar held by short pegs secured in a tree trunk. The line continues as a tripwire beneath the weight. Make sure that the line is long enough and tripwire anchor weak enough to allow weight to reach the ground. Set the pegs slightly downward, but keep them short so that the bar disengages easily.

Figure 4 deadfall trap

This looks complicated but once learned is easily remembered and very effective. It can be made to any size. A horizontal bait bar is balanced at right-angles to an upright with a locking bar, which supports a weight, positioned over the bait, pivoted on the sharpened tip of the upright.

Bait bar notched on top to engage locking arm, square cut on side to fit upright. Locking arm sharpened at lower end to release quickly, notched at centre to pivot on upright.

SPEAR TRAPS

DEADFALL SPEAR TRAP

This uses the same mechanism as the deadfall trap (left) but uses rocks to add weight and arms the trap with sharpened sticks. It delivers a stabbing as well as a stunning blow.

Spring spear trap

A very dangerous trap which will kill game. Effective against wild pig. A springy shaft, with a spear attached, is held taut above the trail. A slip ring made from bound creeper or smooth material (not rough twine which could catch against toggle) attached to a trip wire acts as a release mechanism.

A toggle (a) and short line (to a fixed upright) hold the spear shaft in tension. A further rod through ring is tensed between the near side of the spear shaft and the far face of the upright, securing all until tripped.

Pig spear trap

Similar to the spring spear trap but operating horizontally, this trap has the unarmed end of the springy shaft secured and lashed between four uprights. At the business end, the toggle (anchored by a short line) retains the springy shaft so long as the toggle point is held against the horizontal bar by a ring. The ring is on the end of a trip wire, anchored to a post on the other side of the trail.

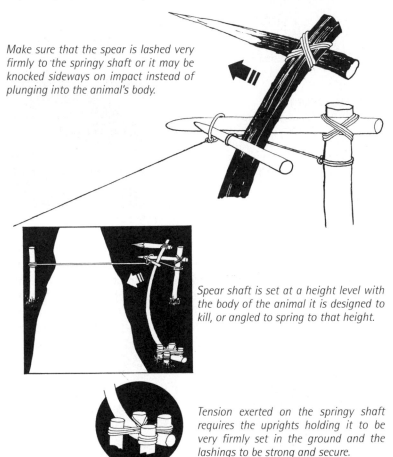

Make sure that the spear is lashed very firmly to the springy shaft or it may be knocked sideways on impact instead of plunging into the animal's body.

Spear shaft is set at a height level with the body of the animal it is designed to kill, or angled to spring to that height.

Tension exerted on the springy shaft requires the uprights holding it to be very firmly set in the ground and the lashings to be strong and secure.

NOTE: Because spear traps are so dangerous, make sure the cord and the knots are strong enough to stand the tension. Never approach these traps except from BEHIND the spear.

Take no risks where these traps are concerned.

Baited spring spear trap

Taking the suspended bait dislodges a retaining ring to release the trigger bar, allowing the spear to fly upwards. The ring holds the upper end of the trigger bar against an upright post, so that it retains the spear shaft. The lower end of the trigger is restrained by a cord. To increase the trap's efficiency use several spear points on the bar.

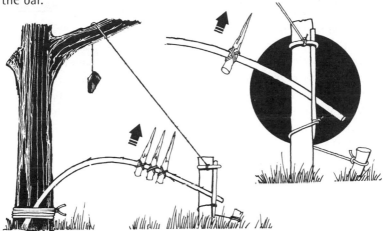

Perch spear trap

This is a good trap for monkeys. It is similar in action to the baited spring spear trap, but uses a perch instead of bait as the trigger mechanism. If the securing ring is around the trunk of a tree rather than a post, make sure that it is on a smooth area and can move easily.

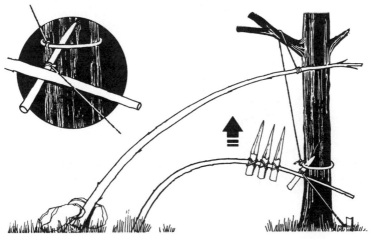

Bow trap

A simple bow made of suitable wood (see *Weapons*) is held taut and angled to shoot slightly upwards by upright posts and a toggle switch with an arrow fitted. The trigger bar is held in place by a toggle

attached to a trip wire, which must be routed round to the point of aim. Keep the first stretch of wire close to the mechanism, for there is no point in it being tripped by an animal approaching from behind the bow. This trap is suitable for large and dangerous animals and can work with animals coming head on to the arrow or approaching from the trip wire side. (The quarry passes across the arrow as it fires.) The arrow may also strike larger animals passing in front of the bow first.

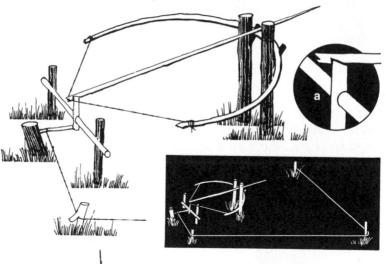

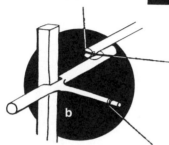

(a) Notch arrow for bowstring and for trigger bar. Angle trigger bar tip to fit arrow notch, cut side to fit cross-bar. Sit toggle between bottom of trigger bar and a fixed post.

(b) An alternative trigger mechanism: Cut a square face on an upright and a square notch on the side of a forked stick to engage it. Notch the upper face of the stick to hold the bowstring. Attach tripwire to other prong of fork.

Baited hole noose

Digging pits disturbs the environment and leaves a permanent mark. This will alarm some animals. In others curiosity may outweigh discretion and they will investigate. Baiting the hole may bring animals sniffing. Foxes, pigs, wild cats and badgers will all dig up rubbish pits and this could attract them. The animal smells the bait and pushes its head down. If it goes past the stakes it will not be able to retract it. If it uses a paw it will become ensnared.

Drive four sharpened pliable stakes through the edges of the pit to emerge below surface where they are less noticeable. Lay a noose across them, attached to a post outside pit.

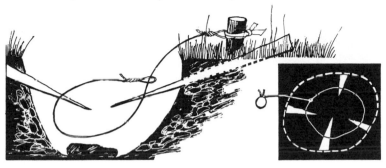

BIRD TRAPS

Nets

A fine net stretched between the trees where birds usually roost is one of the simplest ways of catching them. Instead of a net, fine twine criss-crossed between trees across their flight path will damage birds which fly into it.

Bird lime

Liming is an ancient way of catching small birds. Boil holly leaves and any starchy grain in water and simmer until you have a gooey mess. Spread this on the branches or other perching places before the birds come home to roost and they will get stuck in it when they alight.

Suspended snares

Hang a line of snares across a stream a little above water level. This works best when set among reeds and rushes.

Baited hooks

Fish hooks buried in fruit or other food can be an effective way of catching birds. The hook gets caught in the bird's throat.

Noose sticks

Tie many fine nooses 1.25–2.5cm (1½–1in) in diameter, close together along a stick or branch, use horsehair preferably but any strong material will suffice. Place the stick in a favourite roosting or nesting spot with the nooses uppermost. Birds become entangled when they alight. Do not remove as soon as one bird is caught. It will attract other birds and you will soon have several.

Figure 4 trap

This mechanism (see *Figure 4 deadfall*) can be used with a 'log cabin' type cage, made from a pyramid of sticks tied together, which is balanced over the bait. For small birds you can use a quick method of making the cage: lay all the sticks in position then lay another two sticks, the same length as the bottom ones, on top and tie them tightly to the bottom layer, tight enough to keep all the others in place. Larger animals will soon break out of this and for them each stick must be individually tied in.

Experiment with different ways of making a cage. You may have a suitable box or large tin which would do just as well. It is also possible to prop the raised edge of the cage on a single stick tied to a long line. Take the other end of the line and hide some distance away. If you hold the string taut, you can snatch the prop away as soon as a bird ventures under the cage. Broadcast bait around and under the cage. This works best in areas where birds seem plentiful.

Toggle release net trap

A net laid on the ground and baited to attract birds has lines from the corners to a springy sapling overhead. A tension line extends to a toggle mechanism (see previous traps) notched on to a horizontal bar and operated by a flat bait stick. Set the bait stick off the ground and only just resting against the lower end of the toggle. This trigger mechanism needs to be extremely sensitive if a small bird's weight is to set it off.

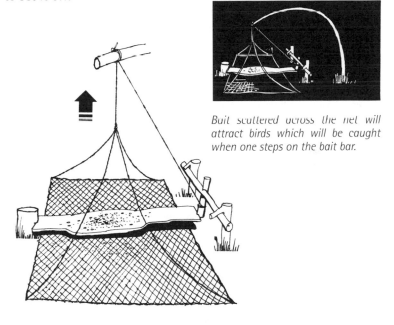

Bait scattered across the net will attract birds which will be caught when one steps on the bait bar.

NOTE: If you set traps in a training exercise make sure that they are clearly marked so that they are not set off by other people. Spear and deadfall traps should be supervised to keep people away for they could inflict serious injury or kill. ALL traps should be dismantled when the exercise is over.

HUNTING

Keen observation of all signs of wildlife and a knowledge of the kind of animals you are hunting are as necessary to the hunter as skillful tracking and accurate marksmanship. They make it easier to be in the right place and to take advantage of the terrain.

Always proceed as quietly as possible. Move slowly and stop regularly. Carry your weight on the rear foot so that you can test the next step with the toes before transferring your weight. Thus you will avoid stumbles and help to reduce the amount of noise you produce from undergrowth and snapping sticks. Fast or sudden movements will startle the game. Sniff the air and listen. Hunt against the wind, or at least across it.

The ideal time to hunt is at first light, when more game is likely to be about. Animals are also about in the evening, but the light will be getting rapidly worse so you need to be sure of the terrain and know your way back to camp. In territory you know well this will not be a problem, particularly if there is a clear sky and moon or starlight to see by.

If hunting in the evening go out at least an hour before dusk so that your eyes will get used to the failing light and you will develop night vision – though your prey will probably be able to see better than you do.

When hunting during the day, try to hunt moving uphill in the morning and return to camp in the afternoon. Signs of animals will be easier to read as you move uphill for those on the ground will be closer to eye-level. Thermal currents build up with the heat of the day and carry scents upwards – so by returning downhill the scent off game comes up to you before your smell reaches it. After a day out hunting and foraging the descent will take less energy than an upward climb and by then you'll welcome the easier going.

INFO.

If you are moving correctly, game often will not see you. If an animal catches a glimpse of you, freeze. You may be the first human it has seen. It will be more curious than frightened. Keep absolutely still until the animal looks away or continues feeding. Avoid large animals, such as bears, unless really desperate or confident of a first shot kill – or you could end up becoming the hunted not the hunter.

Get as close as you can without revealing your presence and take up a steady position, aiming for the area giving the greatest margin of error. An accurate head shot is very effective but risky unless you are very close and the animal still. A point just to the back of the front shoulder is a good target. A firm, accurate strike here will drop most animals instantly. A badly aimed shot may mean unnecessary agony for the animal and a long follow up for the hunter.

If an animal drops first shot, wait five minutes before approaching. Just stand back and observe. If not dead but bleeding, the loss of blood will weaken it and, when you do approach, it will not be able to bolt. If an animal is wounded and moves away wait 15 minutes before following up. If you follow immediately the animal may travel all day.

WEAPONS

Bow and arrow

Most effective of improvised weapons, the bow and arrow is easy to make. It takes only a short time to become proficient in its use.

For the bow a well-seasoned wood is best but you will have to make do without. If you expect to have to stay where you are for many months you could put wood aside to season for future use. The tension in unseasoned wood is short-lived so make several bows and change over to another weapon when the one you are using loses its spring.

Yew is the ideal wood — all the old English longbows were made of yew. There are five kinds of yew distributed across the northern hemisphere but it is not very common and hickory, juniper, oak, white elm, cedar, ironwood, birch, willow and hemlock are all good alternatives.

Making the stave

For your bowstave select a supple wand. It should be about 120cm (4ft) long, but match its size to the individual.

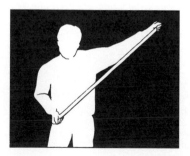

To determine the correct stave length for you:
Hold one end of the stave at the hip with the right hand, reach out sideways with the left hand and mark the extent of your reach as the length of the bow.
This will give you a standard type bow (the longbow requires much more skill in use).

Shaping the bow

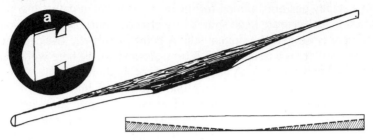

Fashion the stave so that it is 5cm (2in) wide at the centre, tapering to 1.5cm (^{5}/8in) at the ends. Notch the ends (a) to take the bowstring about 1.25cm (^{1}/2in) from the ends. Remove the bark if you choose. When the bow has been whittled into shape rub it all over with oil or animal fat.

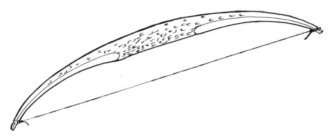

Fitting the string

A rawhide string is best, cut to a width of 3mm (^{1}/8in), but any string, cord or thin rope will suffice. The stems of old nettles provide tough fibres and these can be twisted together to make a satisfactory bowstring. If the bow has a lot of give a shorter string is likely to be needed, but when strung the string should only be under slight tension — the main tension is added when you pull it back to shoot.

Secure the string to the bow with a round turn and two half hitches at each end. If the wood is unseasoned release one end of the string whenever the bow is not in use to relax the tension or you may find the stave sets in shape.

A properly made bow will be more efficient and more accurate than just bending a pliable wand — but once it loses its spring don't waste time with it. Make another.

Making arrows

Any straight wood will do for arrows, but birch is one of the best. Make arrows about 60cm (2ft) long, and about 6mm (¼in) wide. Keep them straight (a piece of string tied between two points will give you a straight edge to check them against) and as smooth as possible. At one end make a notch 6mm (¼in) deep to fit the bow string.

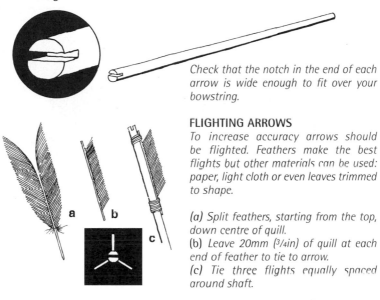

Check that the notch in the end of each arrow is wide enough to fit over your bowstring.

FLIGHTING ARROWS

To increase accuracy arrows should be flighted. Feathers make the best flights but other materials can be used: paper, light cloth or even leaves trimmed to shape.

(a) Split feathers, starting from the top, down centre of quill.
(b) Leave 20mm (¾in) of quill at each end of feather to tie to arrow.
(c) Tie three flights equally spaced around shaft.

Arrow heads

At the business end of the arrow a sharp point is needed. The arrow itself can be sharpened and hardened in fire but a firm tip is better. Tin is excellent or flint can be fashioned into a really sharp arrowhead. With patience even bone can be made into a good tip. Split the end of the shaft, insert the arrow head and bind it tightly. Sinews are good for binding — apply wet, they dry hard securing the head firmly.

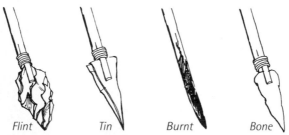

Flint   Tin   Burnt   Bone

WEAPONS FROM FLINT

Arrow and spearheads, axes and knives can all be made by knapping flint, which is a black stone with a dull metallic gleam, often found in association with chalk. Choose a flattish piece of approximately the right shape and size. With another hard stone flake off pieces until it is the shape you want. Chip away at the edges to produce a very sharp cutting edge (see *Tools* in *Camp Craft*).

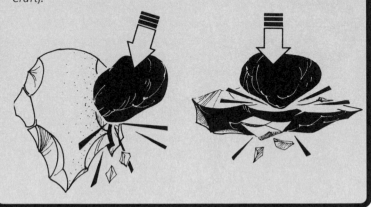

Archery technique

Fit an arrow into the bowstring and raise the centre of the bow to eyelevel. Hold the bow just below the arrow, extending the arm forwards. Keep the bow arm locked and draw the string smoothly back across the front of your body, with the arrow at eye level, and lined up with the target, sighting along the arrow. Release the string — just let go, do not snatch at it as you do so.

Now practise! For rapid fire carry a number of arrows in your bow hand.

ARROW BURNS

Many archers find that the rubbing of the arrow flights against the hand and the cheek can cause friction burns. A scarf or a piece of cloth pulled tight to the face will protect the cheek without interfering with the shot and either a leather mitten worn, or a leather guard fitted between the fingers and the wrist, to protect the hand.

Sling and shot

The simple sling was the weapon with which David slew the giant Goliath and can be armed with ordinary pebbles. It consists of a simple pouch in the middle of a length of rope. Leather is the best material for the pouch but you could make it from any strong fabric and the rope can be a leather thong or twisted from natural fibres. Attach it as one long piece threaded through, or two tied or sewn on.

SLINGSHOT TECHNIQUE

Select smooth pebbles about 2cm (³/₄in) across and as round as possible (jagged pebbles might do more damage but they will not follow such a smooth trajectory).

Swing the sling above the head in a circle lined up on your target. Release one end of the rope and the ammunition should fly with great velocity and, with practise, accurately on target. You will probably need to experiment with sling length to achieve accuracy and distance.

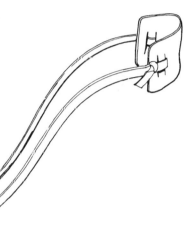

When using either the sling or the catapult against birds, load several pebbles at once.

Catapult

The schoolboy's weapon — but the Romans used giant mechanical ones as siege weaponry. You need a strong forked twig, preferably with some pliability — a hazel prong is excellent — and a piece of elastic material. A piece of innertube from a car or bicycle tyre is ideal (and stronger than the elastic in your clothing, although that could be used).

Make a pouch for the centre of the elastic and thread or sew it into position as for the sling, tie the ends to each side of your twig and use a stone as your missile..

Bola

A weapon that Eskimos use against birds. Stones are wrapped in circles of material and 90cm (3ft) lengths of string knotted around each, the other ends of the string being firmly tied together. Held at the joined end, they are twirled around the head. When released they fly through the air covering a wide area.

The Gauchos of South America use the same weapon and variations have been used in combat.

The bola wraps around a bird in flight or tangles around an animal's legs or neck, bringing it to the ground and giving the hunter a chance to kill it.

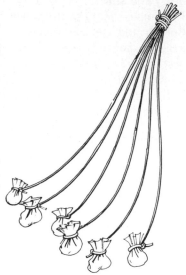

Spears

A staff is a good aid to walking and by sharpening one end can be turned into a useful thrusting or throwing weapon. A straight staff about 1.80m (6ft) is ideal for a jabbing spear. About 90cm (3ft) makes a more manageable throwing spear. A thrower can be made from a piece of wood about half that length — it gives greater accuracy and distance.

To make a spear more effective add a point of flint, knapped to sharpness, or a flattened cone of tin, set into the end — or securely bind on a knife. However, if you only have one knife do not risk it, it could too easily be lost or damaged.

SPEAR THROWER
Spear sits in a groove which runs along most, but not all, of the upper face of the thrower. The end stop adds thrust to the spear.

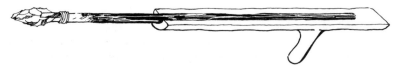

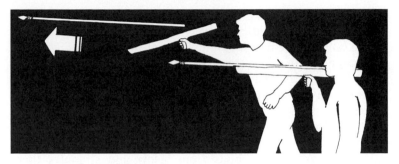

To make the thrower choose a tree limb that is at least twice the width of your spear and with a branch stump which can become the forward sloping handle. Split down the centre using a knife as a wedge. Gouge out a smooth channel for the spear. Make sure it is cleanly cut, leaving a solid portion as a buffer. Experiment to match the thrower length to that of the spear and to suit your own balance.

Held at shoulder level, aim the spear at the target, bringing the holder sharply forwards and then downwards. As you move downwards the butt of the groove adds to the thrust behind the spear.

HUNTING BIRDS

Running noose
A noose attached to a long pole is an effective way of pulling roosting birds down from lower branches. Make a note of roosting and nest sites — remember that droppings will help guide you to them — and if they are within reach return stealthily on nights when there is sufficient light to see them. Slip the noose over the bird and pull, tightening the noose and pulling the bird down at the same time.

Stalking waterfowl
You can get up close by getting in the water and camouflaging yourself around the head with reeds and other vegetation. Very

cautiously, approach an area where fowl nest or are regularly seen. But remember that birds (especially large ones such as geese and swans) can be quite ferocious in defence of themselves.

Another technique in some parts of the world is to use a large gourd worn on the head as cover. Holes are made on one side to breathe and see through and with the gourd just sufficiently above the water the hunter floats with the current among the birds. To prepare the birds several other gourds are thrown into the water first. Having got among the wildfowl the hunter grabs the unsuspecting birds from below and strangles them underwater.

Pit trap

Find or dig a hole about 90cm (3ft) deep in an area where ground-feeding birds are common. Its width depends upon the kind of birds you are after. Spread grain or other bait around the hole, and more concentratedly inside it.

First taking the bait around the hole, birds will enter it to get more. Rush them. In their panic they are unable to spread their wings sufficiently to take off from inside the hole.

SEAGULLS

Seagulls can be caught by wrapping food around a stone and throwing it in the air. The gull swallows the bait while still on the wing, gulping down the stone with it, and the change in weight causes the bird to crash. Obviously this is a technique for use over land rather than at sea. Be ready to dispatch the bird as soon as it hits the ground.

ANIMAL DANGERS

Few animals are likely to attack the survivor unless in self-defence, most will be much more concerned to get out of the way. There is little chance of encountering large animals such as elephants, rhinos and hippopotamus, or the larger big cats, outside wildlife reserves. Nevertheless avoid making camp on a trail, or close to an animal watering place, where you could find you are in the path of a herd of elephants or confronted by a curious cougar.

WARNING

DON'T PROVOKE AN ENCOUNTER. Bears frequently scavenge from homesteads in the northern forests, turning over garbage cans, and are just as likely to come round your camp for easy pickings. Use noise to drive them off — don't try to catch them. Don't get close to them. A bear can easily kill a man and a wounded bear is particularly dangerous. All injured or cornered animals are likely to be dangerous. Most animals will try to escape. If you prevent them from doing so, you are forcing them to fight.

Crocodiles and alligators should be given a wide berth unless very small — and then beware that there is not a larger crocodile behind you! Any of the large-horned animals is likely to be able to wound you with its horns before you can reach it with a weapon. Stags are particularly belligerent in the rutting season. It is not just hooved animals that can deliver a powerful blow with their feet — ostriches can kill with a kick.

Wolves are much more often heard than seen. Tales of large marauding packs are probably wild exaggerations. A wolf may get curious and look at you from a distance, but you can take with a pinch of salt the idea of hunters being chased by packs of ferocious wolves. If you are badly injured and unable to defend yourself, wolves might finish you off. Hyenas also hunt in packs. Although basically cowardly, they are very powerful and, as scavengers, are attracted to camp sites. They will probably turn tail and run, but drive them off rather than try to tackle them.

The larger apes can easily kill a man — but they are rarely aggressive animals and will usually give you plenty of warning to back off. Small monkeys are much more often encountered and more immediately dangerous — they have sharp teeth. Mature chimpanzees, in particular, can be very bad-tempered. Thoroughly cleanse any animal bite. All could cause tetanus and some mammals, including vampire bats, can carry rabies.

Snakes will not be a threat, unless you accidentally come into contact with them. You just have to get used to them and to checking clothing, bedding and equipment for any reptile or insect visitors. Occasionally a snake or a centipede may slide into bed with you, attracted by your warmth. Cases have been known of people waking to find an unwelcome visitor nestling in an armpit or even more intimate places. Try to remember that they are not attacking. Move gently and calmly to free yourself from them.

HANDLING THE KILL

Wounded and trapped animals can be dangerous. Before approaching closely check whether an animal is dead.

Use a spear or tie your knife to a long stick and stab a largish animal in its main muscles and neck. Loss of blood will weaken it, enabling you to move closer and club it on the head.

If you have a companion, it is easier to carry a large animal by tying it firmly to a bough, which can be carried on your shoulders, but you should not take it all the way into camp, where it would attract flies and scavenging animals.

Even large animals can be dragged to a more convenient location if turned upon their backs. If the animal has horns cut off its head or they will make this difficult.

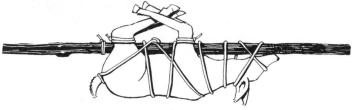

Place the pole along the belly and use a clove hitch around each pair of legs. Lash the animal to the pole and finish with a clove hitch around the pole. If the animal has horns, tie these up out of the way.

It is preferable to butcher all game on the trap line. It will attract predators and carrion eaters that in turn may become trapped. Use the entrails to rebait traps. Only carry back to camp what you can manage without exertion. In cool climates cache the rest for collection later.

HIDING THE KILL

Suspend a carcase from a bough, too high for scavengers on the ground and out of reach from the branch. A cache in the crook of a tree will keep meat away from ground predators but will still be accessible to felines and other climbing predators.

In territories with vultures and other large carrion eaters it will be almost impossible to protect it, so carry what you can. What you leave behind is unlikely to keep in a hot climate.

Blood is a valuable food, containing vital minerals. Carry a vessel for taking it back to camp. Keep it covered, cool and out of the way of flies.

WARNING

Health Hazards — diseased animals

There are lymph glands in the cheeks of all animals (more noticeable on large ones). If large and discoloured they are a sign of illness. Any animal that is distorted or discoloured about the head (such as a rabbit with the symptoms of myxomatosis) should be boiled there is then little risk of infection from eating it — but care should be taken in preparation when there is a risk. It is essential that any cut or sore in your skin be covered when slaughtering or handling meat, for if an animal carries disease a break in the skin provides easy entry to your body.

PREPARING THE KILL

No part of a carcass should be wasted. Careful preparation will give you the maximum food value and make full use of the parts you cannot eat. Set about it in four stages:

- **Bleeding**, which is essential if the meat is to keep, and without which the taste is very strong.
- **Skinning**, so that the hide or fur can be used for shelter and clothing. (Pigs are not skinned because they have a useful layer of fat under the skin. Birds are plucked but not usually skinned.)
- **Gutting**, to remove the gut and recover offal.
- **Jointing**, to produce suitable cuts for cooking by different methods.

Bleeding
Do not waste blood. It is rich in vitamins and minerals, including salt, that could otherwise be missing from the survivor's diet. Cattle blood is an important part of the diet of many African herdsmen. Cannibals who drank their enemies' blood found vision and general health improved, and giddy spells, induced by vitamin deficiency, cured: the blood provided the missing vitamins and minerals.

Any animal will bleed better if hung with the head down. Tie ropes around the hock (NOT the ankle — it will slip off) and hoist it up a branch or build a frame, placing a receptacle beneath to catch the blood.

For a frame you need a strong structure. Drive the posts into the ground and lash them firmly where they cross to make A-frames and, then rest the horizontal bar on top.

Bleed the animal by cutting the jugular vein or carotid artery in its neck. When the animal is hanging these will bulge more clearly and should be easy to see. The cut can be made either behind the ears, stabbing in line with the ears to pierce the vein on both sides of the head at the same time, or lower down in the V of the neck, before the artery branches. Unless you have a stiletto type knife the latter is best. An alternative is to cut the throat from ear to ear. This has the disadvantage of cutting through the windpipe and food from the stomach may come up and contaminate the blood which you are trying to save, but if your knife does not have a sharp point it may be necessary.

It is particularly important to very thoroughly bleed pigs. If blood remains in their tissues, which have high moisture and fat content, it will speed deterioration of the flesh.

Skinning

It is easier to skin any animal when the flesh is still warm, as soon as it has been bled. First remove any scent glands which might taint the meat. Some deer have them on their rear legs, just behind the knee. Felines and canines have a gland on either side of the anus. It is wise to remove the testicles of male animals, as they can also taint meat. Before attempting to remove hide, cut firmly through the skin, as shown by the broken line in the main illustration:

1 Make a ring cut around the rear legs just above the knee. Take care not to cut the securing rope.
2 Cut around the forelegs in the same place.
3 Cut down the inside of the rear legs to the crotch, carefully cutting a circle around the genitals.
4 Extend the cut down the centre of the body to the neck. Do not cut into the stomach and digestive organs: lift skin and insert two fingers beneath, set knife between them, sharp edge outward and draw it slowly down, cutting away from the body. (See detail illustration.)
5 Cut down the inside of the forelegs.

Cutting in this way, you avoid cutting prematurely into the gut cavity. The fingers lift the skin as you go and the knife, sharp edge outwards, slips in and cuts along. Do not hurry. Do not cut yourself. Do not damage the skin. Taking care will pay dividends later when you want to use the skin.

Now ease the skin of the rear legs from the flesh. Use the knife as little as possible. Roll the skin outwards, the fur inside itself, and pull it down.

Having cleared the back legs, cut around the tail (you have already cut around the genital area). As soon as you can get your hand right down the back of the carcass use your fingers to separate flesh from skin. Now peel the skin from the front legs. You will have a single piece of hide. As you work your thumbs down the neck they become bloody at the point where the throat was cut. A strong twist of the head will separate it. Cut through remaining tissues.

Working on your own

Lifting a large animal takes considerable effort. If on your own you may have to skin and gut the animal on the ground. To prevent the carcass from rolling, cut off the feet of hooved animals and place them under it.

Lay the carcass down a natural slope, scoop an impression in the ground in which to place a collecting tin or other vessel so that the animal bleeds into it. Follow the same pattern of incisions in the hide then skin the animal from one side to the backbone, spread out the hide and then roll the animal onto it to finish skinning the other half — this helps keep the meat from rubbing on the ground.

Skinning small animals

Rabbits and smaller animals can be skinned by making a small incision over the stomach (be careful not to cut into the organs). Insert the thumbs and pull outwards — the skin comes away easily. Free the legs and twist the head off.

If you have no knife available to make the first incision snap off the lower part of a leg and use the sharp edge of the break to cut the skin.

Gutting

With the carcass still suspended remove the gut and recover the offal. Pinch the abdomen as high as possible and in the pouch of flesh you have raised make a slit big enough to take two fingers. Do not stab into the flesh or you may cut through to internal organs. Insert the fingers and use them as a guide for the knife to cut upwards towards the anus. Now cut downwards in the same way, using the hand to hold back the gut, which will begin to spill outwards (see illustration). Cut down as far as the breastbone.

The initial incision, made in the pinched-up flesh, need only accommodate two fingers. Cut in the same way as skinning (previous illustration). First up, then down (the back of the hand prevents the gut from spilling).

Let the gut spill out, allow it to hang down so that you can inspect it. Remove the two kidneys and the liver.

The chest cavity is covered with a membrane and easily missed in small game. Cut through the membrane and remove heart, lungs and windpipe.

Ensure that the anus is clear — you should be able to see daylight through it (push a hand through with large animals). The carcass is now clean.

Jointing meat

Large animals can be quartered by first splitting down the backbone and then cutting each side between the tenth and eleventh rib. The hindquarters will contain the steaks (rump and fillet) and the choicer cuts, the forequarter meat is more stringy and needs slow cooking to make it tender.

The cuts into which a carcass is divided will differ according to the kind of animal and the cook's preference.

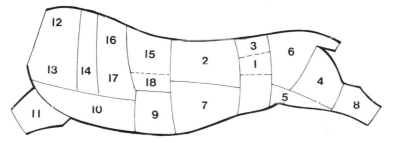

1 **Fillet** or **undercut** *The most tender meat — only 1 per cent is fillet. Ideal for preserving.*

2 **Sirloin** *Next most tender. Fat free strips can be cut for preserving.*

3 **Rump** *Ideal for frying, little cooking needed. Can also be dried in strips.*

4 **Topside** *Muscle from the top of the leg. Cook slowly, it tends to be tough. Cut into cubes for boiling.*

5 **Top rump** *Muscle from front of thigh. As for topside.*

6 **Silverside** *Muscle on outside of thighs. Good for roasting.*

7 **Hind flank** *Belly, ideal for stews and casseroles.*

8 **Leg** *Tough and sinewy, cut into cubes and stew.*

9 **Flank** *Muscular extension of the belly. Ideal for stews. Usually tough so needs long simmering to make tender.*

10 **Brisket** *Same as Flank.*

11 **Shin** *Foreleg, best cubed for stews.*

12 **Neck**

13 **Clod** *Ideal for stews. Contains less tissue than leg. Cook slowly.*

14 **Chuck and blade** *Quite tender but usually cut up as stewing steak.*

15–18 **Ribs** *Ideal for roasting but cook slowly.*

Hanging

Offal should be eaten as soon as possible but the rest of the meat is better hung. In moderate temperatures leave the carcass hanging for 2–3 days. In hot climates it is better to preserve it or cook it straight away.

When the animal is killed, acids released into the muscles help to break down their fibre, making the meat more tender. The longer it is left the more tender it will be and easier to cut, with more flavour too, and harmful parasitic bacteria in the meat will die. You must keep flies off the flesh: if they lay eggs on meat it will quickly spoil.

OFFAL

Liver

Liver is best eaten as soon as possible. Remove the bile bladder in the centre. It is quite strong and can usually be pulled off without difficulty — but be careful, the bile will taint flesh with which it comes in contact. If any animal has any diseases they will show up in the liver. Avoid any liver that is mottled or covered in white spots. If only some is affected, cut it off and eat the remainder.

Liver is a complete food, containing all essential vitamins and minerals. If eaten raw no food value is lost. It requires little cooking.

Stomach (Tripe)

Stomach (tripe) takes little digesting, so is a good food for the sick or injured. Remove the stomach contents (which make ideal 'invalid' food) wash the tripe and simmer slowly with herbs. The contents may sound unpalatable but could save an injured person's life, for the animal has done most of the hard work of breaking the food down. Lightly boiled, stomach contents are nourishing and easily digestible.

In some countries pigs are fed nothing but apples prior to slaughter. They are cooked with the stomach still in. The subtle flavour of apple impregnates the meat. The stomach is removed after cooking and the contents used as sauce.

Kidneys

Kidneys are a valuable source of nourishment and ideal flavouring for stews. Boil them with herbs. The white fat surrounding them (suet) is a rich food source. Render it down to use in the preparation of pemmican.

Melts

Melts are the spleen, a large organ in the bigger animals. It has limited food value and is not worth bothering about in small game such as rabbits. It is best roasted.

Lites

Lites are the lungs of the animal, perfectly good to eat but not of great food value. Any respiratory complaints will show up in the lungs. Do not eat any mottled with black and white spots. Healthy lungs are pink and blemish free and best boiled. They could be set aside for fish or trap bait.

Heart

Heart is a tightly packed muscle with little or no fat. Roast it or use its distinctive flavour to liven up stew.

Intestines

Intestine consist of lengths of tubes and are best used as sausage skins. Turn them inside out and wash them. Then boil them thoroughly. Mix fat and meat in equal proportions and then stir in blood. Stuff the mixture into the skin and boil them well. Before putting them into boiling water add a little cold to take it just off the boil — this will counter any risk of the skins bursting. This makes a highly nutritious food which, if smoked, will keep for a long time. Dried intestines can be used for light lashings.

Sweetbreads

Sweetbreads are the pancreas or thymus gland, distinctive in larger game. Many people consider it a great delicacy and it is delicious boiled or roasted.

Tail

Skin and boil to make an excellent soup for it is full of meat and gelatine.

Feet

Feet are chopped off during slaughter but should not be wasted, boil them up to make a good stew. Clean dirt from hooves or paws and remove all traces of fur. Hooves are a source of nutritious aspic jelly.

Head

On larger animals there is a good deal of meat on the head. The cheeks make a very tasty dish. The tongue is highly nutritious. Boil it to make it tender and skin before eating.

225

All that is left, or the whole head with small animals, should be boiled.

Brain
The brain will make brawn and will also provide a useful solution for curing hides.

Bones
All bones should be boiled for soup. They are rich in bone marrow, with valuable vitamins. They can also be made into tools.

PREPARING SHEEP-LIKE ANIMALS

Follow the instructions for larger animals and then:

1 Split in two down the line of the spine, keeping exactly to the centre of the backbone.

2 Remove rear leg. Try to cut through the ball and socket joint.

3 Remove front leg. There is no bone to cut through, follow the line of the shoulder blade.

4 Cut off neck.

5 Cut off skirt (loose flesh hanging below the ribs).

6 Cut between each rib and between the vertebrae. This gives you chops.

7 The fillet, lying in the small of the back, is the best meat for preserving.

Preparing Pig
Do not attempt to skin a pig. Gut it first then place it over the hot embers of a fire and scrape the hair off. Hot water – just hotter than your hand can bear – will help to loosen the hair. Water that is too hot will make the hair more difficult to remove. Pigs attract many parasites: ticks, crab lice and worms so cooking

must make sure of killing them. Boiling is therefore the best way of cooking pork.

Preparing small animals

Follow the same basic procedure as for larger animals — they all need to be gutted.

Preparing reptiles

Discard internal organs, which may carry salmonella. Reptiles can be cooked in their skins. Large snakes can be chopped into steaks and provide useful skins. To prepare a snake cut off head well down, behind poison sacs; open vent to neck, keeping blade outwards, to avoid piercing innards, which will fall clear. Skewer to suspend and ease of skin towards tail.

Preparing birds

Birds are prepared in much the same way as animals — though they are usually plucked and cooked with the skin on instead of being skinned. Follow the sequence below.

Bleeding:
Kill birds by stretching their necks, then cut the throat and hang head down to bleed. Or kill by cutting just under the tongue, severing main nerve and main artery. The bird dies easily and bleeds well. Handle carrion eaters as little as possible — they are more prone to infection, lice and ticks.

Plucking:
Plucking is easiest straight after killing while the bird is still warm. Hot water can be used to loosen feathers, except in the case of waterbirds and seabirds, in which it tends to tighten them. Keep feathers for arrow flights and insulation. Start at the chest. For speed you can skin a bird — but that wastes the food value of the skin.

Drawing (removing innards):
Make an incision from the vent to the tail. Put your hand in and draw out all the innards. Retain the heart and kidneys. Cut off the head and feet.

Cooking:
Always boil carrion eaters in case they carry any disease. Boiling will make stringy old birds tender but you can roast younger ones on a spit or in an oven.

FISH AND FISHING

Fish are a valuable food source, containing protein, vitamins and fats. All freshwater fish are edible but some tropical ones can be dangerous: keep clear of electric eels, freshwater stingrays and the piranha of South American rivers. It takes skill to catch fish by conventional angling methods but, by considering their feeding habits and following the simple methods given here, you can be successful.

Fish range from tiny tiddlers to some of prodigious size — such as the Nile perch of the tropics. They differ widely in their eating habits and diet. Different kinds feed at different times and at different levels in the water. Some prey on other fish, others eat worms and insects, but they can all be attracted and hooked with appropriate bait.

If you are an experienced angler you can apply your skills, especially if you have plenty of time on your hands, and will probably gain a lot of pleasure, but if you are fishing for survival the sporting angler's techniques are not the most effective. Two of the most useful methods are the night line and the gill net.

Where to fish
Fish choose the places in the water where they are most comfortable and where they most easily find their prey. This will be affected by the temperature of the day.

If it is hot and the water is low, fish in shaded water and where there are deep pools. In a lake fish retreat to the coolness of deep water in hot weather.

In cold weather choose a shallow place where the sun warms the water. Lake fish will tend to keep to the edges which are warmer.

If the river is in flood, fish where the water is slack — on the outside of a bend — for example, or in a small tributary feeding the mainstream if its flow is different — quite possible for the flood may not be due to local rainfall.

Fish like to shelter under banks and below rocks and submerged logs.

When to fish
As a general rule leave lines out overnight and check them just before first light. Some fish feed at night during a full moon.

If a storm is imminent fish before it breaks. Fishing is poor in a river after heavy rain.

228

Indications of fish feeding

Signs that fish are feeding, and therefore likely to take a bait, are when they jump out of the water, or you see frequent clear ring ripples breaking out where fish are taking flies on the surface. Where lots of little fish are darting about they may well be being pursued by a larger predatory fish.

IMAGE REFRACTION
Water refracts light so that the fish sees things above the water at a slightly different angle – and can probably see more on the bank than you think. It is always better to fish from a sitting or kneeling position than standing up so that you are less likely to be in vision. Keep back from the edge. Always try to keep your shadow off the water you are fishing.

ANGLING

Fishing with a hook and line is the popular way of fishing (though others are usually more effective) and they are part of your survival kit. Hooks can also be improvised from wire, pins, bones, wood and even thorns.

Large hooks will catch large fish but small ones will catch both large and small. Near the end of the line you will probably need to attach another short length with a weight to take the hook down and stop the line being carried along the surface of the water, especially if fishing deep. If it is a long line you also need another length with a float which will be pulled down when you get a bite. A rod is not essential (you can fish effectively with a handline) but makes it easier to land fish and to cast away from the bank.

You can improvise hooks from all kinds of materials. Here (from left to right) a pin, a thorn, a bunch of thorns, nails, bone and wood have been used.

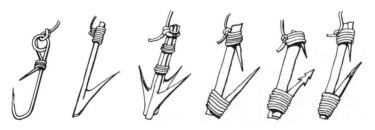

Using floats and weights

Along the line attach a small floating object, easily visible from the bank, and you will be able to see when you have a bite. Its position will help control where the line descends.

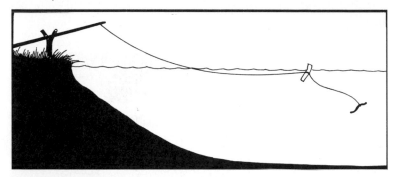

Small weights between the float and the hook will stop the line from trailing along the water or at too near the surface in a current, still leaving the hook itself in movement. You have small split lead shot in your survival kit. Slip the groove along the line and squeeze in to fit closely.

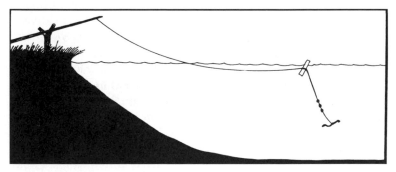

A deeper hook position can be ensured by extending the line to a weight below the hook.

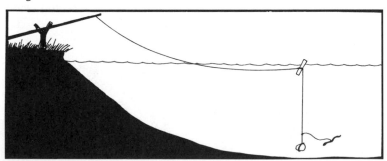

ANGLING WITHOUT HOOKS

You do not even have to use a hook to fish with a line. To catch eels and catfish tie a blob of worms on a line (a). These fish swallow without biting so swallow the bait with line attached. Pull them out as soon as the bait is taken.

Instead of a hook use a small sharp piece of wood tied on the end of the line and held flat along it by the bait (b). When the bait is swallowed the wood will open out and lodge across the gullet of the fish (c).

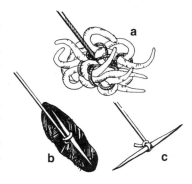

Bait

Bait native to the fishes' own water is most likely to be taken: berries that overhang it, insects that breed in and near it. Scavenger fish will take pieces of meat, raw fish, ants and other insects. Once you have a catch examine the stomach contents of the fish and eliminate the guesswork as to diet. If one bait is unsuccessful, change to another.

Ground bait

Bait scattered in the area you want to fish, will attract fish to it. A termites' or ants' nest suspended over a river is one excellent method. As the insects fall into the river the fish will take them. Bait your hook with them as well and success is sure. Any suitable bait, scattered on the water, can be used to draw fish but it is always best to put the same bait on your hook.

SPINNING

Curious fish will attack a shiny object drawn through the water: try coins, buttons, pieces of tin can, buckles — anything that glitters. Make a propeller shape to thread onto a piece of wire and it will spin with the current. Attach a hook to the end of the spindle.

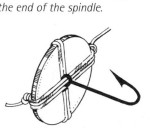

ARTIFICIAL BAIT

Can be made from brightly coloured cloth, feathers and shiny metal. Try to make them look like real bait. A few feathers tied to a hook with thread can simulate a fly, or carve a small fish out of wood and decorate it with colour or glitter (if you make it jointed it will move more naturally). Try to make lures move in the water like live bait. Hazel wood has a soft pith and can easily be threaded through so that you can link segments which will wiggle in the water.

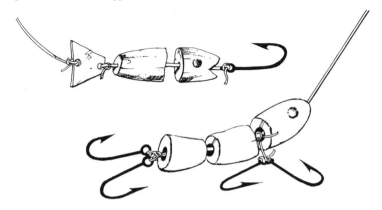

LIVE BAIT

Worms, maggots, insects and small fish can be used as live bait. Cover the hook completely with the bait. You can place the hook through the meaty part of small fish without killing them, or through the body of a grasshopper. Their distressed movement in the water will attract the fish. Tiddlers are easy to catch so you can 'use a sprat to catch a mackerel'.

NIGHT LINES

Weight one end of a length of line and attach hooks at intervals along it. Bait them with worms. Lowered into the water this gives you the chance of catching surface-, mid- and bottom-feeders. Anchor the free end securely on the bank.

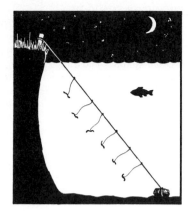

You can put this out at night and leave it until the morning — use it in daytime too — but change the worms at intervals, even if you haven't got a catch, because fresh wriggling worms will attract more attention.

OTTER BOARD

To fish far from the bank, further than you can cast a line — in a lake, for instance, where fish are feeding in the centre — make a board with a moveable, pivoted rudder. Set a bar at the front end of the rudder to which two control lines can be attached. Beneath it suspend baited hooks. Float the board out into the lake.

If winds are favourable you could mount a sail, but then a stabilizing keel will also be needed to stop it blowing over. Gouge holes to fix dowel supports (in water the dowels will expand to make a tight fit) and tie on a flat stone — a big keel might conflict with the rudder.

Undue movement of the board will indicate a bite.

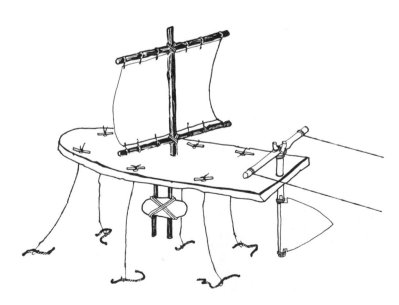

233

JIGGING OR SNAGGING

This is the art of hooking a fish anywhere on its body. It is a good method to use when you can see fish but they are not taking bait. Tie a number of hooks on to a pole and lower it into the water. Suspend a bright object about 20cm (8in) above the pole, and when fish go to inspect the glitter pull the hooks up sharply so that they catch on the fish.

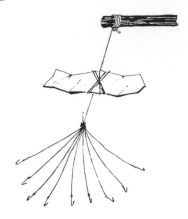

FISH TRAPS

You can make a wide variety of traps, from ones across an entire stream, which you can drive fish into, to bottle traps to capture tiddlers in. Arrows indicate current.

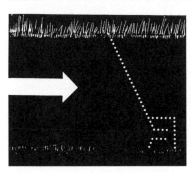
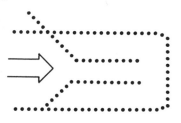

In shallow streams build a channel of sticks or rocks that fish can swim into but not turn around in.

Bottle trap

If you have a plastic bottle you can make an efficient trap for small fish by cutting it off just below the neck and then inverting the neck inside the bottle. Fish swim in but cannot find their way out again. Bait the trap to entice them in.

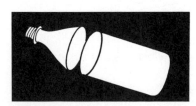
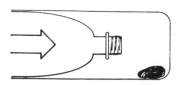

You can make a similar trap for larger fish using a hollow log. Make a lattice cone of twigs for the entrance and block the other end of the log.

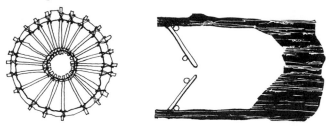

Wickerwork traps

Use young hazel, or other pliant twigs — bamboo bends better if you warm it — to make a trap into which fish can swim but from which they can find no way out. A wickerwork trap allows the current to flow through it, and since it is made of natural materials may seem like a tangle of reeds or stream-bottom debris.

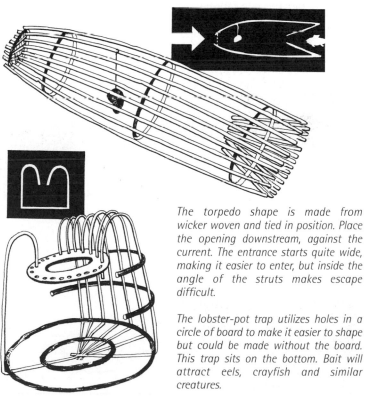

The torpedo shape is made from wicker woven and tied in position. Place the opening downstream, against the current. The entrance starts quite wide, making it easier to enter, but inside the angle of the struts makes escape difficult.

The lobster-pot trap utilizes holes in a circle of board to make it easier to shape but could be made without the board. This trap sits on the bottom. Bait will attract eels, crayfish and similar creatures.

Fish snares

Large fish such as pike, which lay alongside weeds, can be caught in a noose. Fix a noose line to the end of a pole, or pass it down the inside of a length of bamboo. Pass it over the fish from the tail end and pull it up sharply so that the noose traps the fish.

Eel bag

Tie fresh surplus offal or a dead animal inside a sack or cloth bag (plastic will not do) together with a quantity of straw-like vegetation or bracken. Tie a line and a weight to the end of the bag and allow it to sink. Leave it overnight and pull it out in the morning. If there are eels in the water they will chew their way into the bag to get at the offal and will still be wriggling in the straw when you get the bag landed.

Damming

Build a dam across a stream, diverting the flow to one side, and with rocks create a small shallow pool downstream where fish swimming upstream will be trapped. Fix a net below the race at the side of the dam to catch any fish that are carried over it from upstream.

Gill net

Make a net with a mesh size of about 4cm (1½in) between knots (see *Netting* in *Camp Craft*), set floats at the top and weight the bottom, then stretch it across a river. Fish swimming into it get caught by the gills. It is lethal and will soon empty a stretch of water so should not be used for long in an area where you intend to stay (or in a non-survival situation). If the ends of the net are tied to the banks at both top and bottom, weights and floats will not be needed.

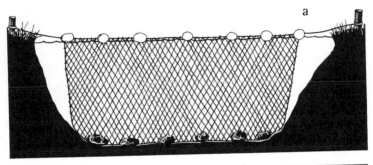

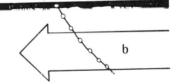

A gill net can be anchored on each bank, (supported by weights and floats (a), or tied to fixed posts. If it is angled across the line of the current (b) there is less likelihood of driftwood building up against it.

OTHER TECHNIQUES

If all else fails try the following methods.

Tickling

This is an old poacher's technique which takes patience but is effective where fish shelter below the undercut banks of fairly shallow streams. Lie along the bank and lower your hands gently into the water so that they can adjust to the water temperature. Keeping your hands as close to the bottom as possible, reach under the bank, moving the fingers slightly, until you touch a fish. Work the hand gently along its belly (fish usually swim against the current when feeding) until you reach the gills. Then grasp the fish firmly and pull it out.

Attracting and driving fish

At night a torch or firebrand held above the water will attract fish. Nets can then be drawn around the area to trap the fish which can be speared or clubbed. A mirror or other shiny material placed on the riverbed will reflect either sun or moonlight and attract fish.

Spearing and shooting fish

Sharpen a long stick to make a spear, adding barbs to make it more effective. If you have multiple points, like Neptune's trident, you give yourself a wider margin of error since it covers a larger area. Try to get above the fish and strike down swiftly.

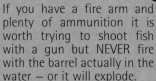

WARNING

If you have a fire arm and plenty of ammunition it is worth trying to shoot fish with a gun but NEVER fire with the barrel actually in the water – or it will explode.

The water seals the end of the barrel and instead of the bullet rushing outwards the force of the detonation blows back at you. It is not just dangerous – it is potentially lethal. Make very sure that the barrel is clear of the water.

Make sure that you are not casting a shadow over the fish you are trying to catch. Aim slightly below the fish to allow for the refraction of its image at the surface.

If you are a good shot use a bow and arrow to shoot fish (the wooden shaft will float and help to bring your prey to the surface, though most dead fish will float, anyway).

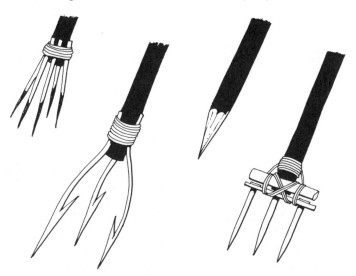

Muddying

Receding floodwater leaves isolated pools which are offer abundant in fish. Stir up the mud at the bottom of these pools with a stick, or by stamping in them. If there are any fish they will try to reach clearer water. Scoop them out.

Explosives

Explosives can be used in the water. They will kill the nearest fish, but by liberating the oxygen in the water will also cause those further away to surface.

FISH NARCOTICS

In many parts of the world fishermen use local plants to poison or stupefy fish to make them come to the surface, where they are easy to collect. This works best in a deep pool where one end can be dammed to contain the fish, but the method can be effective in any slack water.

Some plants daze or narcotize or intoxicate the fish but most have the effect of taking oxygen from the water so that the fish come to the surface in search of aerated water. Various parts of plants are used but in many cases they are simply crushed and thrown into the water. Although the effects are catastrophic for the fish they are not long lasting — the water soon reoxygenates itself. Most of these narcotics take effect more quickly in warmer waters and they are most widely used in tropical countries.

If these methods are used in closed pools you will have cleared out the fish supply and removed a future source of food. When a river or coastal pool is reopened to the main water, however, new fish will move in and restock it.

If seashells, snailshells or coral are burned over a very hot fire they will produce lime which can be thrown into still water to poison fish which will still be safe for human consumption.

WARNING

Dead fish floating on the surface — unless you have caused them to be there — may look like an easy meal but they may be diseased and if they have been there some time will not be fit to eat.

When released in water these poisons are toxic only to cold-blooded animals but this does not mean that they are edible. They are not. Parts of some of these plants are VERY DANGEROUS, if eaten raw. Use them on fish — not yourself — then eat the fish. Many plants are used. The following are effective and common in their areas.

DERRIS PLANTS
Derris (a) are found from south-east Asia to Australia. They are woody, climbing, vine-like plants, usually with small oval leaflets in pairs opposite each other, purple flowers and seedpods. Powder the roots and throw them into the water. Stupified fish will rise to the surface not long afterwards.

BARRINGTONIAS
Barringtonia (b) are trees, found in the same area as Derris, across to Polynesia, and often near the coast. Crush the seeds inside their urn-shaped pods and throw them into the water.

DESERT ROSES
Adenium (c), found in tropical and southern Africa and in parts of Arabia, are shrubs, sometimes small trees, with thick fleshy leaves. One of the most effective, A. obesum (illustrated) from East Africa, has spirals of bluntly oval leaves and clusters of tubular pinkish flowers. Use crushed stems and roots, which contain a highly toxic sap.

SOAP PLANT
Amole Chlorogalum pomeridianum (d) grows in dry open or scrubby country in western North America. It has narrow, grass-like leaves and white star-like flowers. Crush the bulbous root and throw into pools.

GOAT'S RUE
Tephrosia virginiana (e) grows on open ground in North America. Its surface slightly hairy, it has many narrow leaflets and long flat seedpods. Use the crushed stems or the very poisonous roots.

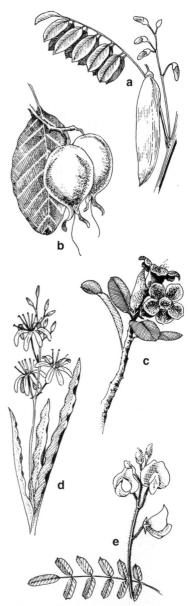

ARCTIC FISHING

On frozen arctic seas fish are likely to be the most accessible food. Even in summer it is safer to fish through the ice than to fish from the edge of a floe which may break up beneath you. The techniques involved are equally effective on any frozen lake or river where the ice is thick enough to bear your weight with ease but not so solid that it cannot be broken through.

First you need to gain access to the water, which means smashing a hole in the ice. If you have an ice saw, use that to cut neat holes which will still leave you with firm edges. If you have to smash the ice there is a risk that it may fracture back into the area where you are standing. Approach the operation carefully.

Hook and line

Bait the hook in the usual way. If the line is being carried back up against the underside of the ice you will have to weight it below the hook.

There is no point in trying out your angling skills at only one hole — far better to set up multiple angling points. In order to cover them effectively, however, you will need an easy way of knowing when you have a bite. Make a pennant from a piece of cloth, paper or card — preferably of a bright colour so that you will see it easily against the snow and ice   and attach it to a light stick. Lash this firmly at right angles to another stick which must extend beyond the maximum diameter of your hole by at least 30 per cent. Now attach the line to the lower end of the flagpole and rest the flag on the side of the hole with the line at its centre.

When a fish takes your bait the cross piece will be pulled over the hole and the flagpole jerked upright. Keep your eye on the markers so you can pull your catch up quickly. The wriggling fish is an easy meal for a passing seal.

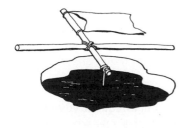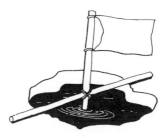

Ice netting

Although fish do not hibernate their metabolism slows down to cope with the reduced winter temperatures and they consequently eat much less, making them less likely to take bait. Netting, always likely to be more certain of producing results, has a further edge on line fishing.

Net through the ice. A net lowered from the edge of a floe would probably end up frozen to the floe and handling it would be a risky operation. Instead make several holes in the ice about 40cm (16in) wide and about twice that distance apart. Attach retaining loops to the top edge of your net at 80cm (32in) intervals, to match the holes, and weight the bottom. Put the retaining loop at one end around a stick or rod of some kind, wider than your holes, and lower one end of the net into the hole at one end of your row.

With a hooked pole (which you can improvise) you now have to fish for the net and haul it through to the next hole where you secure the next retaining loop with another retaining stick — and so on until the whole net is suspended.

If the ice is thin enough, feed all the retaining loops into the hooked pole and lower the entire net through the first hole, anchoring the first loop with a retaining stick. Then, carefully holding the loops, reach the hooked pole through the next hole and slip the remaining loops onto it. Pull the net along and anchor the next retaining loop. Continue until the net is fully extended.

To check your net pull it up with the hooked pole.

If you leave your net for too long, in polar regions, you may find that your catch has been for the benefit of a seal who has stolen most of it.

PREPARING FISH

All freshwater fish are edible. Those under 5cm (2in) long need no preparation and can be eaten whole. Larger fish must be gutted. Catfish and eels are smooth-skinned but others may be descaled. Catfish have a cartilage skeleton. Most other fish have a mass of bones.

Bleeding *As soon as a fish is caught cut its throat and allow it to bleed. Cut out the gills.*

Gutting *Make an incision from the anal orifice to where the throat was cut. Remove all offal — you can use* *it for hook bait or in an eel bag. Keep the roe, which runs down the side of the fish. It is hard in females, soft in males; it is very nutritious. This preparation helps fish keep longer.*

Scaling *is not necessary and fish can be cooked with scales on, but if there is time, scrape them off. Draw knife from tail to head.*

Skinning *Fish skin has good food value and should be left on and* *eaten unless food is plentiful. To skin eels and catfish pass a stake through the fish, lodge it across uprights and, having cut the skin away just below it, draw it down towards the tail.*

243

-5-
CAMP CRAFT

Selecting where to camp and knowing how to make a good shelter are essential skills. A wide range of shelter construction methods, using available materials, are described, from the simplest windbreak to dwellings suitable for long-term occupation.

You will need to make fire and to chose the right type of fire construction. Fires for both general warmth and for cooking purposes are detailed. Guidance on food preparation, cooking and preservation will ensure that food is safe and not wasted. Camp organization and hygiene are as important for health and morale for the single survivor as for a large group.

Methods of making tools, camp equipment, clothes, ropes and nets will all improve survival conditions and skills in knot-making will have many uses.

SHELTER AND MAKING CAMP

Shelter is necessary to give shade, to repel wind and rain and to keep in warmth. Sleep and adequate rest are essential and the time and effort you put into making your shelter comfortable will make them easier to get. If you are the victim of a plane crash or a vehicle that has let you down, it may provide a shelter or materials from which one can be built — but if there is fire or the threat of fuel tanks exploding, wait until it has burned out before attempting salvage.

If you are the unequipped victim of an accident, are trapped by unexpected mist or caught by nightfall in terrain where it is not safe to proceed, or if exhaustion or injury prevents you going further, you may have to make do with any natural shelter that you can find for the night, or until you can more fully assess the situation. In this case, virtually any protection from wind, rain and cold will be welcome. If movement down a slope seems risky, traversing even a short way along the contour may bring you out of the wind. If no cave or crevice is available to give shelter, make use of any hollow in the ground. Add to its height, if you can, by piling up rocks — but make sure that any structure is stable and use a back-pack, if you have one, to increase the windshield before settling down on the leeward side.

If there is still daylight to see by, you have no injuries to handicap you and are not isolated by unnegotiable cliffs or other barriers, it will be worth seeking possible better places in the vicinity. For a long-term camp you should find a secure site with convenient access to your major needs.

Where to camp

If you are on high exposed ground go lower down to find a sheltered spot, but on low, wet ground you will need to climb higher to find

BAD PLACES TO CAMP

1 Hilltops exposed to wind (move down and look for shelter on the lee side).

2 Valley bottoms and deep hollows — could be damp and, especially when the sky is clear, more liable to frost at night.

3 Hillside terraces where the ground holds moisture.

4 Spurs which lead down to water, which are often routes to animals' watering places.

somewhere securely dry. Look for somewhere sheltered from the wind, on rising ground that has no risk of flooding and is safe from rock falls or avalanches.

Hot air rises, cold air sinks, so valley bottoms will often contain pockets of colder air and, in cold weather, be susceptible to frost and damp mist. In areas that get plenty of rainfall, terraces across a slope will often be damper than the steeper ground above and below them, for water collects there before flowing further downward.

Ideally you should be near water, with a plentiful supply of wood near at hand. Pitching camp too close to water, however, may lead you to be troubled by insects, and the sound of running water can hide other noises which might indicate danger, or the sound of search or rescue parties.

On river banks look for the high water mark: in mountain regions streams can become torrents in minutes, rising as much as 5m (17ft) in an hour! Even on plains keep out of old watercourses, no matter how dry they are. Heavy rainfall in nearby hills can easily send water rushing down them in flash floods, with practically no warning. Choose ground that is reasonably flat and free of rocks and make sure that you have space to lay out signals and that you can be easily spotted by rescue parties.

Check above your head for bees' or hornets' nests and for dead wood in trees that could come crashing down in the next storm or high wind. Keep away from solitary trees, which attract lightning, and in forest areas keep to the edges, where you can see what is going on around you. Don't camp across a game trail — you don't want marauding animals as unwelcome guests or to find your bivouac flattened by a herd of animals on their way to a waterhole — but stay near to any obvious human tracks.

TYPES OF SHELTER

The type of shelter you build will depend upon local conditions and the materials available — and upon how long you expect to need it. For immediate protection from the elements, rig up a makeshift shelter while you construct something better and more permanent. If you decide to stay put and wait for rescue, a more long-term shelter can be built and improved on as time and energy permit.

For those walking to safety, on the other hand, temporary shelters can be built at each stopping point. They can even be carried with you if they are sufficiently light and there is a significant risk that suitable materials may not be available at the next campsite.

A more permanent shelter will certainly be worthwhile for the sick or injured, who must rest up in order to regain their strength, or where it is necessary to wait for the weather to clear before attempting a journey. Use the time to stockpile equipment and provisions.

Hasty shelters

If no materials are available for constructing a shelter make use of any cover and protection that is available: cliff overhangs, gradients and so forth, which will help shield you from wind or rain. Incorporate natural windbreaks in quickly constructed shelters. In completely open plains, sit with your back to the wind and pile any equipment behind you as a windbreak.

Bough shelters

Make use of branches that sweep down to the ground or boughs that have partly broken from the tree to give basic protection from the wind — but make sure that they are not so broken that they could come down on your head! Weave in other twigs to make the cover more dense. Conifers are more suited to this technique than broad-leaved trees, as they require less weaving-in to keep out rain.

Make a similar shelter by lashing a broken-off bough to the base of another branch where it forks from the trunk (a).

Root shelter

The spreading roots and trapped earth at the base of a fallen tree make a good wind and storm barrier, if they are at the right angle to the wind. Filling in the sides between the extended roots will usually make the shelter much more effective, and provide a good support for building a more elaborate shelter from other materials.

Use a natural hollow

Even a shallow depression in the ground will provide some protection from wind and can reduce the effort in constructing a shelter. However, take measures to deflect the downhill flow of water around it, especially if it is a hollow on a slope, or you could find yourself lying in a pool.

Make a roof to keep the rain off and the warmth in. A few strong branches placed across the hollow can support a light log laid over them, against which shorter boughs and sticks can be stacked to give pitch to the roof and so allow water to run off. Consolidate with turf or with twigs and leaves.

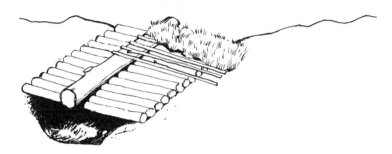

Fallen trunks

A log or fallen tree trunk makes a useful windbreak on its own, if it is at the right angle to the wind. With a small trunk, scoop out a hollow in the ground on the leeward side.

A log also makes an excellent support for a lean-to roof of boughs.

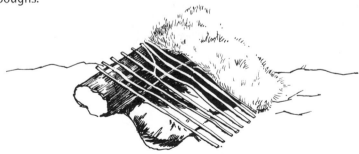

Drainage and ventilation

A run-off channel gouged from the earth around any shelter in which you are below, or lying directly on, ground level will help to keep the shelter dry. Hasty shelters will usually have many spaces where air can enter. Do not try to seal them all – ventilation is essential.

Stone barriers

A shelter is more comfortable if you can sit rather than lie in it, so increase its height by building a low wall of stones around your chosen hollow or shallow excavation. Caulk between the stones (especially the lowest layer) with turf and foliage mixed with mud, and deflect the flow of rainwater around the shelter as shown below.

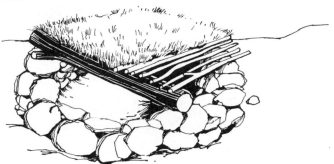

Sapling shelter

If suitable sapling growth is available, select two lines of saplings, clear the ground between them of any obstructions and lash their tops together to form a support frame for sheeting. Weight down the bottom edges of the sheeting with rocks or timber.

You can make a similar shelter from pliable branches driven into the ground.

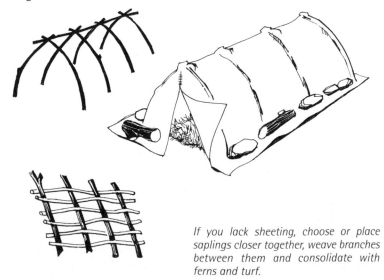

If you lack sheeting, choose or place saplings closer together, weave branches between them and consolidate with ferns and turf.

Shelter sheet

With a waterproof poncho, groundsheet or a piece of plastic sheeting or canvas, you can quickly and easily make a number of different shelters which will suffice until you can build something more efficient. Make use of natural shelter (a) or make a triangular shelter with the apex pointing into the wind (b). Stake or weigh down edges. If it is long enough, curl the sheeting below you — running downhill so that it keeps out surface water (c). Use dry grass or bracken as bedding. Do not lie on cold or damp ground.

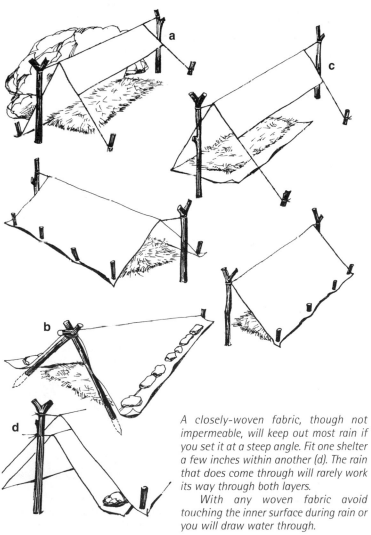

A closely-woven fabric, though not impermeable, will keep out most rain if you set it at a steep angle. Fit one shelter a few inches within another (d). The rain that does come through will rarely work its way through both layers.

With any woven fabric avoid touching the inner surface during rain or you will draw water through.

251

Tepees

Best known from its North American forms, the tepee occurs in many cultures. The quickest type to erect has three or more angled support poles, tied where they cross to make a cone. They can be tied on the ground and lifted into place before covering with hides, birch bark panels or sheeting. Leave an opening at the top for ventilation.

Wider angles will give greater area but shed rain less easily.

Parachute tepee

A parachute, suspended by its centre, makes an instant tepee. Peg out the bottom edge.

Parachute material can be used to cover a tepee, but even simpler is to suspend one from a tree. Give the sides a steep angle and, even when the fabric is not impervious, water will run off. Fold a segment of the chute double for a door flap, slit along a seam and make a tie fastening to close it.

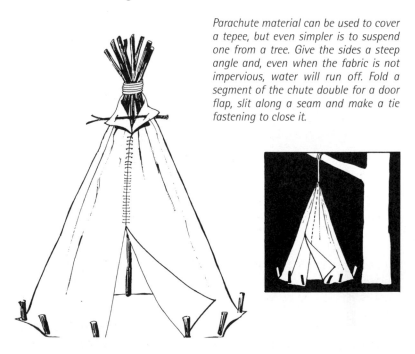

Stick walls and screens

It is easy to build walls by piling sticks between uprights driven into the ground and (if possible) tied at the top. Caulk them well to keep out wind and rain. These are ideal for making one side of a shelter, for blocking a shelter's opening or for a heat reflector behind a fire. If large rocks are not available use this method to dam a stream.

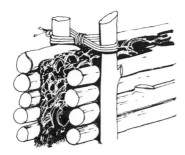

To make a very sturdy stick wall, increase the space between the uprights, use two stacks of sticks and, as you build it, fill the space between with earth.

Coverings

Make wattle and woven coverings for roofs or walls from springy saplings, plant stems, grasses and long leaves (either whole or, if large enough, shredded for tighter weaving). First make a framework from less pliable materials, either *in situ* or as a separate panel to attach later. Tie the main struts in position. Weave in the more pliant materials.

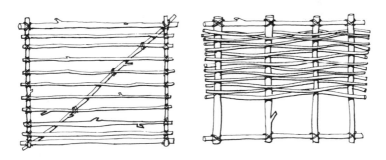

If no ties are available, drive vertical stakes into the ground and weave saplings between them. Caulk with earth and grasses.

If suitable firm cross-pieces are too few, weave creepers between the uprights.

Very large leaves, lashed or weighted down, or hooked over lines of creeper, can be overlapped like tiles or shingles to keep out rain.

Long grass can be bunched and woven, overlap the ends irregularly to make a continuous warp and weft. Or use birch bark to make shingles. Ring a birch tree with even 60cm (2ft) cuts and carefully remove the bark (a). Across a frame fix pairs of canes or creepers in close-spaced pairs (b). Upper ends of shingles are gripped between the canes, the lower ends rest on top of those below (c).

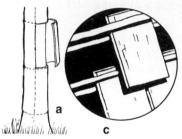

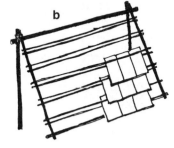

Open lean-to shelter

If there is nothing solid to lean a roof against and you are not trying to keep out heavy rain or a blizzard, use panels of wattle or frames covered in grass for protection.

Erect a horizontal cross-piece between trees or on simple supports. On the windward side lean a panel of wattle, or tie or lean saplings at 45 degrees to make a roof. Add side walls as necessary (a). Site your fire on the leeward. Add side pieces and − this is the trick − build a reflector (b) on the other side of the fire to make sure that you get the full benefit of the warmth.

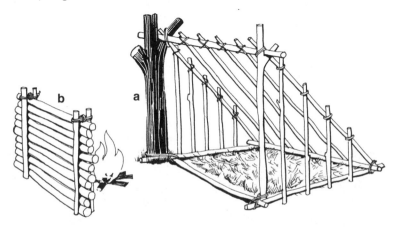

TROPICAL SHELTER

In rain forests and tropical jungle the ground is damp and likely to be crawling with insect life, leeches and other undesirables. Instead of bedding down on the ground you will be better in a raised bed. Consequently you may want to make higher shelters.

Unless you are at an altitude high enough to make the nights cold, you will be less concerned with protection from the wind than with keeping reasonably dry. A thatching of palm, banana and other large leaves makes the best roofs and walls.

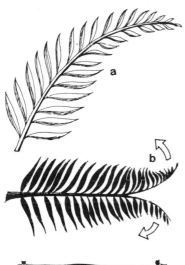

ATAP

Also know as 'Wait-a-while vine', atap is especially useful, despite the barbs at each leaf tip which make careful handling necessary. Look for any plant with a similar structure (a), the bigger the better. The broader the individual leaflets, the better also.

Atap is best used horizontally, splitting each leaf into two from the tip (b) then tearing it into two clean halves down its length. Do not try to split from the thick end or you will end up with a broken branch.

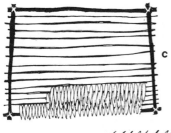

Closely layer halves of atap on your roof frame (c). You can let it be a little less dense on walls.

Woven atap can be particularly effective for the sides of a shelter.

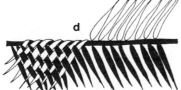

Another method:

Do not split down the leaf but fold the leaflets on one side across to the other and interweave them (d). You will probably find this easiest if you work first from one side then the other — but it does take practise.

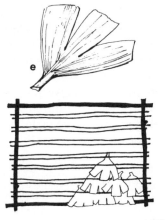

Three-lobed leaves or leaves cut in this fashion (e) can be locked over a thatching frame without any other fixing being necessary to hold them in place (f).

Elephant grass and other large leaves can be woven between the cross-pieces (g). Only a small number are needed to produce a shelter very quickly.

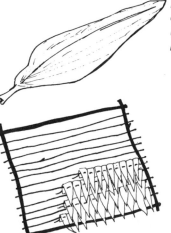

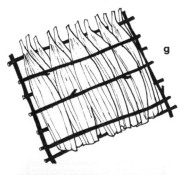

Long broad leaves can be sown along the thatching battens with vines (h).

Palm and other long-stemmed leaves can be secured by carrying the stem around the batten and over the front of the leaf, where it is held in place by the next leaf (i).

Leaves must overlap those below on the outside of the shelter.

Bamboo

This large-stemmed plant, actually a grass, is a very versatile building material and can be used for pole supports, flooring, roofing and walls.

The giant form of bamboo — which can be over 30m (100ft) high and 30cm (1ft) in diameter — is an Asian plant, found in damp places from India through to China both in the lowlands and on mountain slopes, but there are types native to Africa and Australia and two which are found in the southern United States.

Split bamboo vertically to make roofing and guttering to collect rainwater. The split stems, laid alternately to interlock with one another, form efficient and waterproof pantiles.

Flatten split bamboo for smooth walls, floors or shelving by cutting vertically through the joints every 1.25cm (1/2in) or so around the circumference. It can then be smoothed out.

The paper-like sheaths formed at the nodes can also be used as roofing material.

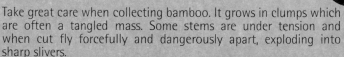

WARNING

Take great care when collecting bamboo. It grows in clumps which are often a tangled mass. Some stems are under tension and when cut fly forcefully and dangerously apart, exploding into sharp slivers.

Split bamboo can be razor-sharp and cause serious injury. The husks at the base of bamboo stems carry small stinging hairs which cause severe skin irritations.

ARCTIC SHELTER

In polar areas simple shelters will be those already waiting for you in natural caves and hollows. If you carry some kind of bivouac in your equipment, you can erect it and increase its protection by piling up loose snow around and over it, so long as it can support the weight. But to build in hard snow — and at very low temperatures snow will be solid — you need some kind of implement to cut into it or make blocks from it. Spades and ice saws are essential equipment for polar expeditions.

Snow or rock caves will be easily recognizable — but not so obvious are the spaces left beneath the spreading boughs of conifers in the northern forests when the snow has already built up around them. A medium-sized tree may have a space right around the trunk (a) or a large one have pockets in the snow beneath a branch (b). Try digging under any tree with spreading branches on the lee side.

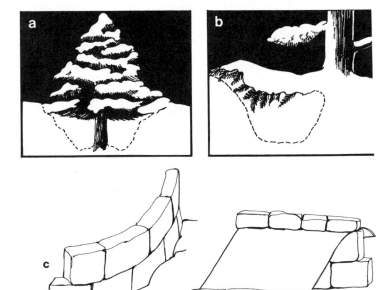

Even soft snow can be built into a windbreak. Those with equipment can cut blocks (c). This is the minimum shelter for the minimum effort.

Anchor a ground sheet or poncho along the top with another course of blocks, use others to secure the bottom edge. Use more snow blocks to close the sides.

BUILDING IN SNOW

A saw, knife, shovel or machete is necessary to cut compacted snow into blocks. The ideal snow will bear a man's weight without much impression being made but be soft enough to allow a probe to be inserted evenly through it.

Cut blocks about 45 x 50cm (18 x 20in) and 10–20cm (4–8in) thick. These will be an easy size to handle, thick enough to provide good insulation and yet allow maximum penetration of the sun's rays.

Snow trench

This is a much quicker shelter to construct than trying to build in snow above the ground, but it is suitable for only one person and then only for short-term use — while you are on the move or making something bigger, for example.

Mark out an area the size of a sleeping bag (including head support) and cut out blocks the whole width of the trench. Dig down to a depth of at least 60cm (2ft). Along the top of the sides of the trench cut a ledge about 15cm (6in) wide and the same deep.

Rest the snow bricks on each side of the ledge and lean them in against each other to form a roof (a).

Put equipment below your sleeping bag so that you are not in direct contact with the snow beneath.

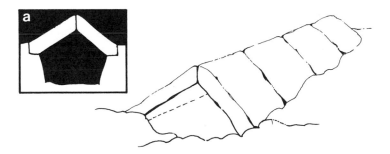

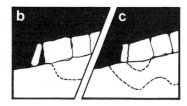

Block the windward end with another block or piled up snow. At the other end (downwind) have a removable block as a door (b), or dig an entrance (c). Fill any gaps with snow. Most effective built on a slight slope, cold air will collect in the entrance leaving warmer air in the sleeping space.

Snow cave

Dig into a drift of firm snow to make a comfortable shelter. Make use of the fact that hot air rises and heavier, cold air sinks. Create three levels inside: build a fire on the highest, sleep on the centre one and keep off the lower level which will trap the cold. Drive a hole through the roof to let out smoke and make another hole to ensure that you have adequate ventilation.

Use a block of snow as a door and keep it loose fitting and on the INSIDE so that it will not freeze up and jam. If it does, a block on the inside will be much easier to free.

Smooth the inside surfaces to discourage melt drips and make a channel around the internal perimeter to keep them away from you and your equipment.

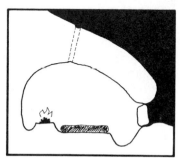

Snow house (Igloo)

An igloo takes time to construct but centuries of use by the Eskimo demonstrate its efficiency. Build the main shelter first then dig out an entrance or build an entry tunnel which is big enough to crawl along. Make sure that its entrance does not point into the wind. You could bend the tunnel or build a wind break to make this less likely.

Mark out a circle on the ground about 4m (13½ft) in diameter and tramp it down to consolidate the floor as you proceed with the rest of the building. Cut and lay a circle of blocks on the perimeter. Be prepared to dig a tunnel (a), leave a space for an entrance (b). Place another layer on top of them but, as when laying bricks, centre new blocks over the previous vertical joint.

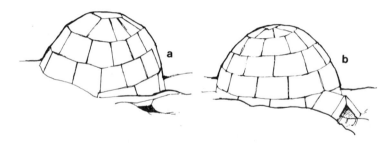

Build up more layers but place each only halfway over the lower tier, so that the igloo tapers in or becomes dome-shaped. Shape out the entrance arch as you proceed. Seal the top with a flat block. Make ventilation holes near the top and near the bottom – not on the side of the prevailing wind or so low that snow rapidly builds up and blocks it. Fill any other gaps with snow. Smooth off all the inside to remove any drip-points. This will allow any condensation to run down the wall instead of dripping off.

Igloo (spiral method)

Lay the first course of blocks and then shape them to the required spiral. You do not have to overhang the blocks if you angle your initial spiral downwards and inwards, and shape the top and bottom faces of subsequent courses to lean inwards. The last few blocks in the centre may need some support as you fit them into position.

Cutting the first course to an even spiral eases the whole process. Angle the top edge slightly down towards the centre.

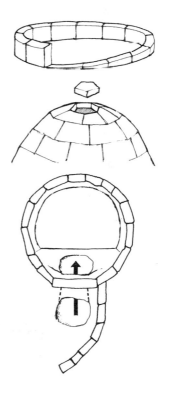

The final block must be cut to fit – unless the space is small enough to leave for ventilation, but this last block helps to keep the structure from collapsing.

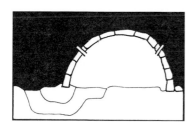

INSIDE THE IGLOO
Build a sleeping level higher than the floor (or dig down when building) to create a lower cold level which can be used for storage.

Cut an entrance way through the lower course of blocks or dig a tunnel beneath them. The central hole can be used as an entrance if you are too exhausted to complete the structure.

BUILDING A SHELTER

The type of shelter you build will depend upon: the materials available, the tools available, what you are sheltering from (WIND, COLD, SNOW, RAIN, INSECTS, and so forth).

How long do you intend to remain at the location? Snow caves and natural holes are ideal if you are on the move and do not need a permanent structure.

Size will depend upon the number in the party.

Take your time over building a complex structure and rest frequently. Over-exertion which produces sweating should be avoided.

All shelters MUST be adequately ventilated to prevent carbon monoxide poisoning and allow moisture to escape. Two holes are needed — have one near the top and one near the entrance. In snow shelters the holes must be regularly checked to ensure that they have not become blocked by snow or ice.

Regularly clear accumulated snow from any entrance tunnel to ensure that it does not become blocked.

The smaller the shelter the warmer it will be inside but, since it will not be possible to heat the shelter to many degrees above freezing, you will need a little time to adapt to the environment.

Parachute snow house

This is a useful structure if stranded on sea ice where sufficient snow for an igloo (or igloos) for a larger party may be hard to find. Look for snow or convenient blocks of ice in the pushed-up pressure ridges of the ice.

Mark out a circle and build up a circular wall of snow blocks about 1m (4ft) high. Leave an entrance space if on ice — you will not be able to dig an entrance tunnel. Dig a lower area in the floor for cold air to sink into.

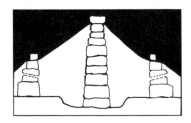

Raise a central column of blocks in the centre about 1–1.5m (3–5ft) higher than the wall. Drape the parachute over this and the wall, securing it with a further row of blocks on top of the wall.

WARNING

The structure of this parachute roof makes it a snow trap, which could become a dangerous weight poised above your head Clear accumulated snow regularly.

If you want a small fire inside, ensure there is adequate ventilation. Site the fire on the outer shelf where it will not affect the canopy, not near the central column.

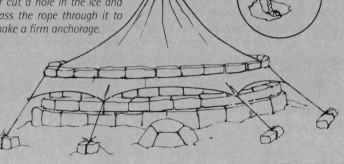

Anchor parachute cords with further blocks of ice or snow or cut a hole in the ice and pass the rope through it to make a firm anchorage.

LIVING IN A SNOW HOUSE

In bad weather make sure that you have a good supply of timber, or liquid fuel, inside the shelter.

Do not carry loose snow into the shelter, knock it off boots and clothing before you enter.

Mark the entrance clearly so that it is easily found.

Keep shovels and tools inside the shelter — you may have to dig yourself out.

Drips in igloos can be stopped by placing a piece of snow on the source.

Relieve yourself inside the shelter — this is usual practice in these conditions and conserves body heat. Use plastic bags, ration tins or other containers and empty when possible. Try to discipline the bowels to work just prior to leaving the shelter in the morning and then remove faecal matter with other rubbish accumulated.

In a shelter with several people organize a rosta of duties. It is important that someone tends the fire at all times. Others can check the vent holes, gather fuel, go hunting when possible, prepare meals and so forth.

Remember that at a low temperature you will need more food.

INFO.

No matter how low the external temperature, that inside a well-constructed snow house will not drop lower than -10°C (0°F). Just burning a candle will raise the temperature by about four degrees. The traditional Eskimo way of heating the igloo was a wick in a bowl of fat. In a large shelter with a wood fire the temperature is cosy. An oil burner or fat on bones are alternatives where there is no wood or Casiope.

LONG-TERM SHELTER

If you decide that any possible search for you has been abandoned and that it is impracticable to make your own way to safety, whether due to distance, time of year, lack of equipment or physical condition, you will want to make the most comfortable permanent shelter possible. Somewhere that you will be able to establish yourself cosily until you can eventually attract rescue or equip yourself to undertake the journey with your own resources.

In a cold climate you will want to be warm and snug. In a warm one, on the other hand, you will want to take advantage of any available breezes. Your shelter will need to provide protection against the changing seasons and night temperatures which may differ from daytime ones.

Caves

Caves are the most ready-made of shelters. Even a shallow cave (in stone usually known, in fact, as a rock shelter) offers an excellent temporary shelter and a larger cave can make an excellent permanent home. People still live in them in many parts of the world, sometimes with all modern conveniences! Caves situated above a valley will be dry even if water seeps through in some places from above. They are weather-proof and require little constructional work, usually simply the creation of a barrier to close off the entrance. Make this of rocks, wattle, logs, turves or almost any material.

If the cave faces into the wind, build a screen out from both sides, one slightly behind the other, overlapping them to provide an entrance (a).

Build the fire at the back of the cave. Smoke will go up to the roof, leaving air nearer the floor. Smoke from a fire near the open mouth of a cave will not escape outwards but will probably be blown in. If you seal the cave entrance make sure you leave a gap for the smoke to escape.

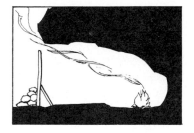

Caves can be cold, and they may already be inhabited by wild animals, so approach any such shelter with caution. Plenty of dry plant matter and pine boughs on the ground will provide insulation. A good fire will usually make animal occupants leave. Allow them an escape route.

Sometimes a cave will have its own fresh water supply, especially if it goes deep into a hillside, either from an underground stream or from water seeping through the rocks above.

WARNING

Check for the possibility of a rock fall inside or outside the cave. You might be desperate for shelter, but your situation will be a lot worse if you are trapped or injured by falling rocks.

Light structures

Follow the methods outlined for the lean-to structure. You can extend it with a less angled roof and a front wall or you can build vertical walls and roof them over with deep eaves to give you extra shade from sun and to ensure that rain runs off well away from the hut. Dig a channel to carry any water away.

If you have bamboo or other strong material available to build a firm frame, raise the floor of your shelter off the ground in tropical climates, so reducing access to ground creatures.

In hot climates you will need to make your roof solid to keep out rain and give good protection from the sun but, if it projects well over the walls, you can leave them as fairly open lattice to allow air to pass through. Grasses and mud will seal cracks and all kinds of material will make a thatch if woven between roof cross-pieces of sticks or cords. In climates with heavy rainfall use leaves or bark like tiles on top.

Building with rushes

When neither trees nor bamboo are available, rushes or other strong stems can be tied in bundles to form structural pillars — a method used by the Marsh Arabs of Iraq.

Tie reeds in long thick bundles by starting and finishing with a clove hitch (see *Knots*). Choose the longest reeds and ensure that their ends are spaced out along the length of the bundle so that they do not cause a weak point by coming all together. The base should be a flat end, the other should taper. Prepare more reed bundles, thinner and longer if possible. They will be used for securing the sides of your shelter.

Range thick columns of reeds on the long sides of your shelter site. Dig the thick ends into the earth and link the columns a short way up each by lashing on thinner bundles horizontally between them.

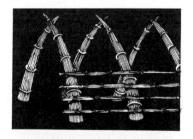

Bend the tops of the columns towards each other, overlapping them and binding them together. Add more thin bundles to link the sides of the columns and carry up over the arches.

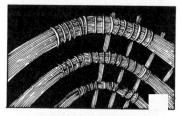

Interweave a wattle of reeds between this framework, using thinner reeds until adequate shelter is provided, or weave separate panels of leaves and reeds to attach to it.

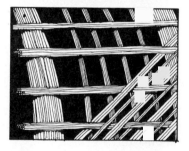

Sod house

Turf-built shelters are an alternative to log cabins when timber is scarce or there are no tools to cut it. Cut sections of turf 45 x 15cm (18 x 6in) and build with them like bricks, overlapping them to form a bond. Slope the sides to give pitch to the roof — to support which you will have to find spars of wood or other strong material. The greater the pitch, the better rain will be repelled. The length of the spars will determine the size of the structure. Lay turves on the roof as well, or cover it with grass.

Unless you have a great deal of turf available keep the structure low, big enough to sit on the floor but not big enough to stand. One side could be open, facing your fire.

Cut the turf in a pattern to leave a permanent distress signal on the ground at the same time as collecting building material.

For a small shelter you could also use turves to make a beehive or igloo-like structure.

If time and resources are available a large hut can be built with turves. Some sort of timber will be needed for a door frame (a) and for roof spars. Build an internal hearth and chimney, but if you use turf for them be careful that they do not catch fire themselves. Plaster the inside of hearth and chimney with clay.

Site the open side or doorway away from the prevailing wind and, with a small turf-built house make your fire outside the entrance and build a reflector on the other side of it to throw heat back inside.

Even with an open side, a short return will make the corners more stable. Bond the corners, as with conventional brickwork, for strength (b).

Log cabin

Scale your cabin to the number it is to house. You can always enlarge it or add on extra rooms later. The size of logs available will determine the length of walls. A square or rectangle will be sturdy and easiest to roof – 2.5m (8ft) square is a sensible small size. You may be lucky and be able to use trees that have already fallen, in which case you could perhaps lash a framework of logs together and fill the spaces in between, but it is much better to joint the corners to fit snugly into each other. Do not finish off the projecting ends. These are the strength of the structure.

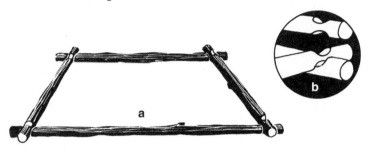

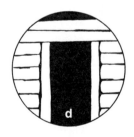

Lay down your first layer of logs in the shape of your hut (a). Joint the corners to fit on top of each other (b) and cut other logs to fit neatly on top. Since logs tend to taper, place them alternately top to bottom to counter this (c).

Once the ground frame is established leave space for a doorway on the side away from the prevailing wind – you may be able to use off-cuts from logs for these sections on either side of the door. Square off the edges and wedge a door frame in place (d). Do not bother with windows, the door will give sufficient ventilation.

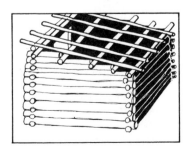

Build up the front higher than the back to give pitch to the roof. The last log front and back should project well beyond the side walls. These will support the roof. Across the hut from side to side notch in one cross-beam to keep short logs in place. Lay a roof of logs, front to back, extending beyond walls. Notch the logs to fit on to the cross-pieces or lash them down.

Choose a flat site for your cabin, or level a slightly larger area. Dig into a hillside if necessary, but the foundations for the walls must be level.

The flexible saw in your survival kit will cut logs of sufficient size, and if you are a survivor from a wrecked plane or boat there will have been a fire axe on board.

There is no need to make a door yet. Hang a piece of blanket to keep the wind out, or make a panel of wattle to fill the gap until you feel equipped to make a permanent door. Don't bother with windows either — the doorway will give enough ventilation.

Caulk between the logs with mud and wood chips, or, if there are big gaps, saplings before applying the mud. Mix it with grass and moss, and use a sharpened stick to force it between the logs. Cover the roof with saplings before adding a layer of mud and turf.

Instead of a complete roof of whole logs you could use lighter materials and mud on a timber frame. Bark from the logs makes an excellent top covering if laid as tiles. These could be pegged through with small supple twigs while the mud is still soft.

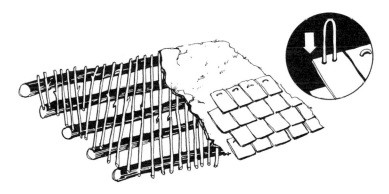

If there is no risk of a build up of water (in which case it would be useful to build a floor later) dig down inside the hut to provide the earth for mud caulking and you will at the same time increase its interior height.

If you leave a hole somewhere in the roof for smoke to escape, you can make a fire inside the hut. But do not leave it unattended — put it out rather than risk your home burning down.

If stone is readily available, you could build a proper chimney and fireplace. You'll retain more of the heat if it is a central structure. Fit stones as closely as possible and use small stones and mud to pack the spaces.

FIRE

Fire can make the difference between living and dying. It will not only cook food but make it go further, for its warmth will save calories being used up in producing body heat. It can be used to signal, dry clothes, provide comfort and act as a morale booster. It can scare away dangerous animals, while its smoke keeps insect pests at bay. It can be used to heat metal to make tools, to sharpen sticks and to bake pots. Make the most of a fire: it can do these things all at the same time.

 It is well worth remembering the Fire Triangle. Its three sides represent AIR, HEAT and FUEL. If any one of the sides is removed, the triangle collapses and the fire goes out.

When lighting a fire, always ensure adequate ventilation, with enough fuel and a hot enough source to ignite this fuel. To produce flame, this temperature must be maintained to keep air and fuel continuously reacting. The more oxygen introduced, the brighter the fire: by using the wind, or forcing a draught, the fire is fanned to a high temperature and rapidly burns fuel. By reducing the ventilation the fire burns less fiercely and embers are allowed to glow, needing less fuel.

If these principles are understood, smoky fires can be avoided. Smoke is the result of incomplete combustion – with care smoke can be virtually eliminated.

PRACTISE FIRE LIGHTING

Fire is essential to survival. It provides warmth, protection, a means of signalling, boils water, and cooks and preserves food. You must learn to light a fire anywhere under any conditions. It is not enough to know all the methods – you have to be expert at them.

Preparation

First make sure that you have sufficient quantities of TINDER, KINDLING and FUEL. Then prepare a fireplace so that you can control the fire. Used carelessly fire can get out of hand and bring disaster.

The fireplace

The fireplace needs to be prepared carefully. Choose a site that is sheltered, especially during high winds. Except for signal purposes (see *Rescue*), or exceptionally to warm a temporary bough or snowhole shelter, do not light a fire at the base of a tree or stump. Clear away leaves, twigs, moss and dry grass from a circle at least 2m (6ft) across and scrape everything away until you have a surface of bare earth.

If the ground is wet or covered with snow, the fire must be built on a platform. Make this from a layer of green logs covered with a layer of earth or a layer of stones.

If land is swampy or the snow deep a raised platform is needed, known as a temple fire.

Temple fire
This hearth consists of a raised platform, built of green timber. Four uprights support cross-pieces in their forks. Across them place a layer of green logs and cover this with several inches of earth. Light the fire on top of this. A pole across upper forks on diagonally opposite uprights can support cooking pots.

IN WINDY CONDITIONS
If there are particularly strong winds, dig a trench and light your fire in it.

Also good for windy conditions: Encircle your fire with rocks to retain heat and conserve fuel. Use them to support cooking utensils. Their heat, as well as that from the fire, will keep things warm and you can use the rocks themselves as bed warmers.

WARNING

Avoid placing wet or porous rocks and stones near fires, especially rocks which have been submerged in water — they may explode when heated. Avoid slates and softer rocks, and test others by banging them together. Do not use any that crack, sound hollow or are flaky. If they contain moisture it will expand faster than the stone and can make it explode, producing dangerous flying fragments which could take out an eye if you are close to the fire.

Tinder

Tinder is any kind of material that takes the minimum of heat to make it catch alight. Good tinder needs only a spark to ignite it.

Birch bark, dried grasses, fine wood shavings, bird down, waxed paper and cotton fluff from clothing all make good tinder. So do pulverized fir cones, pine needles and the inner bark from cedar trees. Dried fungi are excellent, if finely powdered, and scorched or charred cotton or linen, especially ground finely, are also among the best. Where insects such as wood wasps have been boring into trees, the fine dust they produce is good tinder and powdery bird and bat droppings can also be used. The inside of birds' nests are usually lined with down feathers and ignite easily — dry fieldmouse nests are also usable.

Whatever tinder you use MUST BE DRY. It is a good idea to carry tinder with you in a waterproof container. Always keep an eye open for tinder to collect.

Kindling

Kindling is the wood used to raise the flames from the tinder so that larger and less combustible materials can be burned.

The best kindling consists of small, dry twigs and the softer woods are preferable because they flare up quickly.

Those that contain resins burn readily and make firelighting a snip. The drawbacks of soft woods are that they tend to produce sparks and burn very fast. You may need more to get the main fuel going and they are soon consumed if they form the main fuel themselves.

Don't collect kindling straight from the earth, it is almost always damp. Take if from standing deadwood. If the outside is damp, shave until the dry middle is reached.

MAKE FIRE STICKS

Shave sticks with shallow cuts to 'feather' them. Preparing kindling in this way makes it catch light more freely and establishes a fire quickly.

FUEL

Use dry wood from standing trees to get the fire going. Once it is established you can use greener wood or dry out damp wood.

As a general rule, the heavier the wood the more heat it will give — this applies to both dead and green wood. Mixing green and dry wood makes a long-lasting fire, which is especially useful at night.

Hardwoods — hickory, beech or oak, for instance — burn well, give off great heat and last for a long time as hot coals. They keep a fire going through the night.

Softwoods tend to burn too fast and give off sparks. The worst spark-makers are cedar, alder, hemlock, spruce, pine, chestnut and willow.

Remember that damp wood is sometimes advantageous, producing smoke to keep off flies, midges and mosquitoes and burning longer so that it keeps the fire in.

Dry wood across two supports above a fire — not so close that it is set alight. Lay green logs at an angle beside the fire, tapering away from the wind to speed combustion of a sluggish fire while drying them.

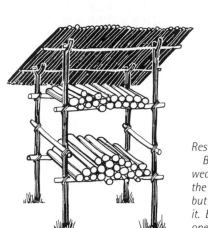

Rest logs against a pot rail to dry.

Build a wood shed — essential in wet weather. Set it close to the fire so that the fire's warmth will help dry the wood, but not so close that a spark could ignite it. Build two bays and use wood from one while the other batch dries.

SAVE ENERGY

Don't waste energy chopping logs:

Break them by smashing them over a rock (a).

If that does not work, feed them over the fire, letting them burn through in the middle (b) or, if they are not so long, feed them end first into the fire.

If it is absolutely necessary to split logs in order to conserve fuel, an axe is not needed. Even quite a small knife placed on the end of a log and hit with a rock may split it (c). Once begun, plug a wooden wedge in the opened gap and drive this downward to complete the split. But if you only have one knife don't take the risk of damaging it.

STAR FIRE

Logs are fed in lengthways. When not required to produce strong heat they can be drawn apart leaving glowing embers and ash for cooking in the centre.

To resurrect the fire push them together and they soon take flame again.

This type of fire is used mainly to conserve fuel but also saves chopping wood.

Other fuels

In areas where wood is scarce or unavailable other fuels must be found.

Animal droppings: These make excellent fuel – frontiersmen of the Wild West used 'buffalo chips' for their fires. Dry the droppings thoroughly for a good smokeless fire. You can mix them with grass, moss and leaves.

Peat: is often found on well-drained moors. It is soft and springy underfoot and may be exposed on the edges of rocky outcrops – looking black and fibrous. It is easily cut with a knife. Peat needs good ventilation when burning.

Stacked with plenty of air around it peat dries rapidly and is soon ready to burn.

Coal: is sometimes found on the surface – there are large deposits in the northern tundra.

Shales: are often rich in oil and burn readily. Some sands also contain oil – they burn with a thick oily smoke which makes a good signal fire and also give off a good heat.

Oils: If you have had a mechanical failure and crashed or broken down with fuels intact you can burn petroleum, anti-freeze, hydraulic fluid and other combustible liquids. Even insect repellent is inflammable. Anti-freeze is an excellent primer for igniting heavier engine oils. With a little potassium permanganate (from your survival kit) you can set it alight in a few seconds.

In very cold areas drain oil from an engine sump before it congeals. If you have no container drain it on to the ground to use later in its solid state.

Tyres, upholstery, rubber seals and much of any wreckage can be burned. Soak less combustible materials in oil before trying to make them burn.

Mix petrol with sand and burn it in a container as a stove, or dig a hole and make a fire pit.

Burn oil by mixing in petrol or antifreeze. Do not set a light directly to liquid fuels but make a wick and let that provide the flame. The same goes for insect repellent.

Animal fats: These can also be used with a wick in a suitably ventilated tin to make a stove. Bones can add bulk when fat is being burned as a fire (sometimes the only available fuel in polar regions).

Start flame with tinder or a candle then place a network of bones over it to support the fat or blubber. Use only a little fat at first. Unless it is surplus, burning fat means sacrificing food value, but seal blubber spoils rapidly and makes good fuel.

BURNING OIL AND WATER

This mixture makes one of the hottest of all fires. Pierce a small hole in the base of a tin can for each liquid and fit a tapered stick into it to govern the flow (a). The oil and water run down a trough on to a metal plate. Pulling the stick out increases the flow, pushing it in reduces it. Try 2–3 drops water: 1 drop oil.

First light a small fire under the plate to get it hot. The mixture becomes highly volatile when heated. Light it above the plate. This fire will burn almost anything.

a

FIRELIGHTING

Make a bed of tinder and form a wigwam of kindling around it. In a strong wind lean the kindling against a log on the leeside. Ignite the tinder. Once the kindling has caught add larger sticks. Or take a bundle of dry twigs, no thicker than a match, light them first and place them in the wigwam.

MATCHES

Matches are the easiest way to start a fire. Carry the non-safety 'strike anywhere' type and as many as possible. Pack them in waterproof containers so that they cannot rub or rattle and accidentally ignite. Waterproofing the matches themselves does both jobs.

Some people split all their matches in half and it has been claimed that one can be successfully divided into six. But do NOT risk wasting them – one that works is more use than six that don't!

Strike split matches by pressing the business end against the striking surface with a finger. If this burns the finger be ready to cool it at once – in cold water, snow or even 'spit on it and blow'.

Damp matches

If your hair is dry and not too greasy roll the damp match in it. Electricity should dry out the match.

Waterproof matches by dripping candle wax on to them. Rip it off with a fingernail when about to strike one.

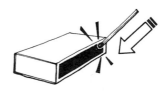

Strike a damp match by stabbing obliquely into the striker strip instead of drawing the match along it.

REMEMBER: Whenever you strike a match light a candle. Many things in turn can then be lit from it — saving matches. Place it in the wigwam of kindling to start a fire and remove it as soon as the flame spreads. Only the smallest amount is burned and even a small candle will last a long time.

However many lighters or fire-makers you carry, still pack as many matches as you can — you can't beat them. So-called everlasting matches can be used over and over again but sooner or later even they pack up. So carry ordinary matches as well. Work out which kind gives you the most strikes for the weight and room they take up.

Using a lens

Strong direct sunlight, focussed through a lens, can produce sufficient heat to ignite your tinder. Accidental fires are caused by the sun shining through broken bottles on to dry leaves or pasture. Your survival kit magnifying glass or a telescope or camera lens will serve instead.

Shield tinder from wind. Focus sun's rays to form the tiniest, brightest spot of light. Keep it steady. Blow on it gently as it begins to glow.

Powder from ammunition

If you are carrying arms you can use the gunpowder propellant from a round to help ignite your tinder.

Break open the round and pour the gunpowder on to your tinder before using your flint (a), or remove only half the powder and stuff a piece of cloth into the cartridge case (b). Chamber the round and fire as usual, into the ground. The cloth will be ejected smouldering. Place it on tinder with the remaining propellant and you will soon have a fire going.

Flint and steel

Flint is a stone found in many parts of the world. If it is struck vigorously with a piece of steel hot sparks fly off which will ignite dry tinder. A saw-edged blade can produce more sparks than an ordinary knife and should be in your kit. A block of magnesium with flint on its side is an even more efficient device — magnesium burns very strongly.

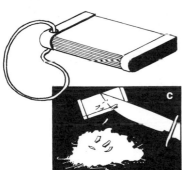

Strike the blade against the flint (a), or draw the saw across the ridged surface of the flint supplied with it (b), close to tinder so that sparks fall on it.

With a magnesium block, scrape slivers of magnesium on to tinder first (c), then use the saw to produce the sparks.

Battery fire lighting

A spark from a car battery can start your fire, and torch and radio batteries should have sufficient power. You need two lengths of wire, which you simply attach to the terminals. If you cannot find any wire you could do it with a couple of spanners or other metal implements. Unless you have long pieces of wire, take the battery out of the vehicle first.

Slowly bring the bare ends of the two pieces of wire together. Just before they touch, a spark will jump across. You must catch it on your tinder. A small piece of cloth with a little petrol on it makes the best tinder, the petrol vapour igniting from the spark.

Fire bow

A simple fire-making technique, but one that needs lots of practise. The friction of a hardwood spindle rotated on a softwood base produces first fine wood-dust tinder, then heat. Balsa, pine and bamboo are typically suitable softwoods; oak, ash and beech are hardwoods. Both must be dry.

Gouge a small depression at the near end of the baseboard and cut a cavity below it in which to place the tinder. Shape the spindle evenly. Make the bow from a pliable shoot such as hazel or bamboo and the string from hide, twine or a bootlace. You also need a hollowed piece of stone or wood, or a small jar to steady the top of the spindle and exert downward pressure.

Wind the bowstring once around the spindle. Place the spindle in the depression, hold the steadying piece over its end and bear lightly down on it while the other hand moves the bow backwards and forwards. This makes the spindle spin. Increase the speed as the spindle starts drilling through the wood. When it begins to enter the cavity apply more pressure and bow vigorously.

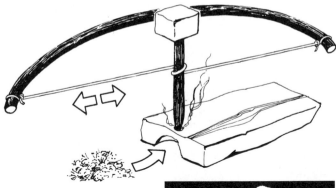

Keep on bowing until unable to continue. If successful the tip, glowing like a cigarette, will drop onto your tinder, which, if you gently blow on it, will burst into flame. You must keep the spindle upright and steady.

It helps to kneel with one foot on the baseboard and to lock the spindle arm on to this leg while bowing with the other hand. Keep the bow strokes very even.

A V-shaped notch, as shown in the baseboard of the hand-drill method, is also recommended.

Hand drill

This variation on the fire bow is particularly useful in dry territories with low humidity and little rainfall — making everything 'tinder' dry.

In a baseboard of hardwood cut a V-shaped collecting notch which will hold tinder, but still allow air to reach it. Make a small depression near it. For a spindle use a stem of hollow softer wood with a soft pith core.

Roll the spindle between the palms of the hands, running them down it with each burst of spinning to press the spindle into the depression in the baseboard.

When the friction makes the spindle tip glow red, blow gently to ignite the tinder around it. Putting a pinch of sand in the spindle hole increases the friction and speeds the heating of the tinder.

A cavity below the spindle, as shown for the fire-bow method, is also recommended.

Fire plough

This method of ignition also works by friction. Cut a straight groove in a soft wood baseboard and then 'plough' the tip of a hardwood shaft up and down it. This first produces tinder and then eventually ignites it.

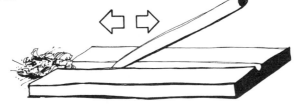

Fire lighting with chemicals

A survivor's pack is not likely to include a complete chemistry set but there are some very common chemicals that, if they are available, can be used to produce combustion. The following mixtures can all be ignited by grinding them between rocks or putting them under the friction point in any of the types of fire drill already described. Mix them carefully, avoiding contact with any metal objects. All are susceptible to dampness and must be kept dry.

WARNING

Handle these chemicals carefully, sodium chlorate in particular — it ignites from percussion, so avoid shaking it up or letting it spill. Spilled weedkiller on a hard path has been known to ignite when stepped on or a watering can put down on it!

Potassium chlorate and sugar in a mixture of 3:1 by volume is a fierce-burning incendiary which can also be ignited by dripping a few drops of sulphuric acid onto the mixture.

Potassium permanganate and sugar mixed 9:1 is less sensitive and temperature is a critical factor in how long it takes to ignite. The addition of glycerine will also produce ignition.

Sodium chlorate and sugar mixed 3:1.
- Sulphuric acid is found in car batteries
- Potassium chlorate is found in some throat tablets — their contents may be listed on the pack. Try crushing one and seeing if it works.
- Potassium permanganate is included in your survival kit.
- Glycerine is a constituent of anti-freeze.
- Sodium chlorate is a weed-killer.

TYPES OF FIRE

However quickly you want to get a fire going take time, while you gather fuel and get the tinder ready, to choose the best location and the best type of fire.

Fires for warmth
With a single fire outdoors only surfaces facing it are warmed. With two fires you can sit between them — but that would use a lot of fuel and, no matter which way the wind is blowing, you are bound to be covered in smoke. Build one fire and use a reflector.

A good reflector, close to the fire, not only reflects heat back to you but also helps to make the smoke go upwards, drawn by hot currents of air, instead of getting in your eyes. Use a reflector to direct heat into a sleeping shelter.

The inexperienced often build a fire up against a tree stump or a rock — don't, build the fire away from it and sit between the two so that the rock reflects the heat and warms your back. Add a reflector.

If there is no ready-made reflector, build one — and build another reflector on the other side of the fire to reflect as much as possible of its heat back to you.

Snake hole fire

This is a shielded fire that produces a good draught and burns almost anything once lit. In the side of a firm earth bank excavate a chamber about 45cm (18in) deep. From above drive a stick down into the chamber, manoeuvre it about a little to make a chimney, removing the spoil that falls below. Build the fire in the chamber.

Good for burning rubbish and for smoke preserving meat and fish. The snake hole fire entrance is best sited downwind in windy conditions.

283

Cooking fires

These cooking fires are also good for heating.

Yukon stove

This fire, once lit, will burn almost anything. It takes a lot of effort to build but is worth it for the whole structure gives off good heat and the top can be used for cooking.

Dig a hole circular in shape and about 24cm (9in) deep with a channel on one side leading down to it. Set rocks up all round the outer edge of the main hole and build up a funnel, bridging over the channel and gradually sloping inwards. Let the upper courses begin to open out again. Seal all the spaces between the rocks with earth. The fire is shielded, the chimney creating a good draught.

Light the fire first in the channel. When it gets going push it beneath the chimney. Fuel is then fed in through the top of the chimney and the rate of burning is controlled by opening or closing the top.

This fire leaves very little ash and will burn a very long time before it needs clearing out.

Trench fire

This fire is sheltered from strong wind by being below ground level. Dig a trench about 30 x 90cm (12 x 36in) and about 30cm (12in) deep plus the depth of a layer of rocks with which you now line the bottom. Build the fire on top of the rocks. Even when it has died down they will remain hot and make an excellent grill.

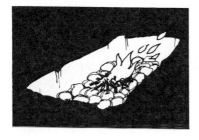

A spit placed across the embers is excellent for roasting.

Hobo stove

This stove provides a heat source several people can huddle around and its top can be used for cooking. To make it you need something like a five gallon oil drum.

Punch holes in the bottom and around the bottom of the sides of the drum for draught to enter. Cut out a panel on one side, about 5cm (2in) from the bottom through which to stoke the fire.

Punch holes in the top if to be used only for heating, but make them on the upper part of one side if you don't want smoke coming through the top.

Set the whole drum on a ring of stones so that there is plenty of draught beneath.

SPONTANEOUS COMBUSTION

Fire sometimes breaks out spontaneously in a compacted heap of wet hay. It can be produced in cotton soaked in linseed oil provided the atmosphere is warm and dry, but temperature can be critical. Either it will burst into flame within a couple of hours or not at all. Not a reliable way of firelighting — but a risk of which to be aware.

COOKING

When food is heated it loses nutritional value — the more the heat the greater the loss — so nothing should be cooked longer than is necessary to make it palatable unless it is suspect and being cooked to kill germs and parasites or to neutralize poisons.

Boiling vegetables destroys their vitamin C content and roasting meat removes its all-important fat, but we are used to eating our food cooked and a hot meal is unsurpassed for raising morale. It would take great discipline to eat many things raw that you had not previously considered foods, but a frog, grubs or rats do not seem too bad once cooked.

Cooking not only makes many foods more appetizing to taste, see and smell, it softens the muscle fibres in meat, makes protein more easy to digest and — most important — it destroys bacteria and parasites that may be present.

If the ground is lush, animal foods are more likely to carry parasites. Pigs, especially, carry worms and flukes. Thorough boiling will destroy them, though at the loss of food value. Some foods must never be eaten raw — nettles and several other plants, for instance — but should always be cooked to neutralize harmful substances which they contain.

Your particular situation will determine whether to cook or not. If you cannot face eating something raw, or if food is plentiful but limited in type, cook it to make it more palatable. Relieve boredom by varying cooking instructions.

Cooking methods will depend upon the foodstuff and the facilities you have or can create. Type of fire, utensil support and cooking methods must all be matched.

Cooking requires a slow heat. Use the flame of a fire to boil water then let the fierce flames die down and use embers and hot ash for cooking.

REMEMBER: NEVER leave your fire unattended when cooking — you cannot afford to ruin food.

Once having lit a fire, ALWAYS have something boiling on it — unless water is in short supply — for hot water is always an asset: hot drinks are always cheering and you will find a multitude of uses from sterilizing wounds to making poultry plucking easier.

Do NOT just balance a can on the fire — if it tips over you could put your fire out, quite apart from losing its contents. Support vessels on firm rocks or suspend them over the fire.

Boiling

Cooking in boiling water requires a container. Tin cans and metal boxes are ideal. Make a handle, hang them from a pot support or use pot tongs to take them on and off the fire (see *Useful utensils*). Puncture holes in pots can be repaired by hammering in small plugs of wood — when wet they will expand and stop leaks. If no metal containers are available, a thick length of bamboo holds liquids well. Containers can also be made from birch bark — but be careful that they do not boil dry.

To cook in a bamboo stem, angle it across the heat of the fire, supporting it on a forked stick driven into the ground.

Although boiling does destroy some food elements it conserves the natural juices and retains all the fat — provided that you drink all the liquid as well as eat the remaining solids. Each time you throw away cooking water you lose valuable nutrients, though you will have to discard it if boiling out toxic substances. Boiling will make tough and stringy roots and old game softer and more edible. It will kill worms and flukes and can even make spoiled meat fit to eat.

If you frighten a feeding animal from its kill, you can eat the remaining meat provided that you cut the meat up and boil it for at least 30 minutes. If desperate for food any dead animal that is not actually decomposing can be risked if you use only the large muscle areas. Cut them into 2.5cm (1in) cubes and then boil briskly for at least 30 minutes. Eat only a little, then wait for half an hour to see if there are any ill effects — most toxins affect the digestive system in that time or less. If there are no ill effects tuck in.

Part-boiling vegetables that you intend to cook by other means will speed up cooking times. (For boiling water when no fire proof containers are available see *Hangi method*.)

Roasting

Roasted meat cooks in its own fat. The easiest method is to skewer the meat on a spit and turn it over the hot embers of a fire or beside a blazing fire where it is hot enough to cook. Continually turning the meat keeps the fat moving over the surface. Roasting makes a very tasty dish but has two disadvantages.

Valuable fat is lost unless a drip tray is placed beneath the spit. Regularly baste the meat with fat from the tray.

Roasting by a fierce fire can cook and seal the outside, the inner flesh remaining undercooked, leaving harmful bacteria alive. A slow roast is preferable, and if cooking continues after the outer meat has been cut off the inner flesh can go on cooking.

The fire should be slightly to one side of food to allow for a drip tray to catch valuable fat.

Grilling

Grilling is a quick way of cooking large amounts of food but it requires a support — such as a mesh of wire — rested on rocks over the embers of the fire. It should only be used when food is plentiful since it wastes most of the fat from the meat. Hot rocks beside the fire can be used as grilling surfaces or food skewered on sticks and held over the fire.

If no wire mesh is available, make a grid of very green sticks or rest a long stick on a forked support so that it can hold food over the fire. Wrap food around the stick. You can also barbecue meat and vegetables on a stick supported across glowing embers by a forked stick on each side.

Baking

You need an oven for baking, but if time and materials are available this is a good way of cooking. Meat should be cooked on a dish and the fat which runs out used to baste it. It is ideal for tough, stringy meat. Cooked for a long time on a steady heat the meat becomes more tender. Baking is also very suitable for root vegetables.

If meat is placed in a tin containing a little water to be cooked in the oven this is a form of braising.

Use an oven to cook several different things at once.

Metal box oven

A large food tin or metal box with a hinged lid makes an excellent improvised oven. Army survivors found an ammunition box ideal. If the lid is hinged and has a catch on it that you can use as a handle, you could set it up to open sideways. It will probably be easier, especially if it has no catch or you have to improvise hinges, to let it open downwards. If you place a rock or other support in front, to rest it on, you will have a convenient shelf. You can always prop it closed if there is no catch, for you do not want a tightly sealed fit — which could build up dangerous pressure inside. If no tin or box is available you could make a clay dome, like an Indian tandoori oven. To make it hot set a fire inside and scrape this out before cooking. Leave a smallish aperture which can be easily sealed while baking.

Stand the tin on some rocks so that a fire can be lit beneath it. Build up rocks and earth — or, better, clay — around back and sides and over it, but leaving a space behind for heat and smoke to move around the back. Use a stick to make a chimney hole from above to the space at the back.

Steaming

Steaming does not overcook so preserves nutritional values. It is an excellent way of cooking fish and green vegetables. Fresh young leaves take very little cooking. The foodstuff needs to be suspended in the steam from boiling water.

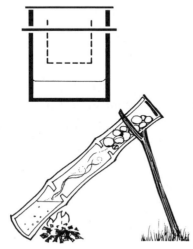

Make a simple steamer by punching holes in a can and suspending it inside a larger can, or putting something in the bottom of the larger can to keep the inner one above the water. Cover the outer can so that steam is not dissipated, but not so tightly that it is sealed or pressure could build up and cause it to explode.

The compartmented sections of bamboo also make an excellent steamer. Make a comparatively small hole between the sections, but big enough to let water through to fill the bottom section. Make a lid (not too tight) for the top. Water boiled in the lowest section will produce steam to cook food in the top one.

Frying

Frying is an excellent way of varying diet, if fat is available and you have a container to fry in. Any sheet of metal that you can fashion into a curve or give a slight lip to will serve. In some areas, you may find a large leaf which contains enough oil not to dry out before the cooking is done — banana leaves are excellent surfaces to fry eggs upon. Try leaves out before you risk valuable food on them and, if you do use one, fry only over embers, not over flames.

Cooking in clay

Wrapping food in clay is a method that requires no utensils and offers a tasty alternative even when you have them. After wrapping in a ball of clay, food is placed in the embers of a fire. The heat radiates through the clay which protects the food so that it does not scorch or burn.

Animals must be cleaned and gutted first but need not be otherwise prepared: when the clay is removed a hedgehog's spines or a fish's scales will remain embedded in it. With small birds, the clay does your plucking for you — but feathers provide insulation and may prevent a big bird being properly cooked. Cooking root vegetables in this way will remove their skins — losing important food value.

Hangi method

This is another way of cooking without utensils. Like the clam bake of the United States and traditional Maori and South Pacific methods it involves heating stones. It requires kindling, logs and round rocks or stones about the size of a fist. Do not use soft, porous or flaky stones which might explode on heating.

Dig an oval-shaped hole with rounded sides 45–60cm deep (18–24in) and place kindling at the bottom. Lay logs across the hole, place another layer of logs at right angles to them, interspersing them with stones. Make another layer of logs and build up five or six more alternating layers, topping them off with stones.

When the kindling is set alight the logs will burn, heating the stones above them, until, eventually, all falls down into the pit. Remove the burning embers and ash. Now, place food on top of the hot rocks, meat to the centre and vegetables towards the outer edge. There must be a gap between the food and the earth. Lay saplings across the pit and place sacking, leaves and so forth on top of them, covering the lot with the earth which you excavated to keep the heat in. The hole now acts rather like a pressure cooker. After 1½ hours remove the cover — your meal will be cooked.

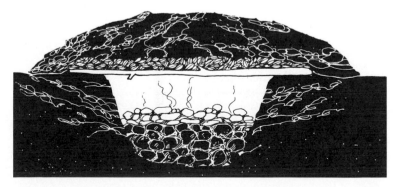

CAMP CRAFT

Boiling water in a hangi

If you have no container in which to boil water you can make use of the hangi. Whatever you have collected water in, provided that it does not melt (so that rules out plastic but includes other kinds of waterproof fabric), can be gathered up and tied so that the water does not spill and placed in the hangi). It will take about 1½ hours to boil but the fabric will not burn through.

USEFUL UTENSILS

TONGS

Choose two branches, both with a natural curve, and lash them together so that they want to spring apart at the free ends. Or use a tapering piece of wood between them under the lashings to hold them apart. If one has a forked end the grip will be improved. Use for holding pots, hot rocks and logs.

POT ROD

To give more variable access to the fire than a rail over it (a), drive a sturdy forked stick into the ground near the fire – but not so close as to catch alight. Rest a much longer stick across it with one end over the fire. Drive the bottom end of the longer stick into the ground and prevent it from springing up with heavy rocks. Cut a groove near the tip to prevent pots from slipping off, or – to be safer – tie on a strong hook.

Two or three sticks could lean over the fire at different heights with meat or vegetables attached.

SWINGING POT HOLDER

This can be made from two forked sticks and a firm upright driven into the ground. Bind the branches together so that the forks fit in opposite directions on the upright. The cantilever action will maintain the height you set it at, and a push sideways will swing the pot away from the flames. With a longer upright you could control cooking height also.

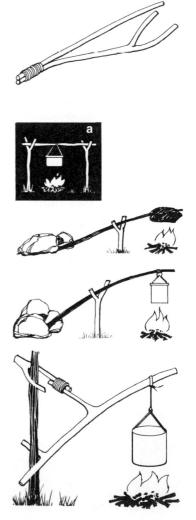

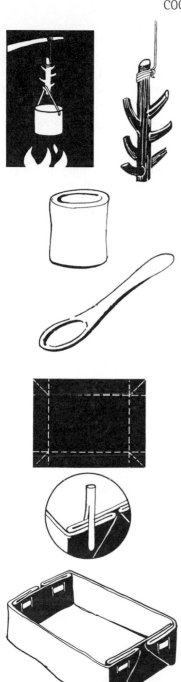

VARIABLE POT HOOK

Since the distance between the fire and the food will affect the speed at which the food cooks, make this hanging device so that you can control your cooking.

Cut a strong piece with several branches from a small tree or bush and trim the branches to 10–12cm (4–5in). Strip off the bark, which may hide a rotten branch.

BAMBOO CUP

Cut a section of bamboo just below a natural joint and then cut just below the next joint up. Smooth the edges to prevent splinters.

SPOON

Start with a flattish piece of wood and scribe a spoon shape on it with the point of your knife. Then whittle away to the required shape. Do not hurry — this will only result in mistakes. Never cut towards yourself or your hand.

BIRCH BARK CONTAINERS

Use the inner layer of birch bark to make storage boxes or temporary cooking vessels — which can be used for boiling. Sew or tie them — near the top — to prevent unfolding. An alternative for temporary vessels is to peg the top edges with split sticks, but you might well spill the contents if the vessel suddenly unfolds.

Make another vessel, but with a larger base, and you will have a lid to fit over the first.

A circle, folded into quarters, will make a cone-shaped cup — or a boiling vessel if suspended.

PRESERVING FOOD

If food is not plentiful or is likely to be limited by season, it is important to ensure that stores keep safely.

Micro-organisms, such as moulds, that spoil food, thrive in warm moist atmospheres. Deterioration can be delayed by keeping food in cool places such as caves or by water, but that is only a short-term measure. More positive action must be taken to ensure long-term preservation. The main methods to use are drying, smoking, pickling and salting. Sugar preserves will not keep for very long unless you can vacuum-seal them, but will keep longer than as soft fruit, and alcohol is an excellent preservative if you set up the facilities to make it.

REMEMBER:

When you have taken time and trouble to preserve valuable foodstuffs, particularly in areas where food is scarce, take equal trouble in storing your food.

Do not store in direct sunlight, near excessive warmth or moisture, nor where scavenging animals may ruin it.

Wrap, where possible, in airtight and water-proof materials – or store in containers (such as birch-bark boxes) with a good seal. Label if you are storing several kinds of food and separate to avoid cross-flavouring.

Check occasionally to see all is well.

Drying

Both wind and sun can dry food but, in most climates, it is easier to force dry food over a fire. Losing moisture shrinks size and weight, concentrating the nutritional value. Many moulds can grow when there is as little as 16 per cent moisture content, but few can grow on foods with 5 per cent or less and these will also be less vulnerable to maggots.

Pork, geese, seabirds and other meat with a high fat content are the most difficult to preserve. It is best to cut off most of the fat and rub salt into the flesh. Salt is a good drying agent. Hang the salted meat in a cool airy place.

Smoke drying

Smoking both dehydrates meat and coats it with a protective layer, like varnishing its surface. The inside is dry so no condensation takes place, and the outside is sealed against bacteria. Smoking can be best effected in a smoke house or a smoke tepee.

SMOKE TEPEE
Drive three sticks into the ground to form a triangle and tie the tops together. Build a platform between them and get a fire going beneath.

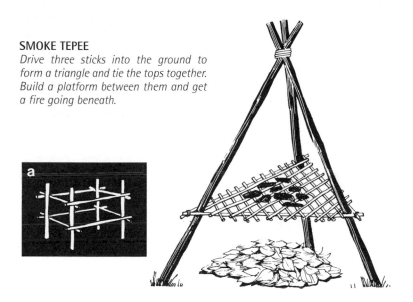

Smoke house

As an alternative to the tepee make a square frame of uprights (a) and cross-pieces supporting a smoking platform with the fire beneath and used in exactly the same way as the tepee.

In both cases meat should be cut into lean, fat-free strips and fish gutted and filleted. The strips can be any length but should only be about 2.5cm (1in) wide and 6mm (¼in) thick.

Get a fire going to produce a pile of hot embers. Have a pile of green leaves ready. Leaves from hardwood trees are excellent, especially oak, but avoid holly and other toxic leaves and conifers which tend to be resinous and may burst into flame. Do not use grass. Some leaves will give meat an individual flavour; pimento leaves are particularly distinctive.

Make sure that there are no flames left in the fire and pile the leaves over the embers. Cover the whole structure with a cloth to keep in the smoke. If you do not have a suitable material, have boughs and turfs ready to pile rapidly on the frame and seal it. Leave the structure sealed for 18 hours ensuring that little or no smoke escapes.

If the embers in a smoke tepee burst into flame, there is a risk that the whole structure may catch alight. This can be avoided by building a fire in a chamber in a bank (see Snake hole in Fire) with the tepee erected over the chimney. This also makes it possible to tend the fire and to ensure a more extensive supply of smoke, which will be cooler than from a fire directly underneath. The food will dry slowly and become coated with smoke without being cooked.

Biltong

This is sun-dried meat. Biltong is the Afrikaans name, it is also known as jerky, from the North American Indian *charqui*. It does not keep as efficiently as smoked meat and should be used only when smoking is not practicable.

Cut strips, as for smoking, and hang them up in the sun. Make sure that they are out of the reach of animals and about 2–3m (6–10ft) from the ground.

It may take two weeks for meat to dry and all this time it must be kept dry, so protection from rain must be provided. The strips must be turned, if necessary, to make sure that all surfaces are thoroughly dried, and, initially at least, flies must be kept off so that they do not lay eggs on the meat.

DRYING FISH
Preserve fish as biltong. Cut off heads and tails and gut. Split open. Remove backbone and lay on hot sun-baked rocks. Score inner flesh to speed up drying.

Small fishes, under 7.5cm (3in) long need not be gutted.

Fish can also be smoked. They should be opened out, but it will be easier to hang if cleaned and gutted without removing the backbone, head or tail. Suspend by one side of the head.

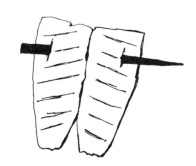

Pemmican

This is a nutritious concentrated food made from biltong — excellent for provisions to carry with you if you decide it is time to trek to safety. It contains all essential minerals and vitamins except vitamin C.

You need an equal quantity, by weight, of biltong and of rendered fat. Shred and pound the meat. Melt the animal fat over a slow fire, without allowing it to boil. Pour the fat over the shredded biltong and mix them well together.

When cold pack the mixture in a waterproof bag. It will keep for a long time, especially in colder climates.

Pickling and salting

Citric acid obtained from wild limes and lemons can be used to pickle fish and meat. Dilute two parts of fruit juice with one of water, mix well and soak flesh in this for at least 12 hours. Now transfer it to a covered, and preferably, airtight container and with sufficient solution to cover all the meat. Vegetables with a high water content are difficult to preserve. Pickling is best for them. Alternatively, if salt is more easily available than citrus fruits, they can be boiled and then kept in brine (saltwater). Boiling kills off bacteria and the brine keeps fresh bacteria away from the food.

The usual way of making sure that a brine solution is sufficiently strong is to add salt until a potato will float in it. In lieu of a potato try a small fruit or root vegetable which fails to float in salt-free water (not apples — they float too easily). Another method of using salt is to pack tightly layers of salt and vegetables such as beans and peas, thoroughly washing off the salt when you need to use them.

Nuts and cereals

These keep reasonably well provided they are not allowed to get damp but will keep better if dried. Place them on hot rocks from the fire, turning them frequently until thoroughly dried. They should then be kept in damp-proof containers.

Fruit, fungi and lichens

Fruit and berries can be dried whole or cut into slices and dried by sun, smoke or heat. Fungi also dry very readily — the Boletus species especially. Fruit can usually be eaten dry. Fungi can be added to soups and stews or soaked in water for several hours to regain some of their texture if being used in other ways.

To store lichens, soak them overnight, boil well and dry. Grind to a powder then boil again to form a thick syrup, which can be kept in a sealed container and used to give body to other foods.

COOKING TIPS

Meat

Meat is best cut into small cubes and boiled. Pork is particularly suspect in hot climates: wild pig is usually infested with worm and liver fluke. Venison is also prone to worms.

Put excessively tough meat in a solution of juice from citric fruit for 24 hours. This marinading helps to make it more tender. Bring to boil and simmer until tender.

Offal

Check liver especially carefully. If firm, odourless and free from spots and hard lumps it can be eaten. Boil first, then fry if you wish. Hearts are best par-boiled then baked. Brain (if not used for preserving hides) makes an excellent stew. Skin the head and boil, simmering for 90 minutes. Strip all the flesh from the skull, including the eyes, tongue and ears.

Blood

Leave in the container in which it is collected but keep it covered. A clear liquid comes to the top. When separation seems complete drain it off. Dry the residue by the fire to form a firm cake. Use it to enrich soups and stews.

Sausages

Thoroughly clean intestines, turning them inside out to wash. Fill with a mix of half meat/half fat bound with enough blood to hold the ingredients together. Tie the ends and boil. Once cooked they can be preserved by cold smoking in a smoke tepee over a chimney.

Fish

Usually germ-free if caught in fresh water. Fish take little cooking and are best stewed or wrapped in leaves and placed in hot embers — chickweed and butterbur are good for this: avoid toxic leaves.

Birds

Boil all carrion. Old crows, blackbirds and parrots are tough and best boiled. Young specimens can be roasted — stuff the bird with herbs and fruits.

Reptiles

Best gutted and then cooked in their skins which are rough and leathery. Place in hot embers and turn continually. When the skin splits the meat can be removed and boiled. A few snakes have poisonous secretions on the skin and others may have venom glands in their head, so cut this off before cooking. If you are not sure whether they are safe, take care in handling them.

Skin frogs before cooking (many frogs have poisonous skins). Roast on a stick.

Turtles

Boil turtles and tortoises until the shell comes off. Cut up the meat and cook until tender.

Shark meat

Has a bad taste unless correctly cooked. Cut into small cubes and soak overnight in fresh water. Boil in several changes of water to get rid of the ammonia flavour.

Shellfish

Crabs, lobsters and shrimps, crayfish, prawns and so forth are safer boiled since they may contain harmful organisms. All seafood spoils quickly and must be cooked as soon as possible. Drop into boiling salted water and boil for ten minutes.

If you are sure the food is fresh, a clambake is a delicious way to prepare mussels, clams and similar creatures. Dig a hole in the sand and light a fire alongside with stones on top. When the stones are hot place them in the hole, put the shells on top and cover with wet seaweed or grass, then a 10cm (4in) layer of sand. The hole will develop a lot of steam which cooks the molluscs.

Insects and worms

Best boiled. Cook and mince them by crushing in a can.

More acceptable dried on hot rocks and then ground into a powder with which to enrich soups and stews.

Eggs

Boiling is the best way of cooking, but if no container is available roast after first using a sharpened stick or the very sharp point of a knife to pierce a small hole in one end. Place on warm embers to cook slowly. Slow cooking reduces the risk of cracking. Remember that banana leaves, which are full of oil, make an excellent frying pan. Place over hot embers and crack the egg onto the leaf. If a boiled egg contains an embryo chick remove the embryo and roast it.

Green vegetables
Wash in clean water and boil for just long enough to make them tender — they are often and easily overcooked. Tender plants can be gently steamed if you are sure that they are safe to eat. Add to stew after the meat is cooked and already tender. Eat fresh greens raw as salad.

Roots
Some are toxic but the toxins are destroyed by heat. Always cook roots; boiling will make the toughest ones tender. Roast roots are tasty — but boil them first. Try boiling for five minutes then place them in a hole dug beneath the fire, cover with ash and embers and leave until tender.

Lichens and mosses
Soak overnight in clean water. Add to stews.

Sago
Proper sago comes from the sago palm, but buri, sugar, fishtail and, in the American tropics, cabbage palms can be used in the same way. The average sago palm yields about 275kg (600lb) of sago — enough to feed one person for a year. Cut down the palm at the base of the trunk, trim off the tip just below the last flowering line. Divide a large trunk into sections.

Cut lengthwise — hard work, for the outer bark is 5cm (2in) thick and hard as bamboo. Using each section as a trough, pound pith into a mash, then knead in a container of water (the bole of the trunk will do) and strain through a cloth. A starchy paste will precipitate in the water. Roll this into sticky balls and cook.

Sap
Palm sap is extracted from flowering parts, not the trunk. Choose a fat stalk carrying a flowering head (at the base of the crown of the

trunk). Bruise with a club to stimulate flow of sap, then cut off head. Sweet juice will flow from the end of the stalk — 1·5 litre (3pt) per day. Bruise and cut daily to stimulate flow. Drink raw or boil then cool it to produce toffee-like lumps of almost pure sugar. Sugar, nipa, coconut and burl palms can all be used in this way. (Extracting resinous sap is dealt with under *Trees* in *Food*.)

Grains and seeds

Grains are enclosed in a husk. Dry them thoroughly to allow the grain to crack out. Thresh (or thrash) it with a flail, stick or rock, or, if the grain is very malleable, rub it between your hands. Shake out on to a flat container and occasionally toss into the air in a breeze (winnowing). The husks (chaff) will blow away leaving the heavier seed behind.

Pinole

Parch husked seeds on hot stones by the fire. The heat will cook and dry seeds without roasting them. This pinole will keep well. Eat cold or reheat. Add to stews or place a handful in a mug of hot water — tasty and nutritious. Dry they will not be properly digested, but they will fill the belly. It is better to grind them into flour.

Flour

Grinding flour without a proper mill is hard work but can be done by pounding with a smooth stone on a hard surface. Look for a large stone with a depression in the middle to place the grain in. Use a circling action as with a mortar and pestle. Another way to grind flour is to hollow a tube of hardwood and to pound a stick up and down inside it on the grain.

Mix flour with a little water and knead into a dough. Bake in an oven or make into thin strips, wrap around a shaven green stick and cook over hot embers. Another method is to make the dough into fist-size balls, flatten them and then drop hot pebble-size stones into the centre and wrap the dough around them. Lick your fingers before picking up the pebbles — if you are quick the moisture stops the pebble from burning you — or use sticks or tongs (see *Useful utensils*) to lift them.

Flour does not have to be made from cereal grains. Use the flowering heads of cat's tails or boil and mash up peeled roots, of wild calla for instance, or edible barks. Those that are not harmful raw can be steeped in water and crushed with a stick or stone to free the starch. Remove fibres, leave starch to settle, then pour off the water and you will have your flour.

ORGANIZING THE CAMP

In many survival situations there will already be someone in a position of responsibility who will head the organization of the camp and lead the development of survival plans. If no established command structure exists among a group of survivors, an organizing committee should be established and individuals nominated and elected with particular responsibilities, perhaps on a rotational basis if it is a large group and rescue does not come quickly. Experience must be pooled and immediate steps taken to discover what skills individuals can contribute.

A rosta is essential for such daily chores as collecting firewood and water, foraging, cooking, latrine digging and maintenance tasks, and for hunting and trapping.

In a group of survivors there may be all kinds of people of different ages and experience. People will have varied skills and enjoy doing different tasks. Everyone who is fit and able should take their turn at the unpleasant tasks, unless their skills are so much in demand that it would be a waste of their abilities, but individuals should do what they are good at — and be encouraged to develop skills for which they show an aptitude.

Not only should everyone do their fair share but keeping busy eliminates boredom and keeps up morale. Anyone who is sick or injured gets the lightest jobs and is best employed around camp until they have recovered. In a group there should always be someone in camp, and they should be able enough to operate the signals should a search aircraft appear. If you have sufficient numbers do NOT venture from the camp in less than pairs.

Except in the desert, where the day will be largely spent sheltering from the sun and early morning and evening are the times for activity, daytime is likely to be fully occupied. Evenings, however, may drag if not occupied by hunting. A gathering around the camp fire will help establish a pattern and provide a sense of discipline and normality. It will give an opportunity to debrief on the day's events, to plan for tomorrow and to discuss new strategies.

Music can be a great morale booster. If no instruments were carried or survived, simple ones such as percussion or pan-pipes can easily be improvised, and everyone can sing after a fashion.

Sing-songs, dancing, charades, quizzes and story-telling all have their place and you may have talents which can create more elaborate entertainments. For private recreation any books will be invaluable and you can make pieces for board games such as draughts and chess, using stones for counters or carving simple playing pieces.

Even the lone survivor requires discipline and order. A regular routine will help morale and exactly the same care must be taken to ensure that the camp is kept in good order. At first there may be so much to do that the individual is too tired to think of recreation, but boredom is even more dangerous for a person on their own and objectives should be set each day whether practical or for amusement.

CAMP HYGIENE

Keeping healthy is an important factor for survival, so strict hygiene should be practised, not only personally but in the planning and running of a camp. Rubbish and latrines must be kept away from the camp to reduce the threat from flies and, since most of the common diseases in a survival situation are water-borne, pollution of drinking water must be rigorously avoided. Food scraps and other rubbish should be burned in the fire if possible.

Camp layout
Select sites for all camp activities so that they do not interfere with each other or pollute the living and cooking areas. If you are camped by a river or stream, fix specific sections for activities and keep to them.

Latrines should be dug downhill of the camp and away from the water supply so that there is no possible risk of seepage polluting either.

Activity areas
Establish a water point from which drinking water will be collected and ensure that no one washes, cleans pots, scrubs clothes or otherwise uses the stream upstream of this point. Downstream choose a wash point for personal ablutions and clothes washing and further downstream of that select a place to be used for cleaning cooking utensils.

Latrines and rubbish disposal should be well away from the camp — and preferably downwind — but not so far away that it is inconvenient and people are tempted to go elsewhere. If necessary cut a track to it to make access easier.

REMEMBER: NEVER urinate or defecate in or near your water supply.

Latrines and rubbish disposal

It is important that proper latrines be established, even for the lone survivor. With a group separate latrines for the sexes may make a mixed group feel more comfortable, and as much privacy as possible should be provided. Rubbish, after checking that it really has no useful value, should be burned, and what cannot be burned should be buried.

Even if you have it, do NOT use disinfectant in a latrine. Lime or disinfectants would kill the useful bacteria that break waste down and then it WILL start smelling! After defecating cover the faeces with earth. Add small amounts of water which will promote the bacteria.

Make a latrine cover to keep out flies and remember always to replace it, or flies that have walked all over faeces may walk all over your food and start a cycle of infection.

If, after a time, a latrine starts to smell, dig a new one. Fill in the old latrine. Build a new seat and burn old timbers and covers.

DEEP TRENCH LATRINE

Dig a trench about 1.25m (4ft) deep and 45cm (18in) wide. Build up the sides with logs or rocks and earth to make a comfortable sitting height sealing the gaps between them. Lay logs across to leave only a hole for use (or several if you are a large group and making a communal latrine). Empty wood ash on the logs to make a seal — it will also deter flies.

Make a lid of smaller wood to cover the opening or use a large flat rock or a large leaf weighted down with stones. Always remember to replace it.

URINAL

Dig a pit about 60cm (2ft) deep. Three-quarters fill it with large stones and then top up with earth with a cone made from bark set into it as a funnel. Site it close enough to the camp to ensure that people bother to use it.

Incinerator

If there is too much waste for the camp fire to burn, make a separate fire in the latrine area. If a large can is available use it as an incinerator. Bury any unburned refuse in a garbage pit.

CAMP DISCIPLINE

- Do not prepare game in camp: bleed, gut and skin on the trap line. This attracts game to the traps where you want them, not into your camp.

- Keep food covered and off the ground. If kept in trees make sure it is proof from tree-dwelling animals.

- Replace lids on water bottles and containers immediately after using them.

- Stow spare clothing and equipment in your shelter. Do not leave it lying where it can get wet or burned.

- Have a place for everything and keep things tidy: a tree for mess tins and cooking utensils — hook them on twigs and branches, a place for mugs and spoons — and keep everything off the ground. Fit a box as a cupboard on a tree trunk.

- Never leave the fire unattended.

Soap

Washing with soap removes natural oils, leaving the skin less waterproof and more prone to attack by germs. In survival circumstances it is a mistake to wash with soap too often. However, soap is the most widely used antiseptic, better than many others, such as iodine, which destroy body tissue as well as germs. It is ideal for scrubbing hands before administering first-aid for wounds. Save supplies for this.

Soap-making

Two ingredients — an oil and alkali — are needed to make soap. The oil can be animal fat (including fish) or vegetable, but not mineral. The alkali can be produced by burning wood or seaweed to produce ash.

METHOD: Wash ash with water. Strain and boil with the oil. Simmer until excess liquid is evaporated and allow to cool. This soap will clean the skin but is not antiseptic. Adding horseradish root or pine resin to the brew will make it antiseptic.

Experiment will be necessary to get the balance in the mixture right. Start with more oil than alkali because too much alkali will dry the skin, leaving it sore.

TOOLS

Before humans discovered metals, and learned to work them, tools were made from stone — especially flint, obsidian, quartz, chertz and other glassy rocks, bone and other natural objects. Stones can make efficient hammers, alone or lashed onto a handle if a shape that can be easily secured. The glassy stones can be knapped (chipped and flaked) to make a sharp edge; some other kinds of stone, such as slate, can also produce a knife edge, though they may not have the strength to be used for percussive blows.

The best start for a stone implement is a split cobble, perhaps from a stream bed, or split by a blow from another smooth, hard pebble, so that a flat face is produced. The blow should be at an angle of less than 90 degrees or the shock will be absorbed within the pebble. Once the split is made, other layers can be broken off. Flakes can be removed around the edge of the flat face by hitting edge-on with another stone. Delicate work can be produced by hitting and pressing with a softer tool such as deer's antler. If a flat face is produced end-on blows can make thin blades.

Making stone implements is not a skill that can be quickly acquired and you may have to be very persistent.

Bones can be used as tools — antlers and horns make useful digging implements, gougers and hammers. They can also be cut with stone tools or ground with coarse stones. You may have the advantage over the prehistoric toolmakers, whose skills you are copying, of having a knife or other metal implement to help you to carve bone.

Some woods, such as the Mulga tree of Australia, used by the Aborigines for spears, are hard enough to make effective blades for hunting and cutting.

STONE TOOLS

One technique for producing an axehead: First the stone is split and the edges partly shaped (a), then a platform is created on one side (b) from which a series of flakes can be struck vertically down (c).

The final shaping can then be done. Hit with softer stones, and hit and press small flakes away with a piece of antler or hard wood.

It may take a lot of patience to acquire tool making skills but even practise flakes may be useful as scrapers, for cutting edges and as arrowheads.

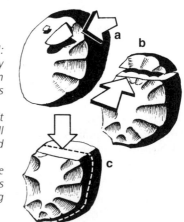

BONE TOOLS

A shoulder blade provides a good shape for an effective saw (a).

First it should be split in half then teeth can be cut along it with a knife.

A small bone scraper (b) could also be made, the edge ground sharp.

Ribs are good bones for shaping into points (c).

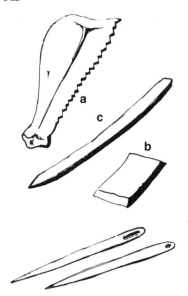

BONE NEEDLE

Choose a suitably-sized bone or flake of bone and sharpen to a point. Burn an eye with a piece of hot wire, or lacking that, scrape with a knife point or piece of flint. DON'T heat the knife in the fire.

AXES

A fire axe is part of the equipment of any boat or plane, but an axehead, to be fitted to an improvised handle, is a useful additional piece of equipment for anyone to carry. One of about 500–750g (1–1½lb) is ideal. Use your knife to fashion a handle when needed.

AXE HANDLE

Any straight, knot-free hardwood is suitable – ash and hickory are ideal. In the tropics the flukes of a buttress tree (a) are excellent: slightly curved, straight-grained and easy to work.

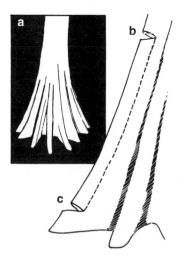

Cut two notches into the fluke of a buttress spaced to the desired handle length (b to c).

Hit along the side of fluke close to the cuts. It will split away at their depth.

FITTING THE HEAD

Whittle the handle into shape with one end cut to fit the hole in the axehead, cutting a notch in that end. Make a wedge to fit the notch.

With the head in place drive in the notch then soak the axe in water overnight to tighten the head on the shaft.

Always check axeheads for tightness before using them.

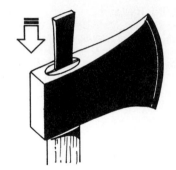

FITTING A STONE AXEHEAD

Select a hardwood handle. Tie a band of cord around it about 23cm (9in) from one end. Split the end down as far as this band (use your knife and a wedge or the piece of flint you have made for the axehead). Insert the flint and tie the end to secure.

This mounting will split wood but will not be very effective for chopping it.

Sharpening an axe

An axe with a blunt edge becomes no more than an inefficient hammer so keep it sharp, it will save energy. A file is best for getting rid of burrs, and a whetstone for imparting the sharp edge. A file is a one-way tool — it works when pushed, not pulled.

Prop axehead between a log and a peg (a). Always try to sharpen INWARDS from cutting edge to avoid producing burrs.

Use file or rougher stone first to remove rucks and burrs (b). Then finish with a smoother stone, using a circular motion. Don't drag the stone off the cutting edge. Push ONTO blade. (See Knives in Essentials).

Turn the axe over. Repeat the process circling in the opposite direction.

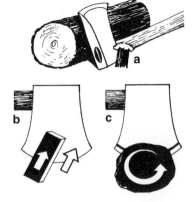

Using an axe

Most people have a natural prime hand and swing. Use an axe in a way that is comfortable to you, swinging it in an arc that feels natural with a firm grip and ALWAYS away from your body, hands, and legs. Make sure that, if you miss the tree or other point of aim and follow through, the axe will not strike you or anyone else. NEVER throw an axe on the ground. Sheath it or bury the blade in a log.

Tree felling

Check overhead for dead branches, which may fall and injure you, and for hornets' nests. Clear branches or creepers which could deflect your blows. If roots or the bole spread out at the bottom, build a platform to reach thinner-diameter trunk and reduce the effort of chopping. Ensure such a platform is stable and that you can jump off it quickly if the tree falls the wrong way!

Work at a comfortable height and try to cut downwards at 45 degrees, although every now and then a horizontal blow is needed to clear the cut.

Cut from both sides of the tree, first chopping out a notch at an angle of about 45 degrees and another on the opposite side at a lower level, ON THE SIDE TO WHICH YOU WANT THE TREE TO FALL (a). Do not cut through more than half the tree before starting the other notch.

If two people are at work on opposite sides this is particularly important. A leaning trunk or a tree with most of its branches on one side will fall in the direction of its weight and the placing of the cuts will not affect it.

A steady rhythm of blows will cut more effectively than trying to make fewer big blows. If you put too much effort behind the axe your aim will suffer and you will soon tire. Let the weight of the axe do the work.

Alternating the angle of stroke will prevent the axe from jamming. Too steep an angle will cause the axe to glance off the trunk (a). Dead-on will make it jam or be inefficient (b). Aim for 45 degrees (c).

TO REMOVE BRANCHES

Cut off branches from the outside of the fork (a), not the inside (b).

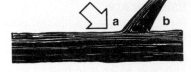

SPLITTING LOGS

Stand behind a large log with feet well apart. Swing down to cut the side away from you (a).

Do NOT chop downwards (b).

To split a smaller log, angle against another log (c). DO NOT PUT YOUR FOOT ON IT.

Alternatively, hold smaller log against cutting edge of axe and bring both down together (d) on to a larger log. (Not to be tried holding too short a log for safety.)

If in doubt split larger logs with a wedge and a rock (e). DO NOT HOLD WOOD UPRIGHT IN YOUR HAND AND ATTEMPT TO SPLIT WITH AXE.

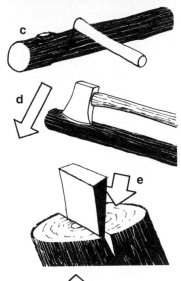

BROKEN HANDLES

Using an axe takes practice and while gaining experience axe handles often get broken — usually because the head misses the target and the handle takes all the blow (a). To remove a broken handle, the easiest way is to put it in a fire, burying as much as possible of the metal in the earth to prevent it losing temper — single-headed (b), double-headed (c).

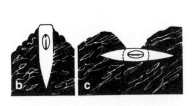

USING A FLEXIBLE SAW

Always use a flexible saw so that the cut opens up (a) rather than closes tight (b) on the saw, causing it to jam. Do not pull too hard or the saw may break.

At all times keep the wire taut (c) pulling in a straight line, never at angles (d).

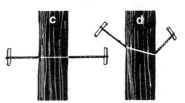

With two people the rhythm must be carefully maintained. If a kink is produced in the saw (e) it may break.

It is usually easier for a single person to cut a log by pulling upwards (f). Support the log to keep it off the ground and give it an angle to keep the cut open.

Alternatively, to remove a branch, pull down from above the head (g). This could be dangerous.

Very high branches can be removed by attaching strings to the saw toggles to give extra reach. This is dangerous. Keep your eye on the branch and be prepared to jump out of the way.

FURNISHING THE CAMP

BEDS

Sleep is the great regenerator and a comfortable bed is worth a little effort. Some form of bedding should always be used to avoid lying directly on cold or damp ground. In tropical climates it is always better to raise the bed into the air, both to keep off wet earth and to provide a current of cooling air. In cold climates, when no permanent shelter has been erected, choose fuel which will keep the fire going through the night and build a screen to reflect heat back on to your sleeping space.

When the ground is dry, or under shelter, stones heated in the fire (but see *warning* in *Fire*) and then buried under a thin layer of soil beneath the bedding will keep their heat through most of the night, adding to your comfort.

A-frame beds

An A-frame forms a strong construction and will keep you off the ground. Drive two pairs of posts into the ground at an angle, leaving a little more than your height between the pairs. Lash the tops together. If the ground is hard, cross-members will be needed between the feet of each A-frame and between the two A-frames.

Tube bed

This simplest form depends on having or making a tube of strong material, sewn or thonged together. A large heavy-duty plastic bag is suitable, but not thin plastic. Really toughly made clothing could serve but would usually make a rather narrow bed.

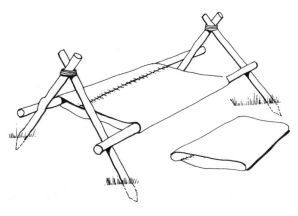

Do not risk this method with any fabric that might give under your weight or with seams that might come apart.

Make A-frame supports and choose two fairly straight poles, each slightly longer than the distance between the frames, and pass them through the tube of plastic or fabric. Place them over the frames so that they rest on the sides, the tube preventing them from slipping lower.

Bough bed

Where conifers are growing, fir tree branches arranged in alternate layers will be comfortable and their fragrance will ensure a good night's sleep.

Ladder bed

Make A-frame supports and select poles as for the tube bed, but you will also need a number of cross-pieces — how many will depend upon the size of the sleeper and the kind of bedding to be used. Springy saplings will be more comfortable than boughs, provided they are strong.

Lash the end 'rungs' to the A-frames, jutting out either side. Make these of strong timber and lash them securely. Fit the ladder over the frames and lash in place. Lay bedding of bracken, ferns or leaves.

Hammocks

It takes a little practice to sleep in a hammock — in a string one you must push the sides outwards so that it cups around you.

PARA-HAMMOCK
It is possible to make a hammock from a parachute. The rigging lines run through the fabric right up to the apex. Cut five panels as shown but do not cut the rigging lines above.

313

Overlay the panels as shown (a) and flatten out.

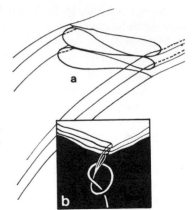

Grasp the three rigging lines in the corner and tie, close to the fabric, in an overhand knot (b).

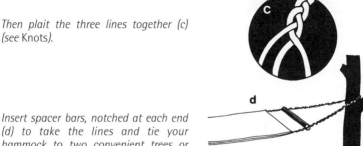

Then plait the three lines together (c) (see Knots*).*

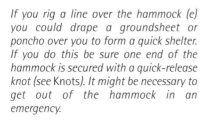

Insert spacer bars, notched at each end (d) to take the lines and tie your hammock to two convenient trees or stout posts.

If you rig a line over the hammock (e) you could drape a groundsheet or poncho over you to form a quick shelter. If you do this be sure one end of the hammock is secured with a quick-release knot (see Knots*). It might be necessary to get out of the hammock in an emergency.*

If you have another piece of rope, or plait some from unused rigging lines, you could tie both the hammock strings to a fixed loop, such as a bowline (see Knots*). Experiment with different ways of suspending your hammock, until you find the most stable and comfortable.*

SEATS

Never sit on damp ground. Use something, even if it is only a log. If there is no ready-made seat available, lash together a couple of low A-frame supports and rest another bough across them.

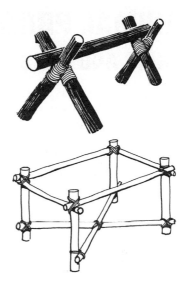

Make a simple box frame with cross-members linking legs from short lengths of wood. To make a seat: weave vines or twine back and forth or sew on a piece of canvas or plastic with thongs. Failing these, try a flat piece of wood or metal laid across, or thin springy saplings lashed to the frame and interwoven.

LADDER

Food-collecting, shelter-building, trap-setting and a whole lot of other tasks will be easier with a ladder. This one is easily made by lashing cross-pieces to two long poles. Because these are set at an angle, not parallel, the rungs will not be able to slip down.

TRAVOIS

For bringing fuel or your prepared kill back to camp, or for other loads, a travois will work if the ground is fairly smooth — it will not on rough and boulder strewn terrain. Choose two boughs with some spring to them and lash cross-pieces, as for the ladder. Add additional struts to provide closer support.

Pull the load on its 'runners' like a sled. If you are pulling loads over a short distance, lash the runners to come to a single grip (a). For a larger version leave the last space clear or fit leather or fabric shoulder straps to haul it by (b).

(For carrying equipment and sledges see **On the Move**).

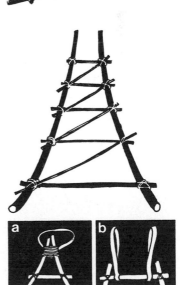

ANIMAL PRODUCTS

SKINS AND FURS

All animals provide skins. Their condition will depend on how carefully they were removed, the way the animal was killed (which may have damaged the skin), the age of the animal and time of year (mating season, moult and change of season can affect the amount and colour of fur in some species). Common defects are due to parasites, disease, malnutrition and scars from fight injuries.

Snakes, lizards, crocodiles and other reptiles all provide excellent skins. So do large birds such as ostriches. Some aquatic mammals, seals and their relations, are fur-bearing, like land mammals, and the whales and dolphins have strong hides. Sharks also have a hide, instead of scales like most other fish. Birds can be skinned with the feathers attached and used to make warm clothing or bed covers. Skin is a source of food and in circumstances of acute shortage can be eaten, even after being preserved and used for clothing, but it is very tough and takes a lot of digesting. There are cases of people surviving by eating their boots, though it should be emphasized that in all such cases plentiful water was available.

Skins and hides are composed of water and proteins and decay quickly if they are not specially treated to preserve them. How they are treated will depend upon whether you want to retain the hair or fur, but the initial stages will be the same in both. To make moccasins, shelters, laces, thongs, water bags or canoes, the hair is removed, but for warm clothing, bedding or a good insulating groundsheet it should be left on.

Properly prepared skins will be supple, yet strong, and resist tearing, abrasions, deformation or stretching. They are comfortable to wear, with good thermal insulation, but permeable to air and water vapour.

CLEANING THE SKIN

Make cleaning and drying a skin easier by stretching it on a frame. Do not make the holes for the cords too close to the edge. Remove fat and flesh by scraping the skin, using an edge of bone, flint or other rock, or even wood. Take care not to cut the skin. Remove every trace of flesh. Ants and other insects may help you if you lay the skin on the ground. Keep watch that they do not start to consume the skin itself.

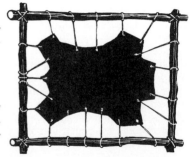

To cure furs

Stretch the skin as tight as possible and leave it in the sun to dry out. All the moisture must be drawn from it so that it will not rot. Rubbing salt or wood ash into the skin will aid the process.

Do not let the skin get wet, or even damp, until the process is complete. Do not leave it where it will be exposed to rain or risk a covering with morning dew.

Keep it absolutely dry. If little or no sun is available, force dry over a fire, but keep the skin out of the flames and use only the heat and the smoke (which will aid preservation). Keep it away from the steam from any cooking pots.

Leather-making

After cleaning, place the skin in water and weight it down with stones. Leave it until the fur can be pulled out in handfuls — usually 2–3 days.

Make a mixture of animal fat and brains, simmered over a fire till they form an even consistency.

Scrape the skin on both sides, removing hair, and grain. Keep it wet. Work sitting down with the skin over your knees. Keep manipulating it.

Work the fat and brains mixture into the inner side of the still-wet skin, stretching and manipulating as you do so.

Dry the skin in the smoke over a fire, keeping it well away from the flames. The smoke sets up a reaction with the solution you have rubbed in to make the skin supple.

Laces and lashings

Hide is one of the best materials for lashings and for thongs to lace things together.

Cut short laces straight from the skin, along its length.

To obtain a greater length cut in a spiral — keep the width consistent or the thonging will have weak points.

Sinew as thread

The hamstring and the main sinews of the legs — especially of the larger animals — can be dried and used as thread to stitch hides together for shelter and clothing. Recognize them by their strong, white, cord-like appearance.

You can also use them for bowstrings and short ropes. They make excellent bindings for arrowheads. Sticky when wet, they dry hard.

Bladder

The normal function of the bladder is to hold water, so naturally the bladder of a large animal can be used as a water carrier — so can the stomach. Tie off the openings to seal them.

CLOTHING

When inadequately or unsuitably clothed for the situation you can improvise or supplement protection in many ways. Weaving fibres will only be practicable in a long-term situation and skins will not be available at first. Salvage towels, blankets, tablecloths, cushions, seat-covers, curtains, sacking from the wreckage — with a bit of initiative any kind of fabric can be used for garments, bedding or shelter.

Improve insulation and increase warmth by adding layers. Wear one sock on top of another and stuff dry grass or moss between them. Grass, paper, feathers, animal hair etc can be stuffed between other layers of clothing — newspapers give excellent insulation.

Waterproofing

Use plastic bags and sheets to improvise waterproofs or cut off large sections of birch bark. Discard the outer bark and insert the soft and pliable inner layer under the outer clothing. It will turn away much of the rain. Other smooth barks that peel easily can be used, but birch is best.

In the longer term, improve water-repellent qualities by rubbing animal fat or the tallow from suet into your clothing. Do NOT do this in situations of intense cold, where the reduction in insulation would be too great a loss and rain rarely a threat.

Footwear

Never underestimate the heavy wear and tear of rough ground on your feet. Climbing over rock and scree can soon destroy a pair of smart city shoes. High heels and sandals will soon break or wear in rough conditions.

- Cut shoe soles from rubber tyres, make holes around the edges for thongs to tie them over wrapped feet, or to sew onto fabric uppers.

- Several layers of wrapping are better than one on the feet. Tie on with thongs or use a triangular shape. Fold one point back over toes, make slits in front. Bring other points from behind heel, through slits and tie around ankle.

- Moccasins can be cut from a single piece of leather, about 8cm (3in) bigger all round than the actual sole of your foot. Thong in and out around the edges and gather them in over wrapped feet. Tie off the gathering thongs, and weave another back and forth over the foot to make more secure. Alternatively, given more time and patience, more traditional moccasins can be made from a thickish hide sole, side strips and an upper. Measure around your foot first.

Goggles

To protect from glare at sea and in snow or desert cut a strip of material, paper, bark — but not metal — to tie over the eyes (or over the whole face in cold climates). Eskimos often carved goggles from wood. Make narrow slits for the eyes. Add extra protection by blackening beneath the eyes with charcoal to reduce glare.

Needle and thread

The Agave plant produces fibres for ropes and mats that are too rough for clothing but the end of the leaf is almost always a hard point which can be extracted with a fibre attached. It makes a perfectly threaded needle!

Clothing tips

- Tie long leaf strips and fibres around a belt or neck band to hang down as a 'grass' skirt or cape.

- Cut a head hole in a blanket or carpet and use as a poncho. Tie at waist or thong sides.

- Small skins are easily thonged or sewn together. Fur on the inside will give greater insulation but on outer garments the suede side sheds snow better.

ROPES AND LINES

There are thousands of uses for ropes and line, from securing constructional joints to making candle wicks, for rappelling down a cliff face to making snares and nets. Traditional materials for rope include hemp, coir (coconut fibre), Manila hemp (from the Abaca plant), henequin and sisal (both from species of Agave). Rope can be made from any pliable, fibrous material producing strands of sufficient length and strength. Much modern rope is made from nylon and other man-made fibres. They have the advantage of great inherent strength, lightness, resistance to water, insects and rot. However, nylon rope should not be the automatic choice if choosing equipment.

Nylon has the disadvantage that it can melt if subjected to heat — and friction on a rope produces heat. It is also slippery when wet. While its tensile strength is good, nylon also tends to snap if subjected to tension over an edge — it does not have to be a very sharp edge.

TYPES OF ROPE

Kernmantel type (a) encloses a central core of strands in an outer sheath. Easier to handle, except when wet or icy, but not so strong as hawser. It can unravel if cut. Traditional hawser-laid rope (b) has three bundles of fibres twisted together. If one is severed the others may hold.

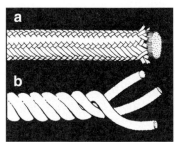

Choosing rope

Match type, thickness and length of rope you carry to the demands you expect to make on it. Nylon will have advantages in very damp climates and when weight is critical but remember its drawbacks. Thicknesses of 7mm (5/16in) and below are difficult to handle.

Rope about 9–10mm (3/8in) is usually recommended for lashings, throwing and mountaineering. It can be used for safety lines and for climbing, provided belay and abseiling techniques are used — it is not thick enough for a hand over hand and foot grip. A length of 30–40m (100–125ft) would then be as much as can be carried without encumbrance.

Climbing rope must be elastic, to absorb some of the shock, without putting enormous strain on anyone who falls. See if it has the approval of official mountaineering bodies or conforms to the British Standard 3184 (for hawser-laid ropes).

Taking care of rope

Rope should be protected from unnecessary exposure to damp or strong sunlight and (in the case of natural fibres) from attack by rodents and insects.

If it does get wet, do not force-dry it in front of a fire. Do not unnecessarily drag it along or leave it on the ground. Dirt can penetrate and particles of grit work away at the fibres from inside the rope. If weather conditions will make drying possible, it is worth trying to wash a very dirty rope in clean water.

Try to keep a rope for the job for which it was intended – do not use climbing rope as clothesline or lashing if you can avoid it – though in a survival situation you may have to use the same length for many purposes.

Whipping the end of the rope (shown later) will prevent it fraying. To prevent a rope becoming tangled, store and carry it in a coil or skein. It will be easier to handle and to pay out when needed.

Rope is valuable equipment. You may have to trust your life to it. Do your best to keep it in good condition.

SIMPLE COIL

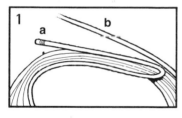

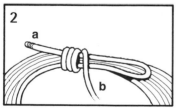

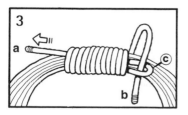

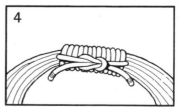

1 *Make a coil of rope 35–45cm (14–18in) in diameter, keeping each circle of the rope alongside the next without twisting or tangling. Leave a length at each end ready for fastening.*

2 *Bend one end (a) back along the coil and wrap it with the other end (b).*

3 *Feed the 'wrapping' end through the loop (c) and pull (a) to secure.*

4 *Tie off with a reef knot – shown later.*

FOR LONGER ROPES

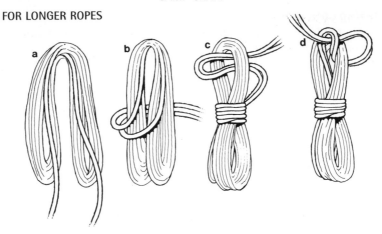

If you wish to carry long ropes over your shoulder or suspended from a belt or from your pack, form a skein.

Loop the rope backwards and forwards over your arm, letting it hang down about 35-60cm (18-24in) long. Leave the ends free (a).

Take both ends together and wrap them several times around the skein (b). Make a loop and take this through the top part of the skein (c) and, finally, pass the ends through this loop (d).

Now tie off on to your pack with a reef knot.

Throwing a rope

It is easier to throw a coil of rope than to attempt to sling a loose end – whether you are throwing upwards or outwards – and it helps to split the coil so that it doesn't tangle. Have a large knot or weight on the throwing end. Make sure that you keep hold of the other end!

Think about the anchored end and what will happen to it when the other end reaches its target. If throwing a lifeline, for example to a fast-moving raft on water, are you going to be pulled into the water yourself? Anchor the end to a tree or weight. Always over-throw a lifeline so that the recipient stands a good chance of catching part of the rope, even if they miss the end.

Coil half the rope onto the fingers and palm of the right hand, then raise the index finger and coil the remainder onto the other fingers only. Pass the second coil back to the left hand.

As you throw, release the right-hand coil a split second before the left. Anchor your end if you think there will be sudden strain on it and your position is precarious.

FOR A LONG THROW

Tie a suitable missile to the end of the rope (a). Coil the rope carefully on the ground or loop it loosely over the other hand so that it will pay out freely as you throw the missile.

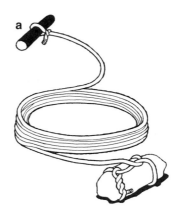

Don't risk loosing your end of the rope. Tie that to an anchor, a heavy stone for instance. Use a killick hitch (shown later).

If throwing a weighted rope over a branch keep out of its path as it swings back towards the throwing point! If throwing a lifeline don't knock out the person that you are trying to help!

ROPE MAKING

Vines, grasses, rushes, barks, palms and animal hairs can all be used to make rope or line. The tendons from animals' legs also make good strings, but they tend to dry hard (very useful for binding on arrow and spear heads).

The stems of nettles make first class ropes and those of honeysuckle can be twisted together to make light lashings. The stronger the fibre, the stronger the rope. Some stiff fibres can be made flexible by steaming or by warming.

While pliable vines and other long plant stems can often be used, as they are, for short-term purposes, they may become brittle as they dry out. A rope made from plant fibres twisted ('spun') or plaited together will be more durable.

Sources of fibres

– Nettles (*Urtica dioica*) are an excellent source of fibres but require preparation.

Choose the oldest available plants and those with the longest stems. Soak them in water for 24 hours, then lay them on the ground and pound them with a smooth stone. This will shred the outer surface exposing the fibrous centre. Tease and comb to remove fleshy matter. Hang to dry.

When dry, remove and discard the outer layer. 'Spin' fibres into long threads. Plaiting or twisting together to make a strong rope.

– Palms usually provide a good fibre. Leaves, trunks and stalks can all be used. The husk of coconut is used commercially to make ropes and matting.

– Dogbane (*Appocynam cannaninum*) stems also provide very good fibre, with which it is easy to work.

– Barks Willow bark especially produces very good fibre. Use the new growth from young trees. The dead inner bark of fallen trees and tree branches should not be overlooked. But if the tree has been down too long it may have decayed too much, so test it for strength.

– Roots The surface roots of many trees make good lashings. Those that run just under, or even on the surface, are often pliable and strong. The roots of the spruce are very strong. The Indians of North America used them to sew birch bark together to make canoes.

– Leaves Plants such as those of the lily family, especially aloes, have very fibrous leaves. Test by tearing one apart. If it separates into stringy layers it can provide fibres to make into rope. Soak to remove the fleshy parts.

– Rushes, sedges and grasses should be used when still green. Pick the longest specimens available.

– Animal tendons are useful for tying one thing to another. They must be used wet.

SPLITTING CANES

Bamboo, rattan, and other types of canes, vines and bark all need to be split to be used for any kind of rope making. If you try to pull away thin strips, these tend to run away to nothing. To avoid this problem pull on the thick part to separate it from the thin. It saves both time and energy.

TESTING FIBRES

Tie two lengths together using an overhand knot. Try pulling it apart, using a reasonable amount of strength. If it snaps the fibre is too brittle. If it is too smooth, it will slip apart. Suitable fibre will 'bite' and hold together.

Plaiting rope

An easy method for the less experienced is to twist and plait strands. If you make three thin plaits, these can then be plaited together again for a thicker, stronger rope. If you are lengthening the strands as you plait, stagger the places at which you feed in new fibres.

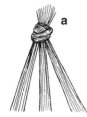

Take a bundle of fibres, tie the ends together, anchor it firmly and split into three separate strands (a). Bring the left strand into the centre (b), then the right over it (c). Then bring what is now the left strand to the centre (d) and so on (e–f). Keep twisting the strands and keep the plaiting as tight and even as you can make it.

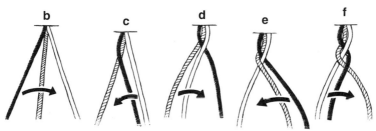

SPINNING A ROPE

Twist fibres together (shown here clockwise, but what is important is to keep to the same direction). Feed in lengths of new fibres as you go so that their ends are staggered.

When you have produced three lengths of fibre, anchor all three at one end and continue to twist each of them until quite tight. Temporarily fastening a toggle to the end of each will make twisting easier.

Now draw all three strands together and twist all three anti-clockwise – the opposite direction.

Continue to add and twist until you have produced the amount of rope you need. You will need to secure a completed section in a cleft stick to keep it tight as you work. Wrap the rope around a tree trunk, to keep the working length short.

To make a thicker rope repeat the process with three 'ropes' you have already made or plait three simple ropes together.

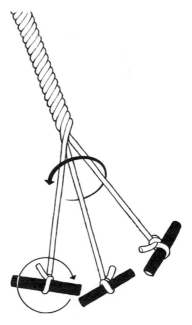

REMEMBER: When making rope try to keep the thickness of the strands equal and even along their lengths. It is where a lay has a thin section that the rope is most likely to break.

Whipping ropes

The end of a rope must be secured in some way so that it does not unravel. To prevent the strands from fraying, bind the rope with twine.

Good binding, or 'whipping', MUST be tight and neat to be effective. If it is too slack it will work loose or fall off. It is difficult to make good whippings with thick cord and very thin is prone to slip. Experience will enable you to match the thickness to the job.

Use the whipping technique to add a comfortable grip to the handles of axes and parangs or, thicker, to replace the handle of a knife.

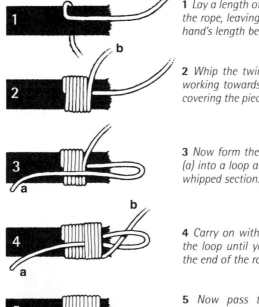

1 *Lay a length of twine along the side of the rope, leaving its end (a) projecting a hand's length beyond the rope's end.*

2 *Whip the twine (b) around the rope, working towards the end and gradually covering the piece you have laid along it.*

3 *Now form the loose end of the twine (a) into a loop and lay it back along the whipped section.*

4 *Carry on with the whipping covering the loop until you have nearly reached the end of the rope.*

5 *Now pass the end (b) whipping through the loop and pull the short end (a) tight. Trim off ends neatly.*

KNOTS

There is a knot for every job and it is important to select the right one for the task in hand. You never know when you may need to tie a knot so learn their uses, and how to tie each one — well enough to tie them in the dark and under all kinds of conditions. Learn to untie them too — the only thing that is worse than tying a knot that comes undone is a knot that CANNOT be undone at a crucial moment.

In the instructions for individual knots that follow the end of the rope or cord being used to tie the knot is referred to as the 'live end' to distinguish it from the other end of the rope, or 'standing part'.

Reef knot

Also known as the square knot, this is perhaps the best known of all knots. It is used for tying rope of the same thickness and will hold firm even under strain, yet may be fairly easily untied.

It is NOT reliable for ropes of different diameters, nor should it be used with nylon — it will slip.

Reef knots can be tied in other materials — it is a good knot to use in first aid. It will lie flat against the patient.

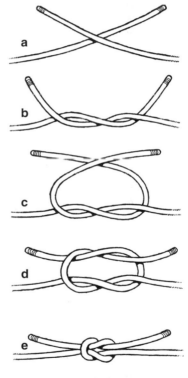

Pass the RIGHT end over the LEFT (a) and then under it (b).

Then take the LEFT over the RIGHT (c) and under it (d).

Check it — the two loops should slide on each other. If you have crossed the wrong way you will have a 'granny', which may not hold and is difficult to untie if subjected to strain.

Tighten by pulling both the strands on each side, or just the live ends, but be sure it tightens properly (e).

To be doubly sure, finish off the knot by making a half-hitch with the live ends on either side of the knot (f).

SIMPLE KNOTS

These are some of the simplest knots. They are quickly made and studying them will help you understand some of the more complicated knots that follow.

OVERHAND KNOT
The simplest of all knots. Make a loop and pass the live end back through it. It has little purpose on its own except to make an end-stop on a rope, but it is part of many other knots.

OVERHAND LOOP
A very quickly made knot for throwing over a projection. The loop is fixed and cannot be tightened so the projection must point away from the direction of strain. Double the end of the rope and tie an overhand knot with the loop.

FIGURE–OF–EIGHT
This makes a much more effective end-stop than the overhand knot. Make a loop. Carry the live end first behind, then around, the standing part. Bring it forward through the loop.

FIGURE–OF–EIGHT LOOP
More secure than the overhand loop, this is made in the same way as the figure-of-eight, but with the line doubled, using the loop as the live end. It can be used over a spike anchor for a belaying rope.

REWOVEN FIGURE–OF–EIGHT
A useful anchoring knot where the top end of a projection is out of reach. Make a loose figure-of-eight along the rope. Pass the live end around the anchor and feed it back around the figure-of-eight, following exactly. Ease tight.

328

JOINING ROPES

SHEET BEND

Used for joining ropes of the same or different thicknesses. It can be more effective than the reef knot with those of equal thickness. It is ideal for joining different materials, especially wet or frozen ropes.

Simple to tie, using up little of the rope length and swiftly unknotted if it has not been subjected to strain. It never slips if correctly made and strain is not erratic.

1 Make a loop in one rope. Take the live end of the other (a) right around behind the loop to the front, where it is carried over itself and then tucked down through the loop.
2 Draw it tight and ease into shape as strain is increased.

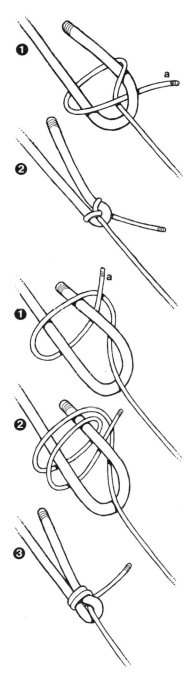

DOUBLE SHEET BEND

A knot that is even more secure than the sheet bend. It is useful with wet ropes, especially if they are of very different thickness, but provides a good strong join in ropes of even thickness too. It is useful where strain is not constant and an ordinary sheet bend may slip.

1 Make a loop in the thicker rope. Take the live end of the thinner rope (a) through the loop, beneath the thicker live end and then forward on the outside of the loop and right around it. Bring the thin live end back between itself and the outside of the thick loop.
2 Take the thin line end completely around the loop again and back through the same place on the outside of the thick loop.
3 Draw it tight and ease into shape.

If not tightened these knots tend to work loose. Do NOT use with smooth materials such as nylon fishing line.

FISHERMAN'S KNOT

A useful knot for joining together springy materials such as vines or wire. It is good for wet or slippery lines and particularly suitable for joining gut fishing line — soak the gut first to make it pliable. Very secure, it will hold well with thin lines but is very difficult to untie. Use when you do not trust the reef knot or sheet bend. It is NOT recommended for bulky ropes or nylon line.

1 *Lay lines beside each other, the ends in opposite directions. Carry the live end of one line around the other and make a simple overhand knot.*

2 *Repeat with the live end of the other line.*

3 *Partially tighten the knots and slide them towards each other. Ease them to rest well against one another, completing the tightening process.*

DOUBLE FISHERMAN'S

This is a stronger version of the fisherman's knot. It should NOT be used for nylon fishing lines, nylon ropes, or bulky ropes.

1 *Carry the live end of one line around the other, then around both.*

2 *Carry the live end back through the two loops you have just made.*

3 *Repeat the pattern with the end of the other line.*

4 *Slide the two knots together and tighten them, easing them to rest well against each other. Apply strain gradually.*

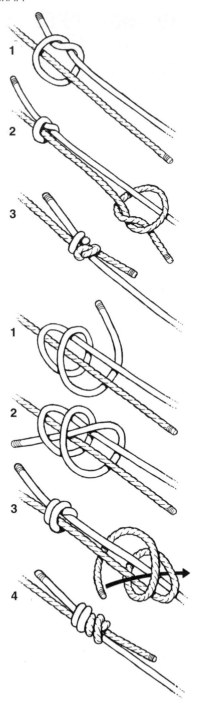

TAPE KNOT

A useful knot for joining flat materials such as leather or webbing straps, tape and possibly even for joining sheets or other fabrics when improvising an escape rope. Experiment!

1 *Make an overhand knot in the end of one 'tape'. Do not pull it tight.*

2 *Feed the other tape through it so that it follows exactly the shape of the first knot.*

3 *The live ends should be well clear of the knot so that they will not slip back when you tighten it.*

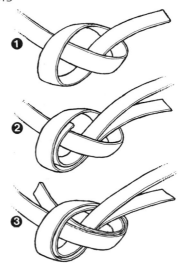

LOOP-MAKING

BOWLINE

This quickly tied knot makes a loop that will neither tighten nor slip under strain. It is used in the end of a lifeline or wherever such a fixed loop is needed.

1 *Make a small loop a little way along the rope.*

2 *Bring the live end up through it, around the standing part and back down through the loop.*

3 *Pull on the live end to tighten, easing the knot into shape. Finish off with a half-hitch.*

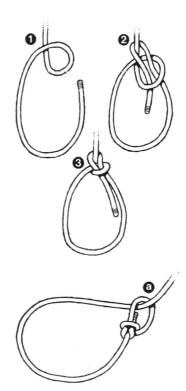

RUNNING BOWLINE

Use in any situation requiring a loop which will tighten easily. Make a small bowline and pass the long end of the rope through the loop.

   Never tie a running bowline around the waist, particularly when climbing. It acts like a hangman's noose and could kill.

TRIPLE BOWLINE

Another bowline, made with a double line. Form a loop, pass the doubled live end through the loop, behind the standing part and back through the loop. This produces three loops which can be used for equipment haulage, or as a sit-sling or lifting-harness with one loop around each thigh and the other around the chest.

It takes some practise to get the proportions right – so learn to tie the triple bowline BEFORE you need to use it.

BOWLINE-ON-THE-BIGHT

This is useful to support or for lifting anyone from a crevasse or elsewhere from which they cannot climb out. Make it with a doubled line, producing two loops which will neither tighten nor jam. It forms a kind of bosun's chair, one loop fitting around the buttocks, the other around the upper body. As with the triple bowline, practise this knot BEFORE you need to know how to use it.

You may find many uses for fixed double loops. House- and ship-painters have been known to support their hanging platforms with a knot like this at each end. If the platform has a pole projecting at each corner, the loops of the bowline-on-the-bight can be slipped over. Notch the poles to prevent the ropes slipping off.

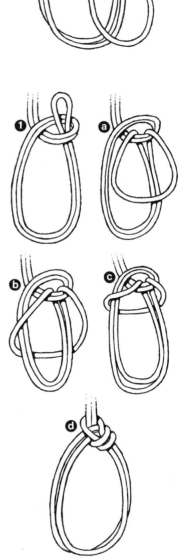

1 *Using the doubled line, form a loop and pass the live end through it.*

2 *Bring this end down (a) and over the end (b) of the larger double loop now formed. Ease it back up to behind the standing part (c). Pull on the large double loop to tighten (d).*

MANHARNESS HITCH

Also known as the Butterfly knot or Artillery knot, this makes a non-slip loop. It has the advantage that it can be made along the length of the rope, but does not require access to an end. Several loops could be put on a rope for harnessing people to pull together in haulage or raising a weight. Also a good way of preparing a rope for climbing. Toes and wrists can be put into the loops to carry the weight so that a rest can be taken when tired.

1 *Make a loop in the rope — but look closely at the drawing.*

2 *Allow the left side of the rope to cross over the loop.*

3 *Twist the loop.*

4 *Pass it over the left part of the rope and through the upper part of the original loop.*

5 *Pull the knot gently into shape, ease tight and test it carefully.*

NOTE: *If this knot is not eased tight correctly it is possible to end up with a slipping loop.*

Different ways of making this knot may be found where the loop is not twisted at 3. The final strength of the loop does not appear to be affected either by making this twist or not, nor if the twist should straighten out in use.

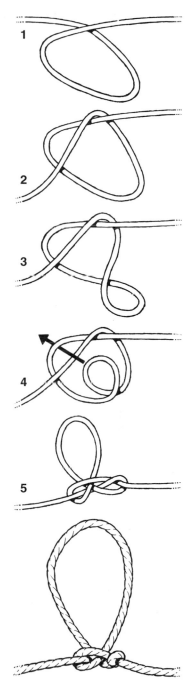

LADDERS

A ladder can be made by simply tying as many manharness hitches in a rope as you need for hand and foot holds. It could also be made with rungs, using strong sticks or pieces of wreckage.

Use two ropes or a long rope, doubled, with manharness hitches placed equally along both sides to make a rope ladder. Pass sticks through the corresponding loops, as you make the loops and ease tight to hold the sticks firmly. Allow the sticks to project a reasonable distance on either side of the ropes for safety and test each for strength.

LADDER OF KNOTS

A series of overhand knots tied at intervals along a smooth rope will make climbing it much easier. There is a fast way of making these, once you have the knack.

1 Leaving a reasonably long free end, make a half-hitch near the end of a short piece of branch or log.

2 Continue making loose half-hitches along the log — the diameter of which will fix the spacing of the knots.

3 Pass the start end back through all the loops and then slide them all off the end of the log.

4 As each turn of rope comes through the centre of the half-hitch loops to the other end, shape and tighten each knot.

If you know the length of your rope you can estimate the number of knots you need. With a half-hitch for every knot, choose a thickness of log to allow the required number of turns — and therefore the required number of knots.

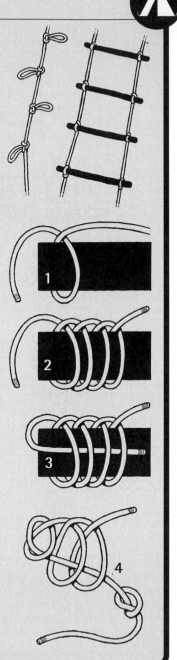

HONDA KNOT

This is another knot that makes a free-running noose — but this one gives a clear circular loop suitable for throwing — it is a lassoo.

You may find a use for this lassoo in many ways but, in a survival situation, if you have only one length of rope, it would be unwise to spend much time and energy trying to catch animals in this way. It takes a lot of practise. When you really need the rope it may be worn and damaged from your lassooing efforts. However, it is worth making one to experiment with so that you have the skill already, should you need it for actual survival conditions.

a *Start with an overhand knot.*

b *Form a loop further down the rope.*

c *Double the rope into a bight between loop and knot.*

d *Pass the bight through the loop.*

e *Tighten the loop around the bight.*

f *Pass the long end of the rope through the new eye formed by the bight.*

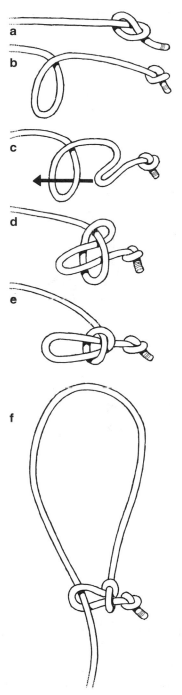

Before trying to use a lassoo on an animal consider its strength against your own. A large animal can — and almost certainly will — run. If you are not holding the rope firmly it may be dragged away and you will lose your meal and your rope. If the rope is anchored to you, YOU may be dragged along and severely injured. Can you make use of a firm anchor to carry the strain? A turn around a tree trunk or a rock may secure what is too powerful for you to restrain on your own.

HITCHES

These are knots for attaching ropes to posts, bars and poles.

ROUND TURN AND TWO HALF-HITCHES

This is the best way to secure a rope to a post. It can take strain from almost any direction.

Carry rope around behind the post, then around again. Bring live end over and back under the standing end and through the loop thus formed. Tighten and repeat the half-hitch to make the knot secure.

CLOVE HITCH

An effective attachment when strain is perpendicular to the horizontal. It is not so good when strain comes at an angle or the direction of strain is erratic – this could loosen the clove hitch.

1 *Pass the live end over and around the bar.*

2 *Bring it across itself and around the bar again.*

3 *Carry the live end up and under itself moving in the opposite direction to the standing end.*

4 *Close up and pull tight.*

It is possible to make a clove hitch in loops on a rope and to put the whole knot ready-made on to the spar – if you have access to the spar end. Many experienced knot makers do this. Make a loose clove hitch and slip it off the spar. Lay it down and copy the loops formed by the rope. Slip onto the spar and tighten.

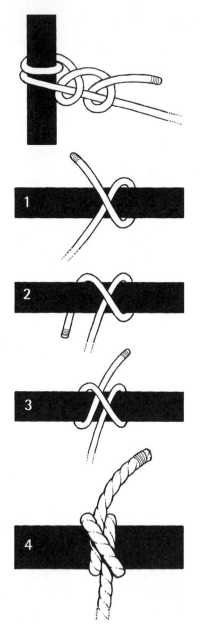

TIMBER HITCH

This knot is used mainly as a start knot for lashings, but can also be used for hoisting and for dragging or towing heavy logs.

1 *Bring the live end around the bar and loosely around the standing end.*

2 *Carry it forward and tuck it beneath the rope encircling the bar. Twist it around as many times as comfortably fit. Tighten the knot by gently pulling on the standing end until a firm grip is achieved.*

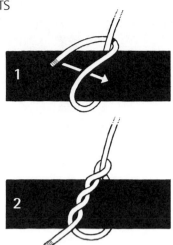

KILLICK HITCH

Also known as the Anchor hitch — use it for securing a line to an anchoring weight. It can be used to secure an actual anchor for use in water or to hold back one end of a throwing line.

Make a timber hitch around one end of the rock or weight and tighten. Carry the line along the weight and make a half-hitch.

MARLIN SPIKE HITCH

This is an instant, but temporary, knot for securing a mooring line to a post, or for dragging over the top of any upright peg or pole. It is particularly useful when tightening lashings. By temporarily attaching a short stout stick to the line it is possible to gain extra purchase on the line to administer a firmer pull.

1 *Form a loop in the rope — study the drawing carefully.*

2 *Bring one side of the loop back up over the standing end.*

3 *Drop this over the pole — the pole coming between the extended loop and the standing part. Pull the live end to tighten.*

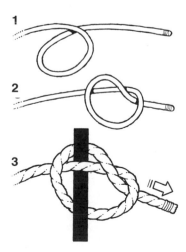

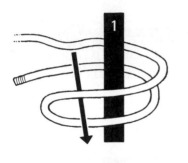

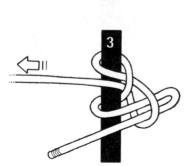

QUICK-RELEASE KNOT

Variously known as the Highwayman's hitch, Thief hitch and Thief knot. This knot is secure but will come untied with a single sharp tug on the live end. It is recommended for temporarily anchoring lines while working – or for situations which need a quick release.

1 *Carry a bight around a post or rail.*

2 *Bring a bight from the standing end through the first bight.*

3 *Form the live end into a further bight and push the doubled end through the loop of the second bight. Pull on the standing end to tighten the knot.*

4 *To release pull sharply on the live end.*

SHORTENING ROPE

SHEEPSHANK

Treble the line. Form half-hitches in the outer lengths and slip them over the adjoining bends. Or, instead of half-hitches, when a loop is formed in the standing part, pull a bight through it and slip this over the bend in the rope. Tighten as you gradually increase tension.

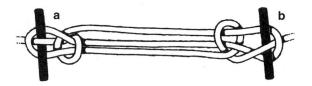

Make a sheepshank more secure by passing a stick through the bend and behind the standing part (a). Or, if you have access to the rope's end, pass that through the bight (b). A stick would make this more secure.

Never cut a rope unnecessarily – you never know when you may be glad of its full length. A knotted rope has only half the strength of a continuous one. Use the sheepshank to shorten it or to exclude a damaged or weakened section.

SECURING LOADS

WAKOS TRANSPORT KNOT

A knot invaluable for securing a high load to boat, raft, sledge etc or for tying down a roof. Maximum purchase is achieved by pulling down with all your weight and finally securing with two half-hitches. If it comes loose undo the hitches, retighten and secure. This knot can also be used for a line across a river or chasm which needs tightening from time to time.

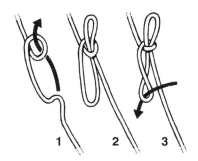

1 Make a loop in the rope. Further down, towards the end of the rope, make a bight.

2 Pass the bight through the loop.

3 Make a twist in the new lower loop. Pass the end of the rope around securing point and up through this twist.

4 Pull on end to tighten.

5 With end make two half-hitches around lower ropes to secure. Undo these to adjust and retighten.

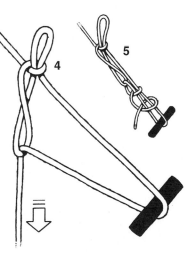

PRUSIK KNOT

A knot that makes a sliding loop, especially useful when attached along a climbing rope. It will not slip under tension, but will slide along the rope when tension is released. Also useful for ropes that need retensioning from time to time, such as tent guylines.

A pair of prusik knots along a rope provide hand and foot holds for climbing or for swinging along a horizontal line. They are slid along the main rope as you proceed.

1 *Pass a bight around the main rope and pull the ends through. Keep this loose.*

2 *Take the ends over again and back down through the loop. Ease tight. Do not allow the circuits to overlap.*

3 *This gives the appearance of four turns on the main rope (a). Mountaineers sometimes take the ends round again and back through the loop to give the appearance of six turns on the main rope (b).*

4 *The prusik knot can be made using a fixed spliced loop — in which case pass the bight over the main rope and back through itself, and repeat.*

5 *For use as a tensioning line attach along the guy rope etc and secure ends (a) to an anchor.*

Note: *When used for climbing, or travelling along a rope, a spliced loop is safest (as 4). If you have no spliced loop, join the ends after the knot is made. Test joins rigorously before relying upon them.*

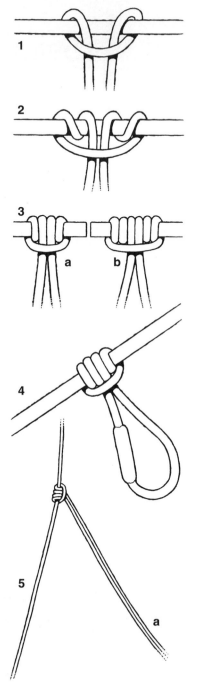

LASHINGS

Methods of lashing spars, logs, poles etc together differ according to the position of the components. Learn these techniques. They will be invaluable in making shelters, rafts and other structures.

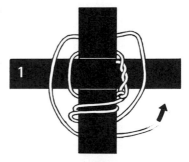

SQUARE LASHING
This is for lashing spars which cross. Most effective when they do so at right-angles.

1 Make a timber hitch carrying the line alternately above and below both spars in a complete circuit before securing it. Then carry the rope over and under both spars in an anti-clockwise direction.

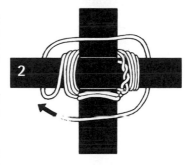

2 After three or four circuits make a full turn around a spar and circuit in the opposite direction.

3 Complete the circuits with a half-hitch around one spar and secure with a clove hitch on a spar at right-angles.

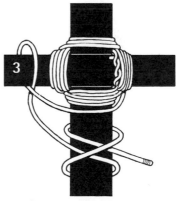

ROUND LASHING
This is for lashing spars alongside each other or extending the length of a spar.

Begin with a clove hitch around both spars (a), then bind rope around them. Finish knot with a clove hitch at the other end (b). Force a wedge under the lashings to make them really tight. If the spars are vertical bang the wedge in downwards.

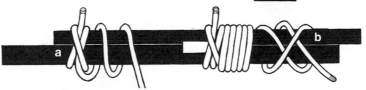

DIAGONAL LASHING

An alternative to square lashing which is more effective when spars do not cross at right-angles, or more especially when the spars are under strain and have to be pulled towards one another for tying.

1 Begin with a timber hitch around both spars, placed diagonally.

2 Frap both spars with a few turns of rope over the timber hitch, then make a full turn under the bottom spar.

3 Frap across the other diagonal, then bring the rope back over one spar and make two or three circuits of the spars above the upper spar and below the lower.

4 Finish with a clove hitch on a convenient spar.

SHEAR LASHING

For tying the ends of two spars at an angle, when making an A-frame, for example.

Begin with a clove hitch (a) around one spar. Bind around both spars – this binding should not be very tight. Bring rope between the spars and frap a couple of times around the binding. Finish with a clove hitch around the other spar (b). Tighten by opening up the shears (c).

A similar method can be used around three poles to make a tripod. Make turns around all three legs and frappings in the two gaps. The feet of A-frames and tripods should be anchored to stop them spreading.

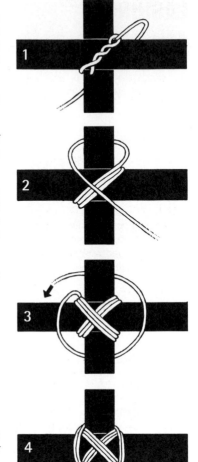

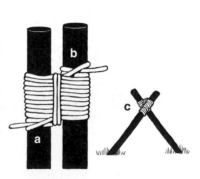

342

NET MAKING

Nets can be made either by making knots along pre-cut lengths of line or by 'knitting' mesh row by row. They are not only useful for fishing. A gill net can also be hung between trees to catch birds and a purse net, made from twine can be placed over animal burrows. Use the same techniques to make a hammock from strong twine.

Gill net

Make this from parachute cords or from two thicknesses of twine. Parachute cord consists of an inner core of fine line within an outer core. Pull the fine inner line out and cut it into manageable and equal lengths (or cut lengths of thinner string). Their length will determine the depth of your net, which will be about 3/8 that of the length of line.

Decide how wide you want your net and set two poles that distance apart. Tie a length of parachute cord outer (or thicker twine) between the two. Cut a piece of wood about 3·5cm (1¼in) across. Use this as a gauge to space out the thinner vertical threads (inner core).

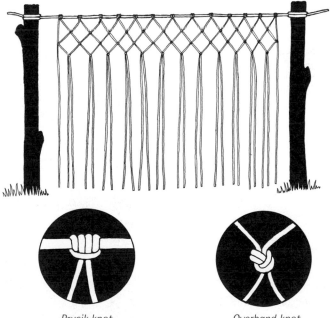

Prusik knot   Overhand knot

Fold each length double and use the bight to make a prusik knot over the top cord and repeat across its length. Slide the prusik knots along to space them out equally using your gauge.

For the first row, working from left to right; ignore the very first individual strand, but take the second of the pair. Hold it with the first strand of the next pair and tie both together in an overhand knot. Take the remaining strand with the first of the next pair and knot. Continue along the line, using your gauge to control spacing.

Proceed to the next row in the same way but this time include the outside lines to produce a row of diamonds. Continue until the line is used up.

To finish off the bottom, stretch another thicker line across between the supports and tie off all the inners (or thinner strings) in pairs around it. Carry each pair around it twice. Separate the pair and tie off around the pair.

Complete the net by securing the top and bottom lines at each corner of the net so that the net will not slip off the ends. Any surplus can be used for attaching the net to supports and weights to keep it in position when in use.

'KNITTING' A NET

A method suitable for nylon fishing line or any other fine line. You need a horizontal string between posts, a mesh gauge, and a 'needle'.

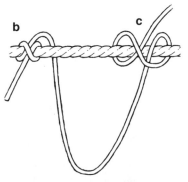

Make the 'needle' (a) about 15cm long x 2·5cm wide (6 x 1in) from hardwood or bamboo. Make a notch at either end and wind line around the whole needle; or try something more traditional like the lower drawing. The needle must be smooth. The line is gradually unwound as you make the net.

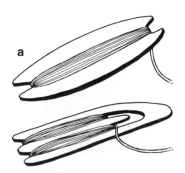

To make the net, tie a top line of required length between uprights. Begin by tying a clove hitch with thinner line (b). Take the needle behind the top line and bring it forward to make another clove hitch (c). Repeat along the line, spacing the knots out with your gauge (d).

When the top row is complete go to the other side of the posts (easier than working backwards) and make the next row. Make each new loop large enough to form a square of the mesh (half-square at each outside edge). Take the needle through the loop of the row above from behind, round the back of the loop and then through the front of the loop it makes (e). Adjust the depth with your gauge before you tighten (f).

Switch sides again and work back in the opposite direction for the next row and continue until the net is the required length.

Tie off the bottom line with another thicker twine using the same knot but keeping the line straight without loops. Leave some free line at both ends. Tie in the ends at the top corners and the net is complete.

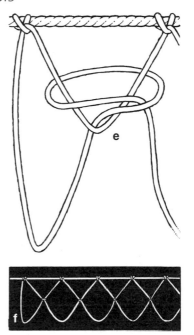

Net hammock

Make a net about 75cm (2½ft) across and wider than your height. Use good strong twine or rope for the top and bottom lines — double twine would be a good idea, the ends have to carry your weight. Leave those ends long enough to suspend the hammock by.

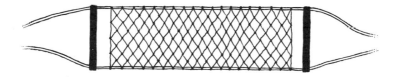

Cut two spacer bars to keep the hammock 'open'. Notch the ends and slip the cords into the notches (a). To simplify hanging the hammock you could tie each pair of end lines to a fixed loop such as a bowline. Then fix one end with a round turn and two half-hitches, the other with a quick-release knot, in case you ever need to leave the hammock in a hurry.

FISHING KNOTS

HOOK ON TO GUT

Turle knot *Soak the gut. Thread it through eye of hook. Make an overhand loop and pass a bight through it (a) to form a simple slip knot (b).*

Pass hook through slip knot (c) and pull tight around shank.

HOOK ON TO NYLON # 1

Half blood knot *Thread end through eye. Make four turns around standing part. Pass live end through the loop formed next to the hook (d).*

Pull taut and snip off fairly close to end (e).

HOOK ON TO NYLON #2

Two turn turf knot *Thread the hook. Pass the live end around the standing part to form a loop and through it. Twist live end twice around side of loop. Hold the loop and pull the twists tight. Pass the hook through the loop (f).*

Pull on standing part to tighten loop on hook (g).

JAM KNOTS

For securing improvised hooks to gut or cord.

With an eye: Thread gut. Make two turns around hook and bring live end up through turns (h). Ease tight and test for strength.

Without an eye: Make loop around lower part of shaft. Make two half-hitches from upper end downwards and pass live end through lower loop (i). Pull on standing part to tighten.

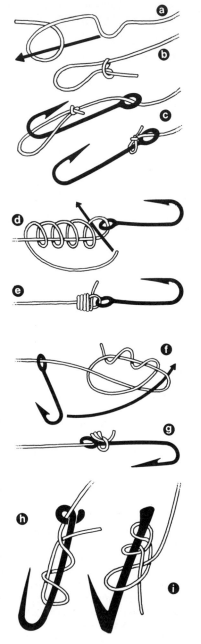

LOOP IN NYLON #1
Double overhand loop *Double the line to make a bight. Tie an overhand in it (a). Twist the end through again (b). Pull tight (c) and snip off end.*

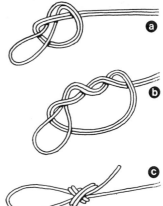

LOOP IN NYLON #2
Blood bight *Form a bight. Twist the end of it back around the standing part (d). Bring end back through new loop (e). Pull tight and snip off loose end.*

JOINING LOOPS
Can be used in nylon line but will work for different strong materials. A fisherman's knot is recommended for gut, which probably could not stand the strain of this method.

With free ends: *Pass each line through the other loop (f) and pull tight (g).*

With only one end free: *Make loop on one line. Take the live end of the other line through the loop, around it and back through and then tie off with either of the knots for hooks on to nylon.*

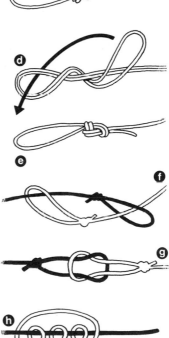

JOINING NYLON
Double three-fold blood-knots: *Place ends alongside and twist one three times around the other. Bring live end back and pass it through the space where the two lines cross over the other line and under its own standing end (h). Do the same in the opposite direction with the other line. The live ends end up pointing in opposite directions (i). Ease tight.*

-6-

READING THE SIGNS

Being able to read and make a map is only the beginning of being able to find your way about. You must learn to interpret the signs found on the ground itself and in the air.

If you do not have a compass, there are a number of ways of creating your own. The sun and stars can provide firm orientation — a variety of methods are available for finding direction in both northern and southern hemispheres.

An ability to anticipate the weather can also be a valuable asset in the wild and simple guidelines for prediction and the interpretation of cloud patterns equip the survivor with more skills.

READING THE SIGNS

READING THE SIGNS

Before embarking on any expedition you will have learned all you can about the terrain, equipped yourself with maps, if available, and worked out routes. Memorize the lie of the land, the direction in which rivers flow, the high ground, the prominent features, the prevailing winds, the weather patterns to expect and any known hazards, check the phase of the moon and times of first and last light — all of which will be invaluable knowledge if you find yourself in difficulties. In a case of accident you may find yourself in a totally unknown territory and have to find out everything about your location from the land itself.

In choosing a camp site, tracing water and finding the other necessities for survival you will need to interpret the surrounding countryside — the other side of a hill may offer quite different conditions — and if you decide not to stay put you will have to interpret both the general geography and the particular landscape as you proceed.

MAPS

Choose maps carefully, making sure that they are to a scale that will be useful to you and show helpful information. A very large-scale map that shows every footpath and building will be no use at all if you are driving a thousand miles along a motorway. Everything will be shown in great detail but only a tiny fraction of the journey will appear on one sheet and you would have to pile the car with maps and change from one to another every few miles. On the other hand few motoring maps give much information about the nature of the terrain or show features which would help a walker choose their route. Sailors must be equipped with accurate charts so that they can keep to safe waters. The surface below the sea can be as varied as that above. Flyers will need to know what altitude obstructions are and what turbulences occur near mountains which make it safer to fly higher. From the air the pattern of the land may show plainly but its contours are flattened out; without interpretation, a map looks rather like that to many people.

Maps and terrain

Height cannot be reproduced on flat sheets of paper so altitudes are recorded at regular intervals — usually every 50ft or every 10m according to the measure used – and every point at this height is joined up by a line – the contour line. In most cases these lines join up to form a complete shape, some sort of irregular oval with bulges here and there. If they suddenly stop against another line that means that there is an abrupt change of height – in fact, a cliff or a very steep fall.

The only contour line that you can see in nature is that of sea level along the coast (and even that is not quite true because of tidal variation) but you can imagine the contour lines as the edges of flat disks and that these are ranged equidistantly above each other. If you threw a cloth to rest over them it would link them together in a shape that would be approximately like a hill or other feature. However, you do not have a record of exactly what happens between those contour lines and there will not necessarily be an even slope connecting them. There could be outcrops of rock, hollows, any manner of variation within that 10m or 50ft. From the relative positions of one height to another you could make a pretty good guess as to what the ground surface was like, but you could not be sure. There may therefore be features that, because they fall between the contour lines, make no appearance on your map.

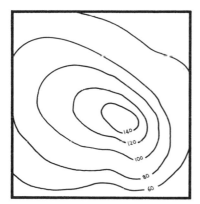

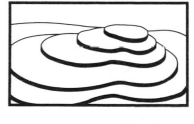

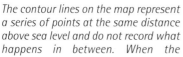

The contour lines on the map represent a series of points at the same distance above sea level and do not record what happens in between. When the

contours are closely grouped the change in height is more rapid (a). Conversely, greater spaces between the contour lines indicate gentler slopes (b).

Interpreting maps

Remember that the intervals between the contour lines are the distances between horizontal points at the same theoretical height – not the actual distance on the slope of the ground. They are measured in units that show relative positions and are not to a scale as is the horizontal plotting.

It is a common error to think of a group of contour lines indicating a rise in the ground comparable to the scale of the distance shown between them — but the scale of a typical walkers' map is 1:50,000 and 10m on that would be only .02mm. Contours spaced 5mm apart on the surface of the map would be at a horizontal distances of 250m and the gradient only 1 in 25.

Scale

Before you can begin to use a map you must understand its scale. This may be shown by a scale bar marked with miles or kilometres to the size that they are shown on the map or it may be given as a ratio — 1:50,000 means that every measure on the map represents a distance 50,000 times greater on the ground.

Key

There will usually also be a key to the symbols used within the map to represent natural and man-made features — rivers, roads, buildings, types of woodland or swamps, types of beach. What is shown, and how, will vary greatly. If there is no key on the individual map or on its wrapping make sure that you find out what symbols mean in that map series. Some will be fairly evident: if the map is in colour rivers will almost certainly be in blue, marshes will usually be indicated by stylized tufts of reed.

Not all features can be shown to exact scale. Roads and paths will probably be given standard widths to match the kind of track they are rather than their exact measurements, and streams and rivers will be similarly standardized. The British Ordnance Survey (OS) maps, for instance, show waterways as a single blue line, gradually increasing in width until it represents a width of 8m (27ft) across a stream, whereupon a double line is used, giving you an immediate indication that you have a river at least that wide to cross. There are similar standardizations on all maps. Once you have mastered the way that information is shown, maps will tell you a great deal.

Grids

Maps almost always carry a grid of lines which divides them up. This is either based on degrees of latitude and longitude or a special grid developed by the mapping authority. The advantage of the special grids is that they are usually planned to form squares based on ground measurement which can help you rapidly assess distances. On the British OS maps, for instance, the grid lines are 1km apart and the diagonal across them is 1½km. If you want to find, or report, a position it can be described by a coordinate made up from the line references from two adjoining sides of the map. To anyone using a map with the same grid this will immediately locate the 'box' in which it appears. Dividing the square by eye into further tenths pinpoints the location. This provides an easy way of telling rescuers of your location or of fixing a rendezvous point with them.

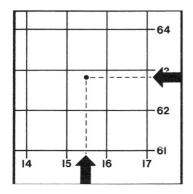

The point marked with a dot can be described as 15.5 x 62.8 using the coordinates from the sides of this grid. This system requires that squares are mentally divided into tenths in each direction. The 'map reference' is normally expressed as six digits: 155628. Any letter area codes on the map should be included.

North on maps

Unless they are lines of longitude, the grid lines on a map are not an indication of north and south, though they may sometimes be close to it. Remember that a compass points not to true north but to magnetic north — and the difference between the two varies both according to where you are in the world and because magnetic north is slowly changing its position. To take accurate bearings you need to know these variations, but even a rough idea of orientation will help you to match you map to the landscape.

If you have an adjustable compass and information on the deviation of it and of your map grid from true north you can carefully match up all of them so that even in poor visibility, or where landscape features are beyond your horizon, you can take accurate bearings and follow them.

Many maps indicate the deviation or the direction of magnetic north. If this is not given you can find it from the North Star or by using the watch method to point to north. Use the Southern Cross in the same way in the Southern Hemisphere to establish south (both are illustrated later).

Local magnetic variation

To find the local magnetic variation, when not recorded on a map, point the compass at the North Star. Note the difference between the pointer and indicated north.

Lining the compass up with the grid lines on the map you can discover their variation, if there is one. If you then propose to walk on magnetic bearings you must remember to compensate for the variation.

Map reading skills should be learned by anyone planning an expedition and are particularly important in mountain country. Compasses are available mounted with calibrations, scales and direction markers which make this kind of orientation easier. Check them out and have them explained to you.

In a survival situation you will probably have to manage without such sophistication. If unable to make appropriate corrections continually check your position against visible features.

Gradients

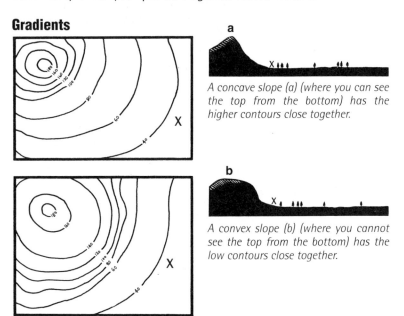

A concave slope (a) (where you can see the top from the bottom) has the higher contours close together.

A convex slope (b) (where you cannot see the top from the bottom) has the low contours close together.

Measuring distances

As-the-crow-flies distances can be measured by using any straight edge and matching it up against the scale bar or multiplying by the ratio of the map's scale. Meandering routes can be followed with a piece of thread which can then be straightened out. Gradients can make an appreciable difference to distances and must be allowed for – a gradient of 45 degrees, for instance, will add another 82m to a horizontal map distance of 200m (500ft becomes 725ft).

Your own maps

The survivor may not be lucky enough to have a map and should then set about making one. With a map you will always be able to find your way back to camp – essential if you are going for help for the sick, children or elderly survivors left behind.

It is not possible for you to measure exact contour heights, but you can devise your own system for indicating the contours.

Find the best vantage point and look out over the terrain. Climbing a tree may give a better view. Note the direction of the ridges, count how many you can see. Between each ridge there is probably a stream or river flowing, you cannot be sure – there will be a lot of 'dead ground', territory you cannot see. Make a general map with blank patches and then fill them in as you gain more information from other vantage points and from your explorations on the ground.

Mark anything of interest on your map: watercourses, rocky outcrops, isolated trees, strangely shaped features that will act as landmarks, and areas of different vegetation. You can plot positions of your traps, animal lairs, good places for foraging for food and fuel or finding useful stones for implements It will be much easier for you or your companions than relying on your memory or vague descriptions.

DIRECTION FINDING

The earth's relationship to the rest of the solar system and the position of the stars in the sky help to locate any position on its surface. Its revolution on its axis produces the changes from light to darkness and its orbit around the sun produces the seasons, for the earth is tilted at an angle to the sun and first the north and then the south becomes nearer to it, the closest point traversing from the Tropic of Cancer (23·5°N) to the Tropic of Capricorn (23·5°S), the sun being above Cancer on 22 June and above Capricorn on 22 December. It is above the Equator on 21 March and 21 September.

The sun rises in the east and sets in the west – but not EXACTLY in the east and west. There is also some seasonal variation. In the Northern Hemisphere, when at its highest point in the sky, the sun will be due south; in the Southern Hemisphere this noonday point will mark due north. The hemisphere will be indicated by the way that shadows move: clockwise in the north, anticlockwise in the south. Shadows can be a guide to both direction and time of day.

SHADOW STICK METHOD #1

On a patch of flat, clear ground place a metre-long (3ft) stick as upright as possible. Note where its shadow falls and mark the tip with a pebble or stick (a). Wait at least 15 minutes and mark the new shadow tip (b). Join the two and you have the directions of east and west (3) – the first mark is west. North-south will be at right angles to this line. This method works at any time of day when there is sunshine and at any latitude. Use it for spot checks as you proceed.

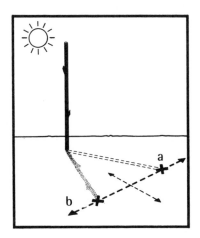

SHADOW STICK METHOD #2

Another, more accurate, method – if you have the time – is to mark the first shadow tip in the morning. Draw a clean arc at exactly this distance from the stick, using the stick as a centre point. As midday approaches the shadow will shrink and move. In the afternoon, as the shadow lengthens again, mark the EXACT spot where it touches the arc. Join the two points to give east and west – west is the morning mark.

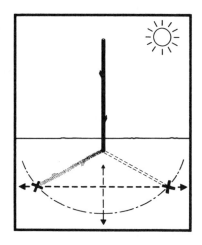

Direction by watch

A traditional watch with two hands can be used to find direction, provided it is set to true local time (without variation for summer daylight saving and ignoring conventional time zones which do not match real time). The nearer the Equator you are the less accurate this method will be, for with the sun almost directly overhead it is very difficult to determine its direction.

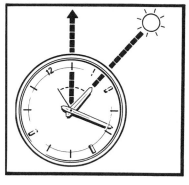

Northern Hemisphere *Hold the watch horizontal. Point the hour hand at the sun. Bisect the angle between the hour hand and the 12 mark to give a north-south line.*

Southern Hemisphere *Hold the watch horizontal. Point 12 towards the sun. A mid-point between 12 and the hour hand will give you the north-south line.*

IMPROVISED COMPASSES

A piece of ferrous metal wire – a sewing needle is ideal – stroked repeatedly IN ONE DIRECTION against silk will become magnetized and can be suspended so that it points north. The magnetism will not be strong and will need regular topping up.

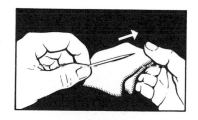

Suspend the needle in a loop of thread, so that it does not affect the balance. Any kinks in or twisting of the thread must be avoided.

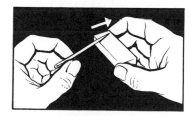

Stroking with a magnet, should you have one, will be much more efficient than using silk – stroke the metal smoothly from one end to the other IN ONE DIRECTION ONLY.

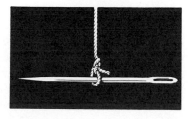

FLOATING NEEDLE

A suspended needle will be easier to handle on the move but in camp or when making a halt a better method is to lay the needle on a piece of paper, bark or grass and float it on the surface of water.

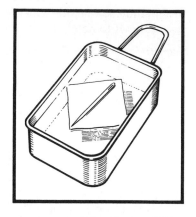

USING ELECTRICITY

If you have a power source of two volts or more (a small dry battery, for instance) the current can be used to magnetize the metal. You will also need a short length of wire, preferably insulated.

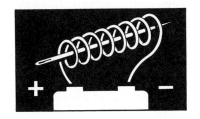

Coil the insulated wire around the 'needle'. If it has no ready-made insulation wrap a few layers of paper or a piece of cardboard around the needle first. Attach the ends of the wire to the terminals of the battery for five minutes.

RAZOR BLADE COMPASS

A thin flat razor blade can also be used as a compass needle because it is made of two metals bonded together. It can be magnetized simply by stropping WITH CARE against the palm of the hand. Suspend it.

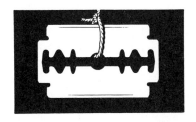

Use other methods to establish which general direction is north and then identify which end of your new compass needle is which and mark one of them. Top up your needle's magnetism from time to time, and always check your reading with the sun. A 'wild' reading may be given if large amounts of ferrous metal are nearby.

Plant pointers

Even without a compass or the sun to give direction you can get an indication of north and south from plants. They tend to grow towards the sun so their flowers and most abundant growth will be to the south in the Northern Hemisphere, the north in the South.

On tree trunks moss will tend to be greener and more profuse on that side too (on the other side it will be yellowish to brown). Trees with a grainy bark will also display a tighter grain on the north side of the trunk.

If trees have been felled or struck down the pattern of the rings on the stump also indicates direction — more growth is made on the side towards the Equator so there the rings are more widely spaced.

There are even species of plant known for their north–south orientation:

North Pole Plant *which grows in South Africa, leans towards the north to gain full advantage of the sun*

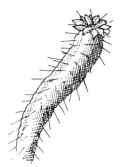

Compass Plant *of North America directs its leaves in a north–south alignment. Its profile from east or west is quite different from that of north or south.*

The wind direction

If the wind direction of the prevailing wind is known it can be used for maintaining direction — there are consistent patterns throughout the world but they are not always the same the whole year round.

Where a strong wind always comes from the same direction plants and trees may be bent in one direction, clear evidence of the wind's orientation. But plants are not the only indication of wind direction: birds and insects will usually build their nests in the lee of any cover and spiders cannot spin their webs in the wind. Snow and sand dunes are also blown into distinctive patterns by a prevailing wind which blows from the outside of the high central ridges.

Making use of the moon

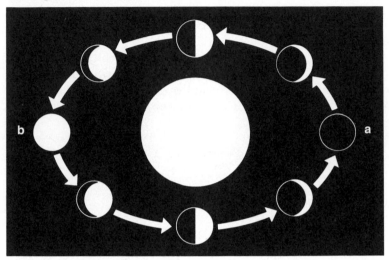

The moon has no light of its own, it reflects that of the sun. As it orbits the earth over 28 days the shape of the light reflected varies according to its position. When the moon is on the same side of the earth as the sun no light is visible – this is the 'new moon' (a) – then it reflects light from its apparent right-hand side, from a gradually increasing area as it 'waxes'. At the full moon it is on the opposite side of the earth from the sun (b) and then it 'wanes', the reflecting area gradually reducing to a narrow sliver on the apparent left-hand side. This can be used to identify direction.

If the moon rises BEFORE the sun has set the illuminated side will be on the west. If the moon rises AFTER midnight the illuminated side will be in the east. This may seem a little obvious, but it does mean you have the moon as a rough east-west reference during the night.

Direction by the stars

The stars stay in the same relation to one another and pass over the same places on the earth night after night. Their passage over the horizon starts four minutes earlier each night – a two-hour difference in time over a month. If you study a star at a certain position at a certain time one evening and then check its position the next evening at the same time you will find that it has moved one degree of arc anticlockwise in the Northern Hemisphere, clockwise in the Southern. Rising in the east, stars attain a zenith and set on the western horizon at the same distance from their zenith as they rose.

The stars have been studied for thousands of years and the groups, or constellations, in which they appear to the naked eye were named in ancient times after animals and mythological figures that their shape suggested.

In the Northern Hemisphere there are groups of stars that remain visible throughout the night, wheeling around the only star that does not appear to move − the Pole Star (a valuable navigation aid, for it is located almost above polar north). In the Southern Hemisphere the Pole Star is not visible and there is no comparable bright and stable southern star but direction finding in the southern hemisphere makes use of a constellation called the Southern Cross, in a way that is explained later.

THE NORTHERN SKY

The main constellations to learn are the Plough, also known as the Big Dipper (a), Cassiopeia (b) and Orion (c), all of which, like all stars in the northern sky, apparently circle the pole star (d), but the first two are recognizable groups that do not set.

These constellations come up at different times according to latitude and Orion is most useful if you are near the Equator.

Each can be used in some way to check the position of the pole star but once you have learned to recognize it you probably will not need to check each time.

A line can be drawn connecting Cassiopeia and the Plough (the Big Dipper), through the Pole Star. You will notice that the two lowest stars of the Great Bear (as shown here) point almost to the Pole Star. It will help you to find these constellations if you look along the Milky Way, which stretches right across the sky, appearing as a hazy band of millions of stars.

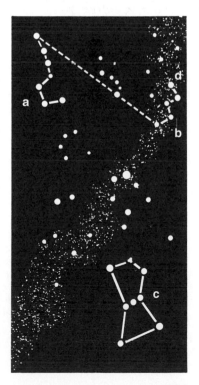

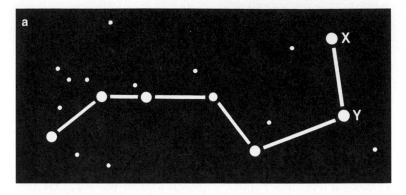

The Plough (the Big Dipper) (a) *is the central feature of a very large constellation, the Great Bear (**Ursa Major**). It wheels around the Pole Star. The two stars Dubhe (x) and Merak (y) point, beyond Dubhe, almost exactly to the Pole Star about four times further away than the distance between them.*

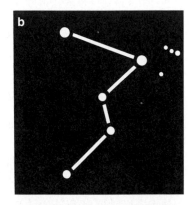

Cassiopeia (b) *is shaped like a W and also wheels around the North Star. It is on the opposite side of the Pole Star and about the same apparent distance away as the Plough (the Big Dipper).*

On clear, dark nights this constellation may be observed overlaying the Milky Way. It is useful to find this constellation as a guide to the location of the Pole Star, if the Plough is obscured for some reason. The centre star points almost directly towards it.

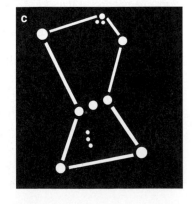

Orion (c) *rises above the Equator and can be seen in both hemispheres. It rises on its side, due east, irrespective of the observer's latitude, and sets due west. Mintaka (a) is directly above the Equator. Orion appears further away from the Pole Star than the previous constellations. He is easy to spot by the three stars making his belt, and the lesser stars forming his sword.*

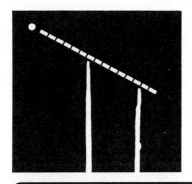

Other stars *that rise and set can be used to determine direction. Set two stakes in the ground, one shorter than the other, so that you can sight along them (or use the sights of a rifle propped in a steady position). Looking along them at any star — except the Pole Star — it will appear to move. From the star's apparent movement you can deduce the direction in which you are facing (See info. box).*

INFO.

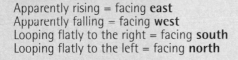

Apparently rising = facing **east**
Apparently falling = facing **west**
Looping flatly to the right = facing **south**
Looping flatly to the left = facing **north**

These are only approximate directions but you will find them adequate for navigation. They will be reversed in the Southern Hemisphere.

Reading the southern sky

There is no star near the South Celestial Pole bright enough to be easily recognized. Instead a prominent constellation is used as a signpost to south: the Southern Cross (Crux), a constellation of five stars which can be distinguished from two other cross-shaped groups by its size — it is smaller — and its two pointer stars.

Finding the Southern Cross

One way to find the Southern Cross is to look along the Milky Way, the band of millions of distant stars that can be seen running across the sky on a clear night. In the middle of it there is a dark patch where a cloud of dust blocks out the bright star background, known as the Coal Sack. On one side of it is the Southern Cross, on the other the two bright pointer stars.

FINDING SOUTH

To locate south project an imaginary line along the cross and four and a half times longer and then drop it vertically down to the horizon. Fix, if you can, a prominent landmark on the horizon — or drive two sticks into the ground to enable you to remember the position by day.

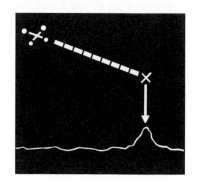

WEATHER SIGNS

Weather is much more localized than climate. Although it is possible to generalize about the weather to be expected in different parts of the world, and in some territories weather patterns are very stable, the geography of one small area may make it differ considerably from that adjoining.

Weather patterns are produced partly by the broad movements of wind and water over the whole globe and partly by localized differences in temperature and air pressure which cause air movements. These produce winds and carry rain.

In general, air moves from high pressure areas into low pressure zones, with warm air expanding and rising, cooler air moving in underneath. The warm air takes up moisture but at higher altitudes, or when some other cause brings down its temperature, the moisture begins to condense as cloud and eventually will fall as rain.

The most obvious example is where mountains force air currents upwards, rain falling on the slopes. In some places so much water is lost that on the far side of the range there is a dry 'rain shadow' territory.

However, that does not necessarily mean that if, from the dry terrain, you climb and cross the ridge you will move into a well-watered zone. The mountain zone may continue some way before the area of great precipitation is reached, or some earlier physical feature may have caused clouds to shed most of their rain.

Coastal areas

In coastal areas, whether of an ocean or an inland sea or lake, there will usually be a wind pattern that reverses from day to night. Water absorbs and loses heat less readily than the land and consequently it tends to be cooler than land during the day and warmer at night. The temperature difference affects the air above it and during the day breezes usually blow from sea to land, at night the wind changes and blows off the land.

Where an island is close to a large land mass these patterns may be overlaid by a broader air movement but a very regular pattern of day-night change in wind direction suggests a large body of water in the direction from which the day wind blows.

Winds

Winds can carry scents with them, providing information about the place from which they blow. Even to the untrained nose the smell of the sea will be recognizable, and to the shipwrecked survivor the smells of vegetation will indicate the direction of land. However, do not rely entirely on the nose, use other evidence to confirm its message.

Where winds tend to maintain direction they can be an aid in keeping to a course, but some other check should also be regularly made to keep direction.

Study the direction of the wind and the accompanying weather. Make a note of them. Dependent always upon barometric conditions, wind from a certain direction is always likely to bring a similar kind of weather. It is a guide for weather prediction.

If a wind is strong and dry the weather will remain constant until the wind drops or veers, then it may rain.

If it is foggy and misty you may get condensation but you will not get rain — but if a wind rises and blows away the fog it may turn to rain.

On a fine day a noticeable increase in the strength of the wind indicates a weather change. (See also *Hurricanes and Tornadoes* in *Disasters.*)

CLOUDS

Watch the way that clouds change, for clouds are the most reliable of weather signs.

Clouds are formed from masses of water vapour which becomes visible as it condenses with cooling. If cooling continues the droplets increase in size until, too heavy to remain airborne, they fall as rain. When their temperature rises sufficiently they evaporate and the cloud disperses.

There are ten main types of cloud formation. Approximate altitudes are given for each type. The same shapes occur at lower altitudes in polar regions.

The higher the clouds the finer the weather.

Small black clouds scudding beneath a dark stratus layer often bring showers.

Clouds hanging on high ground indicate rain, unless they move by midday.

Cirrocumulus clouds *are small rounded masses, looking like rippled sand and often referred to as a 'mackerel sky'. Normally an omen of fair weather, they usually follow a storm and dissipate, leaving a brilliant blue sky.*

Altocumulus clouds *are fair weather clouds, similar to cirrocumulus but on a larger scale, thicker, not so white and with shadows in them. They usually appear after a storm.*

Cumulonimbus clouds *are low thunder clouds. Dark and angry looking, they may tower to 6,000m (20,000ft) with the top flattening out in what is often called an anvil top. This is a cloud that brings hail, a strong wind, thunder and lightning. False cirrus appears above, false nimbostratus below.*

Cumulus clouds *are very easy to recognize: fluffy white clouds, not unlike cauliflowers. They are usually an indication of fair weather when widely separated but, if they become very large and develop many heads, they are capable of producing sudden heavy showers.*

Cumulus clouds at sea in an otherwise cloudless sky are often an indication of land beneath them.

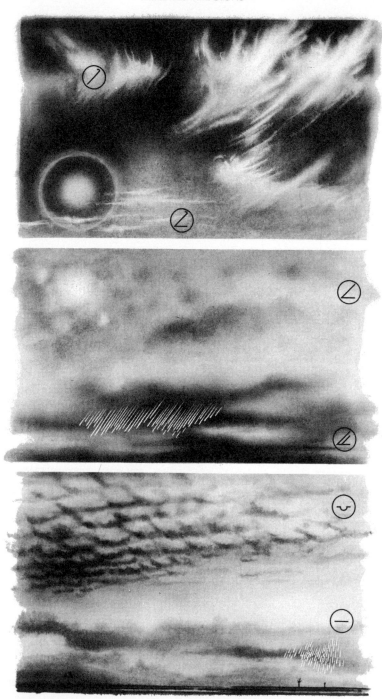

Cirrus clouds *are high, wispy clouds formed from ice crystals which give them a white appearance. Often called 'mares' tails', they are seen in fine weather.*

Cirrostratus clouds *are clouds made up of ice particles and look like white veins. These are the only clouds which produce a halo around the sun or moon. If it gets bigger it means fine weather, smaller a sign of rain.*

If the sky is covered with cirrus clouds and the sky above them darkens and the formation changes to cirrostratus it is an indication that rain or snow are coming.

Altostratus clouds *form a greyish veil through which the sun or moon may appear as a watery disk. If wet weather is approaching the disk will disappear and the cloud thicken and darken until it begins to rain.*

Nimbostratus clouds *form low, dark blankets of cloud and spread gloom. They mean rain or snow within four or five hours and usually the rain continues for hours.*

Stratocumulus clouds *form a low, lumpy, rolling mass, usually covering the whole sky, though often thin enough for the sun to filter through them. Light showers may precipitate from these clouds but they usually dissipate in the afternoon and leave a clear night sky.*

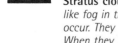

Stratus clouds *are the lowest of clouds and form a uniform layer like fog in the air — they are often described as hill fog when they occur. They are not a normal rain cloud but can produce a drizzle. When they form thickly overnight and cover the morning sky they will usually be followed by a fine day.*

PREDICTIONS

To be caught in bad weather could be fatal to survival. There is a time to go out or move on and a time to shelter. With an awareness of certain signs, short-term weather predictions can be made to help decide which to do.

Before setting out on any activity take note of the weather and any changes that are likely. Learn to observe all wind and pressure changes and keep a record of the weather and the conditions which precede it and what they develop into.

Wildlife indicators

Animals have great sensitivity to atmospheric pressure which aids them in forecasting the weather a day or two in advance.

Insect-eating birds, such as swallows, feed higher in good weather, lower when a storm is approaching.

Unusual rabbit activity during the day, or squirrels taking more food than usual to the nest, may be a prelude to bad weather.

Nature, however, does not go in for long-time forecasting. A squirrel's hoard of nuts is an indication of its industry, not the intensity of the coming winter. The depth of a bear's den has no relation to its severity, but reflects the soil conditions. A particularly big crop of berries is the result of previous bad conditions, the tree producing extra fruit to give the species more chance of survival.

Fireside clues

If the smoke from the camp fire rises steadily the weather is settled and likely to remain fine. If it starts swirling, or being beaten downwards after rising a short way, it indicates the likely approach of a storm or shower.

Wooden tool handles tighten at the approach of stormy weather. Salt picks up increasing dampness in the air and will not run.

'Feelings in your bones'

Curly-headed people find their hair becomes tighter and less manageable as bad weather approaches — and the same happens to animal fur. Anyone with rheumatism, corns or similar ailments can usually tell when wet weather is coming by an increase in their discomfort.

Sound and smell

When wet weather is on the way sounds tend to carry further than usual and distant noises seem more clear — the moisture-laden atmosphere acts like an amplifier. But compare like to like — remember, sound always travels better over water.

The smell of trees and plants becomes more distinctive before the arrival of rain, the vegetation is opening ready to receive it.

Signs in the sky

'Red sky at night, shepherd's delight, red sky in the morning, shepherd's warning' is one of the oldest of weather sayings. Since a red sun, or a red sky at sunset, indicates that the atmosphere holds little moisture it is unlikely that rain or snow will occur within the next two hours, but equally a red sky in the morning is a fair indication that a storm is approaching.

A grey morning is usually the start of a dry day. The dull colour is the result of dry air above the haze formed by the collection of dew on the dust particles suspended in the lower atmosphere.

An evening sky that is grey and overcast indicates rain — the dust particles are so laden with moisture that they will soon drop as rain.

Early morning mist lifting from a valley is a sure sign of fair weather. In hilly country, if mist has not lifted by noon, it is set in for the day and will probably turn to rain during the late afternoon.

A clear night sky is an indication of good, settled weather. At the end of summer it may also be a warning of frost: at night clouds insulate the surface of the earth against loss of heat. Without them frost is more likely. Cold air, being heavy, fills the hollows — avoid camping in them.

A clear sky one night, followed by one with only a few stars visible, indicates a change of weather.

A corona, a coloured circle visible around the sun or moon, can be used to forecast the weather accurately. An enlarging ring is a sign of good weather — the enlarging circle shows that moisture in the atmosphere is evaporating and day or night will be clear.

A shrinking corona around the sun or moon is a sign of rain.

Green light blinking from an afternoon sun indicates fair weather for at least 24 hours. A rainbow in the late afternoon is also a sign of fair weather ahead.

-7-
ON THE MOVE

Having chosen a course and planned a route, you must be able to maintain direction, to match your progress to the type of terrain and the nature of the survival group, and to exploit any techniques that make progress easier. This section deals with skills needed on the move. It should be read in conjunction with the techniques described earlier in *Climate and Terrain*.

Careful reconnaisance may be necessary to choose the easiest routes — which may not be the obvious or the quickest ones. Groups must be organized to suit the least able, or provision made for carrying them.

Waterways can offer the easiest routes to move along, if they are easily navigable and you are able to construct a raft. They can also present formidable barriers if they lie across the route you have to follow. Rivers can be dangerous. You must learn to assess the hazards they present and select the best places and methods of crossing, if crossing is unavoidable.

ON THE MOVE

Whether setting off on a hunting expedition or beginning the trek back to civilization, you will need skills in negotiating terrain and in navigation — either to ensure your return to camp or to keep to your chosen route. Even if you do not have a map, your own reconnaissance will have established your immediate terrain. Guessing what is beyond is much more problematic if you have to assess it for yourself.

On short expeditions take note of the terrain as you move outwards to ensure that you can find your way back to camp. Over short distances physical features will be your guide and you can also mark your trail, but when going further or striking back to civilization you will need all the navigational aids available.

The decision to move

Except when local dangers or the need to find water and food make it imperative that you move away from the site of your accident to make camp, you will stay close in the hope of rescue. If you have injured persons and only limited food and water, it would make sense to send a party to contact help while others stay to care for the sick. The fittest and most able should be chosen to make the trek — unless they include a trained medic, who should stay with the sick.

But what if no rescue comes? Local resources may become exhausted: you go further each day to collect firewood, the game in the area has gone, plants, fungi, fruits and nuts are more difficult to find or require long forays out of camp. Under survival conditions there is also an increased risk of disease from staying too long in one place. Even with the strictest sanitary management the chance of disease gradually builds up.

All these will be pressing you to move. Whether that be a move to new territory or the beginning of a trek back to civilization, many of the same problems will occur and — since there are few situations so idyllic that survivors will prefer their new life to their old — it would be sensible to plan any move as the first stage of the journey out. The exceptions will be where there are still sick people on their way to recovery, or better resources are needed to provision a push through alien territory. A move to a more comfortable camp in a more hospitable area will provide better chances of recovery for the injured or sick and the chance to build up and the necessary surplus and equipment ready for the final trek.

If you have a map or a clear idea of your location make for the nearest known settlement. If you have no idea where you are then the best course is usually to follow waterways DOWNSTREAM, for they will clearly define a route and generally lead to populated areas.

Even if you are simply changing the location of your camp there is no point in just moving a mile away — as you will soon have the same problems that made you decide to leave your first camp. The territory will not be entirely fresh. Move two or three days' journey at least so that fuel, flora and fauna will all be undisturbed.

REMEMBER:

Deciding which way to go will be influenced by all the information you have been able to gather, by the fitness and endurance of the party and by the nature of the terrain. Always remember that the most direct-looking route may not be the easiest to travel.

Although you may expect similar resources to be available, as long as you are travelling through similar terrain, remember that you have been hunting and foraging with experience of where things are best found or trapped and with known supplies of fuel and water. You will have to find your basic needs in new territory and when you move into different terrain availability may change dramatically — for better or worse.

Preparations

Before you finally abandon camp leave signs that will make it clear you have been there and have moved on (see *Signalling* in *Rescue*). Leave a message giving a list of who is in the party and details of your intentions. Mark the trail as you proceed so that if searchers do find the camp they will be able to follow you.

Build up a stock of preserved food, make water bottles and larger containers too if you envisage crossing waterless territory, litters or other means of transporting any remaining sick, the old or very young. Make suitable foot-coverings and clothing for everyone and packs to carry equipment and supplies. Some form of transport may be possible — a sledge or raft. Take shelter material with you — cloth, canvas, ponchos, even sticks if they are likely to be scarce in the terrain you are crossing. A shelter which can be quickly re-erected, will conserve energy for more urgent gathering than roofing materials and supports. Naturally, you will take signalling gear, for you may find an opportunity to make that vital contact which will bring rescue.

Study weather patterns carefully to choose a time for travel when the weather is likely to be settled.

HUDSON BAY PACK

A comfortable and easily improvised way of carrying equipment, this needs strong and preferably waterproof material about 90cm (1yd) square, two small stones and cord or thonging more than long enough to loop across the body.

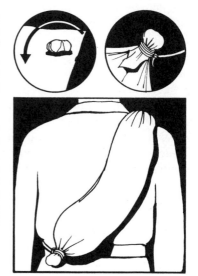

Place stones in diagonally opposite corners of the cloth. Fold ends of cloth over stones. Tie cord below the stones, securing them in position. The stones in turn prevent the cord slipping off. Lay cloth on the ground and roll possessions up tightly. Wrap pack around the body, either across the back or around the waist.

BACK-PACK FRAME

Make a ladder frame to fit against your back, with a right angle projection at the bottom secured by side struts. Add shoulder straps and a belt loop. Use this to support a bag, a bundle of supplies or equipment tied into place.

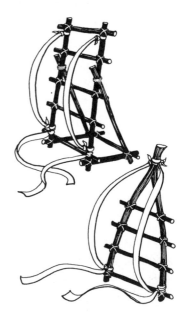

FORK FRAME

A quicker, but less-efficient support can be made from a forked bough with cross-pieces to which baggage can be tied.

BABY BAG

Carry babies and small children papoose style on your back or front. Tie lower corners of a rectangle of cloth around the waist, pop in the child and tie the upper corners around your neck. Pad at neck to ease pressure or chafing.

Carrying people

Pick-a-back and fireman's lifts are impracticable for long distances and stretchers are difficult to handle. Sit small children on a back-pack frame or make carrying chairs on poles to be borne by several people. If you are alone, try a sledge or travois (see *Furnishing the camp* in *Camp Craft*). Equipment can be carried in the same way.

Making a sledge

Sledges are particularly useful on snow and ice, when they will move most smoothly, but may also be used on smooth ground. The shape of the front runners is critical, especially on snow. You can make use of doors and cowlings from a crashed aircraft or vehicle in the construction. Tie lines to the front runners with a bowline to the people hauling — ideally two at the front, and two at the rear as brakemen on gradients. Test thoroughly before using on a long trek.

Choose two forked branches and remove one side of each fork. Make smooth for the runners and lash on cross members. Alternatively, choose two longer supple runners. Bend and brace as shown. This arrangement keeps the lashings off the ground and may be more comfortable for an injured person. Whichever method you use, add at least one diagonal for strength.

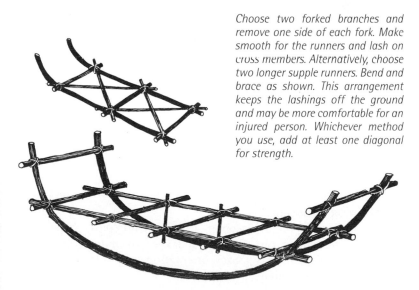

PLANNING

If you are on very high ground, above a large plain, it may be possible to plot out a route with some precision. In most situations visibility will be restricted and you will have to guess what is over the furthest ridge and what occupies the 'dead' ground ahead. Even when you can see the terrain ahead, it is difficult to see the details. What looks like a manageable slope may prove a barrier when you get closer to it. If you have them, make good use of field glasses in studying every potential route.

To see further you may consider climbing a tree — but keep close to the trunk and test each branch before risking your weight on it. This is NO time to risk a fall.

Following rivers

Following a watercourse, however small, offers a route to civilization and a life-support system on the way. Most rivers lead eventually to the sea or great inland lakes. Apart from the rare exception where rivers suddenly descend beneath the earth, they offer clearly defined routes to follow. Sometimes, in their upper reaches, they may cut through gorges and it can be impossible or inadvisable to take a route along their banks, which may be steep, rocky and slippery. In that case take to high ground and cut off the bends, following the general course of the stream.

On more level ground a river is easier to follow and may well have animal trails beside it which you can use. In tropical conditions the vegetation is likely to be denser by the river — for the light can reach below the trees, and the banks may be hard to negotiate. If the river is wide enough it would be worth considering building a raft. Even if there is no bamboo, which makes an ideal raft-building material, there are likely to be sound fallen trees for timber.

When, on flat plains, a river makes huge meanders, the inside of the loops may be swampy and prone to flooding — you can recognize such very wet ground by the lushness of the vegetation and rush-like plants. Avoid marshy areas if you can, and cut across the loop.

Maintaining direction

Having decided upon a direction, try to maintain it. Choose a prominent feature in the distance and keep heading towards it. Travelling through forests makes orientation very difficult and a compass becomes a valuable asset.

If you are in featureless territory, but in a group of three or more, separate to follow each other at wider intervals and look back frequently. If you are following in each other's tracks those behind you will be directly behind each other. If the party always moves on in relay — one moving on ahead, then resting while everyone else moves up from the rear — the straight line will be maintained. On your own you can try to align yourself by looking backwards at your own tracks if they are visible, as they are likely to be on snow or sand. Better still, you can set up sticks or piles of stones in alignment with each other so that you can check that you are not deviating from your route.

If possible skirt rocky outcrops and areas of dense vegetation and, once on high ground, stick to it until certain that you have found the spur down which you can make the best progress in the desired direction.

MOVING IN GROUPS

Always move in an organized manner, in some kind of formation, and not as an unruly gaggle. This way it will be easier to check that no stragglers have been left behind and to ensure that there is help for anyone in difficulty. Before setting out for the day, have a briefing to discuss the route, any obstacles expected and any special procedures.

Divide responsibilities

One person becomes a scout, responsible for selecting the best route, avoiding dead falls, loose rocks etc and finding the best way down a slope.

Number two is responsible for making sure the scout, who will be preoccupied with skirting obstacles, maintains correct overall direction. Others should relieve them frequently, for the lead scout's job in particular is very tiring.

The rest of the party should keep their eyes open for edible plants, berries and fruits and everyone should be responsible for at least one other person to ensure that no one drops by the wayside. A head count and check on everyone's condition is particularly important after a river crossing or negotiating a particularly tricky stretch of terrain. Someone should initiate equipment checks at frequent intervals.

Always travel in at least pairs — and be especially careful in bad weather, and if you have to travel at night, that you do not get split up. It is usually the person in front who gets split off from the group — people are more likely to remember to look for the stragglers. The scout climbs over an obstacle, the second person sees the scout struggling and then sees an easier route to take — the rest of the party follow and the lead person is separated from the group. This is when the benefit of EVERYONE knowing the proposed route, and nominating prominent features as rallying points is apparent. If separated or in an emergency everyone knows where to regroup.

Availability of water, fuel and plants may be an indication of what is available in similar locations further ahead. An eye should always be open for places that offer good shelter — if the weather suddenly turns bad you can backtrack to one of them.

PACE AND PROGRESS

– A large group can send an advance party ahead with the responsibility for clearing the route and setting up the night's camp, ready for the slower-moving injured or less able. A clear trail will make the carrying of baggage and any unfit people much easier. Sick and injured should be provided with fully-fit escorts in case they encounter any difficulties.

– Ensure that the lead man in the party does not go too fast for those behind. After an obstacle wait and allow everyone to catch up before moving on.

– It is best to try to maintain an even pace — smooth, pendulum-like movement tires the legs less than a jerky pace or flexing the knees. It helps to swing the arms — and they should certainly not be pushed in the pockets, especially when going up or down hills for if you then slip you have less chance of stopping yourself falling or sliding.

– Rest frequently (whether in a party or alone). Stop, sit down and see how everyone is doing. Adjust loads which are uncomfortable and repack them if necessary. On average take a break of 10 minutes every 30–45 minutes, depending on the terrain and condition of the group.

– On steep ground the pace should be shortened, on easy ground lengthened. On descents avoid overstepping for this jars the body and increases fatigue.

- On steep or slippery ground ropes can provide a hand hold to help people negotiate a particularly tricky stretch (quite apart from abseiling and other climbing techniques). They will be an asset on scree, as much as on icy slopes.

- You can also use a line with prusik knots attached so that the young and aged can be tied to a fixed rope for extra safety (see *Knots* in *Camp Craft*).

- In estimating distance you have covered allow 3km (under 2 miles) per hour, but going uphill knock off a third.

WALKING AT NIGHT

Negotiating unknown territory at night can be very dangerous, but may be necessary in an emergency, or there are circumstances — in the desert for instance — when it may be more comfortable to travel at night.

The night is never completely dark and outdoor vision is not totally lost, even for man. However, because it is difficult to see things clearly you are easily disoriented, which leads to a feeling of being lost. A compass is a great help in maintaining a heading and dispelling any such fears. It is always darker among trees than out in the open — so keep to open country if you can.

When looking at an object at night it is best to look at one side of it and not directly at it. It is difficult to distinguish anything in a dark central mass but the edges show more clearly and in poor light objects at the edges of your vision are often seen more distinctly.

Once the eyes get accustomed to the dark, more and more is seen as 'night vision' is acquired. It takes about 30–40 minutes for the eyes to get accustomed to the dark. Once this is achieved, the eyes must be protected from bright light or the night vision will be impaired for quite a while. If there is an unavoidable reason for having to use a light, cover one eye so that the vision in that eye at least will be retained. If, for instance, you need to consult a map, a red filter over a torch will help you to retain your night vision.

The ears are good sensors in the dark — the sound of a river, for instance, provides a good guide to how fast it is flowing. Vegetation can be smelt in the dark and familiar smells can aid identification.

Walk SLOWLY in the dark and test each step before putting all your weight forward. If going down a slope use a shuffling step.

UPLAND TRAVEL

In mountainous and hilly country it is best to keep to high ground — it makes navigation easier. Rivers may be in steep-sided gullies and have rapids, falls, and slippery rocks that are difficult to negotiate on foot. You could end up spending an unhealthy length of time in the water.

Use spurs to climb out of valleys and get on to the ridges. If they are very exposed you may have to drop down into the valleys for shelter at night and to find water but you will be able to cover more ground than by negotiating the spurs.

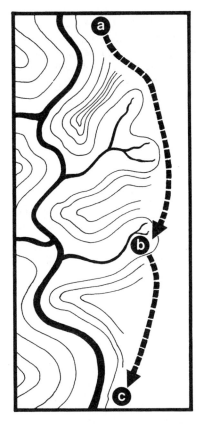

It is no use following a river as it winds in deep valleys through very hilly country. By climbing from the valley at (a) and following the ridge, steep and tiring descents and climbs are avoided.

At (b) a night halt is taken dropping down to the first available water source. This could provide shelter too, which may be unavailable on an exposed ridge.
Be aware of fading light and your own flagging energy. Look for shelter before they are exhausted.
Do not go down to the valley bottom if you can find shelter and water on the way. Not only will you save energy, you may be warmer.
Pockets of cold air are quite often trapped in the bottom of valleys.
If you carry water and shelter materials, stay on the high ground, choosing the most sheltered spot.

Then the route follows the ridge further before dropping down into the widening main valley to follow the watercourse again at (c). Follow the tip of a spur to go down into the valley when a river gets larger and the valley opens out.

Steep slopes

In mountainous country and on high hills, snow and ice may be encountered, and even without them such country can be dangerous with loose scree, steep slopes and crags that have to be negotiated.

Traverse steep slopes in a zig-zag and as you change direction always set off with the uphill foot. This avoids having to cross your legs over each other, which can make you lose balance. When climbing steep slopes lock your knees together after each step – this rests the muscles.

Descending steep slopes, keep your knees bent. Try to go straight down – and if you are picking up too much speed, sit back. Avoid loose rocks and scree but, if you have to negotiate loose surfaces, it helps to dig in the heels and lean back while descending. In climbing test every foothold before putting your weight on it. Don't step on stones or logs on steep slopes, they may dislodge.

With practice it is possible to jump down loose ground – dig in the heels and slide – provided that there are no sudden drops below. Keep the feet square and shoulder width apart and allow yourself to slide. As you increase in speed, dirt will build up under your feet and you will lose control. Jump and start again. If the slope is very steep abandon this method – abseiling (repelling) is the answer (see *Mountains* in *Climate and Terrain*).

JUNGLE TRAVEL

In dense jungle you may have to cut your way through if there is no way of going round. Chop downwards and as low as possible at the stems on both sides so that they fall away from the path you are making, not across it. Avoid leaving spikes standing, bamboo points can be lethal if someone stumbles. High growth and creeper can often be cut and travelled over.

Jungle vegetation seems to be covered in thorns and spikes. You may have to twist and turn to avoid vegetation that seems to surround you. Rushing only makes it worse. Those types of the climbing palms, atap and rattan, that are known as *nanti sikit* – 'wait-a-while' – in Malaya and similar names elsewhere, have thorns like fish-hooks at the end of the leaf. When snared by them you must back off and untangle. Don't try to tear through wait-a-while vine – it will strip you naked. You'll soon see why it got its name! However it has many uses and rattan is one of the best of jungle water vines.

Keep feet covered to protect them from sapling spikes, snakes and chigoes (chiggers). Stop frequently to remove parasites. Chigoes ignored for more than an hour or so will cause infection.

WATERWAYS

If a river is wide enough to be navigable, it will be easier to float on it than to walk beside it. The long-term survivor could experiment with making canoes — burning out the centre of a tree trunk to make a dug-out or covering a frame of willow with birch bark or skins — or copying boats made from reeds like those built by the ancient Egyptians and Mesopotamians, which are also found today on Lake Titicaca in Peru.

All are difficult to make well enough to stand up to water travel and even among the peoples for whom making them is a traditional skill, they are usually the work of specialists.

RAFTS

More practical for the survivor will be to construct a raft, which will not capsize so readily if the structure is not perfect. All boats and rafts must be soundly tested in safe water near the camp before setting out on a journey.

In jungle terrain especially you may find that the river, beside which you have camped, has been swelled by seasonal rains to make rafting a viable proposition. Here, too, you may find ample timber, either bamboo (which is ideal) or uprooted trees which are sound and unrotted. If you have to cut timber choose leaning trees for they are the easiest to drop. With dead falls the top of the trunk is usually sound enough to use for a raft.

You can use oil drums or other floating objects to support a raft, and if there is no supply of strong timber a sheet of tarpaulin or other waterproof material can be used as a man-carrying version of the coracle described later for floating equipment across a river.

Never take chances with a flimsy raft on any water. On mountain rivers there are often rapids which only a really tough structure will survive. On the wide lower reaches there will be a long way to swim to the bank if you have a raft break up under you.

Travelling by raft

Tie all equipment securely to the raft or to the safety line, making sure that nothing trails over the edges where it could snag in shallows.

Everyone aboard should have a bowline attached around the waist and secured to a safety line or to the raft.

BAMBOO RAFT

A single layer will not support you unless it is very long, so go for a two-layer model.

Cut thickish bamboo in 3m (10ft) lengths. Make holes through the canes near the ends and half-way along. Pass stakes through these holes to connect the canes. Lash each of the canes to each of the stakes with twine, rattan or other vines or cable. Make a second deck to fit on top of the first and lash the two together.

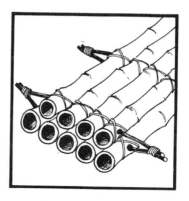

GRIPPER BAR RAFT

This is the quickest raft to build. You need logs for the deck and four thickish stakes with some pliability which are long enough to overlap the width of the deck.

Place two of the stakes on the ground and lay the logs over them.

Place the other stakes on top. Tie each pair of stakes firmly together on one side. Then, with a helper standing on top to force the other ends together, tie these so that the logs are gripped between them. Notching the ends of these gripper bars will stop the ropes from slipping.

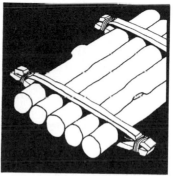

STEERING

To steer the raft make a paddle rudder and mount it on an A-frame near one end of the raft. Secure the A-frame with guy-lines to the corners of the raft and tie the rudder on to it so that it does not slip. The rudder can also be used as a sweep for propulsion. You may need to notch the raft for the base of the A-frame. The guy-lines could be tied to the cross pieces.

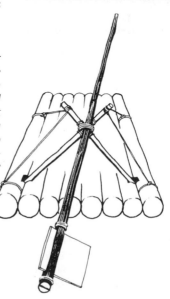

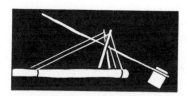

Lifelines should be long enough to allow free movement, but not so long that they trail in the water. In narrow swift-flowing rivers with dangerous rapids and waterfalls it is better not to tie on. If the raft gets out of control and is swept towards dangerous water, it is better to head for the bank.

In shallow water the best means of controlling a raft is like a punt, but preferably with two long poles — with one person poling at one front corner of the raft, and another at the diagonally opposite back corner.

If the survival group is a large one, several rafts will be needed. The fittest should be on the first raft, carrying no equipment or provisions. They can be lookouts and give early warning of hazards to be avoided. If they have to abandon their raft no kit will be lost.

Waterfalls and rapids can be heard some time before you reach them, and often are indicated by spray or mist rising in the air. If uncertain about the safety of the stream ahead, beach or moor the raft and carry out a reconnaissance on foot.

If you reach a difficult or dangerous stretch of water unload the raft and take to the bank, carrying all the equipment downstream of the dangerous waters. Having posted someone downstream where the river becomes safe and manageable to recover the raft, release the raft and let it drift down through the difficult stretch. It will probably need repairing but at least YOU will be safe and have all your equipment.

REMEMBER:

Only raft by day, NEVER in the dark. At night secure the raft firmly — so that it will still be there in the morning — and make temporary shelter on higher ground away from the river.

Bogs and marshes

If you cannot avoid crossing a marsh make your way by jumping from tuft to tuft of grass. If you find yourself sinking into a boa 'swim' with a breast-stroke to firm ground — don't try to jump. Spreading your body over the surface distributes your weight.

Use the same technique in quicksand.

CROSSING RIVERS

The headwaters of a river will be narrow and swift-running. Although banks may be steep and rocky it will usually be possible to find a place to cross. Where the water is shallow you may be able to wade — but test ahead with a pole for hidden depths. You may find rocks to provide stepping stones across or be able to place them for small streams.

Some members of a party may be able to leap across a narrow chasm or from boulder to boulder across the stream bed, but that is not much help if others cannot make it. A slip on a boulder is an easy way to sprain an ankle.

The estuary of a river is wide with strong currents and is subject to tides — which can influence some rivers many miles from their mouths. Avoid crossing there, unless equipped with boat or raft, go back upstream to an easier crossing place.

On any wide stretch, and especially when near the sea, do not set off, even with boats or rafts, immediately opposite the point you hope to reach, but consider how the current will affect your passage and make allowances.

STUDY THE WATER
The surface movement of a stream or river can tell you a great deal about what is beneath. The main flow of the current is usually evident from a chevron shape of smoother water around any rock or projection (a), the V widening downstream.

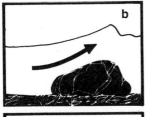

Waves that appear to stay in one position on the surface (b) are usually evidence of a boulder on the bottom deflecting water upwards.

Closer to the surface an obstruction will create an eddy downstream of it where the surface water appears to run back against the main flow. If a large boulder coincides with a steep drop in the level of the bottom (c) these eddies can produce a powerful backward pull downstream of the obstruction and pull swimmers in — they are VERY dangerous.

Wading across

Even quite wide rivers may be comparatively shallow and possible to wade across but never underestimate any stretch of water. Cut a stick to aid balance and cross facing towards the current and you will be more able to avoid being swept off your feet. Roll trousers up, so that they offer less surface to the current, or if they are going to get wet anyway take them off so that you have them dry for the other side. Keep your boots on, they will give a better grip than bare feet. Undo the belt fastening of a back-pack so that you can slip it off easily if you get swept over. But don't lose hold of it. It will almost certainly float and you can then use it to help right yourself.

WARNING

ICE-COLD WATER IS A KILLER
Do not attempt swimming or wading across a stream when the water is at very low temperatures, it could prove fatal. Make a raft of some kind. Only wade if you can do it without getting more than your feet wet and dry them vigorously as soon as you reach the other bank.

Turn at a slight angle, your back towards the bank you want to reach, the current will move you in that direction. Do not take strides but shuffle sideways, using the stick to test for depth and trying each foothold before using it.

Crossing as a group

If a group of people are wading across together, they should line up behind the strongest, who crosses as described above. The others each hold the one in front at the waist and move in step, offering less obstruction to the current.

Alternatively a group can link arms side-by-side and hold on to a pole or branch to keep them in alignment. They cross facing the bank and moving forwards. Only the side of the first person opposes the current and the group provides stability for all of them.

WARNING

Look out for submerged branches. You could get tangled in them and wrench a limb or lose balance. When carried along with the current you do not notice its strength but if it forces you against an obstruction you can be firmly held.

Crossing with ropes

If a rope is available it can make wading safer — but you need a loop of rope three times as long as the width of the stream and there must be at least three people in the party. Two of them always control the rope to keep it out of the water as much as possible and to haul the crosser to the bank if difficulties are encountered.

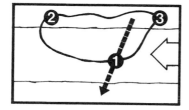

The person crossing is secured to the loop, around the chest. The strongest person crosses first. The other two are not tied on — they pay out the rope as it is needed and can stop the crosser being washed away.

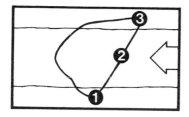

When he reaches the bank, 1 unties himself and 2 ties on. 2 crosses controlled by the others. Any number of people can be sent across in this way.

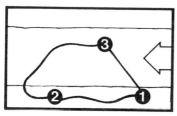

When 2 has reached the bank, 3 ties on and crosses. 1 takes most of the strain, but 2 is ready in case anything goes wrong.

RIVERS ARE DANGEROUS

Never enter the water unless there is no other way of getting across and choose a crossing point carefully.

- Avoid high banks that are difficult to climb out on.

- Avoid obstructions in the water.

- Current is likely to be fastest on the outside of bends and steep banks may be undercut making landing impossible.

- Look for an even section of river bed — shingle is the best surface for wading.

Swimming across

If you can't swim DON'T try — rely on others to get you across with the help of some sort of float. Even the strongest swimmers should make use of flotation aids when crossing a river — and for non-swimmers they will be essential. They will reduce the expenditure of energy and help to keep clothes and kit dry. Do not swim with your clothes on. Once wet they will give you no protection from cold — dry they are something warm to put on when you have crossed.

Always make sure you have found a place on the other side where you will be able to get out of the water. If there are no beaches you will need supports to haul yourself up on to the bank — but avoid tangles of branches in the water where you might get trapped. Enter the water well upstream to allow for the distance that the current will carry you down as you cross. Better to overestimate and be a little longer in the water, than pass your landing place.

Check the strength of the current by watching floating logs and flotsam and study the water surface for hidden obstructions and eddies.

If you hit weed in the water adopt a crawl stroke to cut through it. Once a strong swimmer has cleared a passage others will be able to follow through in the channel made.

Flotation aids

Fuel cans, plastic bottles, logs — anything that floats can be used. If you have a waterproof bag put your clothes and belongings inside, leaving plenty of air space tie the neck and then bend it over and tie again and use it as a float. Hang on to it and use just your legs to propel yourself.

- Without a bag, but with a waterproof sheet, pile twigs and straw into the centre to create air pockets and then pile your clothes and equipment on top before tying up the bundle securely.

- Do not attempt to sit on the bundles or place your weight on them.

- With a group of people, split into fours. Each four should lash their bags together and use them as support for an injured member of the party or a non-swimmer.

- If no waterproof material is available make a small raft or a coracle to float your things on. Bundle your belongings and, if heavy, make the raft two-layered so that only the lower layer sinks into the water and your kit stays dry.

MAKING A CORACLE

There is a real art to building a traditional coracle — and confidence is required to use it. Follow the method below, make a paddle and test your coracle in safe shallow water to see how it handles. Before you begin, make sure you have a waterproof cover for it — tarpaulin, groundsheet, poncho, or animal skins will do. Fats and tree resins are good for waterproofing.

Cut springy saplings 2m (6·5ft) long — hazel and willow are ideal. Stick the ends of one in the ground to form an arch and then add others across it to form a dome at about 25cm (9in) intervals.

Tie them together at the apex. Tie a sapling around at ground level and another half-way up to keep the shape and pull the whole structure free from the ground. Trim off most of the saplings that project above the upper edge.

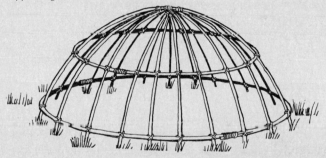

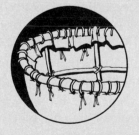

Cover the frame with polythene, tarpaulin, poncho or animals skins, sewn with twine or thonging around the upper edge. Obviously do not pierce below the 'waterline'. To save heavy woodworking a paddle could be made from a sapling loop, tied to a pole and covered in waterproof material.

-8-
HEALTH

When no professional medical help is available, survivors have to undertake medical tasks which should normally be left to those with special training.

Traditional first-aid procedures are designed to cope with minor problems and to sustain a seriously-injured person until they can receive expert treatment. However, if there is no possibility of outside help in time to save a life, the survivor may sometimes have to take drastic measures. Some of the advice given in this section is intended ONLY for such circumstances.

In the treatment of diseases and disorders the experience of centuries of herbal treatments and natural remedies can be put to good use, when no prepared drugs are available — or to reserve supplies for more serious need. Herbal medicines given here use only simple methods of extraction and preparation.

FIRST AID

Maintaining health is of primary importance to the survivor. Do not take any unnecessary risks which could lead to injury. Aim at a varied and balanced diet and make sure that you get adequate rest.

In the initial stages of the survival situation none of these may be possible but, once you have a camp established, food sources and water found, a disciplined approach will enable you to conserve energy and resources. Away from people, you are not exposed to contagious infections, unless you brought them with you. Although some diseases are insect- or waterborne, sensible precautions — especially boiling water and properly cooking food — will protect you from many infections.

Extreme climatic conditions bring their own dangers and an awareness of symptoms will help you to treat yourself and others. Inexperience or ill-luck may lead to injury, however careful you are, and an understanding of practical first aid — improvising where medical equipment is not available — is a basic survival skill. In accident situations such improvisation may be the first key to survival for those involved, when rapid action is essential. Any expedition should have at least one person with suitable specialized medical knowledge — but EVERYONE should know how to deal with basic injuries, disorders and diseases.

PRIORITIES

In an accident, involving many injured people, you must know which patients to treat first. When a patient has multiple injuries, breathing, heartbeat and bleeding should be given priority. Assess the injuries and handle in the following sequence:

- Restore and maintain breathing/heartbeat
- Stop bleeding
- Protect wounds and burns
- Immobilize fractures
- Treat shock

NOTE: Before approaching any accident victim, check for danger to yourself and protect yourself from it. Look out for electric cables, gas pipes, falling debris, dangerous structures or wreckage. Give initial check-up without moving the patient, if possible, but — if there is continuing danger — move the patient and yourself to a safer location.

REMOVE FROM DANGER

First reduce any further danger to the casualty or yourself by moving them to safety — away from a burning vehicle or building. In the case of a road accident, stop the traffic. With electrocution, switch off the current. If you can't, stand on dry nonconductive material and push or lever the patient from the power source with a dry nonconductive pole or stick BEFORE touching them. If gas or poisonous fumes are threatening, turn them off at source and take casualties to fresh air.

There is always a risk in moving patients with unknown injuries but, if they are further threatened, they must be moved to have any chance of surviving. People with spinal injuries are at greatest risk when moved — the spinal cord could be severed. The only safe way to move them requires several people (see *Fracture of the spine*).

Unconscious casualties

If a person is unconscious first check whether they are breathing and begin artificial respiration immediately if necessary. Check for external bleeding and injury, trying to establish the cause of unconsciousness.

BREATHING BUT UNCONSCIOUS

If the patient is breathing, and does not appear to have any spinal injury, check that there are no obstructions in the mouth, deal with any serious bleeding and place him or her in the recovery position. If lying on the back you will need gently to turn the casualty on one side, usually most easily done by grasping clothing at the hip. This produces a stable position so that any liquids or vomit produced from the stomach or nose will not enter or block the lungs and the tongue will not fall back and block the airway.

> ## *WARNING*
>
> Do NOT place a casualty with a suspected spinal injury in the recovery position. Use an artificial airway to maintain their respiration and as a means of administering mouth-to-mouth resuscitation.
>
> **CHECK BREATHING AND HEARTBEAT!**

RECOVERY POSITION

Move the arm and leg on one side of the body outwards to stop the patient lying flat, elbow and knee should both be bent. Turn the head in the same direction. Lay the other arm down along the other side of the patient.

Allow the other leg to bend slightly.
Pull the jaw forward to check that the tongue is at the front of the mouth and not blocking the airway. Loosen tight clothing.

BREATHING AND PULSE

Normal breathing is quiet and easy. Noisy breathing, froth around the nose or lips and blueness around the lips and ears are all signs of difficult or obstructed breathing. Check breathing regularly by listening carefully near the nose and mouth. Remove obstructions and, in the absence of breathing, give artificial respiration. Check at neck or wrist for pulse.

Cessation of breathing
This dire emergency may be caused by:

- Blockage of upper air passages caused by face and neck injuries or foreign bodies
- Drowning or electric shock
- Choking
- Inflammation and spasm of air passages caused by inhalation of smoke, gases or flame
- Lack of oxygen
- Compression of the chest

CHOKING AND BLOCKAGES

If breathing has stopped immediately remove any obstruction in the airway and give artificial respiration.

Clear the airway of any foreign matter: weed, vomit, false teeth or food. Sweep the mouth with a finger and ensure the tongue has not fallen back to obstruct the breathing passages.

If someone appears to be choking, but can breathe and cough, their own coughing is more effective than your aid. A blow on the back may sometimes help. If the victim cannot speak use the Heimlich manoeuvre with adults, but see other methods for special cases.

HEIMLICH MANOEUVRE
Stand or kneel behind casualty, arms around them. Clench one hand over the other, thumb side of fist pressing between waist and bottom of ribs. Apply pressure and jerk quickly upwards four times.

IF THIS DOES NOT WORK
Give four sharp blows to the back between the shoulderblades to loosen object and four more 'hugs'. Stop when victim starts breathing or coughs loudly.

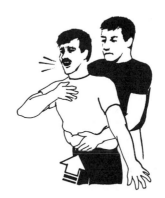

REPEAT if this does not succeed at first. DO NOT GIVE UP! Be ready to give artificial respiration, if the blockage is removed, but the patient does not start breathing. Lay an unconscious patient on his or her back, kneel astride, place your hands, one on top of the other, with the heels resting above the navel, and make quick thrusts up to the centre of the ribcage. If the blockage does not appear to shift, quickly roll patient on to side and strike four times between the shoulderblades. Repeat as necessary.

SELF-HELP

If alone, use the Heimlich manoeuvre by pulling or pushing against a blunt projection — an earth bank, a fallen tree (or a chair back in a domestic situation).

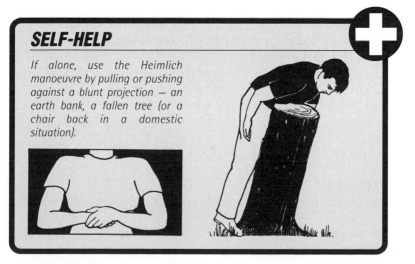

Choking: Special cases
Babies:

Support the baby, face down, straddling your forearm, with the head definitely lower than the chest. Use the heel of the free hand to give four quick blows between the shoulderblades.

Place free hand on back of baby's head and turn over. Use two fingertips to press four times, quickly and fairly firmly, on centre chest. REPEAT. Be ready to give 'mouth-to-mouth (and nose)' if breathing stops.

Children:

With small children hold them upside down and strike four rapid blows between the shoulderblades using the heel of the hand. With older children place across the knee, or bend forward from a sitting position, supporting chest with one hand while administering blows with other. Alternatively, perform Heimlich manoeuvre using two fingers of each hand instead of fists. (Not breathing – see *Artificial Respiration*.)

Pregnancy and obesity:

Abdominal Heimlich manoeuvre impossible. Position fists instead against the middle of the breastbone and follow similar procedure. (Not breathing – see *Artificial Respiration*.)

Drastic action
On the rare occasion when repeated attempts with the Heimlich manoeuvre fail to dislodge an obstruction, drastic action is required: a cut into the patient's throat below the obstruction. Also used in cases where an injury to the jaw prevents the patient from breathing, this is a technique only for a life-or-death situation. It is risky for the untrained, but worth trying to save a life in cases where the casualty will certainly die without it. There is no significant bleeding if you use the Crico thyroid technique, which is superior to a tracheotomy (where the cut is made below the Adam's apple).

Preparation
You need a sharp blade, a scalpel or a penknife, not a wide knife, and a hollow tube (a ballpoint pen case, a CLEAN fuel or hydraulic line from a vehicle, tubing from a back-pack, a small syringe and even a hollow plant stem have been used).

They should be sterilized if boiling water or a flame is available, but do not waste time getting them. WARNING: Contamination with oil or petrol from a dirty vehicle hose could produce chemopneumonia.

1 *Lay casualty on back, shoulders elevated, head and neck presenting a straight line.*

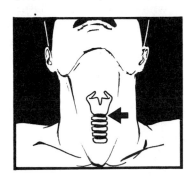

2 *Run a finger down the Adam's apple — the bone-like projection on the front of the neck (more prominent in men than women) and find another small projection just below it. Between the Adam's apple and this smaller projection you will find a central valley.*

3 *Make an incision here at the exact midpoint. Keep the incision small but deep — straight down for about 1–2cm (³/₈–³/₄in) — note the distance on the blade beforehand. You will feel the blade move more easily as it cuts through to the windpipe. Do NOT push down further.*

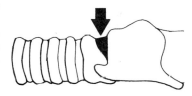

ALTERNATIVE· For the incision, pierce with a wide-bore needle — producing less bleeding (and considered preferable by doctors). A kit is produced and should be included in pare-medical equipment.

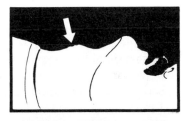

4 *Twist the blade sideways to open up cut.*

5 *Insert the tube in the incision and push it down to keep the cut open and allow air into the lungs. Once in place, secure firmly with adhesive tape or bandage to keep it upright and prevent it falling out.*

Once the airway is clear, whether natural or artificial, if the patient is still not breathing, artificial respiration must be carried out.

Preventing asphyxiation
Pressure:

> Any compression of the chest can cause asphyxiation. A climber who slips and is held suspended by a rope around his chest will find it extremely difficult to breathe. Pass down a rope with a loop (bowline or manharness hitch, see *Knots* in *Camp Craft*) to stand in and relieve the pressure.

> An avalanche of snow, or a fall of earth can exert pressure on the chest and make breathing difficult. Adopt a crouched position if possible, with bent arms and elbows tucked well in and this will protect the chest.

> If a person is trapped under wreckage with pressure on the chest, and the weight cannot be lifted off, use a lever to lift it and prop securely.

Smoke and gas:

> To prevent smoke entering the lungs, place fine mesh material over the nose and mouth to filter it. Smoke can be seen and there is a chance of avoiding it. Gases cannot usually be seen and safety is gained only in fresh air upwind of them, or with a respirator. Casualties must have fresh air.

Lack of oxygen:

> Oxygen can be used up in a shelter which lacks ventilation or becomes blocked and sealed by rubble or snow. This is a danger in igloos especially if draughts are sealed. With a stove or fire, not only is the oxygen used, even more seriously, carbon monoxide is produced. Casualties must have fresh air.

Carbon monoxide poisoning:

> This gas is DEADLY in confined spaces, but the occupants rarely recognize its presence. The symptoms of carbon monoxide poisoning resemble those of an overdose of alcohol: memory and judgment are impaired, an increase in confidence and a disregard of danger.

> Always ensure that you have adequate ventilation, especially when using stoves. Adjust any burning with a yellow flame. Light a candle in your shelter. If the flame gets longer and higher — or in extreme cases shoots to the roof — there is a severe lack of oxygen and it is high time to ventilate. Once again, it is neccessary for casualties to have fresh air.

NOT BREATHING AND NO PULSE

Drowning

Symptoms: Can occur through fluid blockages but generally patient will be in water or have face in liquid. Face, especially lips and ears, livid and congested. Possibly fine froth at mouth and nostrils — it is the froth that is blocking the air passage.

Do not attempt to remove liquid from lungs — you can't. Begin artificial respiration as early as possible. If still in water, support floating body and begin mouth-to-mouth resuscitation after quickly removing weed, false teeth or any other mouth obstructions. On land Holger Nielsen method can also be used.

Electrocution

Symptoms: The cause will usually be obvious. Electrocution may stop the heart and muscle spasms may throw the victim some distance. Electrical burns will be much deeper than their appearance suggests.

Never touch the victim until current is off or contact broken. If an appliance is involved it may be possible to break contact by pulling on insulated cable. But beware of any liquids which will conduct current — victims may urinate. Give artificial respiration and treat for cardiac arrest if necessary before treating burns. TAKE NO RISKS.

Lightning

Symptoms: Another form of electrocution. The victim is usually stunned and falls unconscious. Clothing may catch fire as well as patient having electrical burns, which will be more severe where watches, jewellery, buckles or other metal objects are worn.

Give artificial respiration if necessary and treat burns. Prolonged resuscitation may be needed. Recovery is often delayed.

Poisoning

Symptoms: Poisons which enter the lungs or affect the nervous system can produce asphyxia.

Heart attack

Symptoms: Severe pain in the chest, shortness of breath patient feeling giddy, possibly collapsing to ground, and often anxious. Heavy sweating, irregular pulse, blueness of lips or skin.

If breathing fails give artificial respiration and external heart compression if the pulse stops.

ARTIFICIAL RESPIRATION
Mouth-to-mouth ('Kiss of life')

The fastest and most effective method. Begin as soon as the airway has been cleared. Normal recovery is rapid, except in cases of electric shock, drugs and carbon monoxide poisoning. In these cases nerves and muscles are paralyzd or carbon monoxide has displaced oxygen in the bloodstream. Be prepared to carry on a long time.

If face is injured, or poison or chemical burns are suspect use the Silvester method.

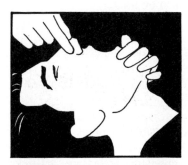

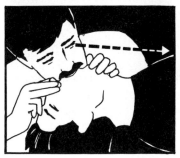

With patient lying on back, hold jaw well open, bending head back (prevents tongue falling and blocking airway). Hold nostrils closed with other hand. Check mouth and throat clear of obstruction. Place mouth over patient's mouth and exhale.

Watch for chest to rise as you blow gentry into patient's lungs. (If chest does not rise, turn him on his side and thump between shoulderblades to remove obstruction.) Remove mouth. Take a deep breath while checking chest falls automatically. You should feel or hear air returning.

REPEAT, as quickly as possible for the first six inflations, then at 12 per minute until breathing is established.

For a child: Do not blow. Exhale normally, or in gentle puffs for a baby. Give first four inflations as quickly as possible. Blowing forcefully into a child's mouth may damage delicate lungs.

Mouth-to-nose: Use if you cannot seal your lips around victim's mouth, holding his mouth closed. For babies, cover both nose and mouth with your lips.

KEEP GOING!

With any form of resuscitation the first five minutes are probably the most critical but, if breathing does not start, keep artificial respiration up for at least an hour. In a group take turns. CHECK HEARTBEAT.

Artificial respiration: with facial injury

Silvester method: Recommended when poisoning or facial injury prevent mouth-to-mouth resuscitation, especially when patient may need cardiac compression (which can be done by the same first-aider).

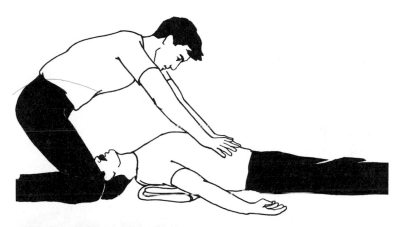

With casualty lying on back, raise shoulders with pad of folded blanket or clothing. Kneel astride casualty's head.

Place hands flat over lower ribs and rock forward to press steadily downwards. Lift casualty's arms upwards and outwards as far as possible.

REPEAT rhythmically about 12 times per minute for adults. If there is no improvement turn patient on side and strike briskly between shoulders to remove any possible obstruction before resuming the cycle.

DON'T GIVE UP! Resuscitation techniques have saved the lives of victims of drowning, hypothermia and electrocution after three hours without spontaneous breathing.

403

Artificial respiration: face down

Holger Nielson method: This is the technique recommended for resuscitating a drowning victim if mouth-to-mouth is not practicable, or if patient cannot be turned on back. Casualty lies face-down, liquids can flow freely from the mouth and will not cause choking.

Place with head turned to one side, arms bent, forehead resting on hands. Loosen tight clothing and ensure tongue is brought forward, mouth clear of weed, mud etc.

Face the casualty, kneeling on one knee at head, placing your hands over shoulderblades, thumbs touching and fingers spread. Perform the following procedure to a count of eight.

1–2–3 *Rock forward with arms straight, producing gentle, even, increasing pressure. (About 2 seconds)*
4 *Rock back, sliding hands to grasp patient's upper arms. (¹/₂–1 second)*

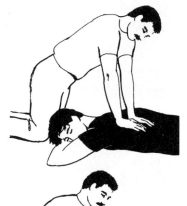

5–6–7 *Pull and raise patient's arms gently by rocking further backwards. (2 seconds) Avoid raising patient's trunk or disturbing head too much.*
8 *Lower patient's arms to ground and slide hands back to initial position. (¹/₂–1 second)*

REPEAT 12 times per minute.

NOTE: If the patient's arms are injured, place a folded garment under the forehead and lift under the armpits. This is not a practicable method if ribs or shoulders are badly damaged.

AFTER BREATHING HAS BEEN RESTORED: Place patient in recovery position — after all forms of resuscitation. But NOT in cases of spinal injury.

IS HEART BEATING?

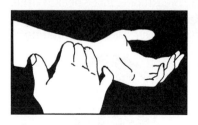 

TAKING PULSE AT WRIST
Rest fingers lightly at the front of the wrist, over the radial artery, about 1cm (¹/₃in) from thumb side at lower end of forearm.

TAKING PULSE AT NECK
Turn face to one side. Slide fingers from Adam's apple into groove alongside. Other pressure points can also be used.

Normal pulse

In a relaxed adult 60–80 per minute (average 72), in young children it is much higher, at 90–140 per minute. Excitement increases rate.

Don't waste precious time — count the beats in 30 seconds and multiply by two. Use a watch with a seconds hand to keep timing accurate and note down result.

If there is no pulse

If you cannot feel a pulse and the pupils of the eyes are much larger than normal, start cardiac compression while artificial respiration is continued. The mouth-to-mouth and the Silvester methods allow both activities to be carried out at the same time.

Cardiac compression

Regardless of which method of resuscitation is used, if there is no pulse and after 10–12 breaths there is no apparent improvement in the casualty's condition, cardiac compression (external heart massage) should be started.

NO TIME TO LOSE!

First place the casualty on a firm surface — let them lie on the ground, chest up. Using the edge of the hand strike firmly on the lower part of the breastbone (the central bone between the ribs). The jarring may start the heart. If there is still no pulse proceed with compression.

Kneel beside the casualty. Place heel of one hand on lower half of breastbone (sternum), the central bone between the ribs. Make sure it is not on the end of, or below, the breastbone. Place heel of other hand over it. Keep rest of hand OFF chest. Keeping arms straight, rock forward and press down 6–8 times after each lung inflation.

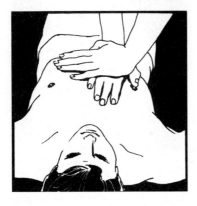

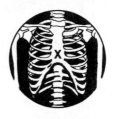

In adults press down about 4cm (1½in). Repeat at least 60 times per minute. Press smoothly and firmly. Erratic or rough pressing could cause further injury.

Infants and children require less pressure and more pushes. For babies and small children light pressure with two fingers is enough at a rate of 100 times per minute. For older children up to ten years, use the heel of one hand only and push 80–90 times per minute.

Note: Check for dilation of pupils of eyes and return of pulse in neck artery which indicate success. ARTIFICIAL RESPIRATION MAY STILL BE NEEDED.

Artificial respiration with compression (Cardiopulmonary resuscitation)

If alone: Use mouth-to-mouth or Silvester methods of resuscitation, giving a repeated pattern 15 heart compressions followed by two rapid lung-inflations.

If two first-aiders: Give five heart-compressions followed by one deep lung-inflation. Repeat. First-aider giving inflations should also note neck pulse and pupils.

Once breathing has been restored, it must be maintained. Lay the patient in the recovery position (EXCEPT when spine or neck injured) which reduces risk from liquids they may bring up as they recover. Check condition regularly.

If available use ARTIFICIAL AIRWAY to keep airway open in unconscious patients.

RECOMMENDED EQUIPMENT

ARTIFICIAL AIRWAY

Before use inspect both patient's and artificial airway.

Insert the artificial airway to a third of its length, end pointing to the roof of the mouth, then turn it through 180° to point down the throat.

Once it is in place patient will be able to breathe. A mucus build-up may start coughing and gurgling. Clear it with an extractor.

MUCUS EXTRACTOR

Placed down artificial airway, its one-way valve allows mucus to be sucked out without risk of swallowing. One was probably used on you first thing after birth! Without one you can use any tube or straw (preferably sterilized), trying NOT to swallow the mucus yourself.

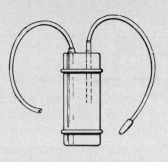

DANGEROUS BLEEDING

An average person has up to 6·25 litres (11pt) of circulating blood. The loss of 0·5 litre (1pt) causes mild faintness, 1 litre (2pt) faintness — with an increase in pulse and breathing, 1·5 litre (3pt) collapse. More than 2.24 litre (4pt) may even cause death. Immediate steps must be taken to stop the flow of blood. However, once a small haemorrhage has been stopped, blood volume is quickly restored with fluid from the tissues — the resulting slight anaemia is not important. Body fluids must be replaced by giving water, so that the fluid balance is restored.

PRIORITIES

Blood transports life-giving oxygen. When bleeding is coupled with cessation of breathing treat both concurrently. Get the patient breathing AND staunch the bleeding.

Bleeding from veins and capillaries can be stemmed by simple pressure over the bleeding point, with or without a dressing, and minor arterial bleeding may also be controlled with local pressure. Extremity wounds should be elevated above the heart, still applying pressure.

You can use anything to staunch the flow of blood – a hand, handkerchief, blouse – but use the cleanest material possible and apply it rapidly and firmly. There is danger of infection from unsterile material but, if a person is bleeding to death, there is no time to worry. Death is more certain from serious bleeding.

Maintain a continuous, firm pressure for 5–10 minutes and you will stop the bleeding. Resist the temptation to lift and look. If blood seeps through the pad place another on top.

Large dressings of absorbent cotton wool (known in the army as shell dressings) are ideal for stopping bleeding. Include them in your medical kit.

Secure with the attached bandage and then with a further crepe bandage which will maintain the steady pressure required.

Arterial bleeding

This is the most serious type of bleeding and speed is essential to stop it. Bleeding from an artery comes in powerful, rapid spurts, in time with the pulse. It can be temporarily controlled by compressing an artery where it crosses a bone, against that bone, at pressure points. Precautions must be taken, if at all possible, to prevent the spread of diseases such as HIV, but it is accepted that if you are faced with this emergency you are unlikely to have gloves etc.

PRESSURE POINTS

These are places where arteries run close to the surface over a bone so that they can be pressed against it, cutting off the flow of blood. Each is effective for arterial blood loss from the area specified. Watch the wound. If blood flow is not immediately reduced, move fingers until it is.

- **Temple or scalp:** Forward of/above ear (a)
- **Face below eyes:** Side of jaw (b)
- **Shoulder or upper arm:** Above clavicle (c)
- **Elbow:** Underside of upper arm (d)
- **Lower arm:** Crook of elbow (e)
- **Hand:** Front of wrist (f)
- **Thigh:** Mid-way on groin/top of thigh (g)
- **Lower leg:** Upper sides of knee (h)
- **Foot:** Front of ankle (i)

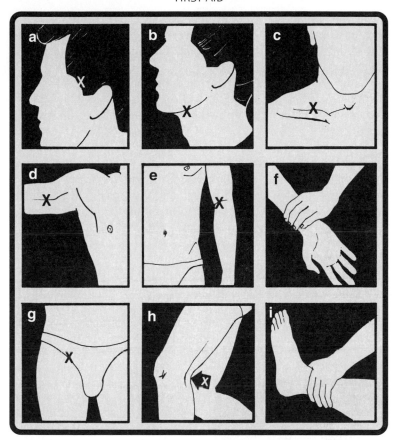

Tying arteries

In the case of major wounds to which a pressure dressing cannot be applied, where access is restricted or a limb partially severed, trace the bleeding artery and tie it off.

This is hazardous for the untrained — arteries often have accompanying nerves and including them in a clip or tie could cause permanent damage, such as loss of function of a limb.

Apply a temporary tourniquet to control the bleeding — but you may have to release spurts of blood to find the artery.

Sterilize a piece of fishing line, thread or fine string by boiling or soaking in alcohol. The contents of a hip flask or a perfume bottle will remove bacteria. Cleanliness is essential. Boil all dressings and bandages. Scrub the hands thoroughly in boiled water, using soap if available.

409

Clean the wound with sterile (boiled) water and gently explore it with a clean finger to locate the severed artery. Tie it securely with the sterilized thread. This is the one time that an open wound is touched.

If the artery is completely severed, its ends may retract making them more difficult to locate. If you are sure the bleeding vessel is in a piece of tissue then the whole area can be sewn up, using a large needle.

Cautiously relax the tourniquet as soon as possible to check whether your handiwork has been successful. Make sure there is not more than one major bleeding vessel. If you see more bleeding, immediately tighten the tourniquet and try again. Other smaller vessels will supply sufficient blood to maintain the life of the limb.

Do NOT leave the tourniquet in position.

Tourniquets

There are only two places where a tourniquet may be placed: on the upper arm, just below the armpit, and around the upper thigh. Preferably use a piece of cloth at least 5cm (2in) wide. If you have to use anything thinner (wire or cord), you MUST apply over a fold of clothing to reduce discomfort and avoid damage to nerves or flesh.

Wrap around limb three times and tie half knot. Place stick, or similar object over knot and tie double knot over it. Twist stick, tightening band until bleeding stops.

Tourniquet must be tight enough to arrest blood supply but relaxed frequently, so after applying WORK FAST.

Release COMPLETELY when job is done.

WARNING

A tourniquet cuts off the blood flow and if left on too long can cause serious damage — even loss of a limb.

- **ONLY** use a tourniquet on a limb. **NEVER** on head, neck or torso.

- **NEVER** cover a tourniquet. If you have to leave one unattended write TK and time applied on victim's forehead with felt-tip or lipstick.

Check circulation

After bandaging a limb, check frequently that neither toes nor fingers are blue, cold or numb. If they are, loosen the dressing. If you do not GANGRENE MAY DEVELOP, perhaps resulting in the loss of a limb.

For the same reason do NOT use a tourniquet (except when tying arteries). First try direct pressure. Then use pressure points, still keeping direct pressure on the wound. If wound is at an extremity keep it elevated at all times.

RECOMMENDED EQUIPMENT

HAEMOSTAT

This instrument, like a pair of lockable pliers, can be clamped on a blood vessel, stopping the flow and making it easier to tie off. Haemostats have many applications and are worth including in a medical kit. They are ideal for holding needles while sewing — even tough leather can be stitched. AVOID clipping nerves.

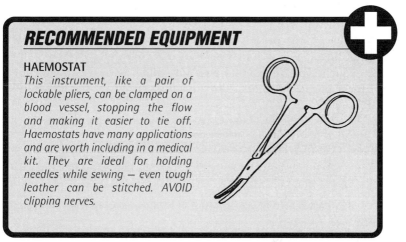

LESSER BLEEDING

Venous bleeding

Bleeding from a vein is not so dramatic as arterial bleeding. The darker venous blood flows more slowly. There is time to select the best available dressing. If blood welling up from a deep wound makes the exact point of haemorrhage difficult to locate, use a large pad and apply pressure over as wide an area as possible. After 10 minutes you will probably be able to secure this pad in place — you can use a tie or strips torn from clothing, the broader the better so that they do not cut into the casualty's flesh.

Capillary bleeding

Capillaries are tiny blood vessels that will stop bleeding by themselves. Do not waste time on capillary bleeding, it is never serious. Deal with essential things first and dress later.

INTERNAL BLEEDING

This serious condition is common after a violent blow to the body, broken bones, bullet or deep penetration wounds. At first there may be little evidence of internal injury, perhaps only slight bruising under the skin. The patient will feel light-headed, restless and faint, and look pale with the skin cold and clammy to touch and the pulse weak but very fast.

Bleeding into the tissues occurs with all fractures and bruises and a fractured thigh may result in the loss of one or more pints of blood at the fracture site.

Symptoms

Subsequent signs of internal bleeding, which also give an indication of the source of haemorrhaging, include:

- From kidneys or bladder: red or wine colouring to urine

- From lower bowel: blood passed with faeces

- From upper bowel: partly digested blood gives black tarry appearance to faeces

- From stomach: blood vomited. If bright red from fresh bleeding.

  If like brown coffee grounds, has been in stomach some time

- From lungs: coughed up blood, frequently as red froth.

Treatment

Lie the patient flat with the legs elevated, making it easier for the heart to pump blood to the head. Keep patient moderately warm but do not overheat — this would result in blood being diverted to the skin. Serious internal bleeding may occur if an organ such as a kidney, liver or spleen has been damaged. The only treatment is nursing care. Hope for early evacuation.

NOSE BLEED

Treat by sitting patient up with head slightly forward and pinch the soft part of the nostrils for five minutes. Encourage patient to breathe through the mouth. They must not sniff. Loosen any tight clothing.

WOUNDS AND DRESSINGS

Open wounds are always a hazard because of the risk of infection by bacteria. Most important of these is the *Tetanus bacillus*, which causes lockjaw. Tetanus immunization is a wise precaution for everyone, and essential for outdoor adventurers and travellers.

Wounds caused by glass, metal or burns are usually clean wounds. All foreign bodies must be extracted. This is usually left for trained medics — but should be done in a survival situation. Sterile haemostats or tweezers are the best tools for the job. A wound that has been in contact with the ground or dirty clothing MUST be cleaned and ALL dead flesh removed.

Cut away the clothing from the wound site, clean the vicinity and irrigate the wounds to wash out all the dirt. Clean a wound from the centre outwards, do NOT swab from outside in. Dry and apply a clean dressing. Immobilize the wound in a position that is comfortable.

Dressings should be changed if they become wet, omit an offensive smell, or if pain in the wound increases and throbs, indicating infection.

Local infection can be treated by soaking in hot salty water, or applying poultices. Poultices will draw out the pus which accompanies infection and help to reduce swelling. Anything that can be mashed can be used for a poultice: rice, potatoes, roots, shredded tree bark and seeds are all suitable. Clay can also be used. Boil them up and wrap in a cloth. Apply to the infected area as hot as can be tolerated — do not risk scalding. The human body has a tremendous capacity for resisting infection if given proper rest and nutrition.

Applied heat also aids healing. A warm rock wrapped in cloth can be used to provide it.

SOAP IS ANTISEPTIC

Soap is an excellent antiseptic and good for washing wounds. Use boiled water to wash your hands before cleaning a wound. Wash the wound in boiled water — if none is available use urine. Urine is a sterile fluid and will not introduce infection. It also has the slight beneficial effect from the uric acid which helps to clean the wound.

Stitching wounds

Minor wounds can be closed by suturing, if there are no medics available to do it. (Haemostats are again useful for this.) It is recommended where a clean cut caused by a knife needs closing and for facial injuries which interfere with eating or breathing.

First clean the wound thoroughly, then stitch across it, or use butterfly sutures (from your survival kit) which can be applied without any special skills. Some tribal peoples use the Fire ant to do the job, making it bite across the wound and then snapping the head off so that its mandibles hold the wound together.

STITCHES

With a sterilized needle and thread or gut, make each stitch individually, beginning across the mid-point of the wound.

Draw the edges together and tie off thread, then proceed working outwards.

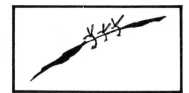

ADHESIVE SUTURES

Use butterfly sutures or cut adhesive plasters in butterfly shape. Draw edges of wound together. Apply plaster to one side of wound, close up as much as possible and press down other side of plaster.

If the wound becomes infected — red, swollen, tense — remove some or all the stitches to let pus out. Leave to drain.

Open treatment

'Open treatment' — covering with a dressing but not suturing — is the only safe way to manage survival wounds, apart from those mentioned. If unable to thoroughly clean a wound it must be left open to heal from the inside. It will form infection resistant tissue, recognized by its moist red granular appearance — a healthy sign in any wound.

Despite precautions there will always be some degree of infection. Deep wounds may have to be drained and occasionally it may be beneficial to open an abcess (an accumulation of pus) and insert sterilizd loose packing in the form of bandage or a ribbon of cloth. Leave a tail hanging out, preferably with a safety-pin in the end. Allow wound to drain for a few days. If lancing or reopening a wound, sterilize the blade of the scalpel or knife to prevent the introduction of new bacteria. Packing keeps wounds covered, but allows them to drain as they heal from inside. Reduce packing as healing progresses, until able to remove it all and cover with a dressing.

Chest wound: One of the greatest dangers with a chest wound is, if the chest cavity is penetrated, air is sucked into the wound as the patient breathes. This can cause collapse of the lungs. Place palm of hand over such sucking wounds to prevent air entering. Lay casualty, head and shoulders supported inclining to injured side. Plug with large loose, preferably wet dressing, or cover with plastic film or aluminium foil (preferably coated with petroleum jelly), and bandage firmly.

Abdominal wounds: These are serious because of the danger of damage to the internal organs and of internal bleeding. No solids or liquid must be given. Thirst can be relieved by using a damp cloth to moisten the lips and tongue of the patient. If the gut is extruded it must be covered and kept damp. Do not attempt to push it back into place. (That would make difficulties for surgeon after rescue.) If no organs extrude dress and bandage firmly.

Head injuries: Head injuries pose problems of possible brain damage and wounds may interfere with breathing and eating. Ensure that the airway is maintained and that the tongue has not fallen to the back of the throat. Remove any false or detached teeth. Control bleeding. The conscious casualty can sit up, but the unconscious patient must be placed in the recovery position, provided that no neck or spinal injuries are present. (See *Fracture of the skull*).

Amputation: If a person is trapped by a limb in a burning wreck, or similar situation, drastic action may be required to extricate them. You may have to trade a limb for a life, if otherwise they would be burned to death, for example.

Time is critical if you are working under pressure with increasing risk to yourself and the patient, from fire or other danger. But you must still take as much care as possible.

If a limb is trapped, cut as close to the wound site as possible — which will probably mean cutting through bone. A saw of some sort is required. The flexible saw in your survival kit was originally a surgeon's tool and will do the job. If no saw is available, or amputation is because of gangrene, sever at the nearest joint.

First apply a tourniquet and be ready to tie off arteries as they are exposed, or use haemostats if available.

Make an incision in the skin and into the underlying tissue. Allow the skin to retract, then sever the muscles. They will retract too, leaving the bone or joint exposed. Saw through the bone or cut through the joint. Tie off arteries, if not already done, but leave the stump open to allow for drainage. Apply a light bandage to protect the stump.

Traumatic amputation
If a limb is torn off as a result of accident there is very little bleeding. The damaged muscle in the wall of the artery goes into spasm and shuts off the artery. You will be able to examine the wound and tie off all the arteries exposed.

USE OF ANTISEPTICS

If antiseptic is available use it for cuts and abrasions. Do NOT use antiseptics on deep wounds. They cause further tissue drainage. Clean the local area with antiseptic, but wash the wound with boiled water.

BURNS

Burns, which are a common injury in aircraft accidents, cause severe pain and fluid loss. Victims are VERY susceptible to shock and infection.

The skin area of the body affected can be used to assess the possibilities. Burns extending over 50% or more of the body are usually fatal, if extensive medical facilities are not available. As a rough guide to area affected:

Head = 9%
Arms = 9% each
Front of torso = 18%
Back of torso = 18%

Genital area = 1%
Front of legs = 9% each
Back of legs = 9% each

Extinguish burning clothing

It is vital to extinguish burning clothing without fanning the flames. Most people will instinctively run away from the danger but, as they do so, the draught will encourage the flames to increase.

Get the victim down on the ground and roll over, if possible covering him or her with a blanket, poncho or sleeping bag. If necessary roll on the victim yourself to extinguish the flames (this is when you find out who your real mates are!).

Remove the victim's smouldering clothing and any constricting garments, jewellery etc which may become tighter if swelling occurs. It is important to remove smouldering clothes at once, for they retain heat and can be hotter than the flames themselves.

Reduce the temperature

Drench the burned tissues with water to cool them. Ideally submerge under slowly-running cold water for at least 10 minutes.

Do NOT even think of using anything to soothe the burns. Neither antiseptic, butter, grease, lard, calamine lotion, Vaseline nor anything like them should be applied. Resist the impulse! Cooling should continue until it produces no further relief and withdrawal from water does not lead to increase in pain.

After the initial cooling leave burns alone except for applying dressings, as dry and sterile as possible, to resist infection. Put dressings between burned fingers or toes before bandaging to prevent them sticking to each other.

Later, hardwood barks such as oak or beech, which contain tannin can be boiled up in water. When cool it can be applied to the damaged areas to soothe burnt flesh.

Give fluids

Fluids must be given to replace those lost. Give small cold drinks frequently. If possible add a half teaspoonful of salt — or even better a pinch of bicarbonate of soda — to a pint of water. If you have no salt, give the patient small amounts of boiled animal blood to drink.

Types of burns

Deep burns are charred or white in appearance, possibly with bone and muscle visible. By a merciful act of nature these burns are painless as the nerve endings have been destroyed. Superficial burns are very painful and, if covering a large area,

417

fluid loss can create even greater shock than for deep burns. The skin will blister but these blisters should NEVER be deliberately burst. If there are burns about the face and neck ensure airway is clear.

Scalds:

Are wet burns caused by hot liquids, whether water, steam, oil or even a poultice, treat as for dry burns.

Mouth and throat burns:

Possible from inhaling flame or hot gases, accidentally drinking from a very hot vessel — or swallowing very hot liquids or corrosive chemicals. Give sips of cold water to cool. Swelling in the throat may affect breathing and artificial respiration may be required.

Eye burns:

Spitting fat or corrosive chemicals may burn the eyeball. Hold the lids open and pour plenty of water over it to wash out chemicals. Tilt head so that chemical is not washed into mouth or nose or into other eye if only one is affected.

Chemical burns:

Use copious amounts of water to dilute and wash off chemicals. Remove clothing that may retain corrosive substances. Do not attempt neutralizing acid with alkali or vice-versa, chemical interaction will produce more heat. Continue to treat as for heat burn.

Electrical and lightning burns:

Check respiration. Treat as for heat burns. Take no risks if current still live.

BURNS AND SHOCK

All except small or superficial burns and electric burns are likely to result in shock, the degree dependent upon the amount of plasma fluid lost. Flooding with cold water in the case of extensive burns could increase shock, but that must be weighed against dramatically reducing tissue damage. Keep up cooling for at least 10 minutes.

FRACTURES

Accidents may produce sprains and bruises, broken arms and legs and compression fractures of the back. Broken bones should be examined early, before swelling complicates location. Always look before touching and moving an injured person. However, treat asphyxia and bleeding first and do not seek to set a fracture in an urgent emergency when there are others with more pressing injuries to treat. Immobilize before moving, if possible, and finish treatment later.

There are two types of fracture: open and closed. In an open fracture the bone may push through the skin or there may be a wound leading down to the fracture. In these fractures infection can gain direct access to the bone and they must be treated very seriously. If the limb is grossly distorted by the fracture it must be straightened before splinting. It will be painful. If the patient is unconscious do it straight away.

Fractures which neither penetrate the skin nor are exposed to the air are known as closed fractures.

Symptoms

- Pain, usually severe, aggravated by attempted movement of injured part.
- Tenderness, even with only gentle pressure.
- Swelling (caused by loss of blood into the tissues), later showing discoloration or bruising.
- Deformity: apparent shortening of a limb, irregularity either visible or to touch, unnatural movement, limp and wobbly limbs — compare a suspect area with the unharmed opposite side.
- A grating sound when limbs are moved (do NOT move limbs deliberately to check for this).

Compare injured limb with opposite sound limb.

Reduction

If medical help is expected, immobilize closed fractures and leave them for professional treatment, but — if none can be expected — 'reduce' them as soon as possible after injury, before a painful muscle spasm sets in.

Apply traction (a slow, strong pull — not a tug) until the overriding edges of fractured bone are brought into line. Check alignment with the other limb. Then splint and immobilize, keeping up the traction to ensure it does not slip back. A splint will now be needed and can be made from all sorts of material — ski sticks, branches, ships spars, parts of wreckage, driftwood, rolls of newspaper etc.

NOTE: Separate all hard splint material from the skin with padding — moss is useful for this — or pressure sores may develop.

IMMOBILIZATION

Immobilize the whole length of the limb. Use slings to support bent-arm fractures. If no splint is available, or to increase immobilization, strap injured limb to uninjured limb or to body. Insert padding in any natural hollows to keep limbs in position. Secure firmly above and below fracture and below nearest joints. Tie with any soft materials available. Place all knots on same side, giving easy access, and use reef knots or reef bows.
CHECK CIRCULATION PERIODICALLY.

Sling materials
Triangular bandages are excellent for making slings (See 11 Bandaging) — but slings can also be improvised from pieces of clothing, belts etc. as shown in these illustrations. Do NOT tie splints directly over injury or allow knots to press against the limb.
CHECK CIRCULATION.

- FRACTURE OF ARM BELOW ELBOW
- FRACTURE OF HAND OR FINGERS
Place sling (in this case a long-sleeved sweatshirt) between arm and body. Immobilize from elbow to mid-fingers with a padded splint. Take one arm of shirt behind head and tie to other on opposite side to injury. Knot below elbow to stop slipping.

    Arm is elevated to prevent severe swelling.

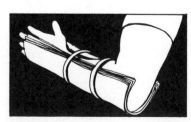

FRACTURE AT ELBOW

 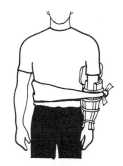

If elbow is bent: *support in narrow sling. Bind across upper arm and chest to prevent movement. Check the pulse to ensure that an artery has not been trapped. If no pulse try straightening the arm a little to see if it will return. If there is no pulse medical aid is urgently needed.*

If elbow is straight: *do not bend it. Place pad in armpit and strap arm to body or place padded splints either side of arm.*

FRACTURE OF UPPER ARM

Place pad in armpit. Splint from shoulder to elbow on outside of arm.
   Narrow sling at wrist. Bind arm and chest.

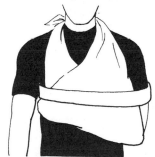

– FRACTURE OF SHOULDERBLADE
– FRACTURE OF COLLARBONE

Make sling to take weight off the injured part.
   Immobilize with bandage across arm and body.

WARNING

CHECK periodically that circulation is not impeded. Blue or ashen fingers and toes are the obvious danger warnings that straps and dressings are too tight.

For any fracture of the thigh or lower leg a figure-of-eight bandage should be applied, binding the feet and ankles of both legs. This controls rotation and counters shortening.

FRACTURE OF HIP OR UPPER LEG

Place splint on inside leg and another from ankle to armpit. Use a stick to push tying bands under hollows of injured leg.

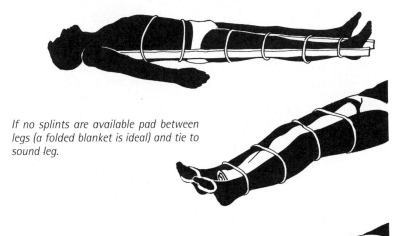

If no splints are available pad between legs (a folded blanket is ideal) and tie to sound leg.

FRACTURE TO KNEE

If leg is straight: place splint behind leg. Apply cold compress to knee (ice if possible).

If leg is bent and you cannot straighten: bring legs together, place padding between calves and thighs and strap in those places.

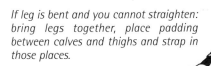

This can only be a temporary measure until proper medical help is available. If help is out of the question, the leg must be made as straight as possible.

FRACTURE TO LOWER LEG

Splint from above knee to beyond heel, or pad between legs and tie together (see Fracture of hip).

FRACTURE OF ANKLE OR FOOT

Not usual to splint. Elevate foot to reduce swelling. Immobilize with pillow or blanket folded around ankle and under foot, strapped twice at ankle and once under foot. Alternatively: if no wound, leave shoe or boot to provide stability. Do NOT allow casualty to put weight on foot.

FRACTURE OF PELVIS

Symptoms include pain in the groin or lower abdomen. Pad between thighs. Tie at knees and ankles. Place pillow support beneath bent legs and strap to flat support (door, tabletop, stretcher) at shoulder, waist and ankle.

OR

Place padding between legs. Bandage around feet, ankles, knees and with two overlapping bandages over pelvis.

Fracture of the skull

Blood or straw-coloured fluid seeping from the ear or nose may indicate a fractured skull. Place the casualty in the recovery position, with the leaking side down. Allow the fluid to escape — bandaging or plugging could cause a build-up in the skull and pressure on the brain.

Keep a careful check on the casualty's breathing. Completely immobilize and keep comfortable.

Fracture of the spine

Must always be suspected when a casualty complains of pain in the back or neck, with possible loss of sensation in the lower limbs. Test for 'feeling' by gently touching the limb. Ask casualty to move fingers and toes. Warn the patient to lie still. If medical assistance is expected and the area is safe, immobilize by placing soft but solid objects such as luggage or padded rocks to prevent movement of head or body.

Fracture of the neck

If a neck fracture is suspected, it is ESSENTIAL to immobilize it with a cervical collar, or to place a bag of earth or something similar against either side of the neck to prevent movement.

CERVICAL COLLAR
Make from rolled up newspaper, folded towel, car mat etc. Fold to about 10–14cm (4–5¹/₂in) wide — distance from top of breastbone to jaw. Fold in edges to make narrower at back than front. Overlap around neck. Secure in place with a belt or tie.

Whilst the patient's shoulders and pelvis are firmly held, place pads of some material between the thighs, knees and ankles. Tie the ankles and feet together with a figure-of-eight bandage. Apply broad bandages around the knees and thighs. Keep completely immobilized and hope for early rescue.

SPRAINS/DISLOCATIONS

Sprains

A sprain occurs at a joint and is caused by the wrenching or tearing of tissues connected with the joint. The symptoms are pain, swelling and the later appearance of bruises. If in doubt whether a sprain or a break, treat as a fracture.

Sprains are best exercised through a full range of movements, but NOT put under very painful stress, which could cause permanent damage. Bathe sprains with cold water to reduce swelling. Support with a bandage — crepe if possible (it should not constrict). Elevate the affected limb and rest completely.

If you sprain an ankle and have to keep on walking keep your boot on. If you take it off, the swelling will stop you putting it back on. Left on, the boot acts like a splint.

Dislocations

Dislocations are usually caused by a fall, blow or sudden force applied to a joint which pulls it apart. There is pain and obvious deformity, often with one end of the bone clearly felt under the skin. There is no grating sound, for the bone ends are not usually damaged. Muscle spasms 'fix' the bone in position, making it very painful to replace. Shoulders are especially prone to dislocation.

Dislocated shoulder: Take off your shoe and put foot in patient's armpit. Pull on arm.

An alternative, but more risky method, flexes the elbow at a right-angle and uses it as a lever.

Support arm with a sling and immobilize with a bandage across chest and rest completely.

Dislocated finger: Replace by pulling on finger, then gently releasing it so that the bone slips back into place. It helps if someone else can hold the patient's wrist.

Try this only gently with the thumb. If it does not work first time on the thumb, leave well alone or you will do more damage.

Dislocated jaw: Usually caused by a blow — though sometimes by yawning!

Place pad of cloth over lower teeth on each side. With patient's head resting on a firm support, press downwards on these pads with your thumbs, simultaneously rotating the dislocated side of the jaw backwards and upwards with your fingers. It should snap into place.

Bandage around the head and under jaw and leave supported for two weeks. Feed soft foods.

SHOCK

Shock can kill. Its prevention and treatment must be a major object of first aid.
The signs of all types of shock are:

- State of collapse

- Extreme pallor

- Cold sweaty skin

- Feeble but rapid pulse

- Excitement and apprehension

Nervous system: This initial shock produces an acute slowing of the heart with dropping blood pressure. In severe injuries, it can stop the heart. Pain and excessive nerve stimulation are the main causes.

Shock from blood loss: Delayed shock may occur a few minutes to many hours after an injury. It is brought on by blood loss, burns, abdominal injuries and continuing considerable loss of fluid due to vomiting or diarrhoea. Blood poisoning from injuries and infection produces another kind of shock.

Treatment

Lay the survivor flat and elevate the legs. Loosen tight or restrictive clothing around the neck, chest or abdomen. Rest and reassure.

Do NOT give liquids. Maintain body heat but do not add heat — warming the surface of the body will draw blood away from the internal organs which need it most.

Your attitude and actions are very important in treating shock. If you appear calm and in charge of the situation the patient will feel cared for and respond. Stay with them if you can, do not leave a shock victim on their own. Holding a hand is calming and reassuring and a moist cloth wiped occasionally across the forehead often helps.

Stand by to give mouth-to-mouth resuscitation and cardiac compression, if the patient's breathing or heart stops. Treat all injuries and relieve pain with drugs if available. Shock can take a long time to pass, do NOT move unnecessarily and encourage rest.

BANDAGING

Triangular bandage

A triangular bandage, with its short sides not less than 1m (1yd), is a versatile dressing. Use for slings, or folded to make a wide range of bandages and supports.

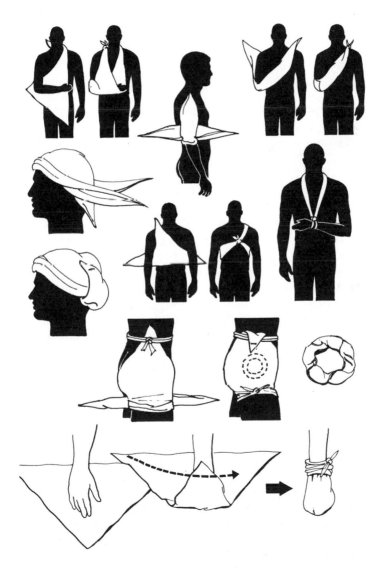

427

Roll and improvised bandages

Roll bandages are usually of open weave gauze but those of crepe material (which stretch) are easier to apply, less likely to come loose and apply pressure more evenly. Adhesive tapes can be useful for fixing dressings to areas that are difficult to bandage. Some people are allergic to them – in which case use the tape to fix bandage to bandage.

All kinds of material, especially clothing, can be used to improvise bandages and supports, but they should never exert more pressure than is required, nor cut into the flesh.

Dressings

Dressings usually consist of a pad of cotton wool covered with gauze and attached to a bandage or an adhesive strip, in a sterile wrapping. Apply without touching the dressing pad. Improvise dressings from the cleanest material available. Do not use cotton wool directly on an open wound. It will adhere to the surface. Change dressings when they become wet, smell or throbbing of the wound indicates infection.

Simple bandaging

Bandages should be applied firmly enough to stop slipping, but NOT so tight as to interfere with circulation or cause pain. Even with improvised bandages you will find application easiest if you roll the bandage to begin with. Unrolling the bandage as you apply it will help to keep the bandage smooth and evenly applied.

Always begin bandaging with a firm oblique turn to anchor it. Each turn should overlap the previous one by two-thirds, with the edges lying parallel. Tuck in the ends of bandages below the last layer and secure with a safety pin or adhesive tape, or split the end, take ends in opposite directions and tie in a reef knot away from the wound.

- **Hand:** Begin at wrist. Carry bandage over back of hand, around fingers (just below finger nails), across the palm and around the wrist. Repeat until the hand is covered and the bandage secure.

- **Foot:** Begin at ankle to prevent slipping. Follow technique for hand bandaging.

- **Forearm or foreleg:** Begin at the lowest point. Work upwards.

- **Elbow or knee:** Begin with a turn around the joint then alternately above and below it.

- **Upper arm or leg:** Apply as a figure-of-eight spiral. If bandaging begins over knee or elbow simply carry on upwards in this manner.

REMEMBER:

- Do not join bandages with knots. If you need to use separate strips, bind new one over that already applied to hold it in position.

- Always tie a finishing knot or bow over the uninjured side or uninjured limb, or the casualty will be uncomfortable.

- Use reef knots or bows which are easy to untie. Try to keep knots or fastenings on the outside so that they are easily accessible to remove or change dressings.

- Check regularly that bandages are not too tight. Look for any sign of blueness at extremities that would indicate restricted circulation.

- Pass bandages under a casualty making use of the natural hollows of the body: neck, waist, crotch, knees.

MINOR AILMENTS

In a survival situation even the most minor ailment should NOT be ignored. Small problems become larger if they are untreated. Anything which puts strain upon the body will make you less able to deal with other problems and stresses.

Do NOT be tempted to deal with corns and callouses by cutting them out. You risk opening up a channel for infection which could be worse than the corn.

Blisters

Usually a problem on the feet, though hands not used to survival tasks and tools may blister too. Reduce the risk by wearing gloves or wrappings on the hands. Choose tool handles carefully and shoes that fit perfectly! Badly fitting boots can skin you. Break them in by soaking in water and rubbing in oils to make them supple.

One of the main causes of foot blisters is socks falling down and rucking. This is frequently a problem after wading through water.

Pull them up and, if necessary, tie them to the top of your boots. It is preferable to wear two pairs of socks — an inner of nylon, next to the skin, and an outer pair of wool. This stops them from slipping. **Treatment:** Wash the area of the blister. Sterilize a needle. Pierce the blister near its edge. Gently press out fluid. Cover with cloth and tape or bandage into place.

Objects in the eye

First inspect the eyeball and the lower lid, pulling it downwards to see the inside surface (ask the patient to look upwards). Remove any foreign body with a moist corner of cloth.

If you can see nothing there, and the problem is under the upper lid, you may be able to brush it out by pulling the lid down over the lower lashes and letting them brush it out. If that does not work, grasp upper lashes between thumb and index finger and pull lid up. If doing this for someone else, it is best if you place a matchstick or small twig over the lid and fold the lid back over it. Get the patient to look down. Inspect both eye and underside of lid. Remove with a moist corner of cloth, a clean watercolour brush or even a feather. If doing this to yourself, look in a mirror, rather than try to work by touch.

Earache

Unless due to an infection this is usually due to the pressure of wax on the eardrum — but it can be unbearable. Warm up a few drops of any edible oil available, pour it into the ear and plug with cotton wool. The heat alone will be soothing and the oil will soften any wax.

Toothache and tooth loss

Usually caused by a cavity in a tooth or by a filling falling out, exposing a nerve, toothache is a problem you can well do without in a survival situation.

Treat it by plugging the hole to cover the nerve and the pain will subside. The resin from a pine or similar tree will help. Scar the trunk and gum will ooze out. Soak up a small amount on cotton wool and use this to plug the hole.

If a tooth is knocked out in an accident, put a cloth pad on the empty socket and apply pressure by biting down on it to stop bleeding.

Take care of your teeth. Use splintered soft woods and plants for brushing. Strip the inner core of parachute cord to use as dental floss.

PAIN-KILLERS

Morphine

Morphine is the standard accepted analgesic carried as part of the medical kit of planes and ships and by the military. A very powerful pain-killer, usually given by injection, it is excellent for treating casualties in great pain and minimizes the effect of shock, but it has several side-effects.

It depresses the breathing, indeed may stop it altogether. It causes nausea. It should NOT, therefore, be given to cases already likely to be affected in these ways.

Morphine comes in tubonic ampoules which contain 10–15mg. The needle is fixed and can be self-injected. Choose the largest muscle available for the injection. If self-administered, the upper quadrant of the thigh. If injecting a patient, the upper outer quadrant of the buttocks.

USE MORPHINE FOR:

- Fractures
- Amputations
- Serious burns
- Abdominal injury of a straightforward perforation by a sharp object

DO NOT GIVE MORPHINE TO:

- People with respiratory difficulties, such as head and chest wounds
- Snake-bite victims (snake venom affects the respiratory system)
- Children or pregnant women
- Casualties who have lost a lot of blood
- Crush type injuries with suspected internal damage

WARNING

MORPHINE CAN BE LETHAL
An overdosage of morphine will kill. Do NOT repeat for at least three hours. Once a patient has been injected record the time and dosage, preferably on the forehead of the parent, and pin the empty syrette to their collar.

Temgesic tablets

These are an alternative to morphine. They are slower to take effect but can be used when morphine cannot, when there are abdominal wounds for instance. They are placed under the tongue and should not be chewed or swallowed. Give 1 tablet for moderate pain, 2 when severe, not more than 4 times a day. Can produce drowsiness and hallucinations. Do NOT give to children or pregnant women.

Drugs for minor pain

Aspirin and Paracetamol are the best drugs for general pain relief. Aspirin will also help to control fever in 'flu-like illnesses. Do NOT give aspirin to people prone to indigestion, stomach ulcer etc — it can cause irritation to, and bleeding from, the lining of the stomach.

MOVING THE INJURED

Anyone with injuries to the spine or lower limbs should be carried on a stretcher if possible.

A stretcher can be improvised by passing two poles through pieces of sacking, heavy plastic bags or clothing — jerseys, buttoned jackets, shirts etc. Or from blankets folded around one pole, then wrapped under and over another. Or from doors and table tops. If no poles are available roll in the sides of a blanket and use the rolls to give a firm grip when carrying. Always test an improvised stretcher with a fit person before using it for the injured.

REMOVING FROM DANGER

You may have to move even a person with spinal injuries, if they are in further danger. If three or four people are available roll on to an improvised stretcher. Do not bend or twist. One person should be responsible solely for maintaining stability of the head and neck. Another holds the shoulders. If there is no stretcher or board roll onto a blanket or coat. Support the head and torso steady even if the legs drag.

If working alone do not attempt to turn casualty over. Pull by the shoulders if face down, by the ankles if face up, in the direction in which the body is lying. Do not twist. On rough ground or steps drag from behind, pull by shoulders, resting head on your forearms.

Loading a stretcher

If the patient is on a blanket, or can be rolled on to one, the edges of the blanket can be rolled to give a firmer grip. Methods of lifting without a blanket depend upon the number of helpers. When lifting with others, agree signals first for synchronizing movements.

WITH 4 PERSONS

Three lift from same side, C supports head and shoulders. D hooks fingers with adjoining hands of B and C to aid lift. A, B, C support while D places stretcher in position. D helps lower casualty.

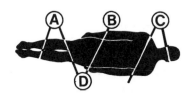

WITH 3 PERSONS

Place stretcher at patient's head. C lifts at knees. A faces B, locking fingers under shoulders and hips. Move casualty from foot of stretcher to over it.

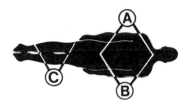

WITH 2 PERSONS

Both stand astride casualty. B links arms beneath shoulders. A lifts with one hand beneath thighs the other beneath knees. Both move forward to above stretcher. Use this technique in narrow spaces, even if more help is available.

Lifting on your own

If help is available do NOT attempt to move an injured person on your own. If there is no alternative, relate the method to the weight and condition of the casualty – and the distance to be carried. Do not choose a method you cannot sustain. Dropping the patient will not only risk worse injury but will reduce the victim's trust in you. If the victim is too heavy to lift drag them on a blanket or a coat.

Cradle: Suitable for small children or the very lightweight. Lift with one arm beneath the knees, the other around the shoulders. With some weights it will be easier to support in a sitting position.

Crutch: Place and hold casualty's arm around your neck (not an injured arm). Put your arm around casualty's waist. Give extra support by grasping clothing at hip.

Pick-a-back: Crouch while casualty puts arms around your neck. Lift legs on either side of your body. Casualty must be conscious and injuries must permit them to maintain hold onto your shoulders or around your neck.

Fireman's lift

Not a suitable method with a heavy casualty. With conscious person help them to an upright position. If on a chair allow them to fall forward over your shoulders. Otherwise, the method is as for the unconscious.

If casualty is unconscious: *Place face down. Kneel at head. Slide hands under shoulders.*

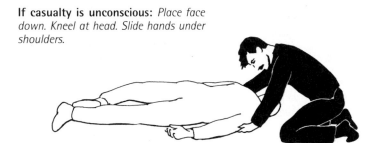

Lift casualty under armpits to kneeling position, then to upright. Raise casualty's right arm (with your left hand).

Alternatively: *With casualty on back, lift from behind. Stand astride casualty, facing head. Lift under armpits, to kneeling position. Then drag back to straighten legs. Manoeuvre forward to standing and support under armpits. Raise casualty's right arm and quickly move under it, release it and end up face-to-face, still supporting him. Raise his right arm (with your left hand).*

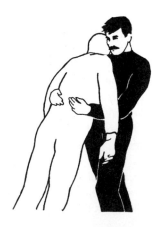

Conscious casualty: Start here

Bend to place your head under casualty's arm (at same time lifting it over your head). Bend further, placing your right shoulder level with casualty's lower abdomen.

Go down on to your right knee if you wish. Allow weight to fall across your shoulders and back. Place your right arm between or around legs.

Transfer casualty's right wrist to your right hand and lift, taking weight on your right shoulder. Press down on your left knee with your left hand to help push yourself up.

This is a relatively comfortable position in which weight is spread across your shoulders. But casualty's head is hanging down — bad for head or facial injuries.

Lifting with a sling

Another method for lifting an unconscious person, and the best one-man carry for a long distance. A sling is needed which is wide enough not to cut into the casualty, and long enough to go over your shoulders and twice across the victim's back. Two triangular bandages, a rifle sling, broad belts or luggage straps of webbing or leather could all be used. If rope is used, it must be padded to prevent it cutting or chafing.

MAKE SLING
Form sling into a continuous loop and place beneath casualty's thighs and lower back.

LIE BETWEEN CASUALTY'S LEGS
Thrust arms through loops. Tighten some of slack in sling. Grasp casualty's hand and grip trouser or leg on injured side of body. Turn away from the injured side rolling over so that casualty lies on top.

ADJUST SLING
To make body comfortable on your back.

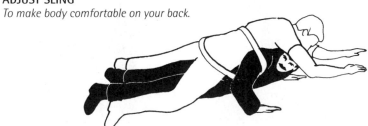

RISE TO A KNEEL

The belt will lift the casualty on your back. If the belt feels loose, or the casualty feels unsafe, return to previous position and adjust straps. Use a hand on the raised knee to help push yourself upright.

CARRYING THE CASUALTY

The weight is now carried over your back. You can hold the casualty's wrists to steady the weight but should be able to proceed with both hands free.

Two persons seats

If the casualty is able to use his or her arms, placed around the carrier's shoulders, two people can make a four-handed seat. Grip as shown: right hand on your left wrist, left on the other person's right.

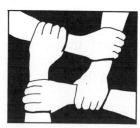

Casualties unable to use their arms can be lifted by the carriers stooping on either side and reaching across the casualty's back, gripping clothing if possible. The forward hand is slipped beneath the thighs and gripped in a padded finger hook-grip.

EMERGENCY CHILDBIRTH

The stress of an emergency sometimes precipitates labour. The signs include a low backache, regular contractions in the lower abdomen, a discharge of bloodstained mucus and sometimes the 'breaking of the waters'.

Sterilize scissors or a knife and three 20cm (9in) lengths of string. Prepare a comfortable and clean surface for the mother. Have plenty of hot water available.

Helpers should scrub their hands thoroughly and should not include anyone with any sign of a cold or infection or with sores on their hands.

First stage of labour

Uterus contracts at 10–20 minute intervals. Increase in bloodstained mucus. Cramp-like pains lasting up to a minute become increasingly more frequent. This stage may last several hours.

Second stage

Half litre (1pt) or more of water flows out in a rush – the 'breaking of the waters'. Mother should lie on her back. During contractions she should bring her knees up and grasp them with her hands, bending her head towards them and holding her breath. She should rest between contractions.

When a bulge appears delivery is near. Mother should adopt a delivery position. Either: Lying on side with knees drawn-up and buttocks near the edge of a bed, table-top etc. Or crouching (which is often a better position if the mother feels strong enough.)

Delivery

Mother should NOT hold her breath and should NOT bear down during contractions. She should take short breaths with her mouth open. By panting she makes it easier for the baby to emerge slowly and smoothly. If mother makes a bowel movement during delivery wipe clean from front to back.

- The baby's head usually emerges first, but not always.

- Tear any membrane covering the baby's face.

- If the umbilical cord is around the baby's neck — ease it over the head or loop it over the shoulder.

- Support the baby's head in the palm of your hands. As the shoulders appear support body under armpits and lift towards mother's abdomen. Be prepared for the baby to be very slippery.

- Ensuring that no tension is put on the cord, place the baby by mother's legs (or if she is lying on back, not side, between them) head lower than body.

- If baby does not appear head-first and delivery is held up for more than three minutes after shoulders emerge, pull very gently.

After delivery

Bind a cloth around baby's ankles. Hook one or two fingers under cloth to support baby, hanging head downwards, to allow fluid to drain from its mouth and nose. Hold head slightly back and mouth open. Wipe away any mucus or blood. When the baby cries lay it by its mother's breast.

If it does not cry and does not show any signs of breathing within two minutes of delivery begin very gentle mouth-to-mouth resuscitation.

Better now for mother to lie on her back, with legs apart, for delivery of placenta (afterbirth), usually about 10 minutes later. After delivery of placenta, or after cord has stopped pulsating the blood should flow out of the cord into the baby, the cord becoming white instead of blue.

Firmly tie a piece of sterile thread around it 15cm (6in) from baby's navel. Then tie with another thread at 20cm (8in). Check that the first tie is really secure or the baby may lose blood. With sterile scissors or knife sever the cord between the two ties. Place a sterile dressing over the cut end. Leave for 10 minutes then check that there has been no bleeding. Tie a further thread 10cm (4in) from the baby.

Wash the mother, give her hot drinks and encourage her to sleep.

BITES

Mammal bites
Animal bites are chiefly dangerous because of the infections that can result from bacteria in the animal's mouth. Rabies, the most serious, is almost always fatal if it has developed sufficiently to produce the symptoms of increasing irritability, dislike of light, hydrophobia (violent aversion to water) and paralysis. Under emergency survival conditions, with no vaccine, there is no hope of treating it. Great care must be taken that the victim does not transmit the disease to anyone else. Felines, canines and apes and many other animals can carry rabies, there is even a form carried by bats.

If you are bitten at any time in a survival situation, even if the bite heals and all seems well, you MUST report the bite when you are rescued. You should be examined by a doctor.

Any bite could also cause tetanus. Anti-tetanus shots are sensible for everyone and rabies vaccine for those travelling in areas where rabies may be expected.

Thoroughly cleanse all animal bites, washing for at least five minutes to remove saliva and wash out any infection. Then deal with bleeding, dress and bandage.

Snake bites
Few snake bites are fatal if anti-venom is available. The victim who is rushed to hospital within an hour or two is usually treated in time, provided the kind of snake is known so that the correct anti-venom can be prepared. Under survival conditions access to anti-venom is unlikely and the victim may not be so lucky but, fortunately, only a small proportion of snakes are venomous.

The fangs which discharge the poison of many snakes are set at the front of the upper jaw and leave distinctive puncture marks as well as the pattern of the bite (those of Coral snakes of the Americas may not be noticeable).

Non-poisonous snakes can also administer a savage bite. If you are not certain whether a snake was poisonous or not, treat as poisonous (though it may calm the patient to say that it was not a poisonous snake).

TREATMENT: The aim is to prevent poison spreading through the body. Reassure the victim. Make them relax, resting with the bitten area lower than the heart. Wash away any venom on the surface of the skin, with soap if possible. Place a restricting bandage — NOT a tourniquet — above the bite, and bandage down over the bite. For instance, if the victim has been bitten on the ankle, start bandaging at the knee. This bandage prevents the toxin from spreading rapidly and being taken up by the lymphatic system.

Place wound in cool water — a stream for instance. Use ice if available to keep as cool as possible.

The casualty will almost certainly need treatment for shock and may also require artificial respiration, keep a check on breathing.

Never cut a snake bite or try to suck out the poison.

Venomous and dangerous animals
For identification and details of SYMPTOMS (see *Dangerous Creatures* colour illustrations.)

Spider bites
Spider bites should be treated in the same way as snake bites. A cold compress (like a poultice, but cold — ice wrapped in a cloth is the ideal, if available) helps to reduce pain.

Stings
Scorpions can inject powerful venom. Bee, wasp and hornet stings can cause severe reactions in some people. Multiple stings are very dangerous — the amount of toxin and the inflammation this causes, may affect respiration.

Bee stings are left in the skin and should be carefully removed. Do not squeeze the stinger end or more venom will be injected. Stroke the sting with the side of a needle to draw it out — DON'T prod with the point.

Treatment is again like that for snake bite.

Chiggers, Ticks, Mosquitoes
Most small insect bites are a nuisance rather than a danger, but some can carry diseases. (See *Warm climate diseases* (this section) and *Tropical regions* in *Climate and Terrain*.)

GENERAL POISONING

The quickest way to remove a poison that has been swallowed is to vomit it up — but this is DANGEROUS in the case of caustic chemicals and oily substances that can produce further damage when being brought up. In cases of suspected plant poisoning always induce vomiting by putting a finger down the throat.

In ordinary domestic as well as survival conditions food and drink containers may have been wrongly used to store toxic substances (despite the fact that it is against the law in Britain). Always check they actually contain what the label says and take particular care that hungry or thirsty children do not help themselves to cream sodas that are actually the camp fuel or bleach reserves.

An effective 'universal' antidote, which will also help to absorb a poisonous liquid can be made up from tea (tannic acid) and charcoal — with an equal part of milk of magnesia if available — or just use charcoal. The aim is to absorb the poison so that it passes out of the system with the charcoal.

Contact poisons

Some plants, such as Poison Ivy, Poison Sumac and Poison Oak, can produce considerable skin irritation. Some people seem to have immunity, but it is not necessary permanent. Some people may have mild or extreme allergic reactions when touching other plants. All skin that has been in contact with the plant should be thoroughly washed with soap and water. It is most important to remove and wash all contaminated clothing since once the irritant oil is on the clothing it can spread to other parts of the body.

Alcohol can then be used to neutralize any oil left on the skin or clothing.

Severe cases may require treatment for shock.

WARNING

If handling a plant has produced a severe reaction, DO NOT PUT YOUR HAND TO YOUR FACE — ESPECIALLY THE EYES OR MOUTH — OR TOUCH THE GENITALS until it has been well washed. These sensitive parts of the body can react with swellings and rashes which can interfere with breathing or cause urinary blockage.

Chemical poisons

Chemical poisons should be sluiced off the skin with water. If skin has been damaged, treat as for burns (see also *Burns*).

> ### WARNING
>
> Sluicing with water may worsen the effects of some chemicals. You MUST know the properties of chemicals to which you are exposed, and the appropriate action to take in case of accident.

GENERAL DISORDERS

Conditions such as constipation and diarrhoea are to be expected, with the jolt to the system that the survivor may have experienced. Failure to defecate or urinate is not unusual in shipwreck situations. Coping with new and perhaps initially distasteful foods may also bring a feeling of nausea.

Small digestive upsets are relatively insignificant in survival conditions, but symptoms which suggest a more serious condition should not be ignored.

Lack of food will itself place a strain upon the body and stress may cause headaches and other disorders. Women survivors may find that menstruation ceases while under severe stress conditions.

However, if food is adequate in quantity the best treatment for digestive problems is to fast for a day and to rest, though in hot climates you should take fluids.

Fevers

Treat the symptom with rest and aspirin and look for the cause of the fever.

Pneumonia

Characterized by a rapid rise of temperature, often with chest pain, sputum mixed with blood, headache, weakness and, later, delirium. Pneumonia has many causes — most commonly a bacteria which attacks the lobes of the lungs. Without antibiotics careful nursing is all that you can do.

Encourage the patient to walk and to do deep breathing exercises. Keep the patient warm and encourage him or her to take frequent sips of hot water. Stay with the patient as much as possible and give verbal encouragement.

DISEASES

There are three main causes of infectious diseases: bacteria, viruses and rickettsiae. Then there are the problems caused by large parasites such as internal worms, scabies and the tropical larvae of the warble fly and the tiny chigoe (chigger).

Diseases caused by bacteria include dysentery, cholera, tuberculosis and diptheria. Viruses cause the common cold, influenza, measles, and poliomyelitis. Rickettsiae, germs which are neither bacteria, nor viruses, cause typhus, scrub typhus and Rocky Mountain spotted fever.

Most of the common infectious diseases which are familiar to everyone from childhood will respond to careful nursing. They are 'caught' from another person. Unless already carried by the party (or humans with whom you come into contact), neither these nor contagious and sexually transmitted diseases are likely to occur. Some human parasites, such as the itch mite which cause scabies, cannot live for very long off a human body so they too will only be a problem if you have brought them with you.

SCURVY

A deficiency disease due to lack of vitamin C, this used to be the scourge of sailors on long voyages. The survivor with access to fresh fruits and vegetables is not at risk. The desert- or sea-survivor is likely to succumb to thirst or hunger well before this problem becomes acute. Symptoms include bleeding gums, loose teeth, easy bruising and breathlessness.

Relying entirely upon hunting and fishing could make this a problem, especially in polar areas, if you have no vitamin tablets left. Always aim for a balanced diet to avoid this and other deficiency diseases.

Precautions

The diseases to which the survivor is most likely to be exposed, especially in tropical countries, are those carried in water or by insects and food animals.

Since the symptoms of tropical disease will be less familiar to most survivors, the most common will be dealt with in more detail so that they can be recognized. Where drugs are not available, treatment of disease will largely be a matter of dealing with symptoms and making the patient as comfortable as possible. Some remedies from natural sources can be prepared.

However, prevention is better than treatment. Measures to avoid diseases should include all suitable immunization before travelling (especially to the tropics) and then giving meticulous attention to the following precautionary procedures:

- Purifying drinking water

- Clean hands when preparing or eating food

- Wash and peel fruit

- Sterilize eating utensils

- Cover the body to reduce risk of insect bites

- Wash clothes and hold over smoke if louse-ridden

- Wash body (but avoid swallowing possibly contaminated water when washing or swimming)

- Bury excreta

- Protect food and drink from flies and vermin

Nursing/Isolation

When infectious disease does occur it is important to isolate it. Contact with other members of the group should be kept to a minimum. All utensils used by the patient should be boiled. Cuts and sores should be closely covered, so that they are not exposed to infection. Hands should be thoroughly washed after treating the patient.

Avoid splashing with mucus from the patient's coughing or sneezing, which may carry germs. Take special care that the patient's faeces are disposed of without risk of infection to the handler and buried where they cannot spread infection or be disturbed.

WATERBORNE DISEASES
EXCREMENTAL DISEASES

The simplest rule to prevent catching these diseases is BOIL ALL WATER – do not even clean your teeth or rinse your mouth when bathing with water that could be impure. Cover cuts and wounds and avoid unnecessary standing in water in areas where you could be at risk. Adopt rigid hygiene procedures, especially with regard to food preparation and cooking and eating utensils.

WORLDWIDE DISEASES

The following are diseases found worldwide. Some of those which occur mainly in warmer climates are dealt with later. See also warnings against animals more likely to carry parasites and food poisoning, such as salmonella, in *Food*.

LEPTOSPIROSIS – Spread by rodents and infected water this causes a serious form of jaundice. It can gain entry through a cut or sore or in contaminated drinking water.
Symptoms: Jaundiced appearance, lethargy and high temperature.
Treatment: Procane penicillin and Tetracycline in medically recommended doses.

INFECTIOUS HEPATITIS – Is passed on through the faeces and urine of infected people and consequently through water and scratches or wounds.
Symptoms: Nausea, loss of appetite and abdominal pain, the skin usually turning yellowish.
Treatment: Rest and good nursing are the only treatment.

POLIOMYELITIS – Is also usually spread through virus contaminated drinking water. It produces paralysis. There is a vaccine available.
Treatment: Hot packs on the muscles coupled with good nursing.

BACILLARY DYSENTERY – Spread by flies, contaminated water and contact with human faeces containing the bacillus.
Main symptoms: Passing faeces streaked with blood and mucous and sudden high temperature. Because of the high temperature and consequent sweating there is a danger of dehydration.
Treatment: Antibiotics coupled with lots of fluids and rest.

ENTERIC FEVER (TYPHOID FEVER) – Caused by a salmonella bacillus.
Symptoms: Similar to dysentery, accompanied by headaches, abdominal pains, fever, loss of appetite and pains in the limbs.
The patient may become delirious.
Treatment: Antibiotics. Innoculation with TAB vaccine gives almost complete protection.

CHOLERA – Sometimes thought of as a tropical disease it is a danger anywhere that insanitary conditions exist and was once the scourge of London. It is especially a danger in the aftermath of flooding, earthquake or eruption, when the strictest measures should be taken to maintain hygiene.

Symptoms: Include vomiting, loss of pulse at the wrist, cold clammy skin and muscle cramps.

Protection: Can be obtained by regular innoculation with cholera vaccine.

WARM CLIMATE DISEASES

In addition to the diseases already described the following are prevalent in warm and tropical climates — although they can occur elsewhere if there are carriers of the infection.

Waterborne diseases

BILHARZIA — A disease of the bowel or bladder, caused by a microscopic fluke or worm, which spends part of its life cycle in a water snail and part in the human liver. It is endemic in parts of Africa, Arabia, China, Japan and South America. It enters the body either through drinking infected water, or through broken skin.

Main symptom: An irritation of the urinary tract.

Can be treated: With the drug Niridazole in recommended doses.

HOOKWORMS — Another parasite that can enter the body in infected drinking water or penetrates bare skin, usually through the feet. The larvae travel through the bloodstream to the lungs, where they may cause pneumonia, are coughed up and swallowed to develop into worms, about 1·25cm (½in) long, in the intestine, causing anaemia and general lethargy. Common in many warm countries including the southern United States. Keep your boots on!

Can be treated: With the drugs Alcapar and Mintazol in recommended doses. A decoction of bracken is also a powerful de-wormer.

AMOEBIC DYSENTERY — Transmitted through contaminated water and uncooked food, this form of dysentery is largely found in the tropics and subtropics, though sometimes encountered in the Mediterranean.

Symptoms: It does not necessarily produce a temperature, but the victim will feel fatigued and listless. Faeces may be solid, but will smell foul and carry blood and mucus looking like red jelly.

Treatment: Administer fluids, maximum rest and correct dosage of Flagyl.

Insectborne diseases

Dengue, malaria and yellow fever are all transmitted by mosquito bite. A course of tablets, begun before exposure, can protect you from malaria.

There is no defence against the others, except keeping the skin covered by wearing long sleeves and trousers, especially at night, sleeping under a mosquito net if possible and using insect repellents.

Remember: Do NOT increase risk by camping near stagnant water and swamps.

MALARIA – Not restricted to the tropics, although probably the first disease the tropics call to mind. It could occur anywhere the anopheles mosquito is found, and was once prevalent in swampy areas of southern Italy and other parts of Europe. Transmitted through the saliva of the female mosquito.

It produces: recurrent fever. Although sweating, the patient feels intensely chilled and shivers violently. There are four kinds of infection. One produces almost continuous fever, accompanied by delirium or coma. Two kinds produce fever every 48 hours and the fourth kind, fever every 72 hours.

Quinine is the traditional treatment but paludrine, chloroquine, darapryn and other anti-malarial drugs are now available. Protection can be obtained by starting a course of tablets before visiting an infected area. This is so the body can get used to the tablet and if any of the symptoms are unbearable an alternative found.

Taking 2 Paludrine daily and 1 Nivaqin tablet weekly is still recommended and now comes as a pack. But take advice from your doctor on their effectiveness. They must be continued even after returning from abroad. Follow pharmacist's instructions carefully.

However, in certain areas of the world, conventional anti-malarial drugs like Paludrine are now ineffective. Different species of mosquito have become immune. Areas in particular include Africa and the Far East. Check your travel agent for up-to-date information.

Larium is now the drug to take for complete cover, but has some nasty side effects. These include nausea, vomiting, diarrhoea, abdominal pain, dizziness, loss of balance, anxiety, hallucinations and sleep disorders. The dose is 1 tablet per week and should be started 2–3 weeks before the trip.

There is another way to use Larium, which a lot of overseas workers practice. They don't take anything so the signs and symptoms of malaria are not masked in any way. At the first sign of malaria they begin immediately on a course of Larium which is a cure. It should be taken 4 weeks after return from abroad.

A new drug is coming out called Malarone, which is 100% effective with less side effects.

DENGUE (BREAKBONE FEVER) – Dengue fever lasts for about a week, with headaches, pains in the joints and a rash. Unlike malaria, one attack by this virus usually confers immunity. The type of mosquito that carries dengue is just as likely to bite in day and night. There is no drug to treat dengue.

YELLOW FEVER (BLACK VOMIT) – Prevalent in Africa and South America, Yellow fever first produces headaches, limb pains and fever. The mouth feels swollen, vomiting may produce blood and the eyes are bloodshot. After three or four days the fever is reduced but there is constipation, pain in the kidneys and urination becomes less and less. There is increased vomiting and the skin takes on a yellowish tone before recovery.
Treatment: Rest and nursing.

SANDFLY FEVER – A disease mainly of the grasslands of the sub-tropics and the Mediterranean. A small fly bite, usually on ankles, wrist or neck, produces an itching which is aggravated by scratching and can lead to sores which are an entry for further infections. Headache, bloodshot eyes and 'flu-like symptoms may also occur. The fever usually lasts about three days before subsiding.
Treatment: Rest and liquids.

SCRUB TYPHUS (TSUTSUGAMUSHI DISEASE) – Also known as mite fever, and occurring widely through eastern Asia and Australasia, this is carried by mites whose larvae live on rodents. The mites transmit the disease by biting, often in the groin or on the neck. The bite usually goes unnoticed, but a sore will develop in a few days in the bite area. Severe headache, shivering and fever develop within 10 days.

The disease is similar to other forms of typhus, with a rash appearing after about a week, and is treated in the same way. Infection is more likely in areas of thick dry vegetation. Avoid such places, sleep at least 30cm (1ft) from the ground and use insect repellent to avoid this disease.

TYPHUS – There are two forms. Epidemic typhus is carried by body lice which transmit it to humans. Endemic, or murine, typhus is transmitted by the rat flea. Both are diseases associated with dirty, overcrowded conditions and more likely to be diseases of disaster aftermath than survival in remote places.

Symptoms: Both forms produce headache, nausea and, after about four days a rash which spreads from the armpits to the chest, abdomen and thighs. Victims may recover after about 12 days, or fall into delirium, coma or death.

Treatment: Antibiotics. There is also a vaccine available.

ROCKY MOUNTAIN SPOTTED FEVER – Also known in Brazil as São Paulo fever, this is another type of typhus, spread by ticks. As the name suggests, it is also found in the western United States.

Symptoms and Treatment: As for typhus, but the rash tends to be most severe on wrists and ankles.

Small parasites which burrow beneath the skin, such as the tear-shaped, bristly larvae of the warblefly, or the tiny chigoe, which makes red pinpricks where it lodges on the skin, should be removed before they can open up a route for further infection.

WARM CLIMATE AILMENTS

PRICKLY HEAT

Miliaria, or prickly heat, can occur whenever people are exposed to very hot conditions without acclimatization. Heavy sweating, coupled with rubbing by clothing, can produce blockages in the sweat glands and an uncomfortable skin irritation. Heavy exertion may precipitate miliaria, which is aggravated by sunburn and eczema. Babies are very vulnerable.

Excess sweat does not clear sufficiently quickly, the glands are blocked and the cooling effect of sweating is lost. Taking more liquid, especially hot drinks may produce more sweat, and make the situation worse. Remove clothing, wash the body with cool water and put on dry clothes. Small amounts of tiger balm applied to the upper lip may distract from the itching and antihistamine relieves the discomfort.

HEAT CRAMPS – These are usually the first warning of heat exhaustion and occur in the muscles which are doing most work: arms, legs and abdomen. Usually due to lack of body salt (produced by excessive sweating – especially if no salt has been taken).
Symptoms: Shallow breathing, vomiting, dizziness.
Treatment: Move to shade. Rest. Drink water with a little salt dissolved in it – only a pinch to a half-litre or pint.

HEAT EXHAUSTION – Exposure to high temperature and humidity, with loss of body fluids through excessive sweating, produces heat exhaustion. It can occur without direct exposure to the sun – lying on hot ground with poor ventilation for instance.
Symptoms: Face pale, skin cold yet sweating, pulse weak. Accompanied by dizziness, weakness and perhaps cramps. Patient may become delirious or unconscious.
Treatment: As for cramps.

HEATSTROKE – The most serious result of overexposure to or overexertion in the sun.
Symptoms: Hot dry skin, face flushed and feverish – but sweating stops. Temperature rises, pulse becomes fast and strong. Severe headache, often with vomiting. Unconsciousness may follow.
Treatment: Lay in shade, head and shoulders slightly raised. Remove outer clothing. Cool body by wetting underclothing with TEPID water (cold water would push the core temperature up) and fanning. Do NOT fully immerse in water – sprinkle it over the patient. Then lay in a damp hollow with plenty of ventilation. When consciousness returns give water to drink. When temperature returns to normal, replace clothing, keep warm to prevent chill.

Immediate immersion in cold water is very dangerous but in extreme cases, where risk of death or brain damage outweighs shock from immersion, could be used AFTER initial cooling begins to take effect. Slowly lower the body into water, feet first, massaging extremities to increase blood flow and aid dispersal of heat from body's core. Remove as soon as temperature falls – be prepared to cover patient if it plummets. You may need to cool and cover several times before temperature becomes stable.

SUNBURN – Actual burn, with blistering (not just tanning) is a real danger, especially with pale and sensitive skins. If more than two-thirds of the body is affected it can prove fatal.
Treatment: Avoid further exposure – keep in the shade. Take pain killers if available. Cover all blisters with dressings but DO NOT BURST.

451

SORE EYES – Sore eyes may be due to glare – especially at sea and in desert and snow-covered locations (see *Snow-blindness* below) – or to excessive exposure to the sun or dust particles.

Treatment: Rest in shade, covering eyes after washing out foreign bodies and bathing in warm water. Use a mask and darken below eyes with charcoal to avoid recurrence.

DEHYDRATION

Dehydration becomes increasingly noticeable as more body fluid is lost. Water makes up 75% of the body weight – about 50 litres (11 gallons) for the average man. Survival is unlikely if more than one fifth of this is lost.

Fluid loss 1-5%: Thirst, vague discomfort, lack of appetite, flushed skin, impatience, sleepiness, nausea.

Fluid loss 6-10%: Dizziness, headache, laboured breathing, no salivation, indistinct speech, unable to walk.

Fluid loss 11-20%: Delirium, swollen tongue, unable to swallow, dim vision, numb and shrivelled skin.

In the latter stages: There is gross muscular weakness and mental capacity is impaired – you must make your plans at the start when you can think clearly – and then stick to them.

COLD CLIMATE HAZARDS

It is not only in the polar regions that low temperatures create health hazards. Prolonged exposure to cold is dangerous anywhere. Take precautions against all these conditions.

HYPOTHERMIA – Technical name for the condition where the body cannot generate heat as fast as it looses heat and its temperature falls below normal. It is caused by exposure to wind, rain and low temperatures and also brought on by:

- Exhaustion

- Inadequate clothing

- Inadequate shelter

- Inadequate food intake

- Lack of knowledge and preparation

The conditions which aggravate hypothermia are exactly those likely to occur in the polar regions — though it can occur under any cold conditions, especially as a result of wind chill. It is a common problem of any very cold spell, especially among the underprivileged elderly. It is a killer and must be treated as soon as it is recognized.

Prevent it by sheltering when conditions are bad and by keeping dry. Avoid over exertion and if in a group use the 'buddy system'. Watch each other carefully, so that you recognize symptoms early.

If one person goes down with hypothermia others in the group may also be near to it. Check everyone for symptoms.

Signs and symptoms: Irrational behaviour, typified by sudden bursts of energy followed by lethargy. Slowing down of responses, failing to respond to questions or instructions. Sudden uncontrolled fits of shivering. Loss of coordination, stumbling and falling. Headaches, blurred vision and abdominal pains. Collapse, stupor or unconsciousness.

Aggravating factors: Soaked clothing, with high winds. Low air temperature accompanied by high winds. Immersion in water. Any injury that immobilizes and reduces the ability to produce heat. Anxiety and mental stress. Unusual thinness.

Treatment: Prevent any further heat loss. Shelter from wind and weather. Replace wet clothing with dry. Do NOT strip off completely, remove one garment at a time and replace it with a dry one. Insulate patient from the ground and apply warmth (other bodies, hot rocks). Give warm fluids and sugary foods — but only if conscious.

In advanced hypothermia the body loses the power to rewarm itself. However, it must still be rewarmed from the inside, because fast external heating would drive cold blood into the core, further aggravating the situation. Place warmth in the following places: pit of stomach, small of back, armpits, back of neck, wrists, between thighs. These are places where the blood is near the surface and will carry the heat through the body.

Do not apply or administer alcohol. It opens blood vessels at the surface of the skin, allowing heat to be lost more rapidly.

The patient is NOT cured when his or her temperature reaches normal. Body reserves must be built up until the ability to generate heat internally returns.

A foil blanket will reflect heat and aid care in sub-zero conditions.

HEAT LOSS: GENERAL RULES

If heat is lost rapidly — rewarm rapidly
If heat is lost slowly — rewarm slowly

FROSTBITE – Frostbite occurs when the skin and flesh freeze – when reduced to a temperature of -1°C (30°F). Frostbite affects all exposed parts of the body and the regions furthest from the heart which have the least powerful circulation: hands and feet, nose, ears and face. It can be light or deep according to the degree of exposure.

The first signs are often a prickly feeling as the skin freezes. Then rather waxy-looking patches on the skin which feel numb – and later hard and pebbly with considerable pain, swelling, reddening and blistering before the deadening and dropping off that is the final stage.

Frostnip: Affects only the skin. To treat it place the affected part in a warm area. Put hands under your armpits or in your crotch. Put feet against a

> ## REMEMBER:
>
> Keep a continual lookout for signs of frostbite on yourself and your companions. Act at the first appearance of any waxy signs. Exercise the face by pulling grimaces to combat its attack.

friend's stomach (you may not stay friends for long!). Thawed out frostbite will be painful.

Deep frostbite: A much greater problem. Protect the affected area from greater injury. Do NOT rub with snow. Do NOT expose to an open fire. The best treatment is to thaw the injured area gradually with warm water at a temperature of about 28-28·5°C (108-109°F) – about the temperature which your elbow can comfortably bear. If too hot, cool down to the right temperature than apply to the affected areas.

Advanced frostbite: May cause blisters to form which can become infected and form ulcers. These tissues become grey, then black and die and will eventually fall off. Do NOT burst blisters and NEVER rub the affected part. Severe pain is an indication that the part has been warmed too quickly. Use 'animal warmth' only.

SNOW BLINDNESS – A temporary form of blindness, caused by the high intensity and concentration of the sun's rays, which are reflected from the snow-covered ground or ice (and also from ice crystals in the clouds). It occurs most frequently when the sun is high, but can also occur when there is no direct sunlight – during a bright overcast period in polar and alpine regions.

Symptoms: First the eyes become sensitive to the glare and then blinking and squinting begins. Vision takes on a pink hue, becoming redder. If not checked at this stage the eyes begin to feel as though they had sand in them.

Treatment: Get into a dark place and blindfold the eyes. Heat aggravates the pain so apply a soothing cool wet cloth to the forehead. The condition corrects itself in time. Prevent further exposure by wearing goggles and black beneath the eyes with charcoal to reduce the glare (see *Climate and Terrain*).

CARBON MONOXIDE POISONING – A risk that is a byproduct of incomplete combustion in a badly ventilated area – which may result from overzealous efforts to prevent draughts. All forms of fire and stove are a potential cause, if used in confined spaces without adequate ventilation. The carbon monoxide which builds up is colourless and odourless, so is difficult to detect. It may cause slight headache, dizziness, drowsiness, nausea or even vomiting – but these signs can go unnoticed and progress to unconsciousness without warning. Unless discovered promptly it will be fatal.

Treatment: Simple – and prevention even simpler – VENTILATE. There is no treatment if you are on your own so ensure that such conditions cannot develop. Remove the patient to fresh air and encourage him or her to breathe evenly and regularly. If unconscious, and not breathing apply artificial resuscitation. Keep patient warm and ventilate the offending shelter.

TRENCH FOOT – This occurs when feet are immersed in water for long periods, or are damp and cold for a long time. Tight-fitting boots accelerate the condition. This is a serious malady and its onset is hastened by exhaustion, coldness and lack of food, drink or sleep.

Prevent trench foot developing by keeping the feet dry. Wear boots that fit correctly, exercise the legs and toes and inspect feet regularly.

Symptoms: Feet feel as though they have pins and needles. Numbness sets in and is interspersed with sharp pains. On inspection feet appear purple with swelling and blisters.

Treatment: Dry the feet, but do not rub or damage blisters. Elevate feet and cover to keep warm – but improvise a cage to take weight of coverings. Do NOT apply artificial heat. Do NOT massage. Rest and warmth are the cure.

NATURAL MEDICINE

Natural remedies are available for many human illnesses if you know where to look. For thousands of years drugs and treatments have made use of all kinds of herbs, plants and natural substances and many of the drugs still in use today are derived from plant sources. Not all the traditional medicines are endorsed by modern doctors, some were based more on an association of the plant than with its medical properties – though strangely colour and appearance does often seem to be indicative. Plants such as scarlet pimpernel and burdock, used to clear the blood, are mainly red; those that treat jaundice, including agrimony, hawkweed and dandelion, are yellow. Sometimes a name reminds us of the old medical usage – lungwort for instance, or eyebright.

Cruel to be kind

Sick survivors need your care and attention, but they must also be kept interested and optimistic. If a man with pneumonia is left to curl up in a corner of the shelter, he will probably die. Get him on his feet and keep him occupied with minor tasks. Give him plenty of fluids and coax him to eat. Do not let him lie down. The hepatitis case must be forced to eat. You cannot allow either strength or morale to be depleted.

It is not only plants that can replace your medical supplies, or to supplement your store. Urine can be used as an antiseptic to wash out wounds. If the patient is fussy, use their own. If sick enough, they won't care whose. Maggots too, have been used to clean wounds. In tropical countries an open wound is soon infested with them – but they do keep it open and clean until better treatment can be given. Keep watch that they do not devour good tissues.

Fire has been used for centuries to clean wounds. Cauterizing with heat requires fortitude in the patient – but, if they can stand it, and you have ammunition, placing powder around a wound and lighting it can prevent gangrene. Some people believe that the best way to seal a stump after an amputation is to cauterize (as used to be done to criminals who had their hands chopped off) – but the shock of this on top of the shock of injury will kill some people.

Modern drugs

Many modern drugs such as cocaine, morphine and digitalis are derived directly from plants, but extracting them is NOT straightforward. Often poisons are involved which could be VERY

DANGEROUS if any attempt was made to use such plants in treatment. What follows is a list of plants and the medical uses to which the survivor can put them – in simple preparations. Although many modern drugs are made from tropical plants, and indigenous medicine has many plant ingredients, most of these plants are found in temperate regions for they are the ones which have been most documented and which you have a reasonable chance of recognizing.

Plant preparations

Leave all poisonous plants alone and be sure that you have properly identified the plant. As a general rule plants will be most potent when in flower. Note that different parts of a plant may have different uses.

Infusions are usually made from leaves or flowers and decoctions from roots. The methods are described below. Divide the amount made into three doses to take in one day Always prepare infusions, decoctions and poultices freshly, just before using. Never keep for more than 12 hours.

Plants vary in potency depending on season when picked. Do not think you will do more good by taking or administering larger doses – you won't and you may do harm.

Don't expect miracles overnight. Give the treatment a fair chance to work.

To make an infusion

Cut and crush the herb so that juices and oils are more readily available. You need a slack handful of herb to a half-litre (1pt) of water (30g to 50cc/1oz to 20fl.oz). Pour boiling water over it. Stir. Leave to cool. There is no need to strain – the herb will sink to the bottom.

If you cannot boil water use half the amount of cold water and stand the vessel in the sun. If there is no sun or no water try sucking or chewing the leaves, extracting as much of the juices as possible, then spit out the pulp.

To make a decoction

Usually a preparation from roots. Cut, scrape and mash root. Soak in water (handful to 85cc/1½pt) for at least half an hour. Bring to boil, simmer until liquid reduces by one-third.

To make a poultice

Mash up root, leaves or all of the herb and make into a flat pad. If too dry add water. Apply to affected part and cover with a large leaf, bind in position. Poultices can be applied to stiff joints, sprains and pus-filled sores.

Expressed juice

Reduce stem and leaves of the plant to a juicy mush by crushing with hands, rocks or sticks. Squeeze juice only into a wound and spread pulp around infected area. Keep in place with a large leaf and bind.

Splinting agents

The roots of Comfrey and, to a lesser extent, Solomon's seal, are so rich in starch that they will set hard when they have been well boiled and reduced. Allow to cool slightly and pack around an injured limb or joint. Good for holding poultices.

REMEDIES

STOPPING BLEEDING

Dove's-foot crane's-bill: Expressed juice
Giant puffball: Packed as poultice
Periwinkle: Expressed juice of leaves
Plantains: Pounded leaves as poultice
Self-heal: Expressed juice
Stork's-bill: Expressed juice of leaves
Woundwort: Expressed juice

CLEANSING RASHES/ SORES/WOUNDS

NOTE: *Use these plants externally to bathe the skin or where indicated, as a poultice. Apply two or three times a day.*

Burdock: Decoction of root; crushed raw root and salt for animal bites
Camomile: Infusion of flowers as poultice
Chickweed: Expressed juice of leaves
Cleavers: Infusion of whole plant, except roots
Comfrey: Decoction of root as poultice
Dead-nettle: Infusion of flowers and shoots
Docks: Crushed leaves

Elder: Expressed juice of leaves
Elm: Infusion of bark
Horehound: Infusion of whole plant, except roots.
Mallow: Decoction of leaves and flowers as poultice
Marsh mallow: Decoction of root infusion of leaves and flowers; as poultice
Oak: Decoction of bark
Sanicle: Infusion of whole plant, except roots
Scurvey grass: Crushed leaves
Shepherd's purse: Infusion of whole plant, except roots; as poultice
Silverweed: Infusion of whole plant, except roots
Solomon's seal: Decoction of roots; as poultice
St John's wort: Infusion of flowers and shoots
Sorrel: Crushed leaves
Tansy: Crushed leaves
Watercress: Expressed juice
Woundwort: Infusion of whole plant, except roots
Yarrow: Infusion of whole plant, except roots

ANTISEPTIC

NOTE: *These plants can be used externally or internally. They are particularly useful for wounds that become infected.*

Garlic: *Expressed juice*
Mallow: *Infusion of leaves and flowers*
Marsh mallow: *Decoction of root; infusion of flowers and leaves*
Horseradish: *Decoction of root*
Thyme: *Infusion of leaves and flowers*

ACHES/PAINS/BRUISES/STIFFNESS

NOTE: *Where indicated, use externally.*

Balm: *Infusion of leaves*
Birch: *Infusion of leaves*
Borage: *Infusion of whole plant, except roots*
Burdock: *Decoction of root*
Camomile: *Expressed juice of flowers applied to swellings*
Chickweed: *Infusion of whole plant, except roots*
Comfrey: *Decoction of root applied to swellings*
Cowberry: *Infusion of leaves and fruits*
Dock: *Crushed leaves applied to bruises*
Dove's-foot cranc's-bill: *Infusion of whole plant, except roots, applied to swellings*
Elm: *Infusion of bark*
Figwort: *Decoction of whole plant except roots; use externally to draw bruises and blood clots*
Garlic: *Expressed juice applied to swellings*
Horehound: *Expressed juice or leaves to earache*
Poplar: *Infusion of leaf buds*
Solomon's seal: *Decoction of root; use externally*
Sorrel: *Crushed leaves applied to bruises*
St John's wort: *Infusion of flowers and shoots applied to bruises*
Tansy: *Crushed leaves applied to bruises*
Willow: *Decoction of bark*

FEVERS

NOTE: *These plants will induce perspiration to break a fever.*

Camomile: *Infusion of leaves and flowers*
Elder: *Infusion of flowers and fruit*
Elm: *Decoction of bark*
Feverfew: *Infusion of whole plant, except roots*
Lime: *Infusion of flowers*

COLDS/SORE THROATS/ RESPIRATORY

Agrimony: *Infusion of whole plant, except roots*
Angelica: *Decoction of root*
Bilberry: *Infusion of leaves and fruits*
Bistort: *Infusion of whole plant, except roots*
Borage: *Infusion of whole plant, except roots*
Burdock: *Decoction of root*
Camomile: *Infusion of flower; use a gargle*
Colt's-foot: *Infusion of leaves and flowers*
Comfrey: *Infusion of whole plant*
Great mullein: *Infusion of whole plant, except roots; decoction of root as gargle*
Horehound: *Infusion of whole plant, except roots*
Horseradish: *Raw root*
Lime: *Infusion of flowers*
Lungwort: *Infusion of whole plant, except root*
Mallow: *Infusion of flowers and leaves*
Marsh mallow: *Decoction of root; infusion of leaves and flowers*
Mint: *Infusion of whole plant, except roots*
Mountain evens: *Infusion of whole plant; use as gargle*
Nettle: *Infusion of leaves*
Oak: *Decoction of bark, use as gargle*
Plantain: *Infusion of leaves and stems*
Poplars: *Infusion of leaf buds*
Roses: *Decoction of hips*

Sanicle: Infusion of whole plant, except roots
Self-heal: Infusion of whole plant, except roots; use as a gargle
St John's wort: Infusion of flowers and shoots
Thyme: Infusion of leaves and flowers
Willow: Decoction of bark
Yarrow: Infusion of whole plant, except roots; use as inhalant

SETTLING STOMACH

Balm: Infusion of leaves
Bilberry: Decoction of fruit
Bracken: Infusion of leaves
Bramble: Infusion of leaves
Dandelion: Decoction of whole plant
Horseradish: Infusion of root
Mint: Infusion of whole plant, except roots, with crushed charcoal
Solomon's seal: Decoction of root
Sanicle: Infusion of root
Yarrow: Infusion of leaves and flowers

DIARRHOEA

NOTE: Take two or three times daily until symptoms subside.

Bilberry: Decoction of fruit
Bistort: Infusion of whole plant, except roots
Bramble: Infusion of leaves or decoction of fruit
Cowberry: Decoction of fruit
Elm: Infusion of bark
Great burnet: Infusion of leaves and shoots
Hazel: Infusion of leaves
Marsh mallow: Infusion of leaves and flowers; decoction of root
Mint: Infusion of whole plant, except roots
Mountain evens: Infusion of whole plant, except roots
Oak: Decoction of bark
Plantain: Infusion of leaves and stems
Periwinkle: Infusion of leaves; NOT to be used for long periods
Silverweed: Infusion of whole plant, except roots

CONSTIPATION

Agrimony: Infusion of whole plant, except roots
Barberry: Expressed juice of fruit
Common cleavers: Infusion of whole plant, except roots
Couch grass (Elymus): Decoction of root
Dandelion: Decoction of whole plant
Elder: Expressed juice of fruit
Feverfew: Infusion of leaves and flowers
Rowan: Expressed juice of fruit
Rose: Decoction of hips
Walnut: Decoction of bark

HAEMORRHOIDS

NOTE: Apply externally, two or three times a day.

Bilberry: Expressed juice of fruit
Camomile: Infusion of leaves and flowers
Elm: Decoction of bark
Lesser celandine: Expressed juice of leaves
Oak: Decoction of bark
Plaintain: Expressed juice
Poplar: Decoction of leaf buds
Silverweed: Infusion of whole plant, except roots
Solomon's seal: Decoction of root

REMEMBER:

For Headaches: Willow leaves and bark make a decoction containing Salicin, a constituent of Aspirin.
For Healing: Express the juice from Comfrey leaves to aid tissue regrowth.

EXPELLING WORMS

Bracken: Infusion of roots
Feverfew: Decoction of leaves and flowers
Figwort: Infusion of whole plant, except roots
Tansy: Infusion of leaves and flowers; use sparingly in small amounts

Tropical Medicinal Plants

Many thousands of tropical plants are known to have medicinal properties and are used by tribal peoples. Relatively few have been studied by Western scientists or are widely known. The following are a few of the many plants which may be of use, but lacking accurate information on medicinal plants you will do better to take medicines with you. NEVER experiment with something you cannot positively identify.

Copperleaf *(Acalypha indica)* is one of several similar shrubs in India and southeast Asia, reaching 2–3m (6½–10ft), with oval to heart-shaped leaves that are often variegated in shades of red, bright pink and green. In Malaya, the leaves are dried and drunk like tea. A decoction of roots and leaves is laxative and restorative.

Alstonias, including Alstonia scholaris are found from India east to Phillipines and south to Indonesia and parts of Australia. Boil the bark in water to produce a tonic, reduce fever, relieve diabetes and kill internal parasitic worms.

Antelaea azadirachta occurs from India to China and Indonesia. A decoction of leaves and bark will help to suppress malaria and dysentery. Use oil from seeds to treat ulcers and skin complaints.

Bruceas occur in many, fairly similar forms from India east to China and south to Australia. All parts are bitter tasting. Take seeds of Brucea sumatrana for diarrhoea and dysentery. Crushed leaves relieve external bleeding and sooth boils and insect bites.

Elettaria cardamomum, is a relative of ginger, found in India and parts east, is a tall, herbaceous plant with thick, fleshy rhizomes and a long, branched head of flowers. Use seeds or expressed juice of fruit for settling the digestion and relieving nausea.

Cinchonas, China Barks or Red Barks *(Cinchona),* large trees, typically with red-brown trunks, wild in tropical South America, have been taken all over the world. Take a decoction of the quinine-containing bark to suppress malaria.

Horseradish Tree *(Moringa oleifera,* see Tropical plants *in Food)* is a fairly common edible plant of the tropics Use expressed juice from the roots and leaves to treat skin eruptions and inflammations.

Kibatalia arborea is another Asian tree whose bark, when cut, yields a latex-like sap. Use this sap, in small amounts, to treat worms.

Sida cordifolia is an erect, downy annual, up to 1m (3ft 4in) tall, with oblong toothed leaves and yellowish flowers. It occurs from India east to Taiwan. Use an infusion of the leaves for coughs and fevers. The seeds are mildly laxative.

Pergularia extensa has stems with stiff spreading hairs, broadly oval leaves up to 15cm (5in) long and small greenish-white flowers. It grows in tropical Africa. Use tender leaves and shoots as a potherb or in a strong infusion to treat tapeworm and diarrhoea. Use a poultice of leaves on boils, abscesses and wounds.

Crateava religiosa is found from India east to Papua New Guinea and Polynesia. A decoction of bark and leaves relieves upset stomachs, feverish aches and pains.

Baobabs *(Adansonia, see* Desert plants *in Food)* Scrape gum off the bark. Use to treat worms and diarrhoea.

MEDICINAL PLANTS

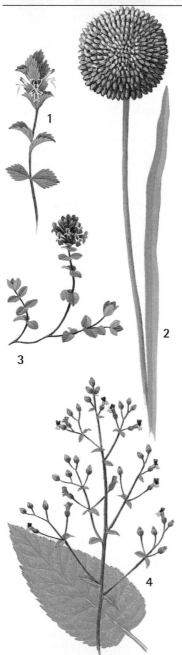

These medicinal plants are found in temperate climates. Many are very common and all are quite safe. Use them to staunch bleeding and heal wounds, for fevers, colds and digestive upsets and other treaments as described. Some have several uses, but they have been grouped here under their most common applications.

GENERAL AND ANTISEPTICS:

1 Eyebright *(Euphrasia officinalis) grows to about 30cm (1ft), with oval, often downy leaves and white flowers tinged violet or purple-veined and with a yellow spot in grassy places, often in mountains, in Eurasia. A strained infusion of the whole plant is excellent for eye infections. It is also said to ease hayfever, catarrh and nasal congestion.*

2 Garlics *(Allium) occur in many varieties in most temperate and, now, tropical parts. The smell will lead you to them; most have long, strap-like leaves arising from the bulb and a tall stem topped with a cluster of small pinkish or white flowers. The bulb is powerfully antiseptic; use as expressed juice externally diluted with water to treat wounds and swellings, and eat garlic to treat and to prevent colds. It also contains a natural antibiotic.*

3 Wild Thyme *(Thymus serpyllum) is small, aromatic, mat-forming, with small oval leaves and reddish-purple flowers; in dry grassy places in western Eurasia, but other species occur elsewhere. Use its antiseptic qualities in an infusion for coughs and colds, or as a potherb.*

4 Figwort *(Scrophularia nodosa) grows to 90cm (3ft), with square stems, pointed oval leaves and red-brown flowers; in woods, clearings and scrub in Eurasia — there are many* *different kinds. Apply as a decoction to reduce swellings, sprains, boils and bruises, to dissipate blood clots, and for treating haemorrhoids.*

BLEEDING:

5 Self-heal *(Prunella vulgaris) is a downy, creeping plant with pointed oval leaves and heads of violet flowers; in dry grassy and waste places in Eurasia. Use as expressed juice to staunch bleeding or by infusion for internal haemorrhage.*

6 Dove's-foot Crane's-bill *(Geranium molle) grows to 30cm (1ft) with a hairy stem, deeply lobed leaves and small, pinkish, five-petalled flowers; in dry grassy and waste places. Use as expressed juice to staunch bleeding or as a decoction for internal haemorrhage.*

7 Marsh Woundwort *(Stachys palustris) is strong-smelling, hairy, up to 90cm (3ft) tall, with toothed, heart-shaped leaves and spikes of dark pink to purple, white-blotched flowers; usually found in damp places; similar species by woodland edges and shady waste place. Use as expressed juice to staunch bleeding or by infusion for bathing aches, sprains and wounds.*

8 Sanicle *(Sanicula europaea) grows to 50cm (20in), with hand-shaped, deeply lobed leaves and tiny white or pinkish flowers in a compact head; widespread in woodland in Eurasia. Use as expressed juice to staunch bleeding or by infusion for internal haemorrhage.*

9 Greater Periwinkle *(Vinca major) grows to 50cm (20in), with leathery, evergreen, broadly spear-shaped leaves and large blue-violet flowers; in woody, scrubby and rocky places in Eurasia. There are many kinds of periwinkle in other parts of the world. Use expressed juice externally to staunch bleeding.*

Plantains (see *Edible plants* in *Food*) *provide juice for treating wounds and for treating chest complaints..*

INTESTINAL PROBLEMS:

1 Mountain Avens *(Dryas octopetala) resembles a creeping wild strawberry, with well-lobed leaves, paler below, and large white, yellow-stamened flowers; in mountainous rocky and northern arctic areas. Use an infusion of stems, leaves and flowers for diarrhoea or as a gargle.*

2 Balm *(Melissa officinalis) is lemon-scented and hairy, growing to about 60cm (2ft), with toothed, oval, greenish-yellow leaves and whorls of small white flowers at the leaf bases; in grassy places in the warmer part of Eurasia. Use an infusion of the whole plant for fevers and nausea. Can also be used to ease painful menstruation.*

3 Water Mint *(Mentha aquatica) is aromatic, hairy, always near fresh water, with toothed, pointed oval leaves, a purplish stem to 80cm (32in) and clusters of pinkish flowers. Use an infusion of the leaves for diarrhoea, as a digestive and heated to induce perspiration in fevers. Similar mints are also effective. If made too strong the infusion may become emetic.*

4 Elms *(Ulmus) are tall trees with large, oval, toothed leaves, green disc-shaped fruits and, often, suckers at the base of the trunk. Use a decoction of the bark for diarrhoea and skin eruptions.*

5 Feverfew *see next column.*

6 Cleavers or **Goosegrass** *(Galium aparine) is straggling, with long prickly stems, whorls of narrow prickly leaves and small white flowers; widespread on moist, woody and waste ground. Young plants can be boiled and eaten like spinach. Use an infusion to ease constipation. Give frequent doses, mixed with an equal quantity of Marsh Mallow for cystitis.*

7 Agrimony *(Agrimonia eupatoria) grows to 90cm (3ft), with a downy stem, toothed, spear-shaped leaflets, greyish below, and a tall spike of yellow* flowers; in dry grassy places — there are several different kinds. Use an infusion of the whole plant to ease constipation and acid stomach. Also use to treat cystitis, giving small doses frequently.

8 Lesser Celandine *(Ranunculus ficaria)* grows to 20cm (8in), with shiny, dark green, heart-shaped leaves and yellow flowers, in wet woodland and damp ground in Eurasia. Apply the expressed juice externally for haemorrhoids; do NOT confuse with its poisonous relatives, the buttercups.

9 Solomon's Seal *(Polygonatum)* are small, patch-forming, with arching stems bearing tube-shaped greenish-white flowers; in woody, scrubby areas. Use a decoction of the root externally for haemorrhoids and bruises, or take an infusion for nausea. The starchy root is edible like parsnips, but when boiled and dried it sets hard as makeshift plaster for a splinting agent. Either an infusion, or a poultice made from the powdered root will ease bruising. Berries are POISONOUS.

Silverweed *(see Edible roots in Food)* also provides an infusion for treating digestive disturbance and haemorrhoids.

FEVERS, COUGHS AND COLDS:

5 Feverfew *(Tanacetum parthenium)* is very aromatic, growing to 45cm (18in), with delicate yellowish leaflets and many daisy-like flowers; in waste and grassy places in Eurasia. Eating the leaves eases headaches and migraines, but in some people this can cause blistering in the mouth. It is safer to use an infusion of the whole plant for fevers, headaches and general pains, or as a tincture for insect bites. Frequent small doses of a hot infusion help regulate contractions in childbirth.

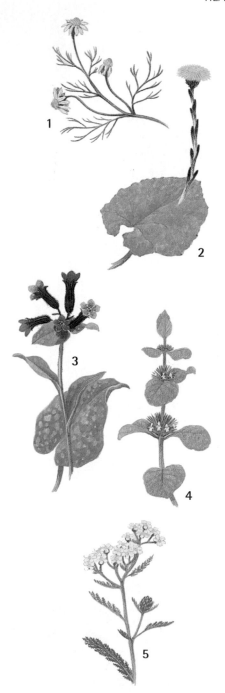

FEVERS, COUGHS AND COLDS CONTINUED:

1 Camomile *(Chamaemelum nobile) is aromatic, creeping, with finely dissected leaves and daisy-like flowers; in grassy places in Eurasia. Use an infusion of the whole plant for fevers, headaches, migraines, and colds, or the expressed juice of the flowers for aches and strains. It has a calming influence especially on nervously excited children.*

2 Colt's Foot *(Tussilago farfara) is common from late winter on bare and waste ground. Large, yellow dandelion-like flowers top asparagus-like stems; heart-shaped leaves follow the flowers. Use the leaves by infusion for colds and coughs.*

3 Lungwort *(Pulmonaria officinalis) is downy, up to 30cm (1ft), with pale-spotted spear-shaped leaves and bell-shaped pink or purplish-blue flowers; in mixed woods and scrub in Eurasia. An infusion of the whole plant is excellent for chest complaints and useful for diarrhoea. For coughs use with equal parts of Colt's Foot.*

4 Horehound *(Marrubium vulgare) is thyme-scented, downy, with squarish stems to 50cm (20in), roundish, crinkly, greenish-white leaves and whorls of whitish flowers; in dry scrubby places in Eurasia. Use an infusion of the whole plant for chills and respiratory disorders; oil expressed from the leaves soothes earache. It is a good cough treatment for children. In large doses it is laxative.*

5 Yarrow *(Achillea millefolium) is downy, aromatic, up to 60cm (2ft), with dissected, feathery, dark green leaves and heads of tiny white or pink flowers; in grassy places. Use an infusion of the whole plant, but NOT the roots, for colds and fevers. It also hastens clotting of the blood in an injury and reduces blood pressure and bleeding in haemorrhoids.*

6 Musk Mallow *(Malva moschata) grows in grassy and scrubby places to about 60cm (2ft), with a hairy stem, deeply divided leaves and large, pink, five-petalled flowers. Mallows are widespread and come in many varieties. Use this like Marsh Mallow (8).*

7 Tree Mallow *(Lavatera arborea) grows to 3m (9ft), with a hairy stem, woody at the base, ivy-shaped leaves and pink-purple flowers streaked darker purple; in rocky coastal areas from Europe to Asia Minor. Use this like Marsh Mallow (8).*

8 Marsh Mallow *(Althaea officinalis) grows to 90cm (3ft), downy grey, with large lobed leaves and pale pink flowers. The cooked root is excellent to eat. Use an infusion of the whole plant for chest complaints or one just of the root to relieve giddiness caused by loss of blood and to clean wounds and sores. A rubbing with bruised leaves soothes insect bites; boiled leaves are a good poultice for skin eruptions. An infusion of the leaves will relax and soothe irritation and inflamation of the alimentary system.*

9 Great Mullein *(Verbascum thapsus) is covered in pale woolly down, growing to 2m (6ft), with large spear-shaped leaves and a dense spike of five-petalled yellow flowers; in dry, warm grassy places. Use an infusion of flowers and leaves for coughs and chest complaints, or a decoction of the root as a gargle. Powder the flowers to make a sedative and pain-relieving tea.*

10 St John's Wort *(Hypericum perforatum) grows to 60cm (2ft), with small, oblong, translucently spotted leaves and a head of golden-yellow flowers that exude a red juice when crushed; in open woods, grassy and bushy places. Use an infusion of the whole plant for colds and chest complaints.*

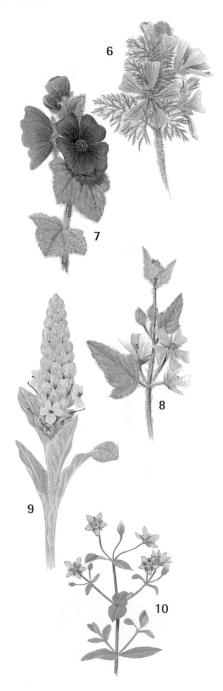

DANGEROUS CREATURES

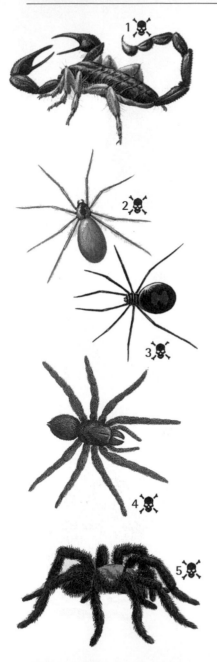

The insects and other creatures shown here are not a major problem for survivors if sensible precautions are taken — but can easily become one if not treated with respect.

1 Scorpion *are found in deserts forests and jungles of tropical, subtropical and warm temperate areas, one kind living at 3600m (1600ft) in the Andes, and are mainly nocturnal. Most desert kinds are yellowish to light green, those from moist or higher mountain areas brown or black. Average size is 2·5cm (1in) but giants in southern Africa and New Guinea reach 20cm (8in). Some burrow but they are usually found under tree bark, rocks, or other shelter, including your gear. The sting is in the tail. Many kinds cause only trivial discomfort, a few produce nerve toxins causing temporary paralysis for 24–48 hours. Some scorpions from the Middle East, Brazil and west Mexico can inflict a fatal bite, but this is very rare and death is more likely in young children and the old or ill, who offer little resistance to it.*

2 Recluse or **Fiddleback Spider** *(Loxoscees reclusa) of North America is recognised by a violin shape on the back of the head. There are several different kinds, but L. reclusa is the worst. Bite produces fever, chills, vomiting, joint pain and spotty skin, within 24–48 hours. Although rarely fatal, tissue degeneration around the wound can cause disfigurement, or even lead to amputation, if left untreated.*

3 Black Widow or **Hourglass Spiders** *(Latrodectus) occur in warmer areas, including deserts, over much of the world. Small, dark, all can be recognized by the red, yellow or white markings on the abdomen, hourglass-shaped in some. Bites produce severe pain, sweating, shivering and* *weakness, disabling the victim for up to a week. Rarely fatal.*

4 Funnelwebs *(Atrax) are large greyish or browny spiders of Australia. Chunky, with short legs, their name alludes to their web's shape. Nocturnal, and not in hot, dry, sunny conditions, but locally common. A bite can kill; symptoms as for the Black Widow.*

5 Tarantulas *(Theraphosidae and Lycosa) are very large hairy spiders of tropical America; one kind occurs in southern Europe. Of menacing appearance, but although a bite is painful the poison is fairly mild and not disabling.*

6 Centipedes and millipedes *are mostly small and harmless but some tropical and desert kinds may reach 25cm (10in). Their feet have sharp claws, which can puncture the skin and cause infections, and a few kinds have a poisonous bite. Brush off in the direction they are moving — there is less chance of them digging into you.*

7 Hornets *occur in swarms and make nests that are guarded ferociously. Some tropical kinds are very aggressive and very poisonous, and should be well avoided. The sting is like being punctured by a hot rivet and several at once could be fatal.*

8 Ticks *are large and common in the tropics; flat-bodied and round, with a small biting head that eats into a wound. Do not pull off; the head will remain and cause infection. Use heat, petrol, alcohol or hot water to make it drop off.*

9 Leeches *are blood-sucking worm-like creatures of tropical jungles and other moist areas, waiting, thread-like, on vegetation before attaching themselves to a victim. Better not to pull off: remove with fire or a pinch of salt. Leeches often carry infections.*

10 Vampire Bats *(Desmodus) occur in Central and South America. Small, nocturnal, they suck the blood of sleeping victims. Their bites may carry rabies. Keep covered at night in these areas.*

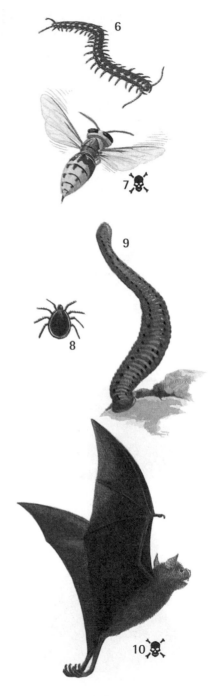

469

POISONOUS SNAKES

WARNING
Unless otherwise indicated to the contrary, these snakes should be regarded as deadly poisonous. Do NOT approach, provoke or handle.

SAFETY RULES
- **Watch where you step:** *On average snakes eat only once a week. After eating and at the times when they shed their skin they are sluggish and more easily trodden on.*
- **Look closely** *before parting bushes, picking fruit, some snakes are arboreal.*
- **Never tease, pick up or corner:** *A few snakes, such as the bushmaster of South and Central America, black mamba of Africa and king cobra of Asia will attack when cornered or guarding a nest.*
- **Use sticks, not hands** *to turn over stones and logs and for digging.*
- **Wear stout boots** – *if you have them. Teeth of many snakes are too small to penetrate them.*
- **Check bedding, clothes, packs** *before putting them on. Snakes may use them as shelter.*
- **Stay calm** *if you encounter a snake. Do not move suddenly or strike at it. Back off slowly. In most cases the snake will be only too eager to escape.*
- **To kill:** *If you have to kill a snake use a long stick, preferably with a spring to it, and a single chopping blow to the back of the head. Make it effective first time – a wounded snake is very dangerous.*

NORTH AND SOUTH AMERICA
1 **Rattlesnakes** *(Crotalus and Sistrurus). Many kinds occur in all parts of North America, varying from 45cm (18in) to over 2·1m (7ft). All have a chunky body, wide head and rattle on the end of the tail that is usually but not always sounded as a warning. The largest are the various Diamondbacks,*

with distinctive diamond-shaped blotches.

2 Copperhead (*Agkistrodon contortix*) averages 60–90cm (2–3ft), with a stout body coloured buff or orange-brown with rich brown bands and a copper-red head; mainly in the eastern United States. Fairly timid; bites are only rarely fatal.

3 Cottonmouth or **Water Moccasin** (*Agkistrodon piscivorus*) averages 60–130cm (2–4ft) with a thick brown or brownish-olive body, sometimes blotched, and a yellowish, also blotched belly; the inside of the mouth is white. Aquatic, in and by freshwater in the southern United States. Belligerent — do not annoy!

4 Tropical Rattlesnake (*Crotalus durissis*) averages 1·5–2m (5–6ft), with diamond-shaped marks, two dark stripes on the neck and a rattle on the tail; nocturnal, in drier areas from South America north to Mexico. Large, aggressive, very dangerous.

5 Fer de Lance (*Bothrops atrox*) is brownish with paler geometric markings and averages 1·3–2m (4–6ft), causes many deaths. Its many relatives vary from grey to brown or reddish with similar markings. Bothrops vipers occur in South America north to Mexico; some are arboreal. All loop their body before striking.

6 Bushmaster (*Lachesis muta*) is large-headed, pinkish-brown marked with large dark brown triangles and averages 2–2·6m (6–8ft) or more; nocturnal, in lowland forests, often using burrows and holes, in Central and South America. Vicious if cornered; the most feared of all New World snakes.

7 Coral Snakes average 45–90cm (1½–3ft), are slender and strikingly coloured in bands of black and red separated by bands of yellow or white; from the southern United States into South America. (Similar kinds occur in south-east Asia.) Small-mouthed, reluctant to bite but deadly.

There are NO rules for identifying poisonous snakes. Cobras usually show hoods and rattlesnakes rattles on their tail, but these are NOT reliable guides. Poisonous snakes must be learned individually. If in doubt, treat every snake as poisonous.

EUROPE

1 Adder *(Viper berus)* averages 30–75cm *(12–30in)*, varying from olive-grey to reddish-brown with a zigzag pattern of darker colouring; especially on heaths, moors and open areas, into mountains. The only poisonous snake of northern Europe, hardly ever fatal, but with larger and more dangerous relatives in southern Europe.

AFRICA AND ASIA

2 Puff Adder *(Bitis arietans)* is thick-bodied, short-tailed and large-headed, straw-brown with darker markings and averages 90–130cm *(3–4ft)*, in semi-arid areas often near water, of Africa and the Arabian Peninsula. Similar relatives occur in other habitats. Many different vipers are found in all parts of Africa and Eurasia, from sandy areas to thick jungle.

3 Saw-scaled Viper *(Echis carinatus)* is rough-scaled, pale reddish to sandy-brown with darker markings and white blotches, and averages 40–55cm *(16–26in)*; in arid areas from North Africa west to India. Vicious, common, causes many fatalities.

4 Russell's Viper *(Vipera russelli)* averages 1–1·25m *(40–50in)*, brownish, with three rows of spots formed of white-bordered black rings with a reddish-brown centre; in most areas except thick forest from Pakistan east to Taiwan. Responsible for most viper bites in the area.

5 Malay Pit Viper or **Moccasin** *(Calloselasma rhodostoma)* averages 60–80cm *(24–32in)* and is fawn, reddish or grey marked with geometric patterns, the belly yellowish or spotted greenish-brown in light growth in south-east Asia and parts of Indonesia. A frequent cause of bites and with many relatives in the area. AVOID any that resemble it.

6 Cobras occur from Africa east through India to Indonesia and the Philippines. They usually average 1·5–2m (5–6ft) and, when alarmed, are recognizable by the raised head and spreading, often marked, hood. Common in some areas, especially rocky and semi-arid ones.

7 Mambas (Dendroaspis) are small-headed, very slender, typically with large green or greyish scales and averaging 1·5–2·1m (5–7ft); in Africa south of the Sahara, usually in trees but the large Black Mamba D. polylepis is largely terrestrial. Often quick to strike, fatal in almost all untreated cases.

8 Boomslang (Dispholidus typus) averages 1·3–1·5m (4–5ft), very slender, varying from greenish to brownish or blackish; in trees and very hard to spot, in savannah parts of Africa south of the Sahara. Highly venomous; it inflates its throat when alarmed.

9 Kraits (Bungarus) average 90–150cm (3–5ft), are small-headed and some have black and white or black and yellow bands down the body, in both open and forested areas from India to Indonesia. Nocturnal, inoffensive, but bites are often fatal.

SPITTING SNAKES

A few cobras, including the ringhals of southern Africa, spit poison as well as bite. This is a purely defensive measure and is not dangerous unless the poison reaches an open cut or the eyes. If it does, wash out immediately with water or, in an emergency, with urine.

473

AUSTRALASIA

1 Death Adder *(Acanthophis antarcticus)* is brownish, reddish or grey with darker banding, thick-bodied and averages 45–60cm (18–24in); in sandy areas of much of Australia, Papua New Guinea and some nearby islands. Well camouflaged; highly venomous, but not so dangerous as the Tiger Snake and Taipan.

2 Australian Black Snake *(Pseudechis porphyriacus)* averages 1·5–2m (5–6ft), slender, bluish-black with a bright red belly; in or near fresh water over much of Australia. There are several different kinds. Very rarely fatal, it flattens its neck when aroused.

3 Australian Brown Snake *(Pseudonaja textilis)* is slender, yellowish-grey to brown with a pale belly and averages 1·5–2m (5–6ft); in drier parts of Australia and Papua New Guinea. There is more than one kind. Aggressive and very poisonous.

4 Tiger Snake *(Notechis scutalus)* averages 1·3–1·6m (4–5·5ft), thick-bodied, large-headed, tawny-ochre banded with greenish-yellow, grey or orange-brown; in semi-arid areas of Australia and in Tasmania. Aggressive, very poisonous, the principal cause of fatal bites.

5 Taipan *(Oxyuranus scutellatus)* is uniformly light to dark brown with yellowish-brown on the sides and belly and may grow to 3·5m (11ft); in open and forested parts of northern Australia. Ferocious when provoked, deadly poisonous.

6 Sea Snakes *occur in the Indian and Pacific Oceans; some are partly terrestrial, in estuaries and coastal swamps. They vary in colour and size, averaging 1·3–1·5m (4–5ft) with a flattened, paddle-like tail. Their scales distinguish them from eels. Not aggressive, but some are the most venomous snakes of all.*

Snakes have excellent camouflage, only movement gives them away. In snake-infested areas you will pass many every day without ever noticing them.

The chances of being bitten are small and all but the worst cases recover. In Malaysia, more people are killed each year by falling coconuts and in India rat-bites produce many more cases for hospitalization!

A bite from a poisonous snake should always be taken seriously, but there are degrees of severity. When biting in self-defence, many snakes inject only a little venom, occasionally none at all. If the snake is out of condition or has recently bitten something else, its venom may not be fully potent and there may be only a little in its venom sacs. Clothing or shoes may have deflected the full force of the bite. In many poisonous snakes the dose of venom needed to kill a man far exceeds the amount that can be injected in one bite.

SNAKE FREE!
There are NO poisonous snakes in New Zealand, Cuba, Haiti, Jamaica, Puerto Rico, Ireland, Polynesia and the polar regions.

LIZARDS
7 Gila Monster *(Heloderma suspectum) is a lizard found only in the deserts of Arizona, Mexico and nearby areas. Large rounded head, thick chunky body, short stumpy tail and brightly patterned in yellow. Averages 37–45cm (15–18in). Bite is poisonous but likely only when handled.*

8 Beaded Lizard *(Heloderma horridum) resembles the Gila Monster but is darker and larger, with a slenderer tail, and spots rather than a mottling of colour; in a few arid parts of Mexico and Central America. Docile, but the bite is poisonous. Do not handle.*

DANGEROUS SEA CREATURES

These fish and sea creatures are dangerous. Most are either poisonous to touch or have poisonous flesh.

RIVER DANGERS

1 Electric Eels *(Electrophorus electricus)* may reach nearly 2m (7ft) long and 20cm (8in) thick, rounded, coloured olive to blackish, and paler underneath, native to Orinoco and Amazon river systems of South America. Often prefer shallow water where there is more oxygen. The shock from a large one can be 500 volts, enough to knock a man of his feet.

2 Piranhas *(Serrasalmus)* occur in the Orinoco, Amazon and Parguay river systems of South America. They vary in size but may be up to 50cm (20in) long and are all deep-bodied and thickset, having large jaws with razor-sharp interlocking teeth. They can be very dangerous, particularly in the dry season when the water levels are low.

SEA AND RIVERS

3 Stingrays *(Dasyatidae)* are a danger in shallow waters, especially tropical ones, and not only on sandy shores. Very variable, but all with the distinctive ray shape though hard for the wader to spot. A few kinds occur in rivers in tropical South America and West Africa. The freshwater stingrays rarely exceed 30cm (1ft) long. They do not occur in rivers that flow into the Pacific. Venomous spines in the tail can inflict severe, sometimes fatal, injury.

SALTWATER DANGERS

4 Rabbitfishes or **Spinefeet** *(Siganidae)* occur mainly on reefs in the Indian and Pacific Oceans, averaging 25–30cm (10–12in); edible but with sharp spines in most fins. These are said to be venomous. Handle with care.

5   Tangs *or* **Surgeonfishes** (*Acanthuridae*) *average 20–25cm (8–10in), deep-bodied, small-mouthed, very colourful, with lancet-like spines on the sides of the tail that can inflict severe wounds when it is lashed. In all tropical waters.*

6   Venomous   Toadfishes (*Batrachoididae*) *occur in tropical waters off both coasts of Central and South America. Averaging 3–4cm (7–10in), they are dull-coloured and large-mouthed. They lie buried in sand and have sharp, very poisonous spines on the back.*

7   Scorpionfishes *or* **Zebrafishes** (*Scorpaenidae*) *are found mostly on reefs in the tropical Indian and Pacific Oceans. Averaging 30–75cm (12–30in), very variable, but usually reddish with long, wavy fin rays and spines. A sting is intensely painful. Less potent relatives occur in the Mediterranean and Atlantic.*

8   Stonefishes (*Synanceia*) *occur in the tropical Pacific and Indian Oceans. Reaching 40cm (16in), their drab colours and lumpy shape make them almost impossible to see. When trodden on, dorsal spines inject venom that is agonizingly painful, in the worst cases fatal.*

The venomous Toadfish, Stonefish and Zebrafish are edible. If you land one strike it on the head and handle only when completely dead, and then with great care.

Though not venomous, there are other fish with dangerously sharp spines, which are not always easy to detect, except at close quarters. The spines usually occur on the back but may also be on fins on the side of the fish. Even a small spine can inflict a bad prick with consequent risk of infection. Large spines — and some spiny catfish grow as large as a man — are as effective as stilettos.

Sea urchins can also inflict painful injuries and Sea anemones can sting.

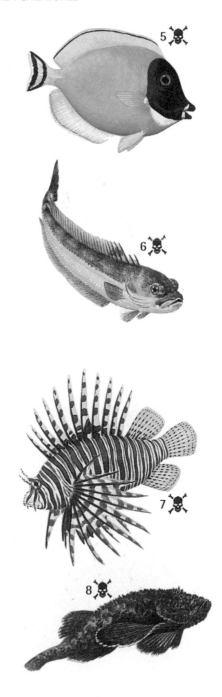

1   Weeverfishes   *(Trachinidae) tapering, dull-coloured, about 30cm (1ft) long, lie buried in sand off the coasts of Europe south to West Africa and the Mediterranean. Venomous spines on back and gills produce disabling pain. Soothe it by applying very hot water.*

POISONOUS TO EAT

Many inshore fish, living in reefs and lagoons, are poisonous to eat. The majority are confined to the tropics but, wherever you are, be wary of eating any fish that you cannot identify.

Some fishes that are otherwise good to eat, such as the Barracuda and Snapper, are inedible when taken from reefs and lagoons, where they will have absorbed poisonous substances with their own food.

The most poisonous kinds, such as puffer fish, usually have rounded bodies with hard, shell-like skins covered in bony plates and spines. They also commonly have parrot-like mouths, small gill openings and either lack pelvic fins or have only a small one.

2 Porcupine Fishes *(Diodontidae) occur in all shallow tropical waters. Variable, reaching 50-60cm (20-24in), but when alarmed all inflate into a very spiny ball. Their flesh is poisonous.*
3 Puffer Fishes *(Tetraodontidae) occur in all tropical and many warmer temperate waters, a few kinds in rivers in south-east Asia and tropical Africa. Stout-bodied, rounded, 15–75cm (6–30in) long, most kinds with spines; when alarmed they puff up into a ball. Their blood, liver and gonads are poisonous; 28mg (1oz) can kill.*

4 Triggerfishes *(Balistridae) occur in huge variety, mostly in shallow tropical seas. Deep bodied, compressed, usually under 60cm (24in), with very large, stout dorsal spines. Many kinds are poisonous to eat. Avoid them all.*

OTHER SEA CREATURES

5 Portuguese Man-of-war
(Physalis physalis), not a jellyfish but a colony of hydroids, is mainly sub-tropical but common in the Gulf Stream which may take it to British shores. Southern currents carry it, for example, to New Zealand. The floating bladder may be only 15cm (6in) long, but the tentacles, which carry stinging cells, can stream out for 12m (40ft). Not fatal but enough to incapacitate, so extremely dangerous.

The Common Jellyfish *(Aurelia aurita), a milky saucer shape with purplish horseshoe marks inside, is not dangerous to humans but many others are, especially the* **Sea wasps** *or* **Box Jellyfish** *(*Chironex fleckeri*), with a cube shaped bell 25cm (10in) long and clusters of tentacles at the corners up to 9m (30ft) long. In big doses venom can be fatal. Avoid all jellyfish streamers — even when washed up on the beach.*

6 Blue-ringed Octopus
(Hapalochlaena lunulata), small, sometimes only fist-sized, found off eastern Australia, particularly around the Great Barrier Reef, is greyish white with iridescent ring-like markings. Very poisonous, potentially lethal bite if trodden on or handled. Treat all tropical reef octopuses with caution.

7 Cone shells *(Conidae), subtropical and tropical gastropods, have a venomous harpoon-like barb. All are cone shaped but shell patterns may be obscured by a membrane. Some very poisonous, a few, in the Indo-Pacific, lethal. DO NOT TOUCH.*

8 Augers *or* **Terebra Shells** *(Terebridae) temperate and tropical seas, particularly the Indo-Pacific also have a stinging barb. They are much thinner and longer than cone shells. The sting is not as serious as the cone's, but do NOT eat.*

479

-9-
SURVIVAL AT SEA

Conditions of survival at sea are perhaps worse than those of any other environment and make the sternest demands. Planes and boats carry survival equipment, but even getting into a dinghy in a heavy sea can be difficult.

Once any emergency supplies of food and water run out, sources are not reliable – so any possibilities of obtaining food from the sea and collecting drinking water must be exploited to conserve supplies as long as possible.

Not all fish are edible and some are even dangerous to handle. Shark dangers are often exaggerated, but should not be ignored. Appropriate action is needed to avoid or deter them. A difficult coast can make even a final landfall hazardous, so heed the advice on lessening the risks.

SURVIVAL AT SEA

SURVIVAL AT SEA

Four-fifths of the earth's surface is open water — probably the most frightening of all environments, and the most difficult in which to survive. In cold water the body soon becomes chilled and even in a boat wind can chill the body rapidly. Alone in cold water your chances are not good without equipment.

If you know your location and the main ocean currents you may be able to predict where they will carry you, though it will be very slowly. Warm currents, such as the Gulf Stream, across the North Atlantic, are rich in fish and sea creatures.

Coastal waters are also often rich in sea foods — but there are dangerous species, such as sharks, and poisonous species, mainly living

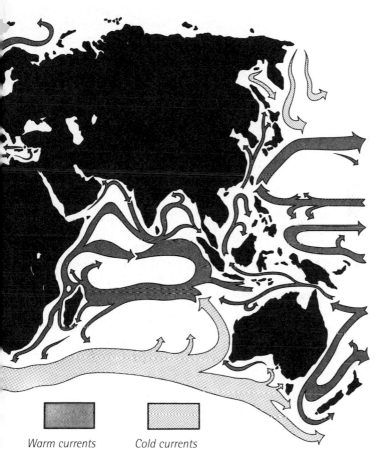

Warm currents   *Cold currents*

in shallower water near lagoons and reefs in warmer climates. Fresh water is a bigger problem if you have no means of distilling sea water.

Lifeboat drill

Lifeboat drill is carried out on every ship soon after it sails and should become a well-rehearsed procedure. Passengers are instructed in how to fit lifejackets, how to proceed to their lifeboat stations and what to take with them. Sailors in small boats should also devise such a drill and instruct everyone on board. Safety equipment could include rigid boats, simple rafts, inflatable dinghies, lifebelts or lifejackets.

If the signal is given to abandon ship put on warm, preferably woollen, clothing including hat and gloves and wrap a towel around your neck. Clothes will not drag you under if you end up in the water and they will help ward off the worst enemy — exposure. Take a torch if you can and grab chocolates and boiled sweets if they are handy. Do NOT push or shout or you may start a panic — an orderly embarkation into lifeboats and on to rafts or dinghies will be faster in the long run and establish a calmer attitude.

Don't inflate your lifejacket until you leave the ship or plane. On small boats lifejackets should be worn all the time. They are brightly coloured and are usually equipped with a whistle, light, marker dye and — when for use in warmer waters — a shark repellent.

If you have to jump overboard, first throw something that floats and jump close to it.

Abandoning ship

Abandoning a ship or ditching from a plane, it is essential that you take what equipment you can with you. A lifejacket or -belt will save a lot of energy that you might otherwise expend in trying to keep afloat. But even without one it is not difficult to float in the ocean. The human body is of lower density than saltwater and anyone who has learned to relax in the water is not in immediate danger from drowning. However, panic or fear make relaxation difficult and many find floating difficult under these conditions. Without a lifejacket or lifebelt, air trapped in clothing will help buoyancy — a good reason for keeping your clothes on despite the frequent advice that you should strip them off.

MAN OVERBOARD!

If you have been swept overboard your first aim, apart from keeping afloat, will be to attract attention. Sound travels well over water — shouting and splashing can be effective. Wave with one arm above the water (not both, you will go under) — movement will make you more noticeable.

If you are wearing a lifejacket — and on a small boat you always should be — it will probably be equipped with a whistle and a light, as regular-issue 'Mae Wests' usually are.

Swimming

Swim slowly and steadily. If you are abandoning a sinking boat or aircraft get upwind and stay clear of it. Keep away from any oil or fuel slick.

If there is a fire and you have to enter the water, or swim through flames, jump into the water feet first and up wind, swimming into the wind using a breast stroke, try to make breathing holes by splashing the flames away from the head. If the fire is not too extensive it is best to swim underwater until clear of that danger.

If there is a danger of an underwater explosion while you are in the water, the risk of injury will be reduced if you swim on your back.

If within sight of land don't battle against the ebb, relax and float until it turns and helps to carry you to land. If the sea is too rough to float on your back adopt this technique.

1 *Float upright in the water and take a deep breath.*
2 *Lower your face into the water (keeping your mouth closed) and bring your arms forward to rest at water level.*

3 *Relax in this position until you need to take in more air.*
4 *Raise your head above the surface, treading water, and exhale. Take another breath and return to the relaxed position.*

Flotation 'bags'

You can improvise a short-term flotation bag from a pair of trousers. Knot the bottoms of the legs, sweep them over the head to fill with air, then hold the waist below the water to trap the air inside, making the legs into water wings to lean on.

Immediate action

Once you are clear of the wreck and have got your bearings inflate your dinghy or look out for a boat or raft or wreckage which can offer support. If there is no boat or dinghy grab as much flotsam as possible to use as a raft. Tie it together with anything that is available — ties, belts, shoelaces, spare clothing. Salvage any floating equipment.

Inflating a dinghy

Aircraft and many boats and ships carry dinghy-type lifeboats. Many are self-inflating and activated by salt water immersion.

If they do not inflate automatically, there is a pump provided. There are several inflation points because the dinghy is built in sections, so that if one compartment is punctured the others will still keep the dinghy afloat.

Boarding an inflatable dinghy

Get aboard as soon as possible. If you are already in the water move to the end (not the side) of the dinghy, place one leg over the edge and roll into the dinghy.

Do NOT jump into a dinghy from above, you may damage it.

To haul someone else aboard a dinghy, raft or lifeboat hold their shoulders and lift one leg over the end, then roll them in. Discourage them from putting their arms around your neck — they could pull you into the water. Then tie yourself and others to the dinghy.

RIGHTING AN INFLATABLE DINGHY
Most dinghies have righting straps on the bottom, and larger ones have a righting line attached to one side. Grab it from the opposite side, brace your feet against the dinghy and pull. The dinghy should rise up and over, pulling you out of the water momentarily. In heavy seas, or a high wind, this can be extremely difficult.

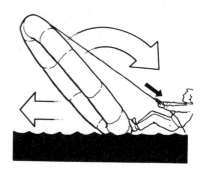

Ensure that the dinghy is fully inflated. It should be firm — not rock-hard. If it is not you will need to inflate it with your own breath or a pump. The valves are one-way and air will not escape when you take off the protective cap.

Check for leaks. Escaping air will cause bubbles under water and above water will make a hissing sound. Deal with them with conical plugs that you will find in the dinghy kit. They screw into holes and seal them. You will probably also find a supply of rubber patches and adhesive.

Make daily checks of inflation and leaks. If you suspect a leak on the underside swim under and insert a plug.

SURVIVAL AFLOAT

Rafts, boats and dinghies are built to carry a limited number of survivors. The lives of those aboard will be even more endangered if these numbers are exceeded.

The safety of the majority must be the priority. Place the infirm, youngsters and any injured in the dinghy or boat first and as many of the able-bodied as the boat is made to accommodate. The rest must hang on in the water. The fit survivors aboard should rotate with those in the water on a regular and frequent change-over rota.

Stow all the gear in any stowage places provided and tie everything securely. Check that there are no exposed sharp objects which will damage an inflatable. Ensure that anything that will spoil if wet is in a waterproof container and kept out of the water.

Check all signalling equipment: flares, rockets, heliographs. If distress signals have already been sent out you will need them to attract the attention of rescue parties when they are searching for you.

If a distress call has gone out giving your position it is best to try to maintain location, so put out a sea anchor. This should look like a large canvas bag. Streamed out from the boat it will keep it into the weather and slow down drift.

You can improvise a sea-anchor from any weighted object securely tied to a line. Even clothing could be used, possibly tied to a paddle with reef knots.

If you do not know where you are do NOT attempt to navigate until you have established your position, but if you can see the shore head towards it.

SURVIVAL PRIORITIES

- PROTECTION from the elements and the effects of exposure.

- LOCATION Try to establish where you are and the best way of attracting rescue.

- WATER Take stock of supplies. Ration it at once. Start collecting any rain.

- FOOD Don't eat, unless you have sufficient water. Check all rations available, stow them securely. Start fishing as soon as possible.

PROTECTION

Even if you are alone keep a log on a daily basis. This will occupy the mind and help keep you oriented. First record names of survivors, date and time and position of accident, weather conditions, equipment salvaged, and record sightings and circumstances daily.

In a cold climate

If the water is cold it is essential to get out of it as soon as possible. You need to counter the chilling effect of the wind, especially if you are wet. Keep the boat or dinghy as dry as possible. Bail out all the water and rig up an awning to keep out spray if you can find any material to use for it.

Dry all wet clothing and if there is no dry clothing to put on squeeze out as much water as possible and then put the clothes back on.

Maintain body heat by wrapping all parts in any available material, such as parachute or canvas. If in a group of survivors huddle together to keep warm. To prevent stiffness to muscles and joints, and to keep the circulation going, do mild exercises, such as stretching and arm circling. Be careful not to disturb the balance of the raft or boat by excessive or sudden movement.

Most modern dinghies have a built-in shelter. If yours does not, rig up a windbreak and a spray shield. Stretch any material that is available across to keep out spray and breaking waves. With adequate shelter and warm clothing, exercise will protect against the risk of frostbite.

In a hot climate

Take off unnecessary clothing, but still keep the body covered. If exposed directly to strong sun always keep the head and neck covered to avoid sunstroke or burn. Protect the eyes from the sun glare by improvising eye shields.

During the day damping down clothes with sea water will help to keep the body cool but make sure that you are thoroughly dried out by evening, for nights can be very cold — and remember that darkness comes quickly in the tropics. Remember also that prolonged contact with sea water can cause sores on the skin.

When it is very hot let out some air from an inflated dinghy, for air expands with the heat — you will need to release the valves. Reinflate in the evening when it cools.

WATCHES AND LOOKOUTS

In a group assign watches. There should be a look-out all the time — even in darkness. Each watch should be for a short period to avoid exhaustion and lack of concentration. It is better for everyone to have several watches a day than for any one person to have long periods on duty.

It is the responsibility of the watch to look out for shipping, aircraft, signs of land — and for seaweed, shoals of fish, birds, wreckage. They should also inspect the raft for signs of leakage or chafing.

IS LAND NEARBY?

When there is no land in sight you may find some of these indicators of land and the direction in which it may be found:

Clouds:

Cumulus clouds in an otherwise clear sky are likely to have been formed over land.

In tropical waters a greenish tint on the underside of clouds, known as lagoon glare, is produced by the reflection of sunlight from the shallow water over coral reefs.

Birds:

A lone bird is not a reliable indication of land, and after rough weather birds can be blown way off course, but few seabirds sleep on the water or fly more than 100 miles from land. Their direction of flight is usually outwards from land before noon and return in the late afternoon. The continuous sound of bird cries is usually an indication that land is not far distant.

Driftwood:

Driftwood, coconuts and other drifting vegetation are often a sign that land is near (though they can be carried right across an ocean).

Sea movement:

The pattern of the swell may indicate land. A change in its direction may be caused by the tide pattern around an island.

Prevailing winds build up a swell pattern and the swell is less if the water is protected by land. If the wind is constant but the swell and waves decreasing you can be fairly certain that land lies to windward.

Sea colour:
Water that is muddy with silt is likely to have come from the mouth of a large river.

TRAVELLING

If an S O S has been successfully sent, or you know that you are in or near regular shipping lanes, it is usually preferable to stay in the same vicinity for 72 hours.

If none of these circumstances hold, then no time should be lost in getting underway to take advantage of initial fitness and energy, especially if land is known to be near and downwind.

If there is no land nearby, assess the nearest shipping lane and head in that direction.

DECIDING FACTORS

Take these factors into consideration in making your decision whether to stay or travel:

- The amount of information signalled before the accident.

- Is your position known to rescuers? Do you know it yourselves?

- Is the weather favourable for a search?

- Are other ships or aircraft likely to pass your present position?

- How many days supply of food and water do you have?

Your craft will move with the wind and current. In the open oceans currents seldom exceed a speed of 9–13km (6–8) miles per day.

Take in the sea anchor. Use the wind if you can. In a craft with no keel it is only possible to sail full tilt with the wind or at most at an angle of 10 degrees off it.

Use a paddle as a rudder. If the wind is against your chosen direction stream the sea anchor to maintain position.

To use the wind

Inflate the dinghy fully and sit high. Improvise a sail if you do not have one. Do not secure its lower edges but hold the lower lines or the bottom of the sail so that if there is a sudden gust of wind you can release them and the raft is not capsized.

In rough water

Stream out the sea anchor from the bow. It will keep the bow always into the wind and prevent capsizing. Keep low in the raft. Do not sit on the sides or stand up. Never make sudden movements. If there are several rafts or dinghies tie them together.

SIGNALLING AT SEA

Flares, dye markers and movement of any kind are the ways of attracting attention at sea. If you have no signalling equipment, wave clothing or tarpaulins and churn the water if it is still. At night or in fog a whistle is useful for maintaining contact with other groups of survivors.

If a radio transmitter is part of the equipment aboard a life-raft instructions for its operation will be found on its side. Frequencies are usually preset at 121·5 and 243 megacycles and the range is about 32km (20 miles). Transmit at frequent intervals but exercise discretion in using battery-operated transceivers. The batteries are precious. (See *Signalling* in *Rescue*.)

Sea markers, which release dye into the water, are only of use in daytime. Unless the seas are very rough they will be conspicuous for about three hours.

Pyrotechnic equipment must be kept dry and secure. Read instructions carefully and beware of fire hazards. Day-and-night flares are particularly useful — one end produces smoke for daytime use. When firing flares and rockets you are holding a dangerous firework in your hand, so be very careful that you do not point them downwards or towards yourself or another person.

Use flares only when you are sure that they will be seen and fire to make sure that they are — when a plane is flying towards you, for instance — not when it has gone past. (See *Signalling* in *Rescue*.)

Most rescues have followed after heliograph signals have

attracted attention. Any shiny, reflective surface can be used to signal in this way.

HEALTH

Exposure and severe hydration are likely to be the biggest problems for the ocean survivor. Seasickness can increase dehydration.

Constipation and, often, either difficulty in urinating or very concentrated urine are not unusual in sea survival conditions. Do not attempt to treat them or you could force further liquid loss.

If feeling sick, try not to vomit and NEVER induce vomiting.

Continued exposure to saltwater can produce skin eruptions. Do not attempt to prick or squeeze any boils or blisters. As a precaution do not damp yourself down too often with salt water to keep cool. If there is any soreness, STOP.

Protect the eyes from glare off the sea with a mask and, if sore eyes are produced by glare, moisten a cloth with sea water and bandage this over the eyes and rest them. Do not do this for too long. The skin may become sore.

Immersion foot (see *Health*) can be a problem if subjected to very long exposure in a boat or dinghy awash with water. Exercise will help protects you from it and from frostbite and exposure. Keep well covered when resting and, when on watch, gently exercise the limbs.

WATER

Although a minimum 1 litre (1¾pts) a day is necessary to keep fit, it is possible to survive on 55–220cc (2–8oz).

Even if you have a good water supply, ration it at once, reflecting these minimum needs until you can replenish your supply. Do not relax the ration until final rescue, for you have no idea how long you will have to last out.

Reducing water needs

Take all the usual precautions against water loss (see *Water* in *Essentials*). Reduce sweating as much as possible. Make use of breezes and use sea water to cool the body. If it is very hot, shade limited and the waters safe take a dip over the side – but first check your safety line. You should ALWAYS be tied on. Beware of dangerous fish and be sure that you can get back aboard.

If seasickness threatens take anti-sickness pills, if they are available, as soon as you start to feel queasy, for vomiting will lose valuable fluids.

If you are low on water do not eat, especially not protein foods — which include fish and seaweed — that require a lot of water to digest. Carbohydrates (sugars and starches) require less water for digestion.

WATER RATIONS

DAY 1:
NO WATER. The body is a reservoir and has a store.

DAYS 2–4:
400cc (14oz) if available.

DAY 5 ONWARDS:
55–225cc (2–8oz) daily, depending on the climate and water available.

When drinking moisten the lips, tongue and throat before swallowing.

Gathering freshwater

Use every possible container to collect rainwater night and day — you will usually see a rain squall coming and have time to rig up a catchment from canvas or plastic, which will hold much more than cans.

At night rig canvas with edges folded to catch any dew.

When it rains drink your fill — but slowly, for if you have been on short water ration you will vomit if you gulp it down.

Stow as much in containers as you can. Drink up puddles in the boat first. But be careful in heavy seas as the water will be contaminated with salt. Water is good ballast in an inflatable — fill it to the brim and it will still float.

Sea Ice

Ice can produce drinking water. But new sea ice is salty. Use only old sea ice, which is blue-grey in colour and with rounded contours. It can be melted or sucked for the ice loses its salt after a year or more. In summer, pools on old sea ice may be drinkable (if they are not wave splashes). Taste very carefully before drinking, for drinking any salt will aggravate thirst.

Water from fish

Drink the aqueous fluid found along the spine of large fish and in the eyes. Carefully cut the fish in half to obtain it and suck the eye. If you are so short of water that you need to do this then do NOT drink any of the other body fluids for they are rich in protein and fat and will use up more of your reserve water in digestion than they supply.

Treatment of sea water

Liferaft equipment may include solar stills and chemical desalination kits. They carry their own instructions. Set solar stills out immediately, but use the desalination tablets only when the weather is unfavourable for the stills and dew or rain catchment is ineffective.

REMEMBER:

DO NOT drink sea water

DO NOT drink urine

DO NOT drink alcohol

DO NOT smoke

DO NOT eat, unless water is available

Sleep and rest are the best way of enduring periods of reduced water and food — but make sure that you have adequate shade when napping during the day.

If the sea is rough, tie yourself to the raft, close any cover and ride out the storm as best you can. RELAX is the keyword — at least TRY to relax.

FOOD

Conserve any emergency food supplies until really needed, even then only taking a small nibble, and try to live off natural foods.

Fish will be the main food source. There are some poisonous and dangerous ocean fish but in general, in the open sea, out of sight of land, fish are safe to eat. Nearer the shore there are fish that are both dangerous and poisonous to eat, including some, such as the Red Snapper and Barracuda, which are normally edible but poisonous when taken from the waters of atolls and reefs.

Flying fish will even jump into your boat!

Fishing

- Do NOT handle fishing line with bare hands and never wrap it around the hands or tie it to an inflatable dinghy. The salt which adheres to it can make it a sharp cutting edge — a danger both to the raft and to your hands.

- Wear gloves if they are available or use a cloth to handle fish to avoid injury from sharp fins and gill covers.

- Fish and turtles are attracted to the shelter from the sun provided by a dinghy or raft and will swim under it. If you have a net pass it under the keel from one end to the other (you need two people to hold the ends).

- Use a torch to attract fish at night — or on a moonlit night lower a piece of cloth, tinfoil or metal into the water to reflect the moon and it may also draw fish to it.

- Improvise hooks from whatever is available. Small folding pocket-knives, pieces of jagged metal, wire. Small bright metal objects may serve as 'bait' — including buckles, spoons and coins.

- If using a metal spoon or spinner keep it moving by paying out and reeling in. Let the 'bait' sink and then retrieve it.

- Use offal from caught fish for bait.

- Fish flesh spoils easily and in the tropics must be eaten fresh unless the air is dry — which is unlikely in the tropical oceans.

- In cooler zones excess fish can be dried in the sun for future meals. Clean and gut before drying.

Birds

All birds at sea are also potential food. They will be attracted to a raft as a potential perching place. Keep still until they settle and you may be able to grab them, especially if they are exhausted by flying in bad weather.

You may also catch birds using lines trailed in the water with hooks or gorges baited with fish.

A diamond-shaped tin gorge, wrapped with fish, and trailed behind the craft will attract birds. When a bird siezes the 'fish', the gorge should lodge across its gullet.

Seaweed

Seaweed not only occurs on shorelines but, far out in some oceans, there are floating forms, especially the *Sargassum* species of the Sargasso Sea and the North Atlantic Drift, which is found in many warm waters, and others which grow in the colder waters of the southern Atlantic and Pacific. Since raw seaweeds are tough and salty they are difficult to digest raw. They absorb fluids so should not be eaten when water is short.

Seaweeds may also provide food in the form of the small crabs and shrimps living on them and small fish that you may shake out from among them if you haul some weed aboard. These small decapods are mottled brown in colour, like the weed, so are not easily seen on it.

Plankton, strained from the water, can also be a useful food source, especially in the cold southern waters (see *Polar food* in *Climate and Terrain*).

Make a grapple hook by lashing pieces of wood or metal wreckage together to form a multiple hook. Attach it to a line and trail it behind, or throw it out to rake in weed. You can use it for gathering other drifting wreckage to consolidate a makeshift raft.

DANGEROUS FISH

Poisonous fish

Many reef fish have toxic flesh, some species at all times and in others only at certain times of year. The poisons are present in all parts of the fish, but especially in the liver, intestines and eggs.

Fish toxins are water soluble — no amount of cooking will neutralize them. They are tasteless — so the standard edibility tests (see *Food*) are useless. Birds are least susceptible to the poisons so do not think that because a bird can eat a fish, it is a safe species for you to eat. Cats appear less affected, though dogs and rats are as susceptible as humans.

The toxins will produce a numbness of the lips, tongue, toes and tips of the fingers, severe itching and an apparent reversal of temperature sensations. Cold things seem hot and hot things cold. There will probably also be nausea, vomiting, loss of speech, dizziness and a paralysis that eventually brings DEATH.

As well as those fish with poisonous flesh (see colour section) there are those which are dangerous to touch. Many kinds of ray have a poisonous barb in their tail; there are also species that can deliver an electric shock. Some reef fishes, such as Stonefishes and Toadfishes, have venomous spines which, although seldom fatal, can be VERY painful, causing a burning sensation or even agonizing pain out of all proportion to the apparent severity of the wound.

Jellyfish, which are sometimes barely noticeable in the water, can carry powerful stings. The Portuguese man-of-war (not a true jellyfish) is a bluish bladder-like creature with a small fluted sail. Do not enter the water if you see these creatures. They trail very long 'streamers' which carry dangerous and painful toxins.

Aggressive fish

There are also a number of ferocious fish which should be avoided. The bold and inquisitive Barracuda has been known to attack man. It may charge lights or shiny objects at night. The Sea Bass, which can grow to 1·8m (5½ft), is another to keep clear of and the Moray Eel, which has many sharp teeth and grows to 1·5m (5ft), can also be aggressive if disturbed. Sea snakes are venomous and sometimes occur in mid-ocean. They are unlikely to bite, but AVOID.

SHARKS

Only a handful of attacks by sharks are recorded each year, and only a minority are fatal. However, the survivor at sea is more vulnerable than the beach swimmer to whom statistics largely refer. Very few types of sharks are considered dangerous to man.

Six sharks account for most human casualties: the Great White, Mako, Tiger, Hammerhead, Bull and Grey Nurse. The Great White is the largest, but size is not an indication of danger and bears no relation to the likelihood of attack. A shark smaller than a man can still kill a swimmer. Basking Sharks and Whale Sharks may be 13·3m (45ft) long but they feed on tiny plankton and are not a problem.

Ocean sharks have the ability to kill but, in the tropics, their food is so abundant that they are not usually ferocious. These sharks are usually cowards and can be scared off by the jab of a stick, especially on the nose. However, making a commotion may ATTRACT sharks from a distance.

Sharks live and feed at considerable depths and for most of the time feed off the ocean bottom, but hungry sharks will follow fish to the surface and into shallow water. When it explores such water a shark is likely to be DANGEROUS.

A shark's usual diet includes fish, squid, crabs and a variety of other marine animals but it seeks food that is EASY to get and especially goes after stragglers from schools of fish or wounded prey. Sharks will follow a ship to scavenge refuse thrown overboard.

The shark feeds most actively at night and at dusk and dawn. Its small eyes have limited vision and it locates its prey by smell and vibrations in the water. It will be attracted by blood from wounds, body wastes and rubbish. Weak and fluttery movements will draw a shark's attention because they suggest a vulnerable, wounded creature. It will be repelled by strong, regular movements and loud noises.

Man's strange appearance is new to a shark and clothing produces a confusing shape. A group of clothed humans bunched together will be safer than a single individual. If a shark keeps its distance, it is only curious. If it circles inwards and begins sudden movement, the likelihood of attack is greatly increased.

Sharks cannot stop suddenly or turn quickly. A good swimmer can evade a single large shark by making rapid changes of direction which the shark cannot match.

FALSE ALARM

Not every fin showing above the surface is attached to a shark! The wing tips of large rays may break the surface and appear to belong to a pair of sharks moving, unnaturally, in perfect synchronization. The fins or flippers of whales may also appear — likewise those of porpoises and dolphins, which are harmless and will probably show themselves more completely.

The sharks shown here have been known to attack man.

1 Great White Shark *(Carcharodon carcharias)* grows to 6m (18ft) but usually less, grey above, white below, very thick bodied, with pure black eyes and a stubby conical snout; in all oceans but mostly off southern Africa, east and west North America and southern Australia and New Zealand.

2 Mako *(Isurus oxyrichus)* averages 2–3m (6–9ft), heavy bodied, ultramarine blue above, creamy-white below; in all oceans but most abundant in warm temperate waters. A very fast swimmer, occasionally leaps from the water.

3 Tiger Shark *(Galeocerdo cuvieri)* averages 3–3.5m (12–13.5ft), heavy bodied, barred or blotched above when young, when mature more evenly greyish above, white below, with a very wide head and jaws and abruptly squared-off snout, in all tropical and subtropical waters, often close inshore.

4 Barracudas *(Sphyraena)* are not sharks but thin, torpedo-like fishes, bluish-barred above, brilliant silver below, with a protruding mouth packed with sharp teeth, some kinds growing to 2m (7ft), in all tropical waters. Very fast, darting, often in shoals, usually dangerous only when there is blood in the water.

5 Hammerhead Sharks *(Sphyrna)* are immediately recognizable by their distinctively flattened hammer-like head. There are several different kinds, the largest reaching 6m (18ft); in all tropical and subtropical waters.

6 Bull Shark *(Carcharhinus leucas)* is found in the tropical west Atlantic with close relatives off southern Africa and in the Indian Ocean. Stout, grey above and white below, up to 4m (12ft). Aggressive, and dangerous in its liking for shallow water and ability to ascend far up rivers.

7 Nurse *(Ginglymostoma)*, such as the Grey Nurse of eastern Australian waters, reach over 4m (13ft) heavily built, large-finned, greyish above and white below. Often found very close inshore.

If you catch a shark

If a small shark is accidentally hooked it can be hauled to the side of the raft or boat, the head pulled clear, and clubbed hard before hauling aboard. Make sure it is really stunned before approaching and finishing it off with more blows to provide shark steaks.

DON'T try this with a large shark. It could injure you and your craft. You must cut your line and sacrifice part of it, for the shark's threshing will soon attract its fellows.

Protection against sharks

Unless wearing a lifejacket or travelling in a craft equipped with shark repellent, the risk is great to anyone in the water, but it is not a foregone conclusion that shark attack will occur. Shark repellent may not be 100% effective – but even so, only use when absolutely necessary. Remember – you can only use it once.

In the water:

If sharks are present try to avoid passing body wastes, which could attract the sharks' interest. If you must urinate do it in short, sharp spurts and allow it to dissipate between spurts. Collect faecal matter and throw it as far away from you as possible. If you vomit try to hold it in the mouth and reswallow it, but if this proves impossible throw it as far away as possible.

If it is necessary to swim use strong, regular strokes, avoiding schools of fish.

If a group of people are threatened they should bunch together and face outwards. To ward off attack kick outwards and punch out with a stiff arm using the heel of the hand – like a sports 'hand-off'.

Make loud noises by slapping the water with cupped hands. Put your head under the water and shout. These measures are more effective with a group but can work even when you are alone and under attack. If you have a knife, be prepared to use it. Let the shark take it fully in the snout, or go for the gills and eyes.

On a raft or boat:

Don't fish when sharks are around and don't throw waste overboard (including excrement and fish offal). Let go of baited hooks. Do not trail arms or legs in the water. If a shark threatens to attack discourage it with jabs to the snout with a paddle or pole. Remember – a large shark could also take a bite out of a boat or raft.

REMEMBER:

If you have shark repellent, follow manufacturer's instructions – but use only if the situation is very grave. The repellent will soon dissipate in the water and become ineffective. Choose your moment well, since you can only use it once.

MAKING A LANDFALL

When you approach land try to select a landing point where it will be easy to beach or where you can safely swim ashore. Take down the sail and keep watch for rocks. The sea anchor will keep you pointing at the shore and will slow down your progress, giving you more time to steer away if you are heading for rocks. Try not to land with the sun in your eyes, which will make it more difficult for you to see rocks and difficulties.

A sloping beach with a small surf is the ideal place to choose — if you have any choice. If you can time it right, ride the back of a breaker. To avoid being swamped or turned sideways by an oncoming crest of a wave paddle hard, but do not overshoot a breaker which is carrying you along. In very heavy surf turn the vessel to face seaward and, as a wave approaches, paddle into it.

As you approach note the lie of the land: the location of high ground, types of vegetation, possible watercourses. You will see features which may be invisible from the shore. If with companions, choose a rendezvous spot to meet at if the boat breaks up and you are separated.

If you reach land at night wait until morning to beach if you can, there are too many dangers you can fail to spot in the dark.

If you float into an estuary make every effort to reach a bank. The turning tide could carry you back out to sea. Take in the sea anchor and, to gain ground, make the boat as light as possible. Bail out an inflatable and inflate it to the maximum. This enables you to make the most of the incoming tide.

If you are being swept back out to sea by the ebb, ballast the dinghy by part filling it with water and stream the sea anchor.

NOTE:

Keep yourself tied to your raft. Even if it is overturned or damaged and you are rendered unconscious, you stand a chance of surviving. Alone in the water and dashed on the rocks — you are DEAD.

Swimming ashore

If you have to swim ashore on to rocks in a heavy sea keep on clothing, shoes and lifejacket if you have it. Raise your legs in front of you to take the shock of impact with rocks on the soles of your feet; absorb it in bending the knees.

-10-
RESCUE

Signalling is necessary to attract rescue and codes may be necessary for communication once a contact has been established. It will help the placing of signals, and increase their effectiveness, if the patterns used for search patrols are understood.

If survivors are being air-lifted out it may be necessary to prepare a landing place for aircraft or helicopter — so suitable locations are described and the precautions you should take in the presence of a helicopter.

SIGNALLING

The first requirement for rescue is to let others know of your situation and, if possible, your location. Once you are in contact you can pass on other information.

The obvious technique is to use a mobile or satellite phone, which should be used sparingly, but if you don't have the luxury of such systems then there are a number of internationally recognized distress signals. The letters S O S (for Save Our Souls) is probably the best known. It can be written, transmitted by radio, spelt out by semaphore or sent in morse code by any method.

The signal 'Mayday' (a phonetic rendering of the French *m'aidez* — help me) is the one used in most radiotelecommunications by ships and planes.

Vehicle or aircraft wreckage

If you are with a stranded vehicle or downed aircraft it may provide many useful signalling aids. If there has been no fire there will be supplies of fuel, oil and hydraulic fluid which can be burned. Tyres and electrical insulation on a fire will generate black smoke.

Glass and chrome make great reflectors, especially engine cowlings and hubcaps. Lifejackets, dinghies, and parachutes are all brightly coloured and eye-catching. Arrange these colourful and shiny objects around your location where they will be most visible and attract attention.

Switch lights on at night — or if batteries are running low keep them in reserve to flash headlamps, sound the horn and otherwise attract attention, when passing aircraft or signs of possible searchers are observed.

Fire and smoke

Fire — both flames and smoke — is an excellent way of attracting attention. Establishing signal fires is one of the primary tasks once the immediate needs for treatment of injury and provision of shelter from harsh elements have been met. In a large group some people should set about gathering fuel for a campfire and for signal fires as soon as possible.

Where to site signals

When siting signals take full account of the terrain. Choose high points for light signals. If you are on a ridge, erecting an unusual silhouette may attract attention. If you are laying out marks on the ground, use level ground or ensure that they are on slopes that are not likely to be overlooked in the usual pattern of aerial search.

NOTE:

It is usual for planes to fly over hilly territory from the lower to the higher ridges. This creates the problem that the slopes behind the ridges may be hidden as the plane approaches. If in doubt, signals nearer the tops of ridges should be seen from whichever direction the rescue aircraft is travelling.

International codes

When contact has been established more complex international codes (shown later) will enable you to signal your basic needs, if verbal communication is not possible.

With air- or sea-rescue it may then be necessary to prepare a landing strip or to help rig lines or apparatus, and some knowledge of basic procedures will greatly facilitate the operation. (See *Helicopter rescue*.)

Transmitters

Dinghies, liferafts and even personal lifejackets are sometimes equipped with transmitters which send out bleeps indicating position, though these are not usually effective over a very long range. Many emergency radio transmitters are also very limited in range and to avoid wasting precious batteries should be held in reserve until there is some chance of their signals being picked up. With effective radio apparatus, however, distress signals should be sent out immediately and transmitted at regular intervals.

Check instructions on all transmitting apparatus. Ship and plane transmitters can operate on many wavelengths, but some emergency equipment is set to fixed distress channels.

Generally speaking, the portable VHF transceivers used by mountaineering teams can communicate only with stations in a direct line of sight and without any intervening obstruction (though sometimes a permanent relay station may be established on a strategic high point). Such sets are usually tuned to a mountain rescue frequency but procedures should be established before departure.

If you have a working transmitter, check the battery situation. Can the vehicle engine still be used to generate electricity or recharge the batteries? Conserve fuel for this purpose and plan your transmissions to a pattern rather than attempting long continuous periods on the air. If anyone picks up your signal they can then work out that they can expect it again.

Noise

Noise is also an excellent way of attracting attention if you know that people are within earshot. The International Mountain Distress Signal, apart from signalling SOS, is six whistles a minute (or six waves, light flashes, etc.) followed by a minute's silence, then repeated. A shout may be enough if you are trapped, or near help but too injured to reach it.

Be imaginative

Do not reject even such ideas as the message in a bottle. This particular method has a low chance of success if you are shipwrecked in the middle of the Pacific but on a river a more noticeable floating object which carries a clear message might well attract attention — a small raft with a bright sail labelled S O S for instance. Use your imagination to think of ways that will attract attention to you and your plight, without using up valuable energy and resources.

Moving on

If you decide that rescue is unlikely, and that your best plan is to make your own way back, you should leave clear signs behind so that if searchers do track down the disaster spot they have an indication of the route that you have taken. On your way you may have more success in attracting attention if closer to regular flight routes or in more open territory.

SIGNALS AND CODES

Fire signals

Three fires is an internationally recognized distress signal. Ideally they should be placed in a triangle at equal distances apart, an arrangement which also makes them easier to feed with fuel, but if that is not possible any grouping serves, provided that the fires are clearly separated. However, if fuel is scarce, or if you are too badly injured or too weak from

REMEMBER:

Almost any signal repeated six times will serve as a distress signal. Depending on your location, this could be six fires, six columns of smoke, six loud whistles, six gunshots — even six flashes of light. If using noises or lights, wait one minute between each group of six signals.

hunger to maintain several fires, use only your campfire.

You can't keep signal fires going all the time but they should be prepared, covered to keep them dry, and maintained, ready to be lit to attract the attention of any passing aircraft. Build them with plenty of easily ignited tinder so that they will get going rapidly when lit. Birch bark makes an ideal tinder. Other tinder materials are described under *Fire* in *Camp Craft*.

Petrol can be used as a firelighter but DON'T just pour it on the fire. Use a piece of rag as a wick, soak it in petrol and lay it to the tinder. Don't light it straight away. Carry the fuel can off to a safe distance and wait a few seconds before lighting the wick. If a fire does not light first time pull the tinder apart, checking that there are no sparks or embers still burning, before adding extra petrol.

REMEMBER:

- Keep a stock of green boughs or supplies of oil or rubber close by to create smoke if needed.
- Among vegetation or close to trees, build an earth wall around each fire to contain it.
- There is no point building fires among trees where they cannot be seen, the canopy will block out the signal. Place them in a clearing.

If by a lake or river, build rafts to place your fires on and anchor or tether them securely in position. Arrow indicates direction of current.

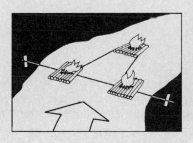

Torch trees

Small isolated trees make excellent fire signals. Build a fire between the boughs. Use plenty of dry twigs — old bird's nests make good fire starters. This fire will ignite the foliage and produce plenty of smoke. If a tree is dead start a fire at its base. It will burn for a long time leaving you free to attend to other signals.

NOTE: Do not risk starting a forest fire. Apart from the damage this will cause, your life will be in greater jeopardy.

Luminous cone fires

On a clear and open site make a tripod with a platform to support a fire. The platform keeps the tinder off damp ground, or you can store more firewood beneath it. Use a covering of evergreen boughs to keep the cone dry; they will burn brightly and give off a good smoke.

Cover the complete cone fire with bright coloured material, if available – a parachute would be ideal. This will not only keep the fire dry and ready to burn, but will itself be noticeable during the day. Whip it off when you ignite the fire – you may not attract attention the first time.

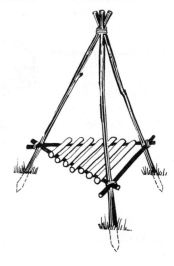

Keep these tripods well maintained, ensuring that wood is dry enough to light at a moment's notice and that the supply is not poached for other uses. Drive the pole ends into the ground to prevent tipping over in strong winds.

When alight the glow of this cone can be seen for miles. In an exposed location a smaller fire inside a conical tent or tepee of parachute fabric will also make a noticeable beacon. Ensure there is a smoke and heat outlet at the top of the tepee and keep the fire under control. If it is on a slope add fuel from the side or above the fire so that you do not excessively mask the firelight – though some flickering of movement before it may help to attract attention.

Use wreckage to help fire signalling

Stand a fire on a piece of metal from an aircraft or vehicle. It will keep kindling from damp ground, when hot will increase convection and make the fire burn brightly and, if polished, will act as a reflector intensifying the brightness. Three such fires become an immediately recognizable distress signal.

Smoke indicators

During daylight smoke is a good locator, so have plenty of smoke-producing material ready to put on your fires. Choose this material to give off a smoke that shows up well against the surroundings.

Light smoke will stand out against dark earth or dark green forest. Produce it with green grass, leaves, moss and ferns. Any wet material will produce a good smudge fire and damp mats and seat covers will smoulder for a long time. This will also keep flying insects at bay.

Dark smoke will show best against snow or desert sand. Use rubber or oil to produce it. If atmospheric conditions make the smoke hang in layers along the ground then build up the fire to increase its heat. Thermal currents will then take the smoke to a good height.

REMEMBER:

Smoke not only helps the pilot of a rescue aircraft find you, it also shows the surface wind direction. Make sure that smoke is downwind of the landing site and of any panel codes that you have laid so that it does not obscure them from above.

GROUND-TO-AIR SIGNALS

These letters are internationally recognized emergency signals. FILL is a useful mnemonic for remembering the main ones. The single bar: I is the most important and the easiest to make. A pilot will risk a great deal to answer such an emergency. Make them as large and as noticeable as possible using colour contrast or shadow. A recommended size is 10m long and 3m wide (40ft and 10ft) for each symbol, with 3m (10ft) between symbols.

Lay or make these panel codes out in the open, avoid steep gullies or ravines and do not make them on reverse slopes. Use the marker panels from your survival pouch (see *Essentials*), or if you do not have these — improvise. Lay out pieces of wreckage or dig out the signs as a shallow trench, banking up the earth so that it increases the depth of the shadow. Use rocks or boughs to accentuate it.

On snow, even tramping out the symbols will show clearly until the next snowfall.

Once contact has been made, a message dropped or signalled by the aircraft can be answered with A or Y (affirmative) and N (negative) signals, or morse code or body signals.

GROUND-TO-AIR CODE

I Serious injury – immediate casevac
(casualty evacuation) – (can also mean NEED DOCTOR)

II Need medical supplies

F Need food and water

N Negative (No)

A Affirmative (Yes) – (Y will also be understood)

LL All is well

X Unable to move on

→ Am moving on this way

K Indicate direction to proceed

⌐L Do not understand

□ Need compass and map

△ Think safe to land here
(Broken at angles, means
ATTEMPTING TAKE -OFF)

! Need radio/signal lamp/battery

⌐7 Aircraft badly damaged

Night signals

These signals will attract attention during daylight, even if you are asleep or injured. If you have a supply of petrol or other inflammable substances, you can make signals which will work at night. Dig or scrape an S O S (or any symbol) in the earth, sand or snow and, when the signal is needed, pour petrol into it and ignite it.

NOTE: You MUST destroy these signals if rescued. They will go on working long after you have gone.

MESSAGE SIGNALLING

You do not need to learn a complicated system of semaphore. The international morse code can be transmitted by flashing lights on and off, by a simple heliograph, by waving a flag or a shirt tied to a stick or using sound.

NOTE: Don't rely upon your memory — carry a copy of the code on your person. Even if you are a regular user and know it backwards others may need it who do not.

There is a procedure to follow when sending and receiving messages. Learn the special codes to make the operation easier.

Heliograph

Use the sun and a reflector to flash light signals. Any shiny object will serve — polish a tin lid, glasses, a piece of foil — though a hand-mirror is best. Sustained flashes are dashes and quick ones dots. If you do not know morse code, even random flashes should attract attention. At least learn the code for S O S.

A flash can be seen at a great distance and even when you do not have a specific contact to aim for may attract someone's attention. It's worth trying, since it requires little energy. Sweep the horizon during the day. If a plane approaches closely make intermittent flashes or you may dazzle the pilot. Once you are certain you have been seen, STOP signalling.

SINGLE-SIDED REFLECTOR
With an improvised reflector pick up the sunlight to get an image on the ground or some other surface and lead it in the direction of the aircraft or other potential contact.

USING HELIOGRAPH

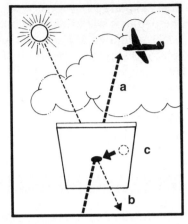

If you have a double-sided reflector and can punch a hole in it you will have something close to a standard issue heliograph.

Sight the person, plane, ship, etc., which you wish to contact through the hole in the heliograph (a) in the general direction of the sun, so that the sun will shine through the hole (b). You will see a spot of light on your face (c).

Angle the mirror so that the dot of light on your face 'disappears' back through the hole in the mirror — still sighting your contact.

If the sun is at such an angle that this manoeuvre does not work bring the mirror close to your eyes and a hand lined up between you and the contact. Angle the mirror to flash on to your hand, then move the hand away.

NOTE: Practise this form of signalling, but unless you are in a survival situation, do NOT signal to aircraft or 'transmit' messages which could cause alarm or danger to others.

Rag signals

Tie a flag or a piece of brightly coloured clothing to a pole and move it left for dashes and right for dots. Exaggerate each movement with a figure-of-eight movement.

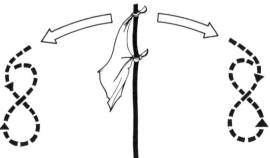

For a 'dot' swing to the right and make a figure-of-eight.

For a 'dash' swing to the left and make a figure-of-eight.

This simple signing may work without figure-of-eight movements at closer range. Keep 'dash' pauses on the left, slightly longer than 'dot' movements to the right.

INFO.

MORSE CODE

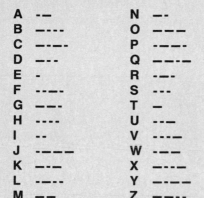

A	-·-	N	--·	1	·----	
B	-···	O	---	2	··---	
C	-·-·	P	·--·	3	···--	
D	-··	Q	--·-	4	····-	
E	·	R	·-·	5	·····	
F	··-·	S	···	6	-····	
G	--·	T	-	7	--···	
H	····	U	··-	8	---··	
I	··	V	···-	9	----·	
J	·---	W	·--	0	-----	
K	-·-	X	-··-			
L	·-··	Y	-·--			
M	--	Z	--··			

SENDING SIGNALS

AAAAA* etc – Call sign. *I have a message*
AAA* – End of sentence. *More follows*
Pause – End of word. *More follows*
EEEEE* etc – Error. *Start from last correct word*
AR – End of message

RECEIVING SIGNALS

TTTTT* etc I am receiving you
K – I am ready. *Start message*
T – Word received
IMI* – Repeat sign. *I do not understand*
R – Message received

* Send as one word. No pauses

USEFUL WORDS

S O S	···---···
SEND	···-·|·-·|--·
DOCTOR	-··-|---|-·-·-|·-|---|·-·
HELP	····-|·|·-··|·--·
INJURY	··-|-·-|·---|··-|-·--|·-·-
TRAPPED	-|·-·-|·-|·--·|·--·-|·|-··
LOST	·-··|---|···|-
WATER	·--|·-|-|·|·-·

BODY SIGNALS

This series of signals will be understood by airmen and can be used to signal to them. Note the changes from frontal to sideways positions and the use of leg and body posture as well as hand movements. Use a cloth in the hand to emphasize the YES and NO signals. Make all signals in a clear and exaggerated manner.

Pick us up **Need mechanical help** **Land here**

All is well **Can proceed shortly** **Have radio**

Do NOT attempt to land here **Need medical assistance** **Use drop message**

Response to body signals

To acknowledge messages received from the ground the pilot of an aircraft will perform one of these manoeuvres:

Message received and understood:
    In daylight – flying the plane and tipping the wings in a rocking movement side to side
    At night – flashing green lights

Message received but NOT understood:
    In daylight – flying the plane in a right-handed circle
    At night – flashing red lights

MOUNTAIN RESCUE CODE

These sound, light and pyrotechnic codes are recognized internationally by mountain rescue services:

Message: S O S
    Flare signal – Red
    Sound signal – 3 short blasts, 3 long, 3 short
        Repeat after 1 minute interval
    Light signal – 3 short flashes, 3 long, 3 short
        Repeat after 1 minute interval

Message: HELP NEEDED
    Flare signal – Red
    Sound signal – 6 blasts in quick succession
        Repeat after 1 minute interval
    Light signal – 6 flashes in quick succession
        Repeat after 1 minute interval

Message: MESSAGE UNDERSTOOD
    Flare signal – White
    Sound signal – 3 blasts in quick succession
        Repeat after 1 minute interval
    Light signal – 3 flashes in quick succession
        Repeat after 1 minute interval

Message: RETURN TO BASE
    Flare signal – Green
    Sound signal – Prolonged succession of blasts
    Light signal – Prolonged succession of flashes

Flares

Any flare will be investigated during a search, regardless of colour, but choose one best fitted to the location.

- In closely-wooded country green does not stand out but red does.

- Over snow white merges — green and red are best.

Familiarize yourself with the types of flare. Make sure you understand the instructions, for some flares eject a white-hot ball of magnesium that will burn a hole in anything it hits — your chest or dinghy if they are misdirected.

Types of flare

Some flares are hand-held and reversible. One end produces smoke for daytime use, the other a flare for use at night. The higher these are held the easier they arc to see. Flares and rockets which are fired into the air will be visible for a greater distance. One type reaches a height of 90m (300ft) where a parachute opens holding the flare suspended for several minutes. Other rockets produce a loud bang and colour balls.

Keep flares dry and away from naked flames and heat sources. Ensure that safety pins are in position and will not accidentally drop out, but also check that they are not bent over in such a way that they could not be quickly removed when necessary.

Handling flares

Hand-held flares are cylindrical tubes with a cap at each end. The top cap is often embossed with a letter or pattern so that it can be identified by touch in the dark. Remove it first. Then remove the base cap to expose a short string and a safety pin, or other safety device. Point the flare upwards and away from you and anyone else in case you accidentally fire it. Remove the pin, or turn to the fire position. Hold the flare at arm's length, at shoulder height, pointing directly upwards. Sharply pull the firing string vertically downwards. Brace yourself as you do so for there will be a kickback. Some flares and maroons have a spring mechanism trigger like that of a mousetrap.

Very pistols fire various cartridges. To fire them load the pistol, point it skywards, cock the hammer and then squeeze the trigger.

Mini-flares are more usual equipment today, lighter than Very pistols but as effective (see *Survival*

> ### DANGER
>
> Hand-held flares get hot. When they burn down do not drop them into the bottom of a boat, where they could start a fire, or burn straight through an inflatable.

kit in *Essentials*). They require handling with the same care. To use, screw a flare of the selected colour into the end of the discharger, aim skyward, pull back striker — FIRE!

INFORMATION SIGNALS

These are signals to leave behind if you leave the scene of the crash or abandon camp.

Make a large arrow shape to indicate the direction in which you have set off which will be visible from the air and other direction markers which can be interpreted at ground level.

Signs on the ground will draw attention to your presence or past presence and the direction markers will help rescuers to follow your trail. Continue to make them, not only for people to follow but to establish your own route if you wish to retrace it and as a guide if you lose your sense of direction and start going back on your trail.

At camp leave written messages in containers to detail your plans. Hang them from tripods or trees and draw attention to them with markers.

Direction markers could include rocks or debris placed in arrow shape (a), stick left in crooked support, top in direction followed (b), grasses tied in an overhand knot with end hanging in direction followed (c), forked branches laid with fork pointing in direction followed (d), small rocks set upon larger rocks, with small rock beside (e), indicating a turn or arrow- or arrowhead-shape notches cut in tree trunks (f).

A cross of sticks or stones (g), means 'Not this way.'

Signal danger or emergency with three rocks, sticks or clumps of grass, prominently displayed (h).

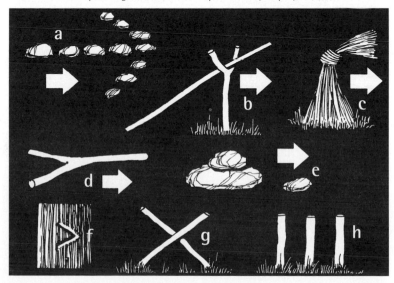

SEARCH

A wareness of search procedures will show how important it is for any expedition or trip to register its route plans and for survivors to stay as close as possible to that course, to set clear signals to draw attention to their location and to mark any camp they have abandoned (leaving information about their subsequent plans).

A search will start from the last known location and sweep on the proposed route. An assessment will be made of probable strategy adopted, given the terrain and the weather conditions. In mountain areas, for instance, it is likely that strong winds would make the survival party use the lee sides of ridges and descend from high ground. If no trace is found of them on the expected route these are the areas in which the search will be concentrated.

The effect of contour will be considered: by studying the ground the search party may assume that survivors were forced off route by the lay of the land. To make the searchers' job easier, make a cairn of rocks or other noticeable construction on prominent ground where it cannot fail to be noticed and leave a message there in a waterproof bag or in the pocket of a colourful piece of clothing. Give information on your intentions and on the state of your party.

If your route has been checked and the obvious refuge places in the locality searched, the rescuers will extend the search to cover the whole area of your disappearance. Ideally this will be done from the air but severe weather which creates bad flying conditions and poor visibility may mean it has to be done on foot, even if planes are available.

The number of searchers and the type of terrain will dictate the search pattern best suited to the situation.

SEARCH PATTERNS

The first search will be made along the route you were supposed to have taken.

BASE LINE

Base line, or box search, is carried out when there has been a high wind or bad weather conditions on your known route (a). Searchers should deduce that you may have veered from the route to the leeside of a slope for shelter.

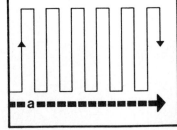

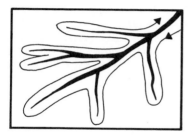

WATERCOURSE
Watercourse search takes in all the tributaries, using the main stream as base-line. This is undertaken when your last known position was on or near a river.

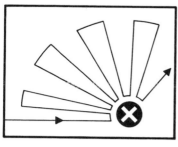

FAN
Fan search is used when your last known position (x) is fairly certain but it is impossible to deduce the direction you may have taken.

Aerial search

Search patterns from the air cover both sides of the intended flight path of missing aircraft or your known route.

If weather conditions are favourable a night search can be made, for lights will be clearly visible and the search can be made from a greater height so that a wider area can be covered in each sweep. If this does not produce results the area will still be rechecked by daylight.

If you are signalling to an aircraft and it turns away — keep watching. It may be following one of those recognized search patterns and you will be able to anticipate critical moments for signalling.

CREEPING LINE
Creeping line search, beginning in a corner of the search area, is particularly useful when only a single aircraft is available. It follows parallels which should be towards and away from the sun for a land search so that any reflection from a missing aircraft or other wreckage and signals will be more easily seen.

521

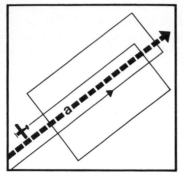

TRACK CRAWL

The primary search pattern, or track crawl search, parallels both sides of a missing aircraft's expected flight path (a), or travelling known land route. After flying for one hour, turn around and fly the reverse pattern.

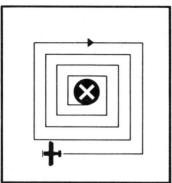

SQUARE SEARCH

Square search is useful when a comparatively small area is to be covered. Search starts in the last known location (x) and works outwards. If unsuccessful fly over last known location and start search in other direction. This ensures both sides are covered.

CONTOUR SEARCH

Contour search allows mountains and valleys to be searched with maximum thoroughness. Steep valleys should be searched several times by flying along them.

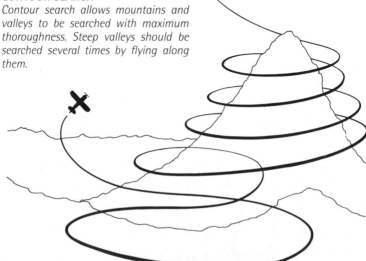

Combined searches

At sea a combined sea-and-air search is desirable. If the aircraft locates survivors the ships can pick them up. The ship can also act as a datum point for all aircraft. Rescue aircraft are equipped with supplies to drop to survivors to help them as they await pick-up by a surface vessel.

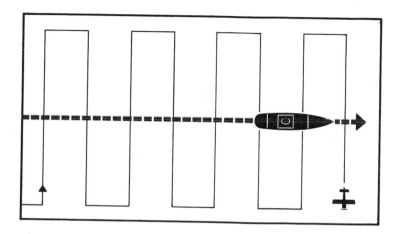

HELICOPTER RESCUE

While aeroplanes are used for the search, helicopters are used in most countries to carry out the actual rescue, especially on land. Where possible the 'copter will make a landing to take on survivors and fly them out. It may be possible for the pilot to find a convenient landing site nearby to which survivors can make their way, but it will be easier for the survivors to check out suitability at ground level and to create a site if necessary.

The helicopter will require an obstruction-free approach and exit path, both INTO the prevailing winds. The ground should be level (the slope should not exceed seven degrees — a gradient of 1 in 10). The touch down surface should be firm and free of loose materials — remove leaves, twigs, everything. There must be no holes, tree stumps or rocks which could cause damage to the aircraft.

Selecting a landing site

Look for a natural clearing. In close country a river bank on a large bend is often the best natural landing place (LP).

Alternatively climb a spur and select a level piece of ground free of large trees. If you need to, cut down trees to clear more space. The trees will fall down the spur without blocking the area and a clear approach and exit path can be obtained across the spur. Do not attempt cutting a landing place on flat ground; it will take forever to create a clear approach and exit.

LANDING PLACE

PREPARING SITE
A level cleared area is needed at least 26m (80ft) in diameter. A further 5m (15ft) is needed all around, cleared to a height of 60cm (2ft). There should be a clear approach path into the prevailing wind with no obstructions within an angle of 15 degrees of the central landing pad.

Mark the touchdown point with an H. You can make it from inlaid rocks (keeping the surface smooth), clothing securely anchored, or panel markers. On snow, trample it down firmly to prevent it swirling and, in dry areas, water the surface to keep the dust down.

READY-MADE PAD
If a spur, mound or area of raised ground is nearby, this will be easier to clear and will provide an easy approach and exit across the spur if the wind direction is satisfactory.

MOUNTAINOUS TERRAIN
The payload of the helicopter is cut drastically with increased altitude so, if possible, make the landing site below 1830m (5000ft).

In mountains updraughts and downdraughts of air can be considerable according to the pattern of the land and its relationship to prevailing winds. Select a site that gives maximum lift in the direction in which the helicopter will take off.

Soft wet snow will cling to the helicopter and hamper its take off. Try to compact the landing surface as much as possible. Powdery snow will swirl under the rotors' downwash and restrict the pilot's vision. Stamp this down, too.

Non-landing rescue

In an emergency helicopters will take considerable risks to rescue survivors. They may hover with one skid on a rock to make embarkation possible — but whenever it can be done create a proper landing place and minimize risks.

Most helicopters are equipped with a winch. If a landing place is out of the question you can be lifted from the ground while the helicopter hovers. All that is needed is an opening or clearing through which to extricate you.

Wind indication

It is important to indicate the direction and strength of the wind at the landing place so that the pilot can select the best approach, and keep the aircraft stable while carrying out the rescue. Smoke is an ideal indicator, but do not place it so that it obscures the touchdown area.

If a fire is not practical make a T sign from contrasting material and place it at the downwind edge of the landing place with the horizontal bar of the T placed upwind.

If there is nothing to make a T shape from, a person standing on the far downwind side of the landing place with their arms outstretched and with their back to the wind can form a living symbol for the pilot. Don't make this signal till you have to — and then only in the correct position. It is very similar to another body signal, which means 'need help'.

Night rescue

The helicopter will itself have powerful lights by which the landing or lift off of survivors can take place but you will need lights to bring the pilot in to the landing place. Flares and fires will give an indication of your position once the helicopter is within range.

If you are illuminating from the ground with torches, vehicle headlights or other beams shine them skyward at first to attract attention but, once the pilot has seen you, keep the beams low so that they do NOT dazzle the pilot, and shine them on to the touchdown or winching area.

Sea rescue

If survivors are being winched up from a ship it will help the pilot to place the deck at an angle of approximately 40 degrees to the right of the eye of the wind. If you can control the vessel give a wind speed over the deck of about 29kph (18mph).

HELICOPTER PRECAUTIONS ON LANDING

– When a helicopter touches down at the LP the rotors will be turning. The approach to the aircraft is therefore particularly important both for your own safety and that of the helicopter.

– NEVER approach from the rear. This is a blind spot for the crew and the tail rotor is unprotected. On sloping ground always approach up the slope – bringing you up below the blades.

– NEVER approach down a slope close to the helicopter. You could be at risk from the blades.

– Make sure that you are not carrying anything which could foul the main rotor. If carrying a radio, stow the aerial.

– Keep all sharp objects away from the body panels of the helicopter. They are of light gauge alloy and easily damaged.

– Sit in the seat allocated to you by the crewman, fasten the seat belt and keep fastened until told otherwise.

– Do not attempt to alight until the engine has been shut down after you have landed – even then, wait for directions.

Winching techniques
A double lift is the usual method but a single lift is sometimes used.

Double lift: With a double lift a crewman is lowered on the winch with another strop for the survivor. During the lift the crewman supports the survivor with his legs, gripping with them around the midsection, and supports the head with his hands. After the strop has been put in place and tightened keep arms down by the sides and do not lift them – just lie back and enjoy it!

Single lift: With a single lift you fit yourself into the strop. When you have placed it under your armpits and securely tightened the grommet give the 'thumbs up' sign. Once acknowledged make no further signals until aboard the chopper – if you raise your arms you risk slipping out of the strop!

When you reach the cabin doorway, let the winchman turn you around and bring you aboard. Do EXACTLY as he directs. Once safely aboard you will be shown where to sit. Do so and tighten your seat belt, or expect to be fastened in some other way.

Wet winching

Both the previous methods can be used on water, employing the same basic techniques.

If you are on a raft disconnect yourself from the lifeline. Fold down a dinghy canopy and lower any sails or other cover you have erected. Stream the sea anchor. These actions will assist the pilot in trapping the raft under the rotor downwash. Stay in the dinghy or aboard the raft until winched out.

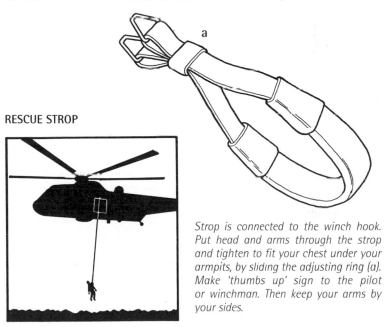

RESCUE STROP

Strop is connected to the winch hook. Put head and arms through the strop and tighten to fit your chest under your armpits, by sliding the adjusting ring (a). Make 'thumbs up' sign to the pilot or winchman. Then keep your arms by your sides.

WARNING

All aircraft build up a considerable charge of static electricity. This is discharged to the earth or water when the aircraft, or the cable from it, touches the ground. Always allow the winch sling or the cable to touch down before you approach it, otherwise you will receive a substantial electric shock.

-11-
DISASTERS

Accidents or isolation are not the only causes of a survival situation. There are many natural and man-made forces which can produce disasters demanding the same survival skills. Drought, fire, earthquake and flood, for instance, can strike both in the remote survival camp and at home. The survivor should know the techniques for dealing with a forest fire but it is just as important to know how to escape from a burning building or even the site of a bomb explosion.

Home front faces the problems of coping with survival on your own doorstep if the services and supplies on which we normally depend are cut off.

DROUGHT

Drought, caused by long periods of dry weather or insufficient rainfall, creates desert in areas where it is a permanent condition. Elsewhere, drought may be a regular seasonal feature for part of the year — and predictable year after year. Where it is balanced by a wet season, water can be stored to last through the dry months. The underground stone-cut or concrete-built cisterns of ancient and modern Mediterranean civilizations collect the rainfall of the wet season for the long dry summer.

In temperate regions, if rainfall drops far below the normal, periodic drought may be produced with vegetation unable to obtain water to compensate for what it loses to the air. In cases where the dry spell may not be so obvious but there is still insufficient moisture to provide that needed by the plants, a condition known as 'invisible drought' occurs. The death of vegetation causes deprivation right through the food chains that are based upon it. If the drought becomes severe, dead and dying animals may even pollute the water supplies that still remain.

Fire risk

The corpses of dead animals should be buried in deep graves. Dry ground can be very hard, but burying is the best way to remove these possible sources of infection. They could be burned, but since drought leaves everything tinder dry, the risk of fire spreading is considerable and it could easily get out of hand. Each year fires rage in southern France, California and Australia and, without water to check the flames, they spread rapidly. If you must have a fire, dig down to bare earth and keep the fire small and attended at all times.

Hygiene

In houses, lack of water for washing and sanitation can bring the risk of infection. If the water level in a water closet no longer seals the S-bend, disease may spread from the sewers and personal hygiene may suffer from lack of washing. Do not use the WC but leave sufficient water in the bowl to form a barrier. Make an outdoor latrine to use instead (see *Hygiene* in *Camp Craft*).

Sweating will help to keep pores open and free of dirt, but, even when you need all available water for drinking, try to clean hands after defecation and before preparing food.

Store and conserve water

If a monsoon does not start at the expected time, or a hot dry summer produces a parching of the earth, take precautions by storing as much water as possible and using it wisely. Keep it covered and shaded to avoid evaporation.

Dig a pit for a storage cistern in a shady spot, avoiding tree roots. Line it with a polythene sheet or with cement if available (but don't fill it up until the cement has had a chance to thoroughly dry). If you live in a clay area, dig a pit and line it with clay. If you build the concrete or clay up into a partial dome, it will help to keep the contents cool and leave a smaller opening to keep covered.

NEVER waste water. Water used for cooking can later be used for washing. Boil all drinking water. If a well runs dry you may gain more water by digging deeper, but the further you dig, the further you deplete the water stored in the earth.

In areas with cold nights the drop in temperature may condense the moisture in the air. Use the techniques to catch it described for desert survival (see *Essentials* and *Climate and Terrain*).

High ground will show greater variation between day and night temperatures

INFO.

If drought persists, especially over more than a year, desert conditions may begin to develop and evacuation may be the only solution, if water supplies cannot be brought in.

and will offer better chance of dew to collect in the early morning. It may also offer the advantage of cool breezes.

Drought can strike anywhere. Even in areas of heavy rainfall, such as Assam, there has been drought when the monsoon has failed.

WARNING

- In conditions of severe drought be especially careful of contamination of water supplies. Disease from dead animals may be rampant. However thirsty you are, boil all water before drinking.

- Flies may be a serious problem at first — ensure that all foodstuffs are covered. Protect from dust, which may become a hazard as top soil is blown away.

- When nature is disturbed in this way, animals act abnormally. Crazed by thirst, normally docile creatures may attack you.

FIRE

Fire requires heat, fuel and oxygen and produces smoke, heat and toxic gases. It may spread by heating its surroundings through direct contact (conduction), through rising gas and smoke (convection) or through heat rays (radiation). Convection is usually the most serious of these forms of heat transfer.

The best protection from fire is prevention. Carelessness with lighted cigarettes and burning matches is the cause of many fires. The sun shining through an abandoned bottle or a piece of broken glass can start a blaze in a dry season.

Fire can strike anywhere — at any time. Precautions should always be taken. Vehicles and buildings SHOULD ALWAYS be equipped with fire extinguishers. Managed forestry plantations are divided by broad paths as fire breaks. Equipment for beating out flames should be found in numerous places. YOU should know how to use it.

FOREST FIRES

If you are present where a fire starts (or where a camp fire accidentally spreads) in woodland, or on heath or grassland, your first action should be to SMOTHER IT.

The first sign of an approaching forest fire will be the smell of smoke. Then you will probably hear the fire before you see flames. You may notice unusual animal behaviour before you realize the cause.

Escape route
If caught in an area where fire is raging, and when it is far too late to put it out yourself, do NOT immediately flee — unless the fire is so close that there is no choice.

Although you may feel that clothing hampers your movement, do NOT discard it for it will shield you from the full force of radiated heat.

Smoke will indicate the direction of the wind — the fire will be travelling fastest in that direction. If the wind is blowing away from you, towards the fire move INTO the wind. Head for any natural fire break — such as where there is a swathe through the trees, where the flames should be stopped. A river is the best break — even if the flames can leap it you will be reasonably safe in the water. In forestry plantations look for the roadways and firebreaks.

Do NOT run wildly. Choose your escape route. Check the surrounding terrain and the wind direction to assess the possible spread of the fire.

If the wind is blowing towards you the fire is likely to travel more quickly — and the flames can leap a larger gap. Fire travels faster uphill so do NOT make for high ground. Try to go around the fire if possible — but some forest fires burn on a front several kilometres wide. If you can neither skirt or outdistance the blaze take refuge in a large clearing, deep ravine, watercourse or gulley.

Into the fire

Sometimes the best escape route may be to run THROUGH the flames. This is impossible if they are very intense and the area covered by the actual fire is great. In a large clearing or on heathland, however, it may be possible to run through less dense fire to refuge on the already burned-out land. Cover as much exposed skin as you can and if you have water available tip some over you to damp down clothing, hair and any flesh you have not been able to cover. Dampen a piece of cloth to cover your nose and mouth.

Thick vegetation will burn fiercely and slow you down — so choose the spot for your breakthrough with care. Make your mind up, then do not delay. Take a deep breath. Cover your nose and mouth to keep out smoke and RUN.

FIGHTING A FOREST FIRE

In areas where there are forestry plantations you should see racks of fire-beating equipment at intervals along the main routes. This consists of bundles of twigs (usually birch), tied in a broom, and spade-shaped beaters with rubber blades. They can be effective in putting out the beginnings of a blaze.

Despite the name, do NOT beat rapidly with them — that will only help to fan the flames and spread sparks. The object is to SMOTHER the fire by bringing the beater down over the flames to extinguish them. The flat blades are particularly effective in smothering a fire beginning among leaves and undergrowth.

If no equipment is available use a coat or blanket to smother the fire and to cut off oxygen from the flames — or use a leafy branch to beat it out.

STAY IN A VEHICLE

If caught in a forest fire in a vehicle, stay inside and keep the windows tightly shut. Turn off the ventilation system. The car will give you some protection from radiant heat. Drive away from the fire if you can but, if immobilized, stay put.

People have survived by staying in a vehicle until the glass began to melt, by which time the fire had moved beyond them. If they had panicked and run into the fire they would have died.

There is a danger of a petrol tank exploding but your chances are much greater than outside, if the fire is intense around the vehicle.

Going to earth

If there is no natural break or gully in which to shelter and the fire is too deep to think of running through it, you may have to seek the protection of the earth itself.

People have survived fierce fires by digging themselves in and covering themselves with earth, allowing the fire to burn over the top of them. The risk is considerable, not just from heat but from suffocation: fire burns up oxygen.

Scrape as much of a hollow as you can, throwing the earth on to a coat or cloth if you have one, then pull the cloth over you with its earth covering. Cup your hands over your mouth and nose and breath through them. This won't increase the amount of oxygen, but it will cool down and filter the very hot air and sparks, which can damage the respiratory system. Try to hold your breath as the fire passes over.

Fight fire with fire

It may be possible to use fire itself to create protection, if there is no way of getting out of the path of the fire or of going through it — but it is still some distance away.

The technique is to burn a patch of ground before the main fire reaches it. With nothing left to ignite, the flames cannot advance, giving you a place of refuge. The main fire must be sufficiently far away for your fire to burn a space it cannot jump before it arrives.

Light your own fire along as wide a line as possible — at least 10m (30ft) wide, but 100m (300ft) would be better. It will burn in the same direction as the main fire, creating a break which you can move into. Make sure you determine the wind direction correctly.

WARNING

Winds may be swirling and fires create their own draughts, so you may still have to make a dash through your own flames. The main fire must be far enough away for your own fire to burn and pass. Do NOT underestimate the speed at which flames travel — they may be approaching faster than you can run. Do NOT light another fire unless you are desperate and fairly certain of the outcome.

BURNING BUILDINGS

Smoke will usually be the first indication of fire. If the fire is still small, attempt to extinguish by covering with a blanket or thick curtain (to deprive the flames of oxygen), or using sand, water or fire extinguisher as available and appropriate.

Electrical fires

If there is any possibility of a fire being caused by an electrical fault, do NOT use water until the power has been turned off, preferably at the mains. Turn off gas at the mains too. If television sets or computer VDUs catch fire do NOT use water on them. Even after being disconnected, there is sufficient residual electrical charge to give you a shock (even to kill you) and the cold water may make the tube explode. Smother them and approach from behind because of the risk of the tube exploding.

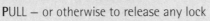

FIRE EXTINGUISHER

PULL – or otherwise to release any lock
AIM – at the base of the fire
SQUEEZE – or press the handle/trigger
SWEEP – from side to side

Check to see what kind of extinguisher you have. Some are designed for small, simple fires and contain water – they are NOT suitable for oil or electrical fires. Others are designed for oil, grease, paint or solvent fires (a chip pan or petrol spillage, for instance). A third type is for electrical fires or those where live cables are exposed. A multipurpose dry-chemical type extinguisher can be used on most kinds of fire.
KNOW HOW TO USE YOUR EXTINGUISHER!

Evacuation

If the fire is already too big to fight with the resources available, evacuate the building. Turn off power at the mains. Close all reachable doors and windows. Try to contain the fire while evacuation is completed and to prevent the fire's spread before fire-fighting services or rescuers arrive.

Fire travels upwards faster than downwards — though a collapsing floor or wall will carry the flames to a lower level. Staircases, lift-wells and ventilation shafts are particularly dangerous.

NEVER use a lift during a fire. If you need to move down a building, use a smoke-free staircase.

Before opening any doors look for smoke around their edges and check for heat. Metal doorknobs are a good test. If they feel warm do NOT open the door — use the back of your hand for the test. Grasping the knob could cause a burn. A stout door can keep back flames for 30 minutes or more (but do not rely on this with thin-panelled modern doors — unless they are fire-doors).

INFO.

If there is no alternative to going into a burning room: brace your foot against the door and open it only a crack — this will help to stop it being forced wide open by the pressure of hot air and gases inside. Crouch low to enter, opening the door as little as possible. This will expose you to less smoke and heat and give less chance for the fire to pass through the gap. Close the door behind you to delay the fire's spread.

Waiting for rescue

If you find yourself isolated and unable to get to safety, go to a room as far from the fire as possible (but NOT on a higher level unless you are certain that rescuers with long-ladders or other equipment are very close). If there is a choice, pick a room with the softest ground outside, no railings below or where there are bedclothes or curtains which you can knot into a rope. Lawns, flowerbeds, even gravel paths are softer than cobbles, concrete or paving. If you are eventually forced to drop down on to hard concrete a sloping surface will be likely to do you less damage.

Close the door and fill any gaps around it with curtains, mats or other thick material, which will take time to catch alight. Wet them if you can. If the alarm has not already been given try to attract attention through the window.

To break the window, use a piece of furniture. You could kick it out, but do not bring your foot back quickly – you will have to negotiate broken glass. If you have to use your hand wrap it first and punch. Alternatively, when protected by a thick jacket, an elbow may be effective.

Preparing to 'jump'

If no rescue is forthcoming do NOT jump – drop. Tie sheets, blankets, mats, loose covers and other strong material together to make a rope – even if it does not reach the ground it will reduce the distance you will have to fall. Tie them with reef knots and test that each is firm by pulling. Push a heavy piece of furniture over to the window and secure one end of your rope to it, or tie your rope to heating pipes – or smash the window and tie on to a thick part of the frame. If the rope is not long enough drop cushions, pillows, a mattress – anything which will soften your landing, below the window.

If there is nothing to use as a rope, lower yourself out of the window and hang from the sill. If there is no sill hang from the bottom of the window frame.

INFO.

Do NOT jump out – unless there is a party of firemen waiting to catch you in a blanket. Where there is something to break your fall make use of it, do not try to drop clear. A car roof makes a good cushion to drop on for it will give slightly to your weight.

BEWARE: Trees may break your fall, but there is a risk of your being impaled on the branches.

Dropping from a height

Having taken every recommended measure to reduce the height of your fall, think of protecting your head – a motor-cycle crash helmet is ideal but a jersey or towel wrapped round your head like a turban will help.

When you are as low as possible, and ready to drop, push yourself away from the building with the side of one foot and, as you let go, turn away from the wall and bend the knees. Leave the arms up to protect the sides of the head.

As you land bend the knees more and roll over on to one side, carrying the roll on to your back (still protecting your head and with your legs in the air). This helps spread the impact over a larger area and increases your chances.

Falling onto a slope

Face down the slope as you drop, with legs together, with the knees slightly bent. Bring the head down on to the chest and the elbows tightly into the sides, the hands protecting the head. Land on flat feet, allowing the knees to bend fully, rolling forward in a tight somersault. It is the method that parachutists use.

WAIT UNTIL THE VERY LAST CHANCE OF RESCUE BEFORE RISKING A DROP GREATER THAN 4M (14FT).

ESCAPING THROUGH FIRE

- If forced to travel through flames to reach safety, cover yourself (including your head) in a blanket, curtain or overcoat — wet it if you can — then take a deep breath and go.

- If your clothes catch alight do NOT stay on your feet when out of the fire. The flames and smoke will travel up your body, over your face and into your lungs.

- Do NOT run — this will only fan the flames.

- Roll on the ground and try to wrap yourself in something that will smother the flames — a mat, blanket or overcoat.

- If someone else comes running out of a fire with their clothes alight, push them to the ground and use the same methods of denying the flames oxygen. Do NOT hug them to you or your clothes may catch fire.

VEHICLE FIRES

The greatest danger with cars is the risk of the fuel tank being ignited — it could explode like a bomb, scattering burning petroleum everywhere. The aim is to control the fire before it can reach the tank. Everything has a flash point and a fuel tank is more at risk than most things. Usually a fuel line (if not armoured) will catch fire first, acting as a fuse which eventually ignites the tank.

In a garage

If a car catches fire in a confined space, such as a garage, smoke and toxic fumes will soon build up. Try to put the fire out first — but if that is not practicable remove the car from the building, before it further endangers life and property.

Do NOT get into the car. You can do everything from outside including steering. If possible, push or pull the car out. If your car has a button starter, select a low gear or reverse and use the starter to bounce the car out. With conventional ignition, turn the key in short bursts. BE PREPARED. The car will jerk forward violently.

FIRE EXTINGUISHER

KEEP IT WHERE YOU CAN REACH IT!
DON'T keep your fire extinguisher in the boot/trunk — keep it in the passenger compartment where you can get at it immediately. Any impact could distort the boot lid and prevent you opening it.

In a crashed car: doors may jam. If it catches fire get through any window or kick the windscreen out.

If the fire is inside the car: use the extinguisher or smother it with a rug or coat. Synthetic materials used in upholstery in many cars burn rapidly and give off thick smoke and toxic gases. These will persist even when the flames are out so get out into the air as soon as possible.

If the fire is also on the outside: amid spilt fuel for example — keep the windows shut and drive out of the danger zone, abandoning the car as soon as it is safe to do so.

FIRES IN THE AIR

Aeroplanes are equipped with automatic extinguishers for engine fires and hand-held extinguishers in the cabin. Action should be taken immediately. On civil airlines summon a steward or air hostess immediately you suspect fire — they know where equipment is and how to use it. Avoid creating panic in other passengers. If you see smouldering or flames, smother with an airline blanket or clothing.

The main fire dangers are: before take-off when there is volatile fuel and vapour around the plane and especially when landing under difficult circumstances when fuel tanks could be ruptured and electrical or friction sparks ignite aviation spirit. Every safety precaution is taken to ensure that fire is not a hazard. You can help. Do NOT smoke, when told not to smoke. Do NOT smoke and doze at the same time.

CHEMICAL AND BIOLOGICAL WARFARE

Terrorism is not new. The destruction of property, murder, threats, fear and panic have long been the tools of those who believe that violence is a means of achieving political and criminal goals. What makes modern terrorists distinct from their historical predecessors is the technology at their disposal and the greater range of opportunities for terrorism which modern life provides.

The global nature of media coverage and the publicity it can give has also fuelled the use of terrorism. There is no doubt, also, that some nations finance and support the activities of terrorists in other countries with which they have political difference.

More value is now placed on the lives of ordinary people, the more innocent the victim, the better for terrorism. The reality is that we are ALL potential targets and that we are ALL vunerable.

Certain countries of the world pose a real threat by producing vast amounts of lethal bacteria and chemicals. These are relatively easy to disperse and threaten large areas of the globe.

Biological agents fall into two groups, pathogens (germs) and toxins. Pathogens are living micro organisms that cause lethal incapacitating diseases like anthrax. Toxins are poisons that are lethal to humans, affecting the nervous system, and causing cell death.

Germs must be inhaled, enter through a break in the skin, or through the digestive tract. They do not react immediately as they must multiply inside the body and overcome the body's defences. This incubation period varies from hours to months depending on the germ. Biological agents are hard to detect, none of our physical senses can detect them. Often the first signs are symptoms of the victims exposed to the agent, and sick-looking plants and animals.

TOXINS

Toxins occur naturally in plants and animals, but can be manufactured and used as weapons which are a thousand times more lethal. Toxins produce a similar effect to chemicals but do not respond to the same treatment. Unlike germs they can penetrate unbroken skin, and their symptoms appear immediately. These include; paralysis, convulsions, fever, blisters/rashes, shock and death.

Protection

If you suspect the presence of biological agents, put something around the mouth and nose to prevent inhalation. It is unlikely that you have a mask so improvise by wrapping a damp cloth around the face. Cover all exposed parts and leave the area as soon as possible. Button/zip-up all clothing. Tuck trousers into socks, and wear gloves. When out of the danger area, wash thoroughly with soap and water. Clean teeth, hair and fingernails. Wash all clothing and equipment in hot soapy water.

ANTHRAX

Anthrax is a disease carried by animals and still kills many humans annually. The disease is transmitted from dead animals in areas like South America, Southern Europe and the Middle and Far East. Signs on the dead carcass include bloating, incomplete rigor mortis, dark coloured blood oozing from nostrils and anus. Avoid all contact and wash thoroughly if accidental contact is made. Seek professional advice soonest. Antibiotics will help, and there is a serum available from the treatment of anthrax.

The early signs of the disease are pustules with dark centres. Anthrax is also produced as a biological weapon.

CHEMICALS

Chemical agents take the form of liquids, gas and aerosols. They may affect breathing, the nervous system or the blood.

Chemical agents are difficult to detect so watch for suspicious signs in your companions. Difficulty in breathing, coughing, itching and tears are the most obvious ones. The landscape will look wasted, with vegetation being discoloured and limp, and maybe dead animals and insects scattered around. Some agents are odourless and others have a distinctive smell. The smell of almonds may indicate a blood agent, newly cut grass a choking agent.

Protection

The whole body must be covered with suitable clothing that will prevent the chemicals penetrating. Waterproof outer garments, goggles and mask are essential. Get out of the danger area and decontaminate as soon as possible, the same as with pathogens.

GASES AND CHEMICALS

Explosive gases can occur and build up in caves and mines, but the main dangers to the survivor in the wild will be oxygen deficiency and carbon monoxide poisoning in restricted spaces and shelters.

In house and vehicle fires and in industrial locations there is risk from toxic fumes being produced when plastic and other materials burn. Industrial and road accidents involving chemicals present another danger.

There is little that can be done to protect yourself in a disaster such as that at Bohpal, in India, once they have happened, other than stay indoors and keep your doors and windows closed. But you can try to discover any risks that are likely from industrial or other plant in your area. There should be government and local authority checks and controls operating to enforce proper safety procedures. Many authorities demand labelling of places where chemicals are used or stored – in London, for instance, by a yellow triangle and/or the sign HAZCHEM.

If handling dangerous materials – not just at work, potentially dangerous substances are used in domestic chores, gardening and hobby pursuits – follow recommended safety procedures. AVOID contact with chemicals and inhalation of fumes and take precautions against spillage, shaking, breakage or accidental mixture with other chemicals which could produce a dangerous reaction.

If exposed to fumes or chemical hazard get to fresh air as rapidly as possible and flush away chemicals with copious quantities of water – BUT adding water to some chemicals can cause even more dangerous reactions. Learn the properties of materials you handle or transport and measures for dealing with accidents.

AVOID touching anyone contaminated with chemicals and do NOT give mouth-to-mouth resuscitation until you know what chemicals are involved.

ROAD AND RAIL

Keep well clear of an accident involving a bulk tanker or other vehicle carrying dangerous substances. You may be able to see spillages on the road surface. Gas escapes may NOT be visible.

Chemical fires may be fought by appropriate techniques. If not properly trained and equipped to handle them you may aggravate the situation, endangering yourself and others.

542

The usual action in such cases will be to cover any flammable substances with foam to exclude oxygen, and to dilute chemicals that do not react dangerously to water with as much water as possible.

There are too many cases on record of public-spirited individuals losing their own lives in such circumstances — like the man who went to aid the driver of an overturned tanker which had been carrying powerful acid. By the time the fire-service arrived his gold wedding ring was all that remained of him.

INFO.

BUT if you do not know what exact substances are involved and the appropriate action — KEEP CLEAR. CALL THE FIRE SERVICE OR POLICE AND LEAVE ALONE.

Vehicles may be painted with a panel warning that they carry potentially dangerous chemicals which includes a code of figures and letters which tell the emergency services what kind of action to take, what kind of protection is essential and whether the chemical is explosive or poisonous. In the British code, for instance, a final E is an instruction to EVACUATE. The figures 1 or 2 at the beginning of the code suggest that water may be used, but that is only part of the information needed — the use of water could produce fumes which demand use of a respirator. Protective clothing may be essential.

Details of these codes are not usually given to the general public, for the information that they provide does not give practical guidance to the untrained, beyond a warning that dangerous materials are carried.

Although the information provided by the codes is valuable to the officers of the emergency services, they do not know the proportions in which spilt chemicals are concentrated, or whether combinations of chemicals could produce results quite unlike those expected. Where dangerous stores and goods in transit are registered with the authorities rescue services may be able to obtain additional information, but uncontrollable elements such as wind direction, temperature and various other factors will all affect the way in which such accidents are handled.

If you see a British hazardous chemical code, an EC Accord Européen Relatif au Transport International des Marchandises Dangereuses par Route (ADR) sign, which gives much less detailed information, or the United Nations International Emergency Action Code (EAC), which only covers a limited number of emergency procedures, KEEP YOUR DISTANCE.

FLOOD

Flooding may be caused by the overflowing of rivers, lakes and reservoirs caused by heavy rains (not necessarily rainfall at the place where the flood occurs); by the build-up of sea or lake water due to the effects of submarine earthquake, hurricanes and freak high-tides and winds; or by the collapse of dams or dykes.

Heavy rain can rapidly produce torrents where there was a dry riverbed, or a build up in a narrow channel or behind a barrier which then gives way to a rushing wall of water that envelopes everything in its path.

Persistent rainfall over a long period after a dry spell and heavy storms should alert you to keep clear of water channels and low-lying ground, but a flood can affect much wider areas. It is always safer to camp on a spur. If the water is rising, move to higher ground. In hilly areas keep out of valley bottoms which are particularly prone to flash floods.

Food is not likely to be a problem, at least at first, for animals will also head for high ground. Both predators and prey are likely to concentrate on getting to safety — but beware of injury from panic-stricken animals in the water.

Drinking water may be difficult to obtain, for the water swirling around you may be contaminated. Collect rainwater to drink and boil any other water before you use it.

Flooded buildings

If you are in a solid building when the water begins to rise, stay where you are if it is rising rapidly. You will be less at risk than trying to evacuate on foot. Turn off gas and electricity and prepare emergency food supplies; warm clothing; drinking water in screw-topped plastic bottles or other well-sealed containers. It is important to keep all water containers sealed to avoid accidental spillage or contamination. If you can, collect a torch, whistle, mirror, brightly coloured cloths, or flags, that would be useful for signalling, and add them to your gear. A camp stove will be valuable for heating food and drinks and for warmth. Candles are also useful — and DON'T forget the matches.

Move upwards

Move to an upper floor, or on to the roof if in a single-storey building. If you are forced to occupy the roof, erect some kind of shelter. If it is a sloping roof, tie everyone to a chimneystack or other solid structure which can be expected to stay firm. If the water looks like continuing to rise, prepare some kind of raft. If you have no ropes to tie things together, use bed sheets. Unless the water threatens to wash your building away, or rises so high that you are forced to evacuate, stay until it stops rising.

Flood readiness

If you live in a river valley or in a coastal area prone to flooding, find out how high you are above normal water levels. Learn the easiest route to high ground — not necessarily the highway route, for major roads tend to follow drainage channels in valley bottoms. In rainy periods listen out for flood warnings which will often predict the levels to which waters may be expected to rise and the areas likely to be affected.

Even a few inches of floodwater can do a lot of damage and it is worth laying sandbags or plastic shopping bags filled with earth along the bottom of doorways and windows to keep out as much water as possible. If you have a really sound building and doorways, windows and other apertures are blocked, water will not enter. The central heating flue, ventilation bricks and other spaces must all be sealed.

If a high flood is likely, there is not much point trying to keep water out of basements. Indeed, in some houses with basements this could cause extra damage due to uneven pressure on the basement walls. If you are bound to be flooded, you could consider flooding the basement yourself with clean water, so that the pressure is equalized. You will have less filth and debris to clear up later.

Evacuation

If you are abandoning your home bring outdoor furniture and other movables indoors — that will reduce the amount of debris floating or being swept along outside.

When walking or driving to a safer location: Remember that a small drop in the level of the roadway down a hill can make a considerable difference to the water depth.

Do NOT attempt to cross a pool (or a stream) unless you are CERTAIN that the water will not be higher than the centre of the car's wheels or higher than your knees.

If you must cross: use river-crossing techniques (see *On the move*).

If crossing bridges which are underwater: Take especial care — you may not be able to see that the flood has already swept part of the bridge away.

Flash floods

In times of sudden heavy rainfall keep out of valley bottoms and stream beds both during and after rainfall. Remember that you don't have to be at the bottom of a hill to be caught by water rushing down it — often carrying mud and a deadly debris of broken trees and rocks.

Coastal flooding

Is usually a combination of high tides and winds which make them even higher. Flood warnings will usually be given and evacuation is the best action.

Flood aftermath

As the waters recede they leave a scene of devastation littered with debris and the bodies of flood victims. With decay and the pollution of the water comes the risk of disease and extra precautions are necessary. Burn all animal corpses — do not risk eating them — and thoroughly boil all water before using. Some crops may still be available after the flood waters recede and birds that have escaped the flood will be safe and good to eat.

TSUNAMI

A tsunami is linked with an earthquake beneath the ocean, creating a series of waves which can reach more than 30m (100ft) high and causing a considerable amount of damage along coasts.

A feature mainly of the Pacific — where over 200 were recorded in the last century — their effect and scale can vary according to direction, shape of shoreline and other factors. One that is quite small on a particular beach can be a giant wave a few miles along the coast. Warnings of tsunami are issued from the National Oceanic and Atmospheric Administration's Pacific Tsunami Warning System headquarters in Hawaii.

Not all earthquakes cause tsunami, but any earthquake could. Keep away from shores and take to higher ground when there are tremors. Do NOT go to look for a tsunami — if you are close enough to see the wave, you are too close to escape it, unless high above its level. There is little defence against a moving wall of water. Evacuate.

HURRICANE

A hurricane is a wind of high speed – above force 12 on the Beaufort Scale – which brings torrential rain and can destroy any flimsy structures. It is a tropical form of cyclone, which in more temperate latitudes would be prevented from developing in the upper levels of the air by the prevailing westerly winds.

Hurricanes are known by various names around the world:

Hurricane: Caribbean and North Atlantic, eastern North Pacific, western South Pacific.
Cyclone: Arabian Sea, Bay of Bengal, southern Indian Ocean.
Typhoon: China Sea, western North Pacific.
Willy-willy: Northwest Australia.

Hurricanes develop over the ocean when sea temperatures are at their highest, especially in late summer. Warm air creates a low pressure core around which winds may rotate at speeds up to 300kph (200mph) or more, circling anti-clockwise in the northern hemisphere, clockwise in the southern. The strongest winds are usually 16-19km (10-12 miles) from the centre of the hurricane but the centre, or 'eye', brings temporary calm. The 'eye' may be from 6–50km (4–30 miles) across and the largest hurricanes up to 500km (300 miles) in diameter. They can occur at any time of year but, in the northern hemisphere, the main season is June to November – in the southern, November to April (especially January and February). Hurricanes are not a feature of the South Atlantic.

Pattern of the hurricane

Out at sea hurricanes will build up force and begin to veer toward the pole, the wind speed usually being greatest on the poleward side of the eye. They can travel as fast as 50kph (30mph) wreaking devastation on islands and along shorelines they pass over, but usually slowing down when they reach the mainland to a speed of about 16kph (10mph).

Hurricane warnings

Satellite surveillance enables meteorologists to see hurricanes developing far out in the ocean, to track their progress and to give warning of their approach. Some hurricanes move very erratically, so sailors particularly, should monitor forecasts in hurricane areas.

Without radio to alert you, the growth of swell can be an indication of a hurricane — when coupled with other conditions such as highly coloured sunsets or sunrises; dense banners of cirrus cloud converging towards the vortex of the approaching storm; abnormal rises in barometric pressure followed by an equally rapid drop.

SAFETY PRECAUTIONS

Get out of the hurricane's path if you can.

- Hurricane warnings are usually issued when one is expected within 24 hours and will give you plenty of time to evacuate its path, if you are prepared.
- Keep away from the coast, where destruction will be worst, with flooding and a tidal wave, and from river banks.
- Board up windows and secure any objects outdoors that might be blown away.
- At sea take down all canvas, batten down the hatches and stow all gear.

If you are in a solid building and on high ground STAY WHERE YOU ARE — travel in a hurricane is extremely dangerous. The safest place is usually in a cellar or under the stairs. Store drinking water — water and power supplies may be cut off by the storm — and have a battery-operated radio to keep in touch with any instructions issued. If not in a sturdy structure, evacuate to a hurricane shelter. Shut off power supplies before you leave.

Seeking shelter

Outdoors a cave will offer the best protection. A ditch will be next best. If unable to escape lie flat on the ground where you will be less of a target for flying debris. Crawl to the leeside of any really solid shelter such as a stable rocky outcrop or a wide belt of large trees. Beware of small trees and fences which could be uprooted.

INFO.

Stay where you are when the hurricane appears to have passed — there will usually be less than an hour of calm as the eye passes and then the winds will resume in the opposite direction. If sheltering outdoors move to the other side of your windbreak in preparation or move to better shelter if close by.

TORNADO

Tornadoes are violent storms associated with low atmospheric pressure and whirling winds. They apparently develop when air at the surface has been warmed and a column of air descends from the base of cumulonimbus storm clouds above. Air rushing into the low pressure area begins to rotate fiercely.

Tornadoes are the most violent of atmospheric phenomena and the most destructive over a small area. Wind speeds have been estimated at 620kph (400mph).

The diameter of the 'twister' at ground level is usually only 25–50m (80–160ft) but, within it, the destruction is enormous. Everything in its path except the most solid structures is sucked up into the air. The difference in pressure outside and inside a building is often the cause of collapse — or 'explosion'. Tornadoes can sound like a spinning top or engine and have been heard up to 40km (25 miles) away. They travel at 50–65kph (30–40mph).

At sea tornadoes produce waterspouts. Although they can occur elsewhere, tornadoes are most prevalent over the prairies of the United States, in the Mississippi-Missouri valley and in Australia. They can develop in a hurricane.

Tornado precautions

Take shelter in the most solid structure available — reinforced concrete or steel-framed if possible, but preferably in a storm cellar or cave. In a cellar stay close to an outside wall, or in a specially reinforced section. If there is no basement, go to the centre of the lowest floor, into a small room or shelter under sturdy furniture — but not where there is heavy furniture on the floor above. Keep well away from windows.

Firmly close all doors and windows on the side facing the oncoming whirlwind and open those on the opposite side. This will prevent the wind getting in and lifting the roof as it approaches and equalize the pressure to prevent the house 'exploding'.

Do NOT stay in a caravan or car, they could be drawn up by the storm.

Outdoors you are vulnerable to flying debris and to being lifted up — though people have been lowered to the ground again unharmed! You CAN see and hear a tornado coming. Get out of the way. Move at right angles to its apparent path. Take shelter in a ditch or depression in the ground, lie flat and cover your head with your arms.

LIGHTNING

The release of electrical charges built up in clouds can be especially dangerous on high ground or when you are the tallest object. In a lightning storm keep away from hill brows, from tall trees and lone boulders. Make for low, level ground and lie flat.

Insulation

If you cannot get away from tall objects, but have DRY material which will provide insulation, sit on it. Rubber-soled shoes may help insulation but are not a guarantee that you will be safe. A dry coil of climbing rope makes good insulation. Do NOT sit on anything wet. Bend your head down and hug your knees to your chest, lifting your feet off the ground and drawing in all your extremities. Do not reach down to the ground with your hands, that could give a contact to conduct the lightning. If you have nothing which will insulate you from the ground lie as flat as you can.

Stay low

You can sometimes sense that a lightning strike is imminent by a tingling in the skin and the sensation of the hair standing on end. If you are standing up, drop to the ground AT ONCE, going first to the knees with the hands touching the ground. If you should be struck, the charge may take the easiest route to the earth through your arms — missing the torso and possibly saving you from heart failure or asphixiation. QUICKLY LIE FLAT.

Do not hold metal objects when there is lightning about and keep away from metal structures and fences. However, do not jettison equipment if you will lose it altogether (when climbing, for instance). A dry axe with a wooden handle may spark at the tip, but is well insulated. Proximity to large metal objects can be dangerous, even without contact, for the shockwave caused by the heated air — as the lightning passes — can cause damage to the lungs.

Shelter

One of the best places to shelter in a lightning storm is at least 1m (10ft) inside a deep cave with a minimum of 1m (4ft) space on either side of you. Do NOT shelter in a cave mouth or under an overhang of rock in mountainous country. The lightning can spark across the gap. Small openings in the rock are frequently the ends of fissures which are also drainage routes and automatic lightning channels.

EARTHQUAKE

Earthquakes are perhaps the most feared of all nature's violence — they come suddenly with little warning. Unlike other natural hazards, such as flood and fire, little can be done to prepare for them. They range from minor vibrations in the earth, detectable only on delicate measuring instruments, to great upheavals tearing whole mountains apart.

Minor earth tremors can happen anywhere, but major quakes are confined to known earthquake belts where buildings could be planned to withstand them or to cause little damage if they do collapse — like traditional buildings in Japan. Modern cities rarely take this into account.

With constant monitoring by seismologists, major earthquakes can be predicted and some evacuation may be possible. Animals become very alert, tense and ready to run.

A detailed knowledge of local geology may indicate the weak points along major fissures but the tremors and the waves of movement through the earth could extend to almost anywhere in an earthquake zone.

Causes

Earthquakes are caused by the sudden release of tension built up in the Earth's crust, as deep as 700km (400 miles) below the surface — but only a rupture in the upper tens of kilometres is likely to produce movement affecting the surface. The shock wave for the 1964 Alaskan earthquake, for instance, was at about 20–30km (12–30 miles) deep.

The earthquake belts lie along the edges of the semirigid plates that form the Earth's crust. The deepest quakes occur along the ocean trenches, forming and destroying volcanic islands. The most violent tend to occur in areas where one plate is thrusting beneath another, as along the west coast of North America, where the San Andreas Fault is a particularly vulnerable zone.

A succession of preliminary tremors, known as foreshocks, often followed by a seismically quiet period, usually precede a major quake, which they can actually trigger. These initial tremors may not be noticeable.

Domestic earthquake precautions

Stay tuned to a local radio station for up-to-date reports and advice if you have warning of a possible earthquake. Turn off gas, electricity and water if advised to do so. Remove large and heavy objects from high shelves, from which they might fall on you. Put bottles, glass, china and other breakables in low cupboards. Shelves should have a lip or low barrier to stop things slipping off. Cupboard doors should have positive fastening — not just magnetic catches. Secure or remove suspended objects, such as large light fittings and hanging flower bowls.

Have ready in case needed: fresh water and emergency food, a torch, first aid materials and a fire extinguisher.

SAFETY PRECAUTIONS

KEEP AWAY FROM ANYTHING THAT MIGHT FALL ON YOU: trees in the open air, for they may be uprooted; building in towns, for — even if they are stable enough not to be demolished — pieces may come crashing down. Ideally evacuate to an open area but, if that is not possible — and you may have little time — it is safer to stay indoors. In the street ruptured gas mains and power cables may add to the hazards. People going in and out are the ones at most hazard from falling masonry on buildings.

Indoors

If you are indoors when an earthquake strikes, stay there. Douse fires. Stay away from glass, including mirrors, and especially from large windows.

- An inside corner of the house, or a well-supported interior doorway are good places to shelter.
- A lower floor or a cellar probably gives the best chance of survival. An upper floor could come crashing down with you on it. Make sure there are plenty of exits.
- Get beneath a table or other piece of substantial furniture which will give both protection and an air space.
- In a shop keep away from large displays of goods which could come crashing down.
- In high-rise offices stay put. Never go into a lift. Staircases may attract panicking people. Get under a desk.

In a car

Stop as quickly and safely as you can — but stay in the car. It will offer some protection from falling objects. Crouch down below seat level and you will be a further protected if anything falls on the car. When the tremors cease keep a watch for any obstructions and hazards: broken cables, undermined roadways or bridges which could give way.

Outdoors

Outdoors lie flat on the ground. Do NOT try to run. You will be thrown about and could be swallowed in a fissure.

- Keep away from tall buildings.
- Do not go deliberately underground or into a tunnel where you could be trapped by blockage or collapse.
- If you have managed to get to an open space do not move back into buildings for if minor tremors follow they could collapse any structure left unstable by the first quake.
- On a hillside it is safer to get to the top. Slopes are liable to landslide and there would be little chance of survival for anyone caught in the thousands of tons of earth and rock that could move with terrifying speed. People have been known to survive by rolling into a tight ball on the ground.
- Beaches — provided they are not below cliffs — are initially fairly safe but, since tidal waves often follow a quake you should move off the beach to high open ground as soon as the tremor has finished. Further tremors are unlikely to be as dangerous as a tsunami.

Aftermath precautions

Rupture of sewage systems, contamination of water and the hazards of the bodies trapped in the wreckage can all make the risk of disease as deadly as the earthquake itself. Bury all corpses, animal and human.

- Do NOT shelter in damaged buildings or ruins. Build a shelter from debris.
- Take special care over sanitation and personal hygiene. Filter and boil all water.
- Do not strike matches or lighters, or use electrical appliances, if there is any chance of a gas leak. Sparks ignite gas.
- Check sewage services are intact before using lavatories.
- Open cupboards carefully, objects may tumble out.
- Be prepared for after-shocks.

BE CALM! THINK FAST!

Speed is essential if an earthquake strikes. There is little time to organize others. Use force if necessary to get them to safety or pull them to the ground.

VOLCANO

Active volcanoes are found in the areas of the world which are also most prone to earthquakes — where there is most movement beneath the surface. Long dead volcanoes and evidence of ancient volcanic activity can be found elsewhere — such as Arthur's Seat in Edinburgh, Scotland.

A channel is formed when pressure forces molten rock (magma) to the surface through a fault. The channel is usually the main outlet for further eruptions, though other vents may appear. A major eruption may blow the whole top off a mountain.

The molten rock, usually known as lava when it reaches the surface, may be of two kinds: granite lava, which is viscous and slow moving, and basalt lava, which flows more rapidly at speeds of 8–16kph (5–10mph). Granite lava tends to block the vent of the volcano, eventually cleared by an explosion due to the build up of pressure beneath — showering lava and pieces of mountain around for considerable distances and causing fires.

ERUPTION HAZARDS

Lava

Although it is possible to outwalk or outrun most basalt lava flows they continue relentlessly until they reach a valley bottom or eventually cool off. They crush and bury anything in their path. Lava flows are probably the least hazard to life produced by an eruption, for the able-bodied can get out of their way. Other dangers are NOT so easily avoided.

Missiles

Volcanic missiles, ranging from pebble-size fragments to great lumps of rock and 'bombs' of hot lava, can be scattered over considerable distances. A shower of volcanic ash can fall over a much greater area, some dust being carried to great heights and are dispersed around the world affecting weather conditions.

If evacuating from close to the volcano, hard helmets of the kind worn by building workers, motorcyclists or horseriders will give some protection. Over a wider area, where evacuation may not be necessary, protection should be worn against the effects of ash and any rain which accompanies it.

Ash

Volcanic ash is not ash at all, but pulverised rock forced out in a cloud of steam and gases. Abrasive, irritant and heavy, its weight can cause roofs to collapse. It smothers crops, blocks transport routes and watercourses and, combined with toxic gases, can cause lung damage to the very young, old and those with respiratory problems. Only very close to an eruption are gases concentrated enough to poison healthy people. But, when sulphur dioxide in the ash cloud is combined with rain, sulphuric acid (and sometimes others) are produced in concentrations which can burn skin, eyes and mucous membranes. Wear goggles (ski-goggles or a snorkelling mask which seal around the eyes, NOT sunglasses). Use a damp cloth over mouth and nose, or industrial dust masks if available. On reaching shelter remove clothing, thoroughly wash exposed skin and flush eyes with clean water.

Gas balls

A ball of gas and dust may roll clown the side of a volcano at a speed of more than 160kph (100mph). This phenomenon (called by scientists a *nuć ardente* – glowing cloud) is red hot and moves too fast to be outrun. Unless there is a strongly-built underground shelter nearby, the only chance of survival is to submerge underwater and hold your breath for the half-minute or so it will take to pass.

Mudflows

The volcano may melt ice and snow and cause a glacial flood or – combined with earth – create a mudflow, known as a lahar. This can move at up to 100kph (60mph) with devastating effect, as in Colombia in 1985. In a narrow valley a lahar can be as much as 30m (100ft) high. They are a danger long after the major eruption is over and are a potential risk even when the volcano is dormant if it generates enough heat to produce meltwater retained by ice barriers. Heavy rains may cause it to breach the ice.

WARNING

Volcanoes usually show increased activity before a major eruption with rumblings and escapes of steam and gases. Sulphurous smells from local rivers, stinging acidic rain, loud rumblings or plumes of steam from the volcano are all warning signs. Evacuating by car remember: ash may make roads slippery, even if it does not block them. Avoid valley routes which could become the path of a lahar.

NUCLEAR EXPLOSION

The immediate hazards of a nuclear explosion are blast, heat and radiation. The severity of their effects will depend upon the size and type of weapon, distance or height of the explosion, weather conditions and terrain. Heat and blast are like those produced by conventional explosives, but many times more powerful.

Blast

The detonation causes the initial shock-wave. Even more powerful is the compression of the air produced by the rapid expansion of the fireball. The wave of pressure travelling outwards from the point of detonation will collapse buildings, uproot trees and fill the air with flying debris, well before the heat follows. Approximately half the total energy of the explosion is expended in this way.

When the blast wave has passed, air rushes back to fill the void causing further damage. At distances where the initial blast has only weakened structures this vacuum effect will finish the job.

Heat

The thermal radiation (heat and light) produced by a nuclear explosion reaches temperatures hotter than the sun and includes great intensities of ultraviolet, infrared and visible light rays. Close to the point of detonation all inflammable materials are ignited — even vaporized. In the case of the Hiroshima bomb, exposed skin was burned at a distance of 4km (2½ miles). Today's weapons are MANY times that power and their effects comparably more extensive. Even seeing the Dash of the explosion is likely to cause serious eye damage and burns to the skin.

Radioactivity

In addition to the thermal radiation, nuclear fission produces alpha and beta particles and gamma rays. Although radioactive fallout settles to earth, with the appearance of white ash or dust, this is the residue of destroyed matter not the radioactivity itself. That cannot be detected by human senses. A geiger counter is required to register its presence, indicated by a dial or a sound signal which becomes increasingly agitated as the radiation increases.

– **Alpha particles:** have low penetrating capabilities and it is easy to shield them off. They cannot penetrate the skin but they do present serious problems if ingested or inhaled.

- **Beta particles:** are only slightly penetrating and heavy clothing and boots will give full protection. On exposed skin they cause burns. If ingested they attack bone, the gastrointestinal tract, thyroid gland and other organs.
- **Gamma rays:** are highly penetrating. They travel much slower than alpha and beta rays, damaging all body cells.

Residual radiation

The initial radiation given off during the first minute of a nuclear explosion can kill — but it lasts only a short time. Once the blast has passed, so has the initial radiation threat. However, exposure to residual radiation can be equally dangerous.

> **INFO.**
>
> Common symptoms of exposure to radioactivity are nausea, vomiting, general weakness. Ulcer-like sores appear on the skin, which tends to take on a grey hue.

The amount of residual radiation depends on how the bomb was detonated. If it was high above the ground and the fireball did not touch the earth little residual radiation is produced — what the strategists call a 'clean bomb'. If exploded on or near the ground, a huge quantity of soil and debris is sucked upwards to a great height and falls back to earth as radioactive dust. Heavier particles fall in the vicinity of the explosion, but lighter ones may be carried by wind over a wide area — spreading the radioactivity.

In time radiation decays — the cities of both Hiroshima and Nagasaki have been rebuilt and reinhabited. However, while as much as 70% of these particles remain radioactive for only one day or less, it takes others years for their radiation to decay.

> **INFO.**
>
> The radioactivity to which an unprotected person could be exposed in the first few hours will exceed that received during the rest of the week. That in the first week will exceed that accumulated during the rest of a lifetime spent in the same contaminated area. It is therefore important to be shielded during the initial stages.

Radiation shelters

In default of a deep bunker equipped with air, water and food supplies, in which to sit out a nuclear conflict and its aftermath, the best protection is a deep trench with a roof covered by a metre or

SHIELDING

Strictly speaking, it is impossible to shield completely from all radiation but a sufficient thickness of shelter material will reduce the level of radiation to a negligible level. Below are some materials, and the thickness required to reduce radiation penetration by 50%.

Material	Metres/Feet
Iron and steel	0·21/0·7
Concrete	0·66/2·2
Brick	0·60/2·0
Soil	1·00/3·3
Ice	2·00/6·6
Wood	2·60/8·8
Snow	6·00/20·3

more of earth. If the detonation is sufficiently distant not to produce total destruction, the trench and earth will protect from blast, heat and radiation.

Look for terrain that has natural shelter, such as ravines, gullies, ditches and rocky outcrops. If you do not have a trench shelter prepared, start digging — FAST! As soon as the hole is big enough, get inside it to continue digging, to minimize exposure to radiation if you are caught-out while still digging. Rig up a roof. Even if only of cloth, it will stop dust falling on you. Penetrating rays can still reach you so try to get a metre of earth above you.

If caught in the open get to your shelter as quickly as possible. Once under cover, remove outer garments and bury them under a foot of soil at one end of the bottom of the shelter. Do not venture out until absolutely necessary and do not re-use your discarded garments. Under no circumstances move out of the shelter in the first 48 hours.

If desperate for water a brief venture out, lasting not more than 30 minutes, is permissible on the third day. On the seventh day a further exposure, of up to half an hour, can be extended on the eighth up to one hour and then from two to four hours for the next four days and from the thirteenth day normal working hours, followed by rest in the shelter.

Decontamination

If your body, or even your clothing, has been exposed to radiation, it must be decontaminated. Once in shelter scrape earth from the shelter bottom and rub it over the exposed parts of your body and your outer clothing. Brush it off and throw the soil outside. Wipe the skin with a clean cloth if possible. More effectively, if water is available, wash the body thoroughly with soap and water instead of soil.

Medical care

ALL wounds must be covered to prevent alpha and beta particles entering through them. Burns, whether caused by beta particles and gamma rays or by firestorm heat, should be washed with clean water and covered. Urine may be used, if no uncontaminated water is available. The eyes should be covered to prevent further particles entering and a damp cloth placed over the mouth and nose to prevent further inhalation.

Radiation affects the blood and increases susceptibility to infection. Take all precautions — even against colds and respiratory infections.

AFTERMATH

Unless stored in deep shelters, or with special protection, all foodstuffs are likely to have absorbed some measure of radioactivity. Be cautious of foods containing a high salt content, dairy products, such as milk and cheese, and sea foods. After tests it was found that food with salt and other additives had a higher concentration of radioactivity than food without them. The safest canned foods are soups, vegetables and fruits. Cured and processed meat are more readily contaminated than fresh. Bone absorbs the highest levels of radioactivity, then lean meat, with fat lowest.

Water

Unless it is from a protected source, do not drink any water for at least 48 hours after detonation. Avoid water from lakes, pools, ponds and other static surface water. Filter all water and boil it before drinking.

The following sources are the least contaminated (in order of least risk):

1 Underground wells and springs
2 Water in underground pipes/containers
3 Snow taken from deep below the surface
4 Fast-flowing rivers

Dig a hole by a fast-flowing stream and allow water to filter down into it. Scrape off any scum that forms on the surface and scoop up water. Filter it through layers of sand and pebbles (dig deep to obtain these) in a can with holes punched in the bottom, or through a stocking. Boil in an uncontaminated vessel.

Decontaminate utensils by washing thoroughly in fast-flowing or boiled water.

Animals as food

Animals that live underground have less exposure to radiation than those that live on the surface: rabbits, badgers, voles and similar animals are the best bets but, when they venture out, they too will be contaminated. However, such food sources must be made use of. You will increase your own contamination – but the alternative may be to starve.

To reduce contamination from meat do NOT directly handle carcasses, wear gloves or use cloth to cover the hands while carefully skinning and washing. Avoid meat in direct contact with the bone. The skeleton retains 90% of radiation so leave at least 3mm (1/8in) on the bone. Muscle and fat are the safest part of the meat. Discard ALL internal organs.

INFO.

Fish and aquatic animals will have a higher contamination than land animals from the same area. Birds will be particularly heavily contaminated and should not be eaten. However, eggs are safe to eat.

Plants as food

Root vegetables with edible tubers growing underground are safest – carrots, potatoes and turnips, for instance. Wash them well and peel before cooking.

Smooth-skinned fruits and vegetables are next safest. Plants with crinkly foliage are the hardest to decontaminate, because of their rough texture. They should be avoided.

Long-term survival

Predictions of the long-term results on the environment of major thermonuclear conflict differ widely. The possibility of a 'nuclear winter', with consequent effect on climate and plant life far beyond strike areas, would make even subsistence agriculture difficult. In the short-term however, and in the case of limited conflict, much of the advice in *Home front* will be relevant.

HOME FRONT

You do not have to be miles away from civilization to be caught in a survival situation. Natural disaster, civil disturbance or military action could cut you off from all the usual services and food supplies. Until they can be re-established, you would be left to manage on your own resources and skills.

With no power supplies, central heating, hot water, lighting, air-conditioning and refrigeration would all cease. Battery radios and television would for a time give some news of the rest of the world, if the situation is not global, but post, telephone and newspapers would no longer be available. A generator is an essential back up and a short wave radio is useful. As mains water supplies ceased to function, so taps would run dry and toilets would become unusable.

In the countryside there would be natural resources to draw upon. In large cities shops would soon be emptied of food — sold or looted — and plants in parks and gardens would be rapidly stripped, once any private stocks had been exhausted. The population would have to make forays out into the countryside to survive, or abandon the town, if not in a siege situation. Suburban dwellers have more vegetable plots and open spaces to provide foodstuffs. They would be less dependent upon shops. Those away from major centres are more likely to have their own food stocks, because they cannot shop at will.

Most families have some food in store. It should be rationed and supplemented with whatever can be found.

FOOD STORES

Storing food is a good habit to get into, especially if you live in an isolated place, which can become completely cut-off. If you have a year's food supply in store, and add to it as you use it, you will not only be able to survive the worst but will be able to live at last year's prices.

The stock does not have to be established in one go. Build it up gradually, taking advantage of special offers in supermarkets. Buy an extra tin or packet and put it by. Store your foods in a cool, dry, dark place and off the ground — moisture and heat cause bacteria and moulds. If stores are left on the floor insects and rodents will help themselves. Make sure that all containers are insect- and rodent-proof.

REMEMBER: Rotate cans, so that the contents do not settle, and separate. Label each can or packet with a colour-fast waterproof pen, noting contents and date of storage. Use in sequence — the oldest first. Store methodically and if a label falls off, you should still have a good idea of the contents.

Choice of foods will depend upon individual taste, but straightforward products (corned beef in preference to beef stew and dumplings) will keep better and can be used in a greater variety of ways. Wheat keeps better than flour — it is less susceptible to moisture, light, insects and temperature change. Wheat found in the pyramids was found in good condition after thousands of years. However, you must grind it to make flour, so invest in a small hand grinder.

Keep it sealed
Screw-top sweet jars are ideal for storage and plastic containers with tight-fitting lids can also be used. Do not over fill them so that they distort and the lid does not fit correctly. Use adhesive tape to seal the lids. Reseal after using some but remember that once opened the contents will begin to deteriorate.

RECOMMENDED FOODS/SHELF LIFE

Wheat	Indefinitely below 15°C (65°F)
Milk powder	2 years
Honey	Indefinitely
Egg powder	2 years
Salt	Indefinitely if absolutely dry
Canned foods	3–5 years (replace regularly)
Oats	Indefinitely
Cooking oil	2 years (replace regularly)

Rations
Complete rations are available with various menus — either freeze-dried or dehydrated. They are lighter and less space-consuming than canned foods. Freeze-dried are best for both taste and texture and retain minerals which are lost in dehydration. Although both need

water for reconstitution they can, in dire circumstances, be eaten as a dry munch.

Vitamins

Multi-vitamin tablets are also a good investment. The body can store up to a month's supply of most vitamins, then health will suffer if they are not replaced. In stress situations they are more rapidly used up. The B family (and minerals, calcium and zinc) are first to go. Vitamin tablets do not have unlimited shelf-life — check manufacturer's instructions.

Other foods

- **Dried fruit and nuts** are nutritious and should also be included — raisins, sultanas and currants all keep well. Nuts in their shells keep so long as they are dry. Packets of dried salted nuts such as peanuts, brazils and walnuts, are highly nutritious.

- **Potato powder** is a great filler for hungry stomachs and can be prepared in several ways to make it palatable.

- **Brown rice** has more nourishment than long-grain white rice which loses all its goodness when boiled.

Store location

The cooler the storage area, the better the stores will keep — a cellar is ideal but there may be a problem with dampness so keep all the stores off the ground and inspect them regularly. If there is a skylight in the cellar, cover it. The store is best kept dark.

An attic is also convenient for storage — the stores are not in the way of day-to-day activities. However, it may get very warm in summer and access may be difficult — especially if a ladder is the only means of entry — which may be awkward when trying to rotate bulky stores. The roof is also a vulnerable position in most kinds of disaster situations. In an area where hurricanes can be expected an attic is not a good choice. In territory liable to flooding a cellar would be equally at risk. Under stairs is another area that may offer some protection, though perhaps limited space.

Advantage should be taken of wherever is most conveniently available to store not only food but also medical supplies, disinfectants, cleansing materials — and water. If you divide your stores into more than one area, each with a variety of items, you should be well prepared.

ADD TO YOUR STORES

Toothpaste and soap

Disinfectant and bleach

Washing powder

General medical supplies

Medicines: for dysentery, for stomach upsets, for allergies, general pain-killers

Bandages and dressings

Spare batteries

PRIORITIES

In a domestic situation there is likely to be shelter, unless it has been totally destroyed, or the area has become a danger zone and evacuation is imperative. Damage can be patched-up to provide some protection from the elements and more permanent repairs undertaken as soon as possible.

Water supplies are always likely to be a problem — for even during a flood drinking water is scarce. Fortunately there are likely to be some immediate reserves on the premises and, with warning of a crisis, these can be supplemented.

Fire for warmth is less of a problem, since there will be burnable materials in the house and surroundings. Infection may prove the greatest danger and strict hygiene and sanitary practices must be enforced.

WATER

Although a family of four can use a considerable amount of water each week, only a small percentage of this is for drinking — a requirement of about 2 litres (4pt) per day per person. If warned of a crisis, fill as many receptacles as possible, especially in a hot climate. A bath holds many gallons; increase its capacity by blocking the overflow. Use dustbins, buckets, pots — even strong polythene bags if they are only half filled and securely tied off.

Store water in the dark. If light gets to it green algae will develop. Water is bulky and heavy. Do not store it in the attic or it may bring the ceiling down.

Even without advance warning there will be water in the storage tank, heating pipes, radiators, perhaps an aquarium, and the toilet cistern will hold another few gallons — don't flush it. Outdoors you may have a swimming pool, water butts, or a pond — even water from a car radiator can be utilized. Central heating water is usually treated with a de-oxygenizing agent and a car radiator probably contains anti-freeze, so water from these places is best kept for cleaning purposes. If it has to be used for drinking boil it, collect the steam in clean cloths and wring them out. Then reboil. (Also see *Essentials*.)

Boiled water tastes flat and distilled water has even less taste. It is easy to restore some of its sparkle by putting oxygen back into it: simply pour the water back and forth from one vessel to another. A small piece of wood charcoal placed in the vessel while it boils also helps taste.

FILTERING AND STERILIZING

Filter and sterilize ALL water before using it for drinking. If circumstances make it impossible to boil water sterilize it with chemicals.

FILTERING: Allow water to stand in its container so that sediment settles at the bottom. Then siphon it into a filter made up of a nylon stocking (or other porous material) stuffed with layers of sand (bottom), charcoal and moss (top).

STERLIZING: Clear water: add 2 drops household bleach per litre (1 per pint) or 3 drops 2% tincture of iodine per litre (6 per pint)

Cloudy water: double the quantities of bleach or iodine

Large quantities: half teaspoonful bleach per litre (2 teaspoonsful per gallon)

Cooking in water

Water in which food is to be cooked MUST be boiled for at least eight minutes, but water not boiled for as long can be used for heating cans of food provided it makes no contact with the foodstuff.

Stand the can in water, pierce a small hole in the top to avoid the risk of explosion and plug it with a twist of cloth so that water cannot enter the can.

Alternatively, boil the water, remove it from the heat and place the unpierced can in the water. This takes longer for the can to heat through.

Water catchment

- Catch all available rainwater. Break off lower sections of down pipes and divert the flow into a container such as a dustbin. Even if rainwater is pure, guttering may contaminate it – so sterilize.

- Supplement water receptacles with tarpaulins or plastic sheets supported on sticks. Rinse between showers to reduce tainting.

- Dig a hole and line it with a plastic sheet or concrete for water storage. Cover it to prevent evaporation and debris falling in.

- If the local water table is high you may be able to dig down to water – there may even be a well on your property which could be reopened.

- Solar and vegetation stills (see *Essentials*) are other ways of obtaining water.

Water conservation

Do not waste water washing clothes, other than underclothing. Never throw water away after use. Allow sediment to settle and it can be used again.

It is very important to wash the hands before preparing food, but the rest of the body can wait until it rains. The body produces natural oils and, as long as the pores are kept open, health will not be affected. You soon get used to the smell and social occasions are rare in a crisis situation. If showers are few and far between, use a damp cloth for a strip wash – cloths left out on lawns or bushes over night may gather enough moisture for a wipe down without using up your water stores.

Injured persons must receive priority for bathing and all their dressings should be boiled regularly.

FIRE

The warmth and comfort of a fire are great morale boosters, but its most important use will be for boiling water and preserving food. These must take priority in the use of fuel.

Blocked fireplaces should be opened up again and chimneys checked for obstructions. If they are not clear there is considerable risk of setting fire to the chimneys themselves and thus to the house.

To clear a chimney

Tie a holly bush or a similar shrub to a long rope and from the rooftop lower the rope down the chimney (a stone tied on the end will ensure it drops). Now pull down the holly bush and it will clear the chimney.

Improvised fireplaces

Where there are no fireplaces metal containers, metal dustbins lids and central heating radiators can all be used to light a fire on. In flats with concrete floors a fire could be lit directly on the floor. If you have a barbecue stand make good use of it.

Never leave a fire indoors unattended. Even one in a proper grate should be allowed to die down for the night, if no one is going to stay up to watch it.

Fuel

Start with garden furniture, trees, shrubs, bean sticks, swings, ladders, tool handles. When these run out start on furnishings. Carpets, curtains and cushions will all burn. Cardboard, books and rolled up newspapers will also give off a surprising amount of heat. All kinds of vehicle fuel can also be burned as well as the conventional heating and lighting oils.

WARNING

Many modern fabrics and furnishings, especially PVC and foam-block furniture, produce poisonous gases when burned. If burning these items make a fireplace in the garden or, if forced to burn them in a flat, make the fire near an open window. Cover the face with a damp cloth when you need to go near the fire to tend to it and things being heated on it.

FOOD

- Check on all the food in the house and ration it immediately.

- Use the perishable foods first. Fatty foods are the first to deteriorate and canned foods the last.

- Remember that, once electric power fails, the refrigerator and freezer cease to function — though they may take some time to defrost, if you open their doors as seldom and briefly as possible.

- Boil milk and it will keep longer.

- Boil eggs or coat them in a layer of fat – if you have izinglass (a traditional method of preserving fresh eggs) simply immerse them in it.

- Cook meat, wrap it in cloth and bury it in the earth. Cook pork first (which has the highest fat content), then lamb, then beef (which is the best meat to preserve).

- Once meat has been cooked and allowed to cool, do NOT reheat it or you may risk food-poisoning.

- You can only cook so much at a time, so leave the rest in the refrigerator or freezer while they are still cool places.

Food from the garden
The vegetables with four petals, including all the brassicas, from wallflowers to cabbages are edible. Hollyhocks, though not very tasty, are nutritious. Worms, slugs and snails are also edible. AVOID bulbs such as daffodils, tulips and aconites which are all poisonous.

Further afield
Explore parks and open spaces for other vegetation and for hunting and trapping wildlife. Birdlife in cities – especially pigeons and starlings, will often fill the plate, especially if you bait snares and nets. (See *Traps and snares* in *Food*.)

Closer to home
Beware of houseplants – some of them are poisonous, especially the diefenbachia and philodendron – though orchids are good to eat.

NOTE:
If food is short there will be none to spare for pets and you CANNOT afford to be squeamish. If the aquarium water has to be drunk don't waste the fish. In fact they'll probably be the easiest to eat even if you don't need the water. The cat is next in the pot. Once dressed it will be hard to distinguish from rabbit. Gerbils, hamsters, rabbits, budgerigars and parrots can all be added to the diet and, unless the dog is an exceptionally good hunter, it should go too.

Preserving food

For methods of smoking, salting and making pickles and chutneys (see *Food preservation* in *Food.*)

When the fridge no longer functions remove the motor, cut a hole in the bottom, place it on some stones or bricks and with a fire beneath use it as a smoke-house.

SHELTER

The first priorities will be a sound roof over your head and a stable structure. Clear any debris and ensure that there is nothing which could still collapse or fall from above and cause injury. Use slates, tiles and bricks from other buildings to ensure that at least one building is sound.

In cold weather

Conserve resources by living in one room, choosing a ground floor room with a southern aspect (if you live in the Northern Hemisphere). Block all draughts and avoid opening the door unnecessarily.

If there is a fire burning, make sure that there is adequate ventilation to avoid asphyxiation or carbon monoxide poisoning. Wear warm clothing to help conserve fuel. The more people in the room, the higher the temperature. Rest and keep physical exertion to a minimum.

In very warm weather

Use upstairs accommodation and spread out. Open windows on the downstairs windward side and open all windows on the leeside upstairs. Leave all the doors open and a cool breeze will blow through the house. It is best to rest during the day to conserve energy and fluids, and do any necessary work at night.

Moving

If the house proves beyond repair, or other pressures force you to evacuate, take essential items — food, blankets, tools, medical supplies, containers for water and materials suitable for shelter construction — if they are not likely to be available. Use a pram or a shopping trolley as transportation. Either find an empty house or building, or prepare to set up camp in a location elsewhere.

HYGIENE

Sanitation is very important during the aftermath of any disaster. Open sewers, contaminated water and the build up of rubbish all help to cause and spread disease. Germs carried by rats, fleas and other insects, rapidly multiply. All kinds of waste should be carefully disposed of and all the procedures described (see *Hygiene* in *Camp Craft*) should be adapted to the doorstep situation.

Excreta

Urine is sterile but if large amounts accumulate they smell and attract flies. Use the 'desert rose' urinal, of the kind described in *Camp Craft*. Keep the tube covered. If not used directly, pour all collected urine down the tube.

Build a latrine (again see *Camp Craft*), far enough from the house not to be smelt but near enough to be handy for 'emergencies' — there will be many such emergencies in a survival situation. A box with a hole cut in the base can be used as a thunder box. After use, if there is water available, wash yourself rather than using toilet paper. Wash the hands thoroughly afterwards.

Fit a lid to your thunder box, pile earth around the bottom and then you will contain the smells and keep out flies.

Move all muck with a shovel and avoid hand contact.

Animals

Animals pick up diseases which can be transmitted to humans. If you handle animals, make sure you have no breaks in the skin — or wear gloves. Infection can enter through the smallest of cuts. Cook all meat thoroughly.

Kitchen waste

All biodegradable waste should be stacked in a corner of the garden and composted to enrich the soil. Compost heaps are also a great source of worms, which will add protein to your diet.

However, there should not be much kitchen waste. Do NOT peel potatoes, much of their food value is in the skin. The outer leaves of cabbages which you once discarded, will be edible if you cut them up small.

Non-biodegradable waste — cans and plastics that are not useful in some way — should be burned, flattened and buried. This stops them attracting flies. In warm climates burn ALL waste. Put all the ashes in a pit.

FOOD DISEASES

Salmonella and shigella are diseases transmitted through the oral-anal route, by contaminated hands.

Sores on hands can be a source of entry for staphylococcal food-poisoning with severe stomach pains, diarrhoea and dehydration.

Clostridium botulinum, is a frequently fatal bacillus, which can be produced when canning at home if the temperatures are not high enough — it grows only when oxygen is excluded. There is no reliable way of determining whether food is contaminated so TAKE GREAT CARE if you do your own preserving. A related bacillus causes tetanus.

Communicable diseases

Living in close-knit groups after a disaster increases the risk of passing on disease. Good personal hygiene — as good as possible — can reduce the threat. Isolation of patients with colds or fever is advisable.

Seal dressings and discharges in a polythene bag and burn immediately. Dispose of all faeces and urine in the field latrine — and regularly boil the container used for their disposal.

Personal hygiene

Wash with sand if there is no water available. Don't bite your nails — however stressful conditions may be — or put the fingers to the mouth. Don't pick scabs or sores and keep them covered. Change underclothes regularly and wash them (but don't use drinking water to do so).

SOME USEFUL HERBAL PREPARATIONS

Strawberry roots contain a descaler to clean teeth.

Delphinium seeds can be crushed to treat head lice.

Birch bark can be distilled to produce a tar oil which soothes skin complaints.

Lavender makes a decoction to clean the skin.

(See also *Natural Medicine*.)

POSTSCRIPT

Now you have the benefit of knowledge that it has taken me, and others like me, a lifetime of training and experience to gather. But don't think that just reading this book will have made you a survivor. It has shown you the necessary skills, but it is you who must apply them and you who must have the calibre to cope.

When I am personally teaching soldiers or civilians how to deal with survival situations, part of my job is to ensure their safety. I cannot do that for the reader of this book. I can only give information and advice. I am not there to stop you doing something foolish. I cannot deal with individual specific situations, nor can I ensure that what I have written has been properly understood. I do know that what I have written has saved lives in the past and I believe that it could save more in the future. You must apply survival techniques with caution, for it will be your responsibility — not mine — if you inflict injury on yourself or on others.

The human body has an amazing ability to cope with arduous situations and testing environments. People who have come through, after enduring terrible hardship under seemingly impossible conditions, are a living proof of this. Male and female, young and old, they have all had the will to live. Everyone has this basic instinct to some degree and it can be developed by training.

Survival is as much a mental attitude as physical endurance and knowledge. Think of survival skills as a pyramid, built on the foundation of that will to survive. People with it have survived even though they did everything against the rule book. With a little knowledge they could have made their lot much easier. So the next layer of the pyramid is knowledge. It breeds confidence and dispels fears.

The third layer must be training, that does not just mean trying something once but mastering skills and maintaining them. In doing so, you will be keeping your body in training, too.

To cap the pyramid, add your kit. Proper equipment and provisions are common sense, but the survivor does not necessarily know what conditions to equip for. That is where your survival tin will make a tremendous difference to your chances. To the instinct for survival, which you can further develop, add knowledge, training and kit and you will be ready for anything.

INDEX